"Juxtaposing so many law-related films makes a telling point: how many great films, like *The Caine Mutiny* and *To Kill a Mockingbird*, have used the trial process to indict injustice, and how many celluloid clunkers have settled for rehashing clichés such as unidentifiable corpses, surprise witnesses, extralegal justice and forbidden love affairs between lawyers and clients or lawyers and jurors."

—**Allen D. Boyer, *New York Times***

"Why do lawyers in movies do what they do? Films are described thoroughly in cogent prose, analyzed for their handling of the legalities and rated from one gavel to four for their lawyerly perspicacity. . . . So weigh the evidence and go rent the videos."

—**Peter M. Nichols, *New York Times***

"In this informative, entertaining and unique book, the authors, two UCLA law professors, dissect a broad cross section of courtroom films with wit, humor, and professional expertise but without any stilted legal jargon."

—***Library Journal***

"A worthwhile and handy companion at the video store, *Reel Justice* means you'll never be forced to settle for renting *Adam's Rib* again."

—**Jonathan S. Shapiro, *The American Lawyer***

"What makes this book so extraordinary is the simultaneity of legal and film insights offered on each page. . . . The book is replete with wit and good humor. Furthermore, the authors make it plain that they are not interested in keeping anyone from having a good time at the movies."

—**Bruce Barnett, *The Docket***

". . . the non-lawyer filmgoer has no way of knowing that the legal system depicted in the film may be as far from reality as the Death Star in *Star Wars.* Unless, that is, she has *Reel Justice: The Courtroom Goes to the Movies* by Professors Michael Asimow and Paul Bergman of the UCLA School of Law."

—**Professor Thomas D. Griffith, *Entertainment Law Journal***

Reel Justice

The Courtroom Goes to the Movies

Paul Bergman
and
Michael Asimow

Andrews and McMeel
A Universal Press Syndicate Company
Kansas City

For information write to
Andrews and McMeel,
a Universal Press Syndicate Company,
4520 Main Street, Kansas City,
Missouri 64111.

Library of Congress Cataloging-in-Publication Data

Bergman, Paul 1943-
Reel Justice : the courtroom goes to the movies /
Paul Bergman and Michael Asimow.
p. cm.
Includes bibliographical references and index.
ISBN 0-8362-1035-2 (ppb)
1. Justice. Administration of, in motion pictures.
1. Asimow, Michael. II. Title
PN1995.9.J8B5 1996
791.43'655—dc20
95-4421
CIP

00 01 EB 10 9 8 7

To Andi and Bobbi, with love and appreciation

Contents

Foreword

by Judge Alex Kozinski

Scratch almost any lawyer and you'll find a movie buff. That's no coincidence, for the moviemaker's art is not all that different from the lawyer's—especially the courtroom advocate's. Both must capture, in a very short space, a slice of human existence, and make the audience see a story from their particular perspective. Both have to know which facts to include and which ones to leave out; when to appeal to emotion and when to reason; what to spoon-feed the audience and what to make them work out for themselves; when to do the expected and when the unexpected; when to script and when to improvise.

It's not surprising, then, that lawyers and trials are a perennial subject of moviemaking. Trials, by their nature, concentrate human conflict; they force a head-on clash of opposing forces. Any trial has the potential (especially in the movies) to raise difficult questions about the cornerstones of society: law, justice, morality, and the conventions that hold us together. Trials also raise one of the most fundamental doubts of human existence: whether, and to what extent, we can achieve an objective, true account of past events. Fair trials present the tantalizing possibility that the little guy can take on the big guy and win, because brains, wit, and justice count far more than money, power, and influence. Unfair trials make excellent tragedies: The outrage of justice betrayed, coupled with often pitiful consequences, can stir the blood with empathy.

It was while contemplating such matters that I first got the notion of becoming a lawyer. I remember exactly when it happened: It was 1963 or 1964 and I was living in Baltimore. We had come to the United States only a year or so earlier and I was in the process of absorbing American culture (and language) by plugging myself into the endless stream of black-and-white images that materialized in our living room through an ancient round-tube TV set. I found much of what I saw interesting, if strange; some of it funny; but not much of it very memorable.

One exception I still remember vividly: The scene was a small room filled with a bunch of guys sitting around a conference table arguing about the fate of someone who wasn't there to stand up for himself. I almost changed channels when the vote was eleven to one to convict, but there was something in the quiet determination of the lone dissenter that kept me from turning the knob. (For those too young to remember, channels in those days were changed by clicking large knobs on the front of the TV set, rather than by pushing buttons on a remote control.) He wasn't sure the defendant was innocent, the holdout told the others; he wanted to talk about it.

No reader has failed to recognize that I was watching *12 Angry Men,* or that the dissenting juror was the young Henry Fonda. As I sat there watching, struggling a bit with the language, trying to figure out the jury's function in American law (Why, I wondered, didn't they just convict by a vote of eleven to one and go home?), my whole adolescent conception of certainty, of knowledge itself, was shaken. The case against the defendant sounded so airtight; the reasons offered by the eleven sounded so irrefutable. I couldn't imagine how (or why) anyone could reach a different conclusion. Then, as one reason after another started to come apart, as inconsistencies crept into the picture, as jurors began changing their votes, I came to understand that truth does not spring into the courtroom full-blown, like Athena from the head of Zeus. Rather, facts have to be examined carefully and skeptically, moved around and twisted like pieces of a puzzle before they will yield a complete picture. Could it, might it be, that I had the talent for this type of work?

Further research was clearly necessary before I could sort out the realities of law practice. Were real trials, real jury deliberations anything like what I was seeing? As my interest in law grew, and along with it my interest in law-related movies and TV shows, I came up with more unanswered questions: Was the Scopes monkey trial anything like it was portrayed in *Inherit the Wind?* Did the War Crimes Tribunal bear any resemblance to *Judgment at Nuremberg?* I eventually went to law school, passed the bar, and became a judge, but questions of this sort persisted. What *was* the true story behind *Breaker Morant?* Was Sir Thomas More's defense as it was portrayed in *A Man for All Seasons?* To be sure, the answers could be found out there somewhere, given enough time and effort. But, human nature being what it is, I put it off.

And a good thing, too: When Michael Asimow (who taught me most of what I know about tax law) told me about the book he and Paul Bergman were writing, I immediately realized they were on to something that could be quite useful. Selected background material would supply the real story (if there was one) and the historical context of the action. Carefully researched legal analysis would help you figure out what might have happened (or did happen) in a real trial. No longer would inquiring minds have to wonder whether the trial judge's outrageous actions in *The Verdict* were at all plausible, or the procedures in *Whose Life Is It Anyway?* or *Nuts* bore any resemblance to reality. I wondered why no one thought of writing a book like this before.

The book is, of course, more than a disconnected series of answers to questions one might have in watching law-related movies. It is a thoughtful collection of some of the best—and a few of the worst—movies having to do with the legal process. And law-movie buffs desperately need such a guide. The advent of home video as a staple of entertainment in most American households has opened up the possibility of seeing great movies of the past—including movies concerning the law. Video has emancipated our movie viewing from the whims of local TV station program managers. (It took me almost twenty-five years before I saw *12 Angry Men* again.) But freedom can be treacherous without some compass to guide your steps. Stroll into your vast neighborhood video store with no plan and several friends or family members of divergent tastes, and you're likely to emerge three hours later with a made-for-TV comedy about Albanian werewolves. In these challenging times, *Reel Justice* gives you an edge in the movie-selection game. By giving just enough information up front to help you know whether a particular movie is likely to be of interest, it allows you to select a movie you haven't yet seen (or vaguely remember), to cajole your friends and family into concurring, and, later, to fully understand and enjoy the film.

A dog-eared copy of *Reel Justice* will find a place in the living room of most thoughtful movie-watchers. Its only defect, alas, is that it is too short: Where do you get the skinny on *First Monday in October, The Story of Qiu Ju, The Return of Martin Guerre,* and *Hang 'Em High?* I, for one, have already put in my order for *Reel Justice II.*

Alex Kozinski
United States Circuit Judge

Pasadena, Calif.
December 1995

Acknowledgments

Many of our present and former colleagues and students at the UCLA School of Law offered valuable suggestions that enhanced the accuracy of our legal analyses. We're grateful to Alison Anderson, Peter Arenella, Bruce Barnett, Stuart Biegel, Barbara Brudno, David Dolinko, Julian Eule, Ken Graham, Robert Goldstein, Paul Hayden, Steve Heller, Philip Mann, Carrie Menkel-Meadow, Herbert Morris, Fran Olsen, Robert Peroni, Raquelle de la Rocha, David Sklansky, Eugene Volokh, John Wiley, and Eric Zolt. We appreciate the research assistance of Heather Georgakis. Hardy souls that we are, we'll shoulder the blame for any errors.

Our friends and family gave us enormous assistance. We specifically thank Andrea Asimow, Bobbi Asimow, Daniel Asimow, Esther Asimow, Jennifer Asimow, Nathan Asimow, Paul Asimow, Judge Robert Altman, LeAnn Bischoff, our valiant proofreader Andrea Sossin-Bergman, Hilary Sossin-Bergman (especially on *To Kill a Mocking Bird*), Michael Bridge, Tom Griffith, Fred Kuperberg, and Jill Poppe.

We are very grateful to our agent, Angela Rinaldi, for her wonderful efforts on our behalf and to our editor, Donna Martin, for her astute editorial suggestions.

For helping us find still photos, films, laser discs and videotapes, we gratefully acknowledge the assistance of Bob Colman of Hollywood Poster Exchange; Cinema Collectors; Laser Blazer; Eddie Brandt's Saturday Matinee; Collectors Book Store; UCLA Library Film Stills Collection; and the UCLA Film Archive.

We're grateful for support from the UCLA School of Law Dean's Fund.

Introduction

Audiences have an enduring love affair with trial movies. One reason why trial stories work so well is that they provide the drama of one-on-one confrontations—attorney versus witness, attorney versus opposing counsel, attorney versus judge, attorney versus client. And trial movies have a built-in suspense factor. When the judge says, "Ladies and gentlemen of the jury, have you reached a verdict?" we never know whether this mysterious group of twelve strangers will send the defendants to the chair or let them walk out of the courtroom to freedom.

Another reason for the popularity of trial movies is that producers are smart enough not to make movies about the usual grist of the trial court mill, such as slip-and-fall cases or speeding tickets. Instead, memorable movie trials feature such eternally fascinating themes as murder, treachery, and sex—the same topics that Will Shakespeare used to capture his audiences' imaginations a few centuries ago.

Trial movies can also present controversial legal and moral issues in a sugarcoated package that we swallow with pleasure. Would you rather read another book about capital punishment or see it up close and personal in *I Want to Live!?* Browse a treatise on war crimes or see *Judgment at Nuremberg?* Debate whether a quadriplegic has the right to die or watch *Whose Life Is It Anyway?*

Many trial movies are based on true stories—some of them famous or infamous trials of the past. It's enthralling to watch Clarence Darrow and William Jennings Bryan come to life as they square off in *Inherit the Wind,* the story of the Scopes Monkey Trial. The legendary Darrow reprises in *Compulsion,* in which he managed to keep thrill-killers Leopold and Loeb from being sent to the gallows. And *10 Rillington Place* and *Let Him Have It* will introduce you to two of the cases that led to abolition of the death penalty in England.

Trial movies can get away with presenting simple clashes between good and evil, right and wrong. Most audiences today are too sophisticated to cheer the Hero and hiss the Villain. But a movie lawyer fighting for Morality and Justice is the modern counterpart of the 1920s hero who untied the damsel from the train tracks just before the train roared by. Who can forget Atticus Finch in *To Kill a Mockingbird* standing up in a rural southern courtroom for a black man wrongly accused of raping a white woman?

You'll laugh out loud as expert witness Mona Lisa Vito discusses tire tracks and Positraction in *My Cousin Vinny.* You'll reach for the hankies as Ted Kramer loses custody of his little boy in *Kramer vs. Kramer.* You'll tingle with terror in the closing scenes of *Jagged Edge.* And you'll seethe with rage when a kangaroo court-martial sentences three innocent soldiers to death in *Paths of Glory.* Trial movies run the whole emotional gamut.

Our book selects sixty-nine trial movies of the present and from the past. We've written about the great classics of the genre, but we've also covered some not-so-great trial movies that present interesting legal and ethical issues. We hope this book will help you choose which video to rent next Friday night when you feel that gnawing hunger for a good cross-examination along with your microwave popcorn. To help you make the perfect choice, we've ranked each film on a scale of one to four gavels. Our ranking system is based on the quality, dramatic power, and authenticity of the trial scenes in the movie. Four gavels is a classic, three is good, two is just okay, and one means ask for a new trial.

This book is more than just a video guide. Do you ever wonder how much of what you see in trial movies is "real?" When you see a monster devouring a subway train or a fiend chopping off his aunt's head with a chain saw, you immediately recognize it as a movie trick. But legal sleight of hand is harder to detect. We think it's important to know how Hollywood bends the rules to inject drama or humor into trial movies, and we try to alert you to when the filmmakers do so.

Viewers are often left with unanswered questions after they see trial movies. Is the plot legally plausible? Just what is circumstantial evidence or hearsay evidence, and what's wrong with it? Who should wind up with the child when both parents seek custody? Can the devil enforce a contract in which he's bought a soul? Can a lawyer turn down a plea bargain without consulting the client? Would a judge allow evidence about the defendant's prior crimes to be introduced? And what's a mutiny, or a privilege, or a crime against humanity, or an irresistible impulse? Can a lawyer browbeat a distraught witness from a distance of two inches, like Dancer's cross-examination in *Anatomy of a Murder?* Were the cops right not to search for a murder weapon, in *Presumed Innocent?* Are lawyers allowed to interrupt their questioning of witnesses to make speeches, like Joe Miller in *Philadelphia?* If the trial is one drawn from real life, did it really happen that way or did the writer fictionalize it? We try to answer these questions in a way that everybody, lawyers and nonlawyers alike, can understand, enjoy, and learn from.

Trial movies almost always present difficult ethical and moral dilemmas. Should a lawyer represent a client that the lawyer thinks is guilty? What if the client might kill again? Must a lawyer represent a client who is extremely unpopular or who has a repulsive personality or who can't pay a fee or who doesn't even want a lawyer? These are not simple questions, in theory or in practice, and we think that viewers should wrestle with them just as real lawyers do. We don't have all the answers, but we will take our best shot at the questions.

This book is written for everybody, lawyers and nonlawyers, who enjoy trial movies. We'll introduce you to some you haven't seen and, we hope, help you appreciate even more the ones you've already seen. We'll try to answer your questions and bring issues to the surface that you hadn't considered. Writing this book has increased our appreciation of this entertaining and enduring art form, and we hope our descriptions and analyses will do the same for you.

The Gavel Rating System

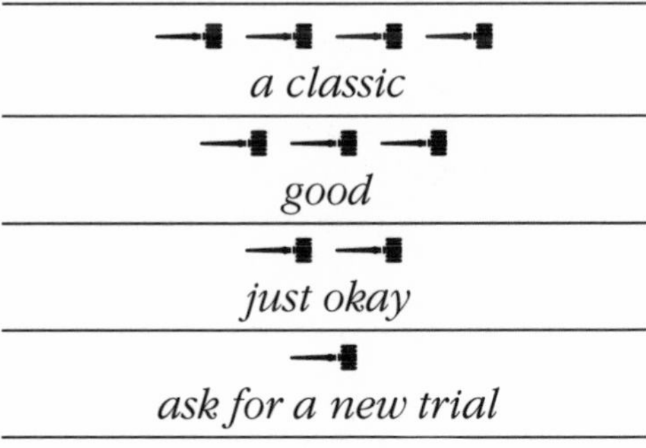

a classic
good
just okay
ask for a new trial

The Story You Are About to See Is True . . .

Dramatic trials have always been great media events. The Scopes monkey trial, dramatized in *Inherit the Wind,* for example, was as much a media circus in 1925 as the O.J. Simpson case was in 1995. Certainly, the Nuremberg war crime trials, in *Judgment at Nuremberg,* were major news stories in the late 1940s. For that matter, the treason trial of Sir Thomas More *(A Man for All Seasons)* was undoubtedly the hottest news story of 1535. Read today's headlines, and imagine next year's movie lines.

Many trial movies are based on real trials. Screenwriters can compress the events of weeks or months into a couple of hours. They cut out the boring details and instead give us insights and perspectives about the defendants, the victims, the lawyers, and the judges that the daily news coverage cannot provide. Failing that, they make up a pack of lies.

This chapter focuses on movies based on real trials (and there are many others throughout the book). Some of them are historically important—the execution of an innocent man in *10 Rillington Place* and of a mentally retarded youth in *Let Him Have It* led to abolition of the death penalty in Britain. Some of them bring to life the great lawyers of the past, like Clarence Darrow *(Inherit the Wind* and *Compulsion)* or Abraham Lincoln *(Young Mr. Lin-*

coln). In each case, we'll tell you what happened in the real trial, so you'll know what is fact and what is make-believe.

The Accused

Synopsis: The victim of a gang rape seeks justice against the barflies who cheered on the rapists.

UIP/Paramount (Sherry Lansing and Stanley Jaffe). 1988. Color. Running time: 110 minutes

Screenplay: Tom Topor. Director: Jonathan Kaplan

Starring: Jodie Foster (Sarah Tobias), Kelly McGillis (Kathryn Murphy), Bernie Coulson (Kenneth Joyce), Leo Rossi (Cliff "Scorpion" Albrecht), Ann Hearn (Sally Frazer), Steve Antin (Bob Joiner), Carmen Argenziano (Paul Rudolph).

Academy Award: Best Actress (Jodie Foster).

Rating: —▮ —▮

The Story

Sarah Tobias has a fight with her boyfriend. To teach him a lesson, she goes to The Mill, a local bar. There, Tobias fires up male fantasies thought to be extinct. She dresses provocatively, smokes dope, and performs a variety of dance steps not generally taught at Arthur Murray. Suddenly Tobias finds herself pinned on the pinball machine getting raped by three men. A number of the barflies cheer them on.

After D.A. Kathryn Murphy charges the three attackers with rape, Tobias learns about another kind of mill—the criminal justice system. Murphy doubts that she can prove rape, and so strikes a plea bargain without consulting Tobias. The rapists plead guilty to "reckless endangerment" and will probably serve no more than nine months in jail. A furious Tobias thinks that Murphy sold her out.

Murphy decides to square things with Tobias by prosecuting three of the barflies for "criminal solicitation." Her boss, D.A. Rudolph, thinks this is a waste of resources and threatens to fire her, but Murphy plunges ahead. Murphy lucks out and uncovers a key witness. Ken Joyce, a fraternity brother of one of the rapists, was at The Mill, saw the rape, and feels ashamed that he didn't interfere. Very reluctantly, he agrees to testify. Joyce's evidence is critical, since Tobias can't identify which bystanders were egging on the rapists. Joyce's trial testimony unfolds in the form of a flashback to the brutal rape scene. The jury believes Joyce, and the three barflies are convicted.

Legal Analysis

Rape is a hard crime to prove. Often, victims have been treated in court as if they were "the accused," rather than the accuser. "Rape shield laws" now exclude most evidence about a rape victim's prior sexual conduct and even their manner of dress. Nevertheless, when rape defendants argue that a victim consented and the victim seems somewhat less than virginal, juries often refuse to convict.

Given this pattern, Murphy's plea bargain probably was a good deal for the prosecution. The rapists stood a good chance of acquittal if they had gone to trial. The prosecution had no eyewitnesses except Tobias (Joyce hadn't yet surfaced), and everyone in the bar was going to testify that Tobias invited the sexual intercourse. Add in some dope, booze, sexy dancing, and making out on the dance floor, and you have both a typical TV family-hour sitcom and a very shaky rape case. Even though Tobias hated Murphy's plea bargain, the deal was pretty good—after all, the defendants did go to jail.

Murphy's relationship with Tobias is entirely different from a private attorney–client relationship. Tobias is not Murphy's client, so Murphy has no obligation to consult her about whether to settle the case or about any other tactic. A prosecutor represents the community at large, not individual victims. This is sensible, since most victims would demand that prosecutors shoot for the maximum possible sentence, regardless of the weakness of the case.

Rudolph, Murphy's supervisor, ordered Murphy not to prosecute the onlookers. He thought it was a waste of resources that would make her and the entire office look bad. Rudolph's job is to make calls like this. District attorneys are always short of resources and can't prosecute every case. They drop the losers. And the solicitation case looked like a loser—especially before Joyce surfaced. When Rudolph tries to stop her, Murphy threatens to quit and to sue everyone in sight, including the prosecutor's office. This is utter nonsense. Prosecutors are immune from being sued for decisions about which cases to prosecute. Rudolph might well have fired her on the spot.

The barflies were charged with "solicitation," which consists of inciting or encouraging another person to commit a crime. To convict someone of solicitation, you don't have to prove the crime was actually committed—just that the defendant encouraged it. Perhaps that's why Murphy chose to prosecute for solicitation—she wouldn't have to prove that rape occurred, just that the onlookers wanted it to occur.

Since Tobias was actually raped, the barflies could have been charged with a more serious crime—aiding and abetting rape. They encouraged the rapists to commit a crime—and the crime was committed. If they were convicted of abetting, the cheerleaders could be punished the same as if they had committed the rape.

The defense at the criminal solicitation trial was very poorly handled. The defense lawyers conceded that a gang rape had taken place. They should have attacked Tobias's testimony that she had not encouraged the rapists. If the jury believed that Tobias wanted to have sex with the men, the barflies would have been urging consensual sexual acts, not rapes. All the negative facts that caused Murphy to plea-bargain the rape case should have been brought out by the defense in the solicitation trial. True, Joyce's testimony was damaging to the defense, but the jury might still have decided that Tobias was asking for it.

Tobias's friend, Sally Frazer, works at The Mill. Frazer tells Murphy that Tobias said that she might take one of the rapists home and have sex with him in front of her boyfriend. Murphy discloses this tasty bit of information to the defense and they use it at the trial. Murphy acted properly in disclosing this information. Under *Brady v. Maryland* (1963), Murphy was obligated to disclose to the defense any information learned from a witness that is likely to be "exculpatory" (i.e., suggests the defendant's innocence).

The Accused is well acted and the rape scene is harrowing and unforgettable. The barflies deserved to be punished, although it seems unfair that they may have to serve longer prison terms than the actual rapists. The defense at the solicitation trial didn't take its best shots and made it too easy for the prosecution.

Trial Brief: The New Bedford Gang Rape

The Accused is based on a notorious gang rape that occurred in New Bedford, Massachusetts, in 1983. The victim, a twenty-two-year-old mother of two, was raped by three men on a pool table in Big Dan's Bar as several others cheered them on. The trial was one of the first covered by live TV and was a national sensation.

The victim testified that she visited the bar to buy cigarettes, had a drink, and was attacked by the men. The defense witnesses, including the bartender, said she had three drinks and was flirting with the men. One of the accused rapists said she agreed to "fool around" with him but he was physically unable to have sex with everybody watching.

The Portuguese-American community in Massachusetts rallied 'round the defendants, but to no avail: The three rapists were convicted and sentenced to nine to twelve years; a fourth man who had tickled the victim during the rapes got six to eight years. The two cheering onlookers were acquitted. The convictions were affirmed by the Massachusetts Supreme Court. The victim moved to Florida and was killed in an auto accident several years later, leaving her two children orphans.

A Cry in the Dark

Synopsis: A woman whose infant daughter was killed by a dingo during an Australian camping holiday is convicted of murder and later exonerated.

Pathe/Evil Angels Films/Cannon International (Verity Lambert). 1988. Color. Running time: 122 Min.

Screenplay: Robert Caswell and Fred Schepisi. Original Book: John Bryson. Director: Fred Schepisi.

Starring: Meryl Streep (Lindy Chamberlain), Sam Neill (Michael Chamberlain), Bruce Myles (Ian Baker), Neil Fitzpatrick (John Phillips).

Academy Award nomination: Meryl Streep (Best Actress).

Rating: —▮ —▮ —▮

The Story

Michael and Lindy Chamberlain live with their three children, including ten-week-old Azaria, in Queensland, Australia. They are a devoutly religious couple; he is a minister in the Seventh-day Adventist Church.

In August 1980 the family sets off for a camping holiday at Ayers Rock, a huge boulder in the Central Australian desert. Together with other families, they enjoy a barbecue as Azaria sleeps in a tent nearby. Lindy goes to investigate a cry coming from the tent area. She sees a dingo (an Australian wild dog, an animal not nearly as cuddly as a koala or a kangaroo) running out through the unzipped front of the tent; Azaria's cot is empty. Lindy screams that the dingo took her baby and a search is undertaken by the other families and police officers, but Azaria is not found.

Over the next few months, the Chamberlains are at the center of a media blitz. Rumors circulate that Lindy killed her child, fed by beliefs that a dingo could not make a child disappear and insinuations that Lindy was a religious nut carrying out a ritual sacrifice. The police also have their suspicions, especially after they find Azaria's sleepsuit in a cave about three miles from the campsite. The sleepsuit is gashed, and a laboratory technician finds no saliva on it and concludes that the gashes were not made by the teeth of an animal. Even after the coroner's inquest clears the Chamberlains of wrongdoing, the rumors and the police investigation continue.

A Cry In The Dark: Prosecutor Baker (Bruce Myles) displays the bloody jumpsuit.

Following a second inquest, Lindy is charged with murdering Azaria; Michael is charged with being an accessory after the fact. Baker, the prosecutor, has no eyewitnesses, no body, and no motive. He therefore builds his case on the testimony of various forensic scientists, including three imported from London. The scientific evidence is confusing, and boring to the hordes of journalists. For example, one scientist claims that she found traces of infant blood in the Chamberlain's camera case and car, but admits that it could have come from various sources, including a runny nose, and could even be rust residue. Dr. Cameron, one of the British experts, claims that special imaging techniques show that small spots on Azaria's sleepsuit are bloody imprints of a small human hand. But if they are human imprints, they are never connected to Lindy. Dr. Cameron also says that it is critical to his opinion that Azaria did not die from a dingo attack that no saliva was found on her clothes. However, Dr. Scott testifies that it is possible that saliva was present. Finally, expert testimony on the attack habits of dingoes is conflicting, though none of it makes dingoes a good choice for a household pet.

Michael and Lindy testify in their own defense. In response to defense attorney Phillips's questions, Michael is confused and inarticulate. Lindy is more responsive and even somewhat abrasive towards Baker. She testifies that she saw a dingo running out of her tent shaking its head, but can't swear that she saw it carrying Azaria. She also testifies that Azaria was wearing a matinee jacket over her sleepsuit, thus explaining the absence of saliva on the sleepsuit. However, no such jacket has been found.

At the conclusion of the evidence, the judge recounts the evidence for the jury in a way that suggests that it should return a verdict of not guilty. However, the jury finds both Lindy and Michael guilty. She receives a life sentence; his eighteen-month sentence is suspended. Lindy is released after serving three and a half years, supposedly out of compassion. However, testing done after the trial casts serious doubt on the prosecution's blood evidence. Moreover, aboriginal trackers find Azaria's matinee jacket while investigating the remains of a climber who fell from Ayers Rock. In 1988, eight years after Azaria's death, judges pronounce the Chamberlains innocent.

Legal Analysis

The popular conception of the Anglo-American adversary system of justice is that it produces truth. But as the Chamberlains' plight dramatically illustrates, all the system really promises are the collection of procedures known as "due process," such as the right to a jury trial, to counsel, and to confront and cross-examine one's accusers. We have to take it on faith that most of the time, those procedures will produce acceptable truth. It would be comforting to blame occasional incorrect verdicts on lying witnesses or venal judges. Or maybe in the Chamberlains' case, while keeping dingoes off the jury, the judge allowed too many dingbats on. But some incorrect verdicts are inevitable when ordinary people try to determine truth by evaluating conflicting versions of the past. The Chamberlains had the benefit of fair processes, but that did not protect them against an unfair result.

What produced the miscarriage of justice in this case? One possibility is that the jurors were unduly impressed by the array of scientific experts that Baker paraded before them. Judges often speak of the dangers of gullible jurors slavishly lapping up any opinion that a scientist puts on their plate. But most judges have little basis for this opinion—they've been on more diets than juries. Anyway, that theory seems not to hold up in this case. The Chamberlains' attorney effectively undermined most of Baker's experts. For example, one expert has to admit that so-called traces of blood could have been left by saliva or nasal secretions, or might even have been rust. Another expert admits that Lindy's nail scissors, supposedly the murder weapon, were incapable of making the cuts in Azaria's sleepsuit. A third expert testifies that a dingo could not pick up a baby by the head without breaking its jaw, but then changes his mind when shown a photograph of a dingo with its mouth encircling a doll's head. And during deliberations, a number of the jurors dismiss all of the scientific evidence as too confusing. Thus, it is unlikely that the jurors were simply sold a bill of goods by a bunch of quacks.

At the end of the day, perhaps the biggest contributor to the verdict was Lindy herself. One factor is her demeanor as a witness. She was not weepy and submissive, the kind of person on whom the jurors might take pity. Instead she was combative when responding to Baker's questions, and she talked objectively and even clinically of Azaria's wounds. The jurors may not have liked her, and they may have allowed their personal feelings to color their evaluation of the evidence.

A more important factor may have been Lindy's telling a story that many people found implausible. Criminal defense lawyers usually tell their clients to keep their mouths shut; Lindy's unjust conviction demonstrates the wisdom of that advice. Assume that instead of claiming that a dingo captured Azaria, Lindy had only said, "I don't know what happened. I heard a cry, ran to the tent, and my baby was gone." This story allows for numerous ways in which Azaria could have come to harm, including kidnapping by a human intruder. The case against Lindy was far from airtight; in addition to the weak scientific evidence, it seems unlikely that she would choose a crowded campsite as the place to murder her child. Thus, if Lindy did not claim to know what happened, the jurors might well have concluded that it was impossible to determine how Azaria was killed, and acquitted Lindy. But after Lindy told the dingo story, the jurors were limited to two possibilities: either Lindy killed Azaria, or a dingo did. Once the jurors decided that the dingo story didn't make sense, convicting Lindy of murder became their only alternative.

The trial judge's "summing up" for the jury before they deliberate is a traditional feature of English and Australian trials. The judges do not simply rehash the evidence for the benefit of jurors who might have been making a mental shopping list during part of the testimony. As in the film, the summary tends to be laced with a heavy dose of the judge's opinion as to how the jurors should decide the case. The practice has drawn criticism, mainly from defense lawyers who complain that judges' summaries almost always favor the prosecution. For example, defense lawyers claim that judges routinely make remarks such as, "The defense theory, if any of you are naive enough to swallow it . . . " Trial judges in the United States retain the inherent power to review evidence for the jury, but they almost never do so. In part, the reason is a noble one: most American judges regard the practice as trampling on the jury's turf. More personally, they also fear that any unbalance in the summary would draw quick and public criticism from an appellate court.

The Chamberlains' case generated immense publicity. Television cameras had to be set up to broadcast the trial to the many journalists who could not be seated inside the courtroom. It was the first trial televised live to the Australian public, undoubtedly a sad event for Aussie soap opera fans. Thus, it is refreshing to see the attorneys limiting their roles to the trial itself, not engaging in a battle to mold public opinion and influence prospective jurors by giving daily interviews and briefings on the courthouse steps. The trend is clearly toward attorneys moving outside the courtroom, however. Like Gilbert and Sullivan's admirals who never went to sea, we may soon see litigators who never go into a courtroom. One will specialize in "top step" interviews, another in "ducking into the limousine" commentary. But all will probably undermine the public's confidence in trial verdicts.

The mistaken conviction of Lindy Chamberlain is the kind of situation that fuels the attack on capital punishment. The judge sentences her to life in prison, which if nothing else gives the judicial system a chance to correct its mistake. Had the jury had the power to choose the death penalty, the enormity of the injustice would have been impossible to calculate.

The Chamberlains were average citizens caught in a web of public suspicion and bad science. The jury system did not protect them. But when the judicial system recognized that a mistake had been made, it was corrected. Perhaps the film's message is uplifting after all.

Trial Briefs

1. Michael was charged with being an "accessory after the fact." This means that he was not accused of committing the crime, but rather of helping the perpetrator escape detection. In most jurisdictions, the penalty for being an accessory after the fact is far less than for committing the crime itself.

2. The film faithfully tracks the critical evidence in the case. The actual trial lasted seven weeks. Not apparent from the film is that the defense called ten witnesses to testify that Lindy was a loving mother of Azaria, and two other parents who testified that dingoes had attacked their children at Ayers Rock around the same time Azaria was killed.

3. Whether to admit evidence based on novel scientific theories can be a difficult yet critical one for trial judges. For many years, judges admitted scientific testimony only if the scientific theory underlying

the testimony was "generally accepted" by other scientists in the same field. The general acceptance test freed judges from having to assess the validity of novel scientific theories; they could just count noses in the scientific community. But many scholars criticized the "general acceptance" test. They mockingly referred to it as the "Galileo Rule," since the rule would have prevented the outcast Galileo from testifying that the earth was round. The case of *Daubert v. Dow Chemical Co.* (1993) eliminated the "general acceptance" requirement in United States federal courts, meaning that many trial judges now have the burden of evaluating the validity of novel scientific theories.

4. Following Lindy's release, the Chamberlains filed a compensation claim against the Northern Territories seeking millions of dollars in damages for their ordeal. Their claims were settled in 1992 when the attorney general awarded about $900,000 to Lindy and about $400,000 to Michael.

5. As depicted in the film, the trial severely strained the Chamberlains' relationship, and they eventually divorced. Azaria's remains have never been found.

I Want To Live!

Synopsis: A harrowing tale of capital punishment, up close and personal.
UA (Walter Wanger). 1958. Black and white. Running time: 120 min.
Screenplay: Nelson Gidding and Don Mankiewicz. Adapted from newspaper articles by Ed Montgomery and the letters of Barbara Graham.
Director: Robert Wise.
Starring: Susan Hayward (Barbara Graham), Simon Oakland (Ed Montgomery), Philip Coolidge (Emmett Perkins), Lou Krugman (Jack Santo), Theodore Bikel (Carl Palmberg), Bartlett Robinson (District Attorney).
Academy Award: Susan Hayward (Best Actress).
Academy Award nominations: Best Director, Best Screenplay, Best Cinematography, Best Sound Direction, Best Editing.
Rating: ⚖ ⚖ ⚖

The Story

Barbara Graham is a happy-go-lucky party girl who has very poor judgment. For example, she supplies a false alibi for some friends—and buys into a perjury conviction. There's some prostitution and burglary in there too. She marries a heroin addict and has a baby. She kicks him out and falls in with a trio of evil guys—Emmett Perkins, Jack Santo, and Bruce King. If Attila the Hun had been around, she might have dated him too.

I Want To Live!: Richard Tibrow (Bartlett Robinson) tries to save Barbara Graham (Susan Hayward) from the gas chamber.

These three characters rob and kill Mabel Monahan. Maybe Graham was involved, and maybe not. She denies it to her dying day, and we never know for sure. The police arrest all four and subject Graham to intense interrogation, but she never wavers.

At the trial, King testifies under a grant of immunity that Graham was a full-fledged participant in the murder. Perhaps he says this because it's true. Or perhaps he says it because that's what the prosecution wants to hear and also because he hates Graham, who rejected his advances.

Unfortunately, Graham has no provable alibi. She claims she was home with her husband and child that night, but the husband is far too doped out to remember. The key testimony against her comes from Ben, an undercover police detective who tricked her into confessing. This came about when another woman in prison told Graham that the woman's boyfriend, Ben, would supply Graham with an alibi. Graham and Ben cook up a fake alibi. Ben then says that he won't go through with it unless she tells him that she actually committed the crime. She says she did—and immediately regrets it.

When Ben plays the tape of this conversation at the trial, Graham's defense is devastated. The incident causes Graham's attorney, Richard Tibrow, to lose faith in her. Still, the truth isn't clear. Perhaps Graham confessed only because she was desperate for an alibi.

Graham is convicted and her case goes up on appeal. Ed Montgomery is a newspaperman who crucified her during the trial as "Bloody Babs." Montgomery has a sudden change of heart and becomes her biggest supporter. Psychologist Carl Palmberg also takes up her case; he is convinced that Graham is a liar and a criminal—but a nonviolent one. Palmberg dies during the appeals process, before he can convince a court or write a book about the case. Graham's conviction is affirmed by the California Supreme Court and the U.S. Supreme Court denies a hearing. She is moved from the comfortable women's prison at Corona to death row at San Quentin to await the result of various habeas corpus petitions. These postconviction remedies fail, and the governor denies clemency. The death row phone rings and Graham gets two last-minute stays as the federal courts briefly consider her attorney's desperate petitions.

Eventually, all remedies fail and Graham goes to the gas chamber with dignity. We see the meticulous preparations for the execution as the workers measure out the chemicals. A gang of reporters gathers to watch the fun. A prison guard says "When you hear the pellets drop, breathe deep and it will be easier that way." Graham replies, "How would you know?"

The cyanide tablets are dropped into the sulfuric acid and we watch the lethal fumes rise. Graham takes her last breath and dies. Viewers may feel like they had a whiff of the gas themselves.

Legal Analysis

Graham's confession to Ben was the key bit of testimony that destroyed her before the jury. Under current law, it is doubtful that this evidence would have been admissible. The use of jailhouse informants is condoned, and it is permissible to get a suspect to confess through trickery, but not through threats. However, Graham already had an attorney at the time of Ben's ruse, and therefore the confession would be barred on the ground that the police denied Graham the right to counsel (*Massiah v. United States,* 1964). Moreover, some cases have ruled out confessions obtained under a threat similar to Ben's (that he would refuse to testify to a fake alibi unless she confessed to him). For example, when a prisoner was told by an undercover informant that he would be protected against prison violence only if he would confess, the confession was considered coerced and thus inadmissible (*Arizona v. Fulminante,* 1991).

The movie leaves us in doubt about Graham's guilt. But let's assume she was guilty. In fact, she probably was. That raises a more profound issue. Should she have been executed? Many people consider the death penalty morally unacceptable. Some people think we need it as a deterrent to violent crime or as an expression of the community's need for retribution.

But people who favor the death penalty never see the gory details of life on death row. They don't see the suffering imposed on the defendant from the ups and downs of the legal process or of the strain imposed on prison personnel who must wait for the death row phone to ring. They don't have to deal, as governors, attorneys, and judges must, with the increasingly desperate last-minute habeas corpus petitions (although recently the Supreme Court has greatly limited the ability to obtain postconviction relief through repeated petitions). They don't get to peek at the macabre details of the execution process itself. *I Want To Live!* is the most powerful antideath penalty picture ever made, and it has to cause every viewer to reexamine his or her position on the death penalty.

Trial Brief: The Real Barbara Graham Case

According to the California Supreme Court decision unanimously affirming Graham's conviction (1954), the crime took place on March 9, 1953. Monahan was a sixty-four-year-old widow who lived alone. Her son-in-law was a prominent gambler, and the Santo-Perkins gang thought there were large amounts of money in her home. Perkins, Santo, Graham, and John True (Bruce King in the movie) went to Monahan's home to rob her. Another man named Shorter was also present but was never found.

True, testifying under immunity, said that Graham's role in the scheme was to gain entry to Monahan's home. True saw Graham enter the house and strike Monahan on the head with a gun. Monahan collapsed and Graham put a pillowslip over her head. Monahan died of asphyxiation.

When Graham heard she was a suspect, she and the other defendants moved several times and were finally caught on May 4, 1953, in an apartment above a machine shop in Lynwood, as depicted in the film. Graham could not give a plausible explanation for her flight.

The key testimony against Graham came from a policeman named Samuel Sirianni (Ben in the movie), who discussed faking an alibi with her. She gave Sirianni specific details about the crime, including the time it took place, and also said that Shorter had been done away with. Thus the Sirianni encounter in real life was much more incriminating to Graham than the conversation with Ben depicted in the movie. The California Supreme Court upheld her conviction based on the testimony of True and Sirianni as well as her flight.

Only four women have been executed in California's gas chamber. One of them was Graham, who was gassed on June 3, 1955, at the age of thirty-one. Graham was the mother of three children, then aged thirteen, eleven, and three. Her execution was set for 10 A.M., but stopped by Governor Goodwin Knight at 9:06 because the Supreme Court had granted a last-minute stay. The stay was lifted at 10:26 and the execution was reset for 10:45, but at 10:41 came a second stay. This was lifted at 11:17 and Graham was finally executed at 11:30. As in the movie, Graham walked to her execution blindfolded but with her hair, makeup, clothing, and jewelry impeccable. The final conversation with the guard is historically accurate.

Santo and Perkins were executed together at 2:30 on the same day. They went with bravado and defiance to the end.

Inherit the Wind

Synopsis: A brilliant recreation of the Scopes monkey trial, focusing on two immortal lawyers and the eternal conflict between science and religion.

UA/Lomitas (Stanley Kramer) 1960. Black and white. Running time: 127 min.

Screenplay: Nathan E. Douglas and Harold Jacob Smith. Original play: Jerome Lawrence, Robert E. Lee. Director: Stanley Kramer.

Starring: Spencer Tracy (Henry Drummond), Fredric March (Matthew Brady), Gene Kelly (E.K. Hornbeck), Harry Morgan (The Judge), Dick York (Bertram Cates).

Academy Award nominations: Best Actor (Spencer Tracy), Best Screenplay, Best Cinematography, Best Editing.

Rating: —▮ —▮ —▮ —▮

The Story

Tennessee passed a criminal statute forbidding any public school teacher to teach that man descended from a lower order of animals. Many people in Tennessee favored the statute, though most animals opposed it. Bert Cates deliberately violates the law by teaching evolution in his high school biology class in Hillsboro. The local district attorney engages three-time presidential candidate Matthew Brady to prosecute the case. The media descend on the town en masse, led by the cynical E.K. Hornbeck. Brady, together with the local fundamentalist preacher, whip the townspeople to a frenzy. Hornbeck's paper

Inherit The Wind: Henry Drummond (Spencer Tracy) examines Matthew Harrison Brady (Fredric March) about nonliteral interpretation of the Bible.

retains the notorious Henry Drummond, champion of hopeless causes, to conduct the defense. Though they find themselves opponents, Brady and Drummond are old friends; Drummond supported Brady in his presidential quests.

At the trial, everyone strips off coats as the temperature soars to a sweltering 97 degrees. Brady's case is a lay down, as Cates was caught with his hand in the monkey jar. Brady makes his case stronger by shouting at Rachel (the preacher's daughter and Cates's fiancée) until she admits that Cates is an agnostic. In this town, that's like admitting to having horns, a pitchfork, and a forked tail.

Meanwhile, Drummond is frustrated at every turn. The court refuses to allow him to introduce expert testimony about evolution. In desperation, he summons Brady to the stand as an expert on the Bible. The judge encourages Brady to decline, but Brady agrees, happy to have another shot at promoting a literal interpretation of the Bible. He insists that the Bible stories are true as written, including the Earth stopping its rotation. But in a dramatic breakthrough, Drummond gets Brady to admit that the first day of creation might have been twenty-five hours long rather than twenty-four, since there was then no Sun by which to measure. So the first day could have been millions of years long, or even as long as *Ishtar.* Through this fatal concession, Brady admits that the Bible can be interpreted in nonliteral fashion, thus making it possible to argue that evolution is consistent with the biblical story of creation.

Nevertheless, the jury convicts Cates. The judge, concerned about the ridicule being heaped on the town by Hornbeck and other journalists, sentences him to pay a fine of only $100. As the court and spectators disperse, Brady stands up to give yet another speech on literal interpretation of the Bible. Bellowing over the crowd noise, he has a stroke and dies.

Legal Analysis

Once again, as in *They Won't Forget* or *To Kill a Mockingbird,* a small town is taken over by lynch mob mentality. There was no way Cates could get a fair trial in what Hornbeck referred to as "heavenly Hillsboro," considering that the townspeople are marching on the jail singing tunefully about hanging Cates and Drummond from a sour apple tree. As a result, had the case not been a setup, Drummond should have requested and been entitled to a change of venue to some other place in Tennessee.

The movie depicts part of the jury selection process, called "voir dire." Needless to say, the jury panel was exclusively white, male, and religious. Brady and Drummond are allowed some leeway during voir dire to tell the jury their approach to the case. But Brady and Drummond break into final argument, going far beyond the proper scope of voir dire.

During voir dire, the judge will excuse obviously biased jurors for cause. In addition, each attorney has a very limited number of peremptory challenges to bump undesirable jurors off the panel. One juror likened Brady to God. The court should have excused this juror for cause. Drummond should not have been forced to use one of his few peremptories to get rid of this juror.

What issues were left for the jury to decide in *Inherit the Wind?* After all, Cates admits that he taught evolution. Doesn't that make him automatically guilty? The answer is that in a criminal case, the jury has the inherent right to nullify a criminal law by finding a defendant innocent, regardless of whether he actually committed the crime in question. This is a vital protection against unjust laws or prosecutorial vindictiveness, though jurors are never explicitly told about it. However, the jury did not take advantage of this opportunity, and considering the attitude of the citizenry, it was unlikely that it would have.

Brady is allowed too much latitude by the trial judge. He constantly makes speeches to the jury when he's supposed to be examining witnesses. Similarly, he asks leading questions of his own witnesses, essentially telling them how to testify. Rachel's highly damaging testimony about Cates's agnostic views is irrelevant. Cates's religious views have no bearing on any issue in the trial. Finally, Brady should not have been permitted to browbeat and intimidate Rachel by shouting at her nose-to-nose. After all, she was his own witness. Even if she were the Marquis de Sade, this technique would still be improper.

The critical dramatic incident at the trial is Brady's admission that the Bible can be read nonliterally. It is normally improper to call one's opposing counsel as an expert witness, since such testimony might involve counsel in a conflict between his views as an expert and the best interests of his own client. Brady was very foolish indeed to take up Drummond's challenge, and the judge was right in trying to discourage him from doing so.

Seventy years after it occurred, the Scopes monkey trial is as fascinating as ever, particularly as immortalized in a wonderful film like *Inherit the Wind*. No viewer can resist the inspired mix of small-town religious hysteria, caustic journalism, profound constitutional issues, and brilliant lawyering by two of the greatest figures in American legal and political history.

Trial Brief: The Scopes Monkey Trial

Inherit the Wind is based on the real Scopes monkey trial that occurred in Dayton, Tennessee, in 1925. The case came about because the American Civil Liberties Union advertised in the Tennessee papers for a teacher willing to cooperate in a challenge of the statute. The businessmen of Dayton thought a trial would bring national attention and increased business to their hick town, so they took up the ACLU's offer.

The merchants were successful beyond their wildest dreams, since several hundred reporters descended on the place, including H.L. Mencken (Hornbeck in the movie). Mencken was a nasty fellow, quite anti-Semitic and even more caustic and cynical in real life than in the film. Indeed, the trial was one of the biggest media events in American history, comparable to the O.J. Simpson trial in our own time. And the forces of evolution won the public relations battle, even though they lost the trial.

Scopes (Cates) was a football coach who never actually taught evolution. During the biology class in question, he discussed football plays, possibly including the "statue of liberty" play. Thus the case was a setup, and Scopes was never called as a witness since he knew nothing about evolution. The schoolboys who testified about the incident in question had to be coached. As far as is known, the part of the story about Cates, Rachel, and her father is fictitious.

A Christian fundamentalist group engaged William Jennings Bryan (Brady) as a prosecutor. Bryan, who had been defeated three times for president, was active in the movement to outlaw the teaching of evolution. Unlike the movie character, Bryan was quite familiar with the details of evolution. His probable reason for resisting evolution was that Darwinian theory was used by some writers such as Nietzsche and Spencer to legitimize human inequalities. Nietzsche's theory of the super race was based on the idea that some men are superior and thus entitled to rule and exploit inferior men.

Clarence Darrow was retained by the ACLU to defend Scopes. He was joined by several other brilliant lawyers (Dudley Field Malone and Arthur Garfield Hays). At the trial, the defense called experts to establish the legitimacy of evolution theory, but the court excluded all such testimony. The film does not make clear why this evidence was relevant. The actual reason for calling the experts was to show that evolution was compatible with the biblical story of creation. To violate the statute, the defense argued, Scopes had to deny the story of the divine creation. The judge allowed none of this testimony, stating that the statute was so clear that no expert testimony was needed.

As in the movie, Darrow actually called Bryan to the stand as an expert on the Bible. Bryan was made to look foolish as he tried to reconcile biblical literalism with scientific truth such as the age of rocks. Bryan willingly volunteered that the first day might have been twenty-five hours long; this was critical since it showed that the Bible need not be read literally and therefore that evolution could be considered compatible with the biblical story. However, the judge struck out the whole Bryan cross-examination as irrelevant.

Both sides agreed that the jury should receive a directed verdict of guilty. Therefore, neither prosecution nor defense made closing arguments, and Bryan especially lost the chance to give his summation, which he had been working on for three months. Bryan lived five days after the trial, and arranged for publication of his summation before he died.

On appeal, the Tennessee Supreme Court reversed Scopes's conviction, but upheld the validity of the statute banning the teaching of evolution. Its decision is not very convincing, however, since it discussed only the Tennessee constitution, not the federal constitution. Scopes's conviction was reversed because fines over $50 had to be imposed by the jury, not the judge. The court recommended that the "bizarre" case not be retried in the interests of the "peace and dignity of the state" and it was not. The Tennessee statute remained on the books until its repeal in 1967; Scopes was the only person ever prosecuted under it.

Trial Brief: The Constitutional Issues in Inherit the Wind

Inherit the Wind presents a difficult constitutional issue that remained unsettled until the United States Supreme Court's decisions in *Epperson v. Arkansas* (1968) and *Edwards v. Aguillard* (1987). Even today, struggles continue in court and in school boards over the issue of evolution versus creationism. In the movie, the trial judge refused even to consider the question of constitutionality of the law. While this was politically astute, it was dead wrong. All judges must decide constitutional questions that arise in cases tried before them.

Like all interesting constitutional issues, the Scopes trial presented two conflicting constitutional rights. On one hand, a state has the constitutional right to decide what should be taught in its public schools. If a state decides to require sex education, or to forbid sex education, a teacher has no right to disregard the law, even if it happens to coincide with the views of some religious group.

Yet there is another constitutional right at stake: the separation of church and state required by the First Amendment. The Tennessee law might be viewed as a deliberate attempt to promote the views of a particular religious group. Of course, any test that turns on the purpose of the legislature in passing a law is hard to apply, since the legislators may conceal their true purpose.

In the *Epperson* case, the Court invalidated an Arkansas law similar to the Tennessee law at issue in Scopes; in *Edwards,* the Court overturned a Louisiana law requiring any teacher who wished to teach evolution also to teach "creation science." In both cases, the Court found that the sole purpose of the law was to promote a specific religious view and thus it was invalid under the First Amendment.

There are some additional constitutional issues lurking in the story. For example, a completely irrational law would violate the due process clause of the Fourteenth Amendment. But since large numbers of people sincerely believed that creationism was right and evolution was wrong, the law would probably be considered rational in 1925 and perhaps even today. It could also be argued that the law interfered with the fundamental liberty of a teacher to teach and a student to learn; this was a view more fashionable in the 1920s than it is today. Perhaps the law interfered with freedom of speech, especially if it is viewed as prohibiting the teacher from even mentioning the existence of evolution. Finally, the law might be void for vagueness, since it was unclear whether it prohibited any mention of evolution or merely prohibited teaching that the theory was valid.

Judgment at Nuremberg

Synopsis: A dramatization of the Nuremberg war crime trials focusing on the moral responsibility of German judges who carried out Nazi laws.

UA/Roxlom (Stanley Kramer). 1961. Black and white. Running time: 190 min.

Screenplay: Abby Mann. TV play: Abby Mann. Director: Stanley Kramer.

Starring: Spencer Tracy (Judge Dan Haywood), Marlene Dietrich (Frau Bertholt), Burt Lancaster (Ernst Janning), Richard Widmark (Col. Tad Lawson), Maximilian Schell (Hans Rolfe), Judy Garland (Irene Hoffman), Montgomery Clift (Rudolph Petersen), William Shatner (Cptn. Byers).

Academy Awards: Best Screenplay, Best Actor (Schell).

Academy Award Nominations: Best Picture, Best Director, Best Cinematography, Best Actor (Tracy), Best Supporting Actor (Clift); Best Supporting Actress (Garland).

Rating: ⚖ ⚖ ⚖ ⚖

The Story

As the Nuremberg war crime trials are winding down, four judges are tried for enforcing Nazi laws. Dan Haywood, a judge from Maine who had been defeated for reelection, and two colleagues are assigned to preside over the trial. The defendants are forcefully defended by Hans Rolfe. The prosecutor, Colonel Lawson, helped liberate the extermination camps and is determined to hold the four judges responsible for their roles in the atrocities.

Three of the defendants are your run-of-the-mill Nazi hacks. The fourth, Ernst Janning, is a fascinating and tragic figure. Janning had been a famous German professor, an author of thirty books, a drafter and strong supporter of the democratic Weimar constitution, and a man who detested Hitler and the Nazis as well as his codefendants. Janning is mute when asked to plead, since he does not recognize the jurisdiction of the court; indeed, he objects to having Rolfe represent him.

The key evidence against Janning is the Feldenstein case, in which Janning condemned an elderly Jew to death for having sex with an Aryan girl named Irene Hoffman in violation of the Racial Pollution law. Hoffman reluctantly appears at the trial at Lawson's urging. She denies she ever had sexual relations with Feldenstein. A cleaning

Judgment at Nuremberg: Ernst Janning (Burt Lancaster) listens as his former mentor, Dr. Wieck, denounces him.

woman, who was an early member of the Nazi party, testifies that she saw Hoffman and Feldenstein kissing and saw Hoffman sitting on Feldenstein's lap. Rolfe's cross-examination of Hoffman is brutal, but Janning interrupts and admits that he decided to condemn Feldenstein before the trial had even begun.

A second claim against Janning is that he approved the sterilization of Rudolph Petersen. One explanation is that Petersen's father was a Communist whose family fought Nazi goons. But Rolfe argues that Petersen was properly sterilized because he was feebleminded. Even in court, Petersen is unable to pass the Nazi intelligence test—to form a sentence using the words "hare," "hunter," and "field." Rolfe argues that this was no war crime, since the Nazi laws requiring the feebleminded to be sterilized were similar to American laws that had been upheld by the U.S. Supreme Court.

In defense, Rolfe argues that Janning served as minister of justice and as a judge only to prevent worse horrors from taking place. Rolfe offers evidence that Janning protected a Jewish doctor at great risk to himself and he reduced many sentences.

Rolfe's closing argument focuses on moral responsibility. He suggests that it's unfair to say that the judges committed war crimes simply by doing their jobs. And if these judges are war criminals, so too are American industrialists who sold weapons to Hitler, or the Vatican that entered into a concordat with Hitler, or the Soviet Union that signed a peace treaty with Hitler and joined him in the invasion of Poland.

With the start of the Cold War, the Russians blockade Berlin, and American appetite for the war crimes trials begins to wane. Military and political authorities pressure Lawson and Haywood to ease up with the highly unpopular case, since the United States will soon need the Germans as friends. Thus Haywood becomes subject to the same sort of political pressure the Nazis placed on Janning.

Unmoved by legal precedents or political expediency, Haywood and Judge Norris (who had lost his son in the war) sentence all four defendants to life imprisonment. Judge Ives dissents, arguing that the defendants were not responsible for carrying out laws made by persons at higher levels.

At Janning's invitation, Haywood visits Janning in prison, and Janning repeats that he never imagined how far things would go under Hitler. Haywood replies, "You knew the first time you sentenced an innocent man to death." In the end, as Rolfe predicts, all the defendants are released within a few years.

Legal Analysis

Judgment at Nuremberg raises profound legal and moral questions about responsibility. Crimes against humanity, with which the Nuremberg defendants were charged, did not even exist as criminal offenses until after World War II, when the London Charter and the Nuremberg trials defined them for the first time. Up to that point, international law condemned nations, not individuals. Individuals could be prosecuted only under domestic laws by domestic authorities.

Thus the Nuremberg trials raise important questions about ex post facto laws—defining an act as a crime after the act has occurred. Under the U.S. Constitution, ex post facto laws are invalid. Nor is it even clear what gave the victorious Allies jurisdiction to try these cases in which Germans committed offenses against other Germans.

But surely it is fair to hold the Nazis to account for behavior that offended every norm of civilized human beings, even if such crimes had never before been defined or punished. After the war, many of the Allies favored rounding up and shooting the top Nazis after hasty courts-martial. It was better to carefully define and prosecute defendants according to due process of law, rather than impose quick and summary justice that the victors have traditionally meted out after wars. If we are to deter and ultimately to punish the international criminals of the present and future, the Nuremberg precedent is vital.

Assuming that Nazi atrocities were crimes against humanity for which individual Germans could properly be punished, were German judges guilty of these crimes? After all, the German judges did not make the policies, they only carried them out. And the policies had been duly adopted by competent authorities. The criminal law usually punishes people who break laws, not those who carry them out. The responsibility imposed by such a standard requires a judge to choose between resigning immediately or becoming an international criminal if he enforces an unjust law or becoming a German criminal if he refuses to enforce it. This is a lot to ask of anyone.

Indeed, were the laws in question in *Judgment at Nuremberg* so clearly unjust that a judge should refuse to enforce them? Remember, for generations American judges enforced laws that required segregation of the races and punished miscegenation (sex between blacks and whites). Such laws were not overturned until the 1950s. And consider the law calling for the sterilization of the feebleminded. As Rolfe points out, such a law had already been upheld in the United States. As the great Justice Oliver Wendell Holmes wrote in *Buck v. Bell* (1927): "Three generations of imbeciles are enough." Was Holmes a criminal too?

Should an American judge, morally and conscientiously opposed to abortion, refuse to enforce laws that establish a right to abortion or punish those who interfere with abortions? Doing so would be an excellent way to get impeached. Or was Germany different, because its unjust laws arose out of the monstrous corruption of the Third Reich in which morality counted for nothing?

Rolfe presents another defense: A judge might hate the situation he is in. Yet, by remaining and perhaps sentencing a Jew or two to death, he might be able to help many others or to prevent even more extreme atrocities from taking place. Haywood rejects this defense, but perhaps it has some merit.

The Feldenstein case established Janning's guilt, for Janning admits that more was involved than merely the injustice of the Racial Pollution Law. Janning admits that he would have condemned Feldenstein regardless of the evidence. Yet there was evidence presented in that case from which a reasonable judge could have concluded that Feldenstein and Hoffman had a sexual relationship. Even if Janning did not believe that evidence, it is not clear that Janning committed a crime against humanity in sentencing Feldenstein to death (and Hoffman to two years in prison for perjury) when the prosecution presented a prima facie case of violation of the law.

Swearing himself in as a witness, Lawson shows the ghastly films of the death camps at Dachau and Buchenwald. This is technically improper; Lawson should have called a different witness. Rolfe's objection is that the films are irrelevant, since the defendants knew nothing of these atrocities and played no role in them. But Janning and the other defendants had signed deportation orders. And, as Janning concedes, they chose not to know, not to see, what was happening all around them. Thus the films are indeed relevant to deciding the judges' moral responsibility. But given their extreme emotional impact, Haywood probably should not have admitted them as evidence.

In convicting the defendants, Haywood rejects all of the claimed defenses. A judge's responsibility, Haywood explains, is to stand for justice when standing for something is most difficult. Using this standard, Janning is guilty. But is this a standard to which we can realistically hold all judges?

There are lingering doubts about the outcome of the trial. One involves selective prosecution. Singling out four judges, when there must have been hundreds of equally guilty judges in Germany, seems unfair. Also, Rolfe devotes most of his efforts to defending Janning, rather than his other three more despicable clients. This seems unfair; perhaps they should have had separate counsel. Indeed, it is unclear whether Rolfe can represent Janning at all since Janning does not want any representation. There is considerable improper ex parte contact between Haywood and other people, including Lawson. Haywood should not be discussing the trial, or any of the defendants, with anyone except his fellow judges.

To its credit, the film does not portray Janning as a vicious thug, for that would be too easy. Instead, Janning is an ethical and intelligent human being caught up in a catastrophic dilemma that is out of his control. To serve the state, he must betray himself. By affirming that even such a man can be punished for executing evil laws, the film makes a powerful and unforgettable moral statement.

Trial Briefs: The Nuremberg Trials

The Nuremberg trials extended from 1945 to 1949. The first and by far the most important of the trials was authorized by the London Charter of 1945. The presiding judges came from the United States, Great Britain, France, and the USSR—the four countries then occupying Germany. The Charter and the trials established for the first time that international law prohibited war crimes and that these crimes could be prosecuted by the victors against individuals rather than against states. The trials also established that it was no defense that a person was acting under the orders of a superior.

The first trial focused on the Nazis at the very top of the Third Reich who had made its policies and had survived the war—people like Goering, Streicher, and Ribbentrop. They were accused, tried, and convicted of crimes against peace (such as waging aggressive war) as well as crimes against humanity. Some were sentenced to death.

There followed twelve more trials conducted exclusively by American civilian judges. German defense lawyers were paid, housed, and fed by the American authorities. *Judgment at Nuremberg* is a fictionalized account of the third of these trials. Other cases were brought against industrialists, military personnel, concentration camp superintendents, and other less prominent Germans. A vast number of suspects were potential defendants in these twelve cases, although ultimately only 185 were indicted.

The trial of the Nazi judges was presided over by James T. Brand of the Oregon Supreme Court. Ernst Janning is a combination of several of the Nazi judges or justice ministry officials who were defendants in the case. One of the defendants, who had been undersecretary of justice, made the argument that if he resigned, his successor would do even more harm. And another, who had been a judge at Nuremberg, presided over a trial just like the Feldenstein case. As in the movie, testimony of various witnesses made clear that the Feldenstein trial was a mere formality since guilt had been decided in advance. Both of these defendants received life sentences along with two others. Six others received prison terms of five to ten years and four defendants were acquitted.

Although it was hoped that the Nuremberg trials would be followed by the creation of an international criminal court which would be available to try war criminals or those who commit crimes against humanity, no such court has ever been created. The future enforcement of these crimes has been left to ad hoc tribunals like the Nuremberg trials or to domestic laws.

Let Him Have It

Synopsis: A mentally retarded nineteen-year-old takes part in a warehouse robbery attempt, and is convicted and hanged when his accomplice kills a police officer. It's a miscarriage of justice and anything else that can be put in a carriage.

First Independent/Vivid/Le Studio Canal Plus/British Screen (Luc Roeg and Robert Warr). 1991. Color. Running time: 115 min.

Screenplay: Neal Purvis and Robert Wade. Director: Peter Medak.

Starring: Christopher Eccleston (Derek Bentley), Paul Reynolds

Let Him Have It: Chris Craig (Paul Reynolds) and Derek Bentley (Chris Eccleston) stand trial for murder.

(Christopher Craig); Tom Courtenay (Derek's Dad, William Bentley), Eileen Atkins (Derek's Mother, Lillian Bentley); Clare Holman (Iris Bentley); Michael Gough (Lord Goddard).

Rating: —▮ —▮ —▮

The Story

Derek Bentley, age nineteen, lives with his working-class family in Croydon, South London. With a mental age of eleven and subject to epileptic seizures because of head injuries suffered in the bombing blitz of 1941, Derek is a recluse. His parents are thrilled when his sister, Iris, finally coaxes him out of the house to buy a Kay Starr record. Unfortunately, the next time out Derek meets Chris Craig, a sixteen-year-old gun-toting gangster wanna-be. Compared to a lifetime of listening to Kay Starr, hanging around with Chris seems exciting to Derek.

The army won't let the mentally disabled Derek enlist. But Chris is an equal opportunity thug, and lets Derek pal around with him. One night Derek and Chris try to break into a warehouse. A witness calls the police, and they are quickly surrounded. Derek gives up immediately, but Chris launches a blitz of his own. He pulls a gun and begins firing wildly, killing police officer Sidney Miles and wounding officer Fairfax. Derek and Chris are both charged with murder.

Since it's obvious that Chris fired the fatal shot, the trial focuses on

Derek's responsibility. The Crown's theory is that Derek is guilty of murder because he incited Chris to shoot. The key evidence comes from Sergeant Fairfax, who testifies that before Chris killed the officer, Derek shouted, "Let him have it, Chris." Asked what Derek meant by that, Fairfax says that he meant, "Start firing." Chris testifies that he owns about fifty guns and is always armed, but that Derek did not know that he had a gun on the night of the planned robbery. Derek also testifies, admitting that he was carrying the brass knuckles that Chris gave him. He didn't know Chris had a gun. He doesn't remember saying, "Let him have it, Chris," but really is too flustered to remember much of anything. Bullied by the judge, Lord Goddard, and the Crown prosecutor, Derek admits that he didn't tell Chris to stop shooting.

Derek's attorney argues that when Derek said, "Let him have it, Chris," he was telling Chris to hand his gun over to Sgt. Fairfax. But the defense offers no evidence of Derek's mental problems; the trial was held so soon after the killing that there was no time to have Derek examined. The jury convicts both Derek and Chris of murder, though it recommends mercy for Derek.

Lord Goddard apparently interprets "mercy" as meaning, "use a smooth rope," because he sentences Derek to death. Dad, Mum, and Iris valiantly and touchingly support Derek and spearhead a national protest. Appeals are filed emphasizing Derek's mental problems, and petitions are sent to the Home Office and Parliament. Nevertheless, Derek is hanged. Ironically, Chris, who fired the fatal shot but is too young to hang, is sentenced to prison.

A postscript tells us that Chris was released in 1963 after serving ten years and stayed out of trouble, and that Iris carries on the fight to clear Derek's name.

Legal Analysis

The film is an emotional account of an apparent miscarriage of justice, one from which no legal system seems immune. As usual, the problem was not in the rules themselves; surely British law provided ample legal bases for reducing the charges against Derek because of his mental limitations. But in a postwar Britain faced with rebellious unemployed youths, judges and politicians apparently felt it necessary to keep stiff upper lips and ropes.

Since Chris fired the fatal shot, the Crown can convict Derek of murder only by pointing to a legal theory that makes Derek responsible for Chris's act. One possibility is the "felony murder rule," which provides that any death that occurs in the course of a felony is murder, and holds all participants in the felony responsible. Unlike most of the United States, England does not have a felony murder rule. Nevertheless, English law would permit the Crown to argue that Derek is guilty of murder because he was engaged in a violent joint criminal enterprise with Chris. But the evidence doesn't support this theory. Derek did not carry a gun, and both Derek and Chris testified that Derek did not know that Chris was armed. And they didn't plan a daylight robbery of a bank filled with people who might try to stop them. Their target was a deserted warehouse, and the crime was to take place at night when nobody would be around. Finally, the Crown offered no evidence that the boys had agreed to kill someone if necessary to escape. Thus, Derek could not reasonably have expected a shooting to occur, and he was not guilty of murder under the violent joint enterprise theory.

Of course, the Crown claimed that not only did Derek join in the burglary attempt, but also he "incited" Chris to fire the fatal shot by telling Chris to "let him have it." As Spencer Tracy said when he let the German judges have it at the conclusion of *Judgment at Nuremberg,* a common thread running through the law of all civilized countries is that people who aid or encourage others to commit murder are themselves guilty of murder. Thus, if the jury believed that Derek was urging Chris to shoot at police officers, then it's fair for them to impute Chris's act to Derek.

But Lord Goddard blundered when he allowed Sergeant Fairfax to give his opinion to the jury that by making this statement, Derek was telling Chris to shoot police officers. A witness is not supposed to give an opinion unless the opinion is the only meaningful way for the witness to tell what happened. For example, a witness can give an opinion that someone was "smiling," because it's pretty hard to describe a smiling face without using the word "smile." (Especially if you're looking at the *Mona Lisa.*) But in this case, Sergeant Fairfax could communicate meaningfully without giving his opinion. For example, he could tell the jury what Derek said, the tone of voice in which he said it, and what was happening on the roof at the time Derek said it. Based on all that, it would be up to the jury to decide whether Derek meant, "start firing," "give him your gun," "turn over your fish and chips," or something else entirely. By giving his opinion, Sergeant Fairfax trampled on the jury's turf.

Even if the jury thought that Derek was telling Chris to "start firing," the jury could not properly decide whether Derek was guilty of murder without knowing about his mental impairment. Punishment for the most serious crimes is supposed to depend on the moral culpability of the criminal. Even though the end results of their acts might be the same, people who are mentally disabled can't be held to the same moral standard as normal individuals. That's why people who are legally insane are not guilty. Since they don't know right from wrong, we don't blame them.

Derek probably didn't qualify as legally insane; he seemed to know that it was wrong to steal from a warehouse. But Derek isn't guilty of murder unless he intended to encourage Chris to shoot a police officer. And that's where the evidence of Derek's mental impairment comes in. Had the jurors known about it, they might have decided that he was incapable of forming an intent to kill an officer. If so, Derek would have been convicted of a less serious crime than murder, and his life would have been saved. (Remember, the jurors recommended mercy even knowing nothing of his mental disability.) The Crown may have been anxious to speed the case along to set an example to others, but the failure of Derek's attorney to seek to postpone the trial to gather evidence of Derek's mental impairment was inexcusable. Once an appeals court became aware of the evidence, it should have reversed the conviction based on the defense attorney's malpractice.

Following British tradition, Lord Goddard "sums up" the case before submitting it to the jury. But though the term suggests otherwise, Lord Goddard's summary is hardly a neutral recitation designed to help the jurors remember the evidence. He points out the bravery of the police officers who must face down armed criminals, and implies that it was treasonous for the defense to suggest that they might be lying. Far from a summing-up, it's a dressing down of the whole defense case. Delivered with pompous authority and constituting the last words the jurors hear before they begin to deliberate, such a summing up could not help but influence the outcome in favor of the prosecution. British defense attorneys claim that such one-sided summaries are common, and they are currently seeking to limit the practice. In the United States also, judges theoretically have the power (if not the bewigged pompous authority) to sum up. But they rarely exercise it, and a one-sided summary such as the one delivered by Lord Goddard would almost certainly constitute reversible error.

Derek's execution was not a proud moment in British legal history. We can only wish that sometime after the trial, Lord Goddard's superiors had let him have it.

Trial Briefs

1. Derek Bentley was executed in 1953; his case and others (such as the *Christie* case, dramatized in *10 Rillington Place*) led Britain to

abolish capital punishment in 1965. Derek Bentley was the first person ever executed in Britain following a jury's recommendation for mercy. Government files which have since been released show that in 1953, senior Home Office officials urged then–home secretary Sir David Maxwell-Fyfe to grant Derek a reprieve. Amazingly, Lord Goddard told the home secretary that "no mitigating factors existed," and the sentence was carried out.

2. In 1991, Chris Craig broke a long silence about the case on the TV show *Thames Reports,* and, as he testified at the trial, denied that Bentley had said, "Let him have it, Chris." He successfully passed a lie detector test.

3. Home Secretary Michael Howard granted Bentley a "partial pardon" on July 30, 1993. The partial pardon maintains Bentley's guilt, but states that the punishment was inappropriate. The partial pardon followed a landmark July 1993 ruling by the Queen's Bench Divisional Court *(Regina v. Secretary of State for the Home Department, ex parte Bentley)* that a pardon may be based on an inappropriate punishment, not just on an erroneous conviction.

4. Iris continues to press for a full pardon for her brother. Her pleas gained momentum in May 1995, when police files were released suggesting a police conspiracy to convict Bentley by making up the fateful words attributed to him.

A Man for All Seasons

Synopsis: A lawyer with a conscience goes up against a king who has none. The treason trial is a sham and it produces a great shame.

Columbia/Highland (Fred Zinneman). 1966. Color. Running time: 120 min.

Screenplay: Robert Bolt. Stage play: Robert Bolt. Director: Fred Zinnemann.

Starring: Paul Scofield (Sir Thomas More), Wendy Hiller (Alice More), Robert Shaw (Henry VIII), Susannah York (Margaret More), Vanessa Redgrave (Anne Boleyn), John Hurt (Richard Rich), Orson Welles (Cardinal Wolsey), Leo McKern (Thomas Cromwell), Nigel Davenport (Duke of Norfolk).

Academy Awards: Best Picture, Best Screenplay, Best Director; Best Actor (Paul Scofield), Best Cinematography.

Academy Award nominations: Best Supporting Actress (Wendy Hiller), Best Supporting Actor (Robert Shaw).

Rating: ⚖ ⚖ ⚖ ⚖

The Story

Sir Thomas More becomes deeply and unwillingly embroiled in King Henry VIII's desperate need to remarry in order to find a wife who

A Man for All Seasons: Sir Thomas More (Paul Scofield) pleads his hopeless case.

will bear a son to carry on his dynasty. Henry had previously secured papal dispensation to marry his brother's widow, Catherine of Aragon. Unfortunately, Catherine proved "as barren as a brick." Now Henry's eye has turned to the vivacious (and hopefully fertile) Anne Boleyn. But not even the king can discard wives like chicken bones. The pope, who has a one-dispensation-per-customer rule, is not about to permit him to divorce Catherine or to annul the marriage.

More, one of England's greatest lawyers and judges, is elevated to the post of lord chancellor after the death of Cardinal Wolsey. Immediately, Henry seeks More's support for the divorce. More refuses to support the king because he believes unshakably in the pope's supreme authority. He does everything possible to avoid a clash with Henry but ultimately is forced to resign. His family's standard of living takes a big plunge.

Henry renounces papal authority and declares himself Supreme Head of the English Church. Now that he's making the rules, he receives an annulment and marries Anne. His faithful administrator Cromwell secures passage of a law requiring all subjects to take an oath of supremacy in which they accept Henry's actions. More refuses to take the oath, although he won't say why. Because of More's enormous reputation, his refusal to take the oath irks Henry more than an unused beheading ax. Even a year of imprisonment in the Tower does nothing to change More's mind. Finally, More is tried for high treason.

The notorious Richard Rich is the key witness against More. More had always distrusted Rich and refused to employ him. Rich, then working for Cromwell, went to More's cell to take him books. Rich testifies that More told him that he rejected the King's seizure of authority over the church. In return for this perjured testimony, Cromwell makes Rich the attorney general of Wales. More is not allowed to present evidence, giving new meaning to the term "speedy trial."

Cromwell asks the jury whether they need to retire. They have a keen interest in hanging on to their own heads, and immediately return a verdict of guilty. Finally, More is free to speak and he passionately denounces the king's actions and affirms papal authority. So much for his chances on appeal. Forgiving his executioner, More is beheaded.

His accusers fare no better, as most of them are beheaded for treason themselves within a few years. They asked for "More" beheadings, and they got them. Sir Richard Rich, however, dies in bed, with head.

Legal Analysis

Early in the film, More's son-in-law Roper declares that the devil should not receive due process of law. Wrong, More argues. "This country's planted thick with laws from coast to coast—man's laws, not God's—and if you cut them down . . . d'you really think you could stand upright in the winds that would blow then? . . . Yes, I'd give the Devil benefit of law, for my own safety's sake." In the end, of course, More is blown down by that very wind. Against a king, even a thicket of laws is unavailing.

More refuses to give in and take the oath, regardless of the consequences to himself and his family. But he uses every trick in the book to try to keep his head. He vouchsafes his views to nobody, not even his faithful and despairing wife Alice. Silence, he argues at the trial, is ambiguous; it can't be considered treason and even could be considered assent to the king's actions.

With all his lawyer's tricks, More cannot overcome Rich's perjured testimony. Of course, More points out an obvious implausibility in Rich's testimony: having refused to speak to anyone on the subject, why would he make the fatal concession to the devious Rich? And Rich's sudden promotion as attorney general of Wales suggests a motive to lie. But when King Henry is out to get you, such small details count for nothing. The verdict against More is a blot on English justice.

Perhaps all countries have had their sham trials, in which the forms of justice are perverted to achieve some political end. This was certainly true of Nazi justice, as stirringly depicted in *Judgment at Nuremberg*. The court system in the USSR dispensed "telephone justice," meaning the judge would call the local party official before deciding what to do. Military justice, as explored in *Breaker Morant* or *Paths of Glory* has often been a political charade. And in America, we might remember the removal of Japanese citizens to concentration camps early in World War II. This terribly unjust and unnecessary action was upheld by courts right up the line. Only a single lonely dissenter in the U.S. Supreme Court refused to buy the government's military necessity argument. So the trial of Sir Thomas More isn't historically unique. And it reminds us once more that any justice system is terribly vulnerable to political pressure.

Most modern viewers are secular in their outlook. Few could imagine sacrificing everything for an abstraction like papal authority, especially when everyone else had long since caved in. So how can we relate to a character like More, whose religious convictions are so powerful that they lead him to martyrdom?

While More may seem to be up on some lonely pinnacle, the fact remains that there are plenty of real heroes in every generation. These are people who are willing to make the ultimate sacrifice for some cause that bewilders their family and neighbors. How about the righteous gentiles who concealed Jews from the Nazis? Or volunteers who willingly marched off to war to preserve the Union? Perhaps each of us can aspire to be persons of conscience like Sir Thomas More, even as we hope never to be called upon to choose personal or professional martyrdom.

Trial Brief: Sir Thomas More

Sir Thomas More (1478–1535) was a true Renaissance man who wrote scholarly books on a variety of subjects (his *Utopia* causes some to regard him as the first socialist). He was a wonderful combination of wily lawyer, loving family man, and heroic defender of principle. His friend, the Dutch philosopher Erasmus, originally called him "a man for all seasons," and so he still seems.

More was admitted to Lincoln's Inn in 1496 and practiced as a barrister until 1503. He served in Parliament and in a variety of diplomatic, judicial, administrative, and educational posts. He was a close and trusted adviser to Henry VIII. The king insisted on employing More after he had won an important case against the Crown. More was a great lawyer and judge. It is said that there was a huge backlog of chancery cases when he became lord chancellor. But he cleared the docket, so that when he called for the next case, he was told there was no man or matter to be heard. As in the movie, More was unflinching in his defense of the Catholic Church. Like many pious people of the time, he favored the burning of heretics.

More is said to have slept only two hours a night, a regimen made easier by the fact that he wore a hair shirt and slept on planks with a log for a pillow. Alice was More's second wife. He married her only a month after the death of his first wife, who had borne him four children ranging in age from two to six years at the time of her death. She also must not have slept much. More insisted on educating his daughters as well as his sons and always corresponded with them in Latin. This gave them a good excuse for not writing back. More's house in Chelsea had eighty-three servants and he often fed one hundred people a day.

More succeeded Wolsey as lord chancellor in 1529. Wolsey did not die, as in the movie. He resigned or was removed by the king because he refused to grant the king an annulment. Wolsey recommended More for the job. More served the king as lord chancellor with great loyalty, supporting policies he loathed, until events relating to Henry's pressure on the church made it impossible for him to continue. He resigned in 1532. The new archbishop of Canterbury upheld the legality of Henry's marriage to Anne Boleyn and she was crowned as queen in 1533. More did not attend the wedding, thus earning the hatred of Anne's family. A revered martyr, More was elevated to sainthood by Pope Pius XI in 1935. He is often considered the patron saint of lawyers, perhaps reflecting what society wishes would happen to lawyers more often.

Trial Brief: The Trial of Sir Thomas More

The conflict between More and the king, as well as More's trial, is quite accurately described in *A Man for All Seasons*. Historical evidence supports the desperate visits of More's family to the Tower. Cromwell and others interrogated More on numerous occasions, but he always refused to say whether he accepted the king's authority as head of the English Church. Richard Rich, by then the solicitor general, did in fact visit More to take him books and he and More engaged in the disputed conversation.

Historical evidence shows that the king had ordered More's execution before the trial even started. The ax was being sharpened even as the trial took place. There were four counts against More, but three were dropped. Only the count for treason remained. The court was an unusual one with seven judges, nineteen councillors, and sixteen jurors. Apparently More was unaware of the indictment, so could not have anticipated Rich's evidence. Rich was discredited when other witnesses called by the Crown could not support his account. More was not permitted to call witnesses in his own behalf.

After fifteen minutes of deliberation the jury found More guilty, and he was sentenced to die. His speech in open court was much as it was presented in the movie. He stated that the Act of Supremacy was repugnant to the laws of God and the church and therefore insufficient to bind any Christian man. On the scaffold, as in the movie, he said that he died "the king's good servant, but God's first."

The Onion Field

Synopsis: Two cop killers tie the legal system in knots. Effective trial scenes, although sometimes it's difficult to know just what's going on in court.

Black Marble (Walter Coblentz). 1979. Color. Running time: 126 min.

Screenplay: Joseph Wambaugh, based on his book. Director: Harold Becker.

Starring: James Woods (Gregory Powell), John Savage (Karl Hettinger), Franklyn Seales (Jimmy Smith), Ted Danson (Ian Campbell), Ronny Cox (Pierce Brooks), David Huffman (Phil Halpin).

Rating: —■ —■ —■

The Story

In March 1963, a scary but highly intelligent psychopath named Greg Powell meets up with Jimmy Smith. Smith recently got out of the slammer on parole and is down on his luck. Powell is totally committed to family values—meaning that he likes being a father figure for the reluctant crooks like Smith who help him with armed robbery and car thefts.

Powell and Smith are pulled over in Hollywood by a police car driven by officers Ian Campbell and Karl Hettinger. Campbell is a veteran cop, but Hettinger is inexperienced. Both men are married with young children. As Powell gets out of the car, he suddenly pulls a gun on Campbell. Although Hettinger's gun is also drawn, he gives it up to save Campbell's life. The crooks then kidnap the two policemen.

They drive to an onion field near Bakersfield, which is about 100 miles and four culture zones away from Hollywood. They get out of the car and Powell shoots Campbell. When Campbell is down but still alive, four more bullets are fired into his chest; these shots kill him. It

The Onion Field: Cop-killers Jimmy Smith (Franklyn Seales) and Gregory Powell (James Woods) on trial for murder.

is unclear who fired the fatal shots; probably it was Smith, although he always denied it. By a miracle, Hettinger escapes into the night as the two killers stalk him. Powell is soon caught and interrogated by Sergeant Brooks. Trying to ingratiate himself with the police, Powell immediately confesses but fingers Smith as the actual killer. Following Powell's tip, Smith is also arrested.

Although some beat policemen defend his decision, Hettinger is heavily criticized by the police brass for giving up his gun. Hettinger has a breakdown, becomes a shoplifter, and is compelled to resign from the force. He nearly kills himself, but finally, years later, pulls out of it and becomes a landscape gardener. He is willing to plant anything but onions. Hettinger's breakdown is caused in part by the legal system which requires Hettinger to testify about the horrible events over and over again. Hettinger is fortunate to have the unwavering support of his wife, who never gives up on him.

At their first trial, Powell and Smith are tried together. Powell fires his public defender and represents himself, infuriating everybody else in the courtroom. He puts his mother and father on the witness stand to testify about his deprived childhood. Both Powell and Smith are sentenced to death. Smith continues to deny ever hurting anyone. "I'm only a thief," he says, not a killer.

Their conviction is reversed by the California Supreme Court and the case is retried. By this time, Powell has become a master jailhouse lawyer and grinds out endless motions. The droning defense attorneys and the endless procedures drive everyone nuts, burning out prosecutor Halpin after six long years. He decides to pursue an ABL (anything but law) career. Ultimately, the two men are sentenced to life imprisonment and Smith is released on parole.

Legal Analysis

One of the bases for the California Supreme Court's reversal of Powell and Smith's convictions was that they were tried together instead of separately. The reason for this decision was that each defendant had made statements incriminating the other one. In a separate trial of A, B's statement incriminating both A and B would be inadmissible under the hearsay rule. But if A and B are tried together, and B's statement is admitted against B, the jury will hear the material that incriminates A. That makes the joint trial unfair (*Bruton v. United States,* 1968). Even aside from the use of the statements, where two defendants are accusing each other, it seems fundamentally unfair to try them both together.

Of course, the use of separate trials permits the defendants to play the self-incrimination game. At Smith's subsequent trial, he calls Powell as a witness. He asks Powell if Powell shot Campbell four times after he was down. Powell takes the Fifth Amendment (which protects him against incriminating himself). That causes the jurors to think that Powell probably fired the four shots rather than Smith.

The big issue for Smith is who fired the four bullets into Campbell's chest after he was down. Apparently, these were the shots that killed Campbell. In terms of guilt, it really shouldn't matter. Even if Smith never fired his gun, he aided and abetted Powell and thus is guilty of first-degree murder. But it would make a difference on the penalty phase of the trial. In California, the jury decides on the penalty in a separate proceeding and is less likely to give the death penalty to someone who was just along for the ride.

Before shooting Campbell, Powell asked Campbell if he'd heard of the Little Lindbergh law. This is a state law (California Penal Code section 209) which calls for life imprisonment without possibility of parole for certain forms of kidnapping. If death or serious bodily harm results, the kidnapping carries the death penalty (this part of the law has since been repealed). The Lindbergh law was inspired by the kidnapping of Charles Lindbergh's son in 1932. Powell thought it applied, so he had to kill the cops to get rid of any witnesses to the crime.

Sergeant Brooks tells Powell that the law wasn't applicable, so he didn't have to kill the cops. Brooks claims the Little Lindbergh law only applies to kidnapping for ransom. However, Brooks is probably wrong. Little Lindbergh could well apply because it covers kidnapping for robbery and Powell and Smith robbed Campbell and Hettinger of money and their guns. If it applied, Smith and Powell would have been subject to life without parole even if they didn't harm Campbell and Hettinger.

Normally, it's foolish to represent yourself in court, especially in a criminal case. However, if the judge finds the defendant competent to represent him- or herself, the defendant must be allowed to do so (*Faretta v. California*, 1975). Powell was intelligent enough to represent himself and by doing so was able to greatly delay and confuse matters. Ultimately, however, the court appointed counsel for Powell on the basis that the case was too complex for him to represent himself. At that point, Powell's disagreements with his assigned counsel delayed the case even more.

The main point of *The Onion Field* is to criticize the criminal justice system for its endless delays and its reluctance to impose the death penalty. By playing the system like a drum, Powell and Smith escape the death penalty and Smith ultimately walks out of prison. Because judges are appropriately concerned that no stone be left unturned when a defendant's life is on the line, the cases often drag on through many rounds of trial, appeal, petitions for habeas corpus, motions for stay of execution and so on.

The Onion Field does a fine job of showing the legal system tied up in knots when it comes to imposing the ultimate punishment. In reality, the death penalty is seldom carried out. It is almost a matter of random chance whether murderers will be put to death. When it is used, the death penalty is disproportionately imposed on minorities, especially blacks who kill whites. The fact that the death penalty is so very difficult and costly to administer, that it imposes great costs on our overloaded criminal justice system, and that its use is capricious, are all arguments often used in support of dispensing with it in favor of a system of life imprisonment without parole.

Trial Brief: Powell and Smith in the California Courts

Joseph Wambaugh, a Los Angeles policeman, wrote the book *The Onion Field* and later the screenplay of this movie. The book and movie are closely based on the facts of the Powell-Smith case. Understandably, Wambaugh was outraged by the fact that the legal system could not bring itself to quickly and efficiently send these two vicious and depraved cop killers to the gas chamber.

The circumstances of the murder of Powell and Smith and their capture by the police are precisely as described in the movie. According to the California Supreme Court (*People v. Powell,* 1967), Smith and Powell each made ten different statements to the police, statements that became more and more incriminating. For example, Powell admitted to thirty-five robberies. By the time the two stopped making statements, about the only thing left in doubt was whether Powell or Smith fired into Campbell's chest after he was down.

The unanimous 1967 decision of the California Supreme Court reversed both convictions because the confessions were made under circumstances that violated the rule in *Escobedo v. Illinois* (1964) and a California case *(Dorado)* that expanded on *Escobedo.* Powell and Smith's confessions were inadmissible because they were interrogated while in custody without being warned of their rights to remain silent and have counsel present. This ruling knocked out all but Powell and Smith's first statements to the police, which were volunteered. There were numerous other grounds for reversal as well. Note: *Escobedo* was later superseded by *Miranda v. Arizona* (1966).

For the second trial, Irving Kanarek was appointed to defend Smith. Kanarek infuriated presiding judge Arthur Alarcon by interrupting him repeatedly during pretrial motions. Kanarek is probably the motormouth heard at one point in the movie whose voice is like fingernails on the blackboard. Kanarek drives everyone in the courtroom berserk and pushes Halpin to make an immediate career change. Judge Alarcon decided that Kanarek was incompetent. He fired Kanarek and appointed William Drake, perhaps confusing him with Perry Mason's trusted investigator, Paul Drake. Smith refused to cooperate with Drake and would accept only Kanarek.

Among Judge Alarcon's reasons for discharging Kanarek was that he had never tried a death penalty case before. This seems a bit odd—if you can't try a death case unless you have tried one before, the number of available attorneys in death cases would shrink to zero as they died off. Anyway, the Supreme Court held that Smith had a right to be represented by the counsel of his choice, regardless of incompetence or bad manners, (*Smith v. Superior Court,* 1968). During the retrial, however, Smith fired Kanarek and yet another attorney was appointed to represent him. Not long afterward, Kanarek represented crazed killer Charles Manson.

In 1969, the two men were retried separately and convicted again without the aid of the incriminating statements. This time Powell got the death penalty and Smith got life imprisonment. However, by the time of the appeal, the California Supreme Court had invalidated California's death penalty statute, so Powell's death sentence was modified to life imprisonment. The Court of Appeal affirmed both convictions against a myriad of technical objections (*People v. Powell,* 1974).

Smith was released on parole in 1982 but continued to have trouble with the law. He served a prison sentence for a drug offense in 1986. By this time, he had amended his spiel, saying "I'm only a thief and a druggie, not a murderer."

In 1977, the Parole Board gave Powell a 1983 parole release date. After *The Onion Field* was shown on television and a public outcry arose, the board canceled the date. The Supreme Court upheld this decision because a psychiatric study considered by the board indicated that there was serious doubt about whether Powell could make it in the outside world. The court's decision also details numerous escape attempts by Powell before his death sentence was modified. Yet he had become an exemplary prisoner once he left death row (*In re Powell,* 1988).

As of this writing, Powell is still in prison. In September 1994, the board refused to parole him, in part because he refused to take part in vocational training. Meanwhile, Hettinger moved to Bakersfield, where he ultimately became a member of the Kern County Board of Supervisors. He died in 1994 at the age of fifty-nine.

Reversal of Fortune

Synopsis: Harvard law professor Alan Dershowitz and an army of law students convince the Rhode Island Supreme Court to reverse the attempted murder conviction of Claus von Bulow.

Warner Bros. (Oliver Stone and Edward Pressman). 1990. Color. Running time: 111 min.

Screenplay: Nicholas Kazan. Book: Alan M. Dershowitz. Director: Barbet Schroeder.

Starring: Jeremy Irons (Claus von Bulow), Glenn Close (Sunny von Bulow), Ron Silver (Alan Dershowitz), Uta Hagen (Maria).

Academy Award: Best Actor (Jeremy Irons).

Academy Award nomination: Best Director.

Rating: —▮ —▮

The Story

Sunny von Bulow is an heiress who's addicted to alcohol, tobacco, and virtually everything else in the drugstore. Husband Claus von Bulow is so icy that he might have been carved from a glacier. Publicly, von Bulow and Sunny are a lovely couple who live like royalty.

Privately, they despise each other, but stay together because he needs her money and she needs his companionship. Von Bulow's quite involved with his mistress, Alexandra Isles, whom he wants to marry. Also, von Bulow wants to start working, but Sunny detests that idea. There is talk of divorce.

Around Christmas 1979, Sunny goes into a coma. Von Bulow lies next to her in bed nearly all day. Her loyal maid Maria is quite concerned, but von Bulow claims she's just sleeping off a hangover. He refuses to call the doctor (Sunny detested doctors) and when he does, he downplays the problem. Finally, when Sunny appears to be having difficulty breathing, von Bulow calls for help, and Sunny is revived. About a year later, Sunny again goes into a coma. She's found unconscious in the bathroom of their "cottage" (actually a palace) at Newport. The window is wide open and the temperature around zero. Sunny never awakes from coma No. 2.

Maria is extremely suspicious of von Bulow and she alerts Sunny's children, Ala and Alexander. They hire an attorney and with an investigator break into von Bulow's closet in Newport. They find a black bag containing some of von Bulow's medications plus a syringe and a container of insulin. This is highly suspicious, since nobody is diabetic and von Bulow hadn't played "doctor" for years. Von Bulow is prosecuted on two counts of assault with intent to commit murder by injecting Sunny with insulin. He is convicted and gets thirty years. Everybody figures he's guilty. Even his mistress testifies against him.

Dershowitz, a hyperactive, motormouth Harvard law professor, agrees to take von Bulow's case on appeal. He does it so that he can use the fee to support his pro bono work on behalf of two black men condemned to death. The streetwise Dershowitz and patrician von Bulow could be from different planets. They barely speak the same language.

Von Bulow maintains that Sunny tried to commit suicide or accidentally took an overdose of something. He claims that she took his black bag and that the contents were hers. Dershowitz tells von Bulow to shut up. He doesn't want to hear any lies; later Dershowitz becomes convinced that von Bulow is innocent. Dershowitz assembles a large team of lawyers and law students to work on von Bulow's case. Some of them are reluctant, regarding von Bulow as an upper-class creep who is obviously guilty. In addition to finding technical errors in the trial, Dershowitz believes that he must make the Rhode Island Supreme Court want to reverse the conviction by finding evidence that proves von Bulow's innocence.

Dershowitz finds evidence that von Bulow did not inject Sunny with insulin. The search of his Newport closet was so sloppy that there was no inventory of what was found and it was unclear what was in the black bag. Moreover, the labels had been scraped off so there was no reason to think there was insulin in the bag. Finally, if the needle had been used to inject insulin into Sunny, it would have been wiped clean when it was withdrawn. Thus the fact that the needle contained traces of insulin suggests that it was dipped into insulin by someone trying to frame von Bulow. Dershowitz's team locates other discrepancies in the medical and scientific evidence against von Bulow.

The Rhode Island Supreme Court justices initially resist Dershowitz's attempt to discuss newly discovered evidence on appeal. However, he persuades them to consider it. The court reverses the conviction and orders a new trial, at which von Bulow is acquitted on all counts. We never know what really happened: Perhaps von Bulow tried to kill Sunny, perhaps Sunny poisoned herself deliberately or by accident, or perhaps it was a little bit of each (von Bulow might have opened the bathroom window when he found Sunny's unconscious body).

Legal Analysis

An appeal in a criminal case is strictly confined to the trial record. It is improper for a lawyer to argue or for the justices to consider new evidence about innocence or any other nonrecord evidence. Therefore, the Rhode Island Supreme Court should not have allowed Dershowitz to make arguments based on affidavits that presented new evidence or to include the affidavits in his appeal brief.

Dershowitz's theory for talking about the new evidence was bogus. In a prior case the court stated that a chain of circumstantial evidence is no stronger than its weakest link. When one of his associates unearths this so-called precedent, Dershowitz reacts like they'd just found the cure for cancer. In fact, this rule is a well-worn cliché. There's no way that it justifies consideration of nonrecord evidence. The weakest-link "rule" simply allows an attorney for the defendant to attack the significance of circumstantial evidence at trial, not to bring in new evidence on appeal.

If a defendant has newly discovered evidence of innocence, it should be presented to the trial judge, who will then decide whether there should be a new trial. If the trial judge refuses to order a new trial, the appellate judges could decide whether the judge's refusal was an abuse of discretion. But appellate justices will not consider the new evidence before the trial judge has done so.

Dershowitz thought that the justices would never reverse the conviction on narrow technical grounds (such as unlawful search and seizure) unless they were first convinced that a real injustice had been done and that an innocent man might have been convicted. This is probably a sound intuition. Appellate court justices want to do justice and generally will try to find a way to overturn a lower court decision that seems unjust. Nevertheless, they are limited to the record when they consider an appeal.

The jury in von Bulow's first trial convicted him because it was convinced that circumstantial evidence established his guilt beyond a reasonable doubt. There was no direct evidence by eyewitnesses who could testify that they'd seen him inject Sunny with insulin. But a conviction based on circumstantial evidence is perfectly proper, (see *Circumstantial Evidence,* p. 193). And here the circumstantial evidence was quite damning. Von Bulow acted quite suspiciously, especially at the time of the first coma. He had a definite financial motive for killing Sunny. Witnesses testified that they found a syringe containing insulin traces in his black bag. Maria had seen a syringe and insulin in his bag a month before. Sunny had an extremely high level of insulin in her blood when admitted to the hospital at the time of her second coma. It seemed like a slam dunk.

Yet there is always a possibility that the inferences of guilt drawn from items of circumstantial evidence can be wrong. Von Bulow's suspicious behavior at the time of the first coma was consistent with his respect for Sunny and her dislike of doctors. The bag might have contained Sunny's drugs, not von Bulow's. Sunny might have injected herself. Worst of all, Dershowitz's newly discovered evidence indicates that a frame-up may have occurred. Someone may have dipped the needle in insulin to create evidence.

The right to an appeal in a criminal case is a vital part of due process. Trial courts can and often do make serious errors of law. Triers of fact come up with decisions that are not supported by the evidence. An appellate court provides a fresh look at the proceedings and one last opportunity to prevent an injustice from occurring.

However, the appeal in *Reversal of Fortune* was unrealistic in the way the Supreme Court considered nonrecord evidence. And very few defendants could afford the full-court press that Dershowitz and his team were able to muster. Nevertheless, the appeal process worked in the film. Von Bulow, who had been sentenced to thirty years in the slammer, won a new trial and ultimately walked out the courthouse door to freedom.

Trial Briefs

1. Alan Dershowitz is a Harvard law professor who's had a long list of celebrity clients. In addition to von Bulow, he's represented Mia Farrow, Mike Tyson, Leona Helmsley, and numerous others. But he's also taken many pro bono cases when he feels the case presents important legal or moral issues. Most law professors live a sheltered life, teaching classes, writing books and articles on legal subjects and trial movies, and seldom if ever represent actual clients. Dershowitz is one of the few exceptions.

2. The film *Reversal of Fortune* mixes fact and fiction. According to Dershowitz's book, von Bulow was Danish, descended from a famous German family. He and his mother fled to England after the Nazis occupied Denmark. Von Bulow was himself an attorney who had apprenticed as a barrister in London. Sunny's father left her an enormous fortune. Her first marriage was to a penniless prince; they had two children, Ala and Alexander, who were twenty-two and twenty-one at the time Sunny went into her second coma. Von Bulow and Sunny had one child, Cosima, who was then thirteen. Cosima took von Bulow's side in the trials and, as a result, was disinherited by her grandmother.

Sunny's faithful maid, Maria Schrallhammer, suspected von Bulow after the first coma and watched him closely. Maria had first seen the black bag in February 1980, after the first coma; she saw it again around Thanksgiving 1980, and claimed that it contained syringes and insulin. Sunny's children hired attorney Richard Kuh to investigate. Kuh interviewed the children and Maria and led the search that uncovered the black bag. However, he refused to disclose his notes and the trial court upheld his decision not to do so.

Maria's testimony was very damaging to von Bulow at his first trial. She described the highly suspicious facts surrounding the first coma (she was not at Newport when Sunny went into her second coma). There was also strong scientific testimony against von Bulow including a Harvard scientist who ruled out all other causes for Sunny's second coma except an insulin injection. Von Bulow did not testify and his defense was ineffectual.

Dershowitz's ploy to get the new evidence before the Supreme Court was innovative. He filed with the Supreme Court the new trial motion that he planned to make in the trial court in the event the Supreme Court affirmed the trial court decision. This motion, of course, included affidavits about newly discovered evidence and possible frame-ups. Thus it drew the attention of the Supreme Court justices to the new evidence, and planted the seeds of doubt about whether an injustice had been done. Dershowitz is convinced that the justices read the motion and decided to order a new trial because they were concerned that an innocent man might have been convicted.

The Rhode Island Supreme Court reversed von Bulow's conviction on two grounds. First, the court held that Kuh's notes had to be disclosed; neither the attorney-client privilege nor the work-product doctrine shielded them. Although the communications between Alexander and Kuh were attorney-client communications, the privilege was waived by disclosing them to the police. Similarly, all of Kuh's notes were his work product, which is normally protected from disclosure. However, he waived it by actually referring to those notes while testifying at the first trial.

The second ground was based on unlawful search and seizure. The Fourth Amendment only prohibits state officials from making unreasonable searches, not private parties. Thus the search by Alexander and the investigator of von Bulow's closet wasn't unconstitutional. However, according to the court, the violation occurred when the police failed to get a warrant before testing the contents of the black bag that Kuh turned over to them. In the book, Dershowitz says he was amazed by this holding; it was an argument he thought so weak that he considered leaving it out of his brief.

Von Bulow was retried and acquitted on both counts. Kuh's notes threw extreme doubt on the whole insulin story; it turns out Maria never mentioned finding insulin when Kuh interviewed her. Dershowitz believes that someone concocted the insulin story (and dipped the needle in insulin) only after it was discovered that Sunny had a high concentration of insulin in her body. All of the test results were dubious (both the insulin on the needle and the insulin in Sunny's body), as was the scientific testimony that the coma could only have been caused by an insulin injection. And the search of the von Bulow bedroom and closet and the black bag was hopelessly inept; no inventory was maintained and it was unclear whether a pill bottle with von Bulow's name on it was found in the bag or elsewhere. Thus on retrial the prosecution's circumstantial evidence case fell apart. Von Bulow may or may not have tried to kill Sunny, but the prosecution failed to prove it at the second trial.

10 Rillington Place

Synopsis: An innocent man receives a fair trial and is convicted and hanged. A cautionary tale about capital punishment.

10 Rillington Place: Murderer John Christie (Richard Attenborough) gives perjured testimony.

Columbia/Filmways (Basil Appleby). Great Britain, 1971. Color. Running time: 111 minutes.

Screenplay: Clive Exton. Book: Ludovic Kennedy. Director: Richard Fleisher.

Starring: Richard Attenborough (John Christie), John Hurt (Timothy John Evans), Judy Geeson (Beryl Evans), Pat Heywood (Ethel Christie).

Rating: ⚒ ⚒ ⚒

The Story

John Christie seems a gentle, kindly sort, always ready to share his medical knowledge with a damsel in distress. In fact he is a psychopathic killer who lures women to his flat at 10 Rillington Place and gasses them to death. Then he has intercourse with their dead bodies, before burying them in the garden.

Tim Evans, his wife Beryl, and their baby Geraldine rent a couple of shabby rooms above Christie's flat. Tim is illiterate and not very bright. The family struggles to get by on his meager salary. Tim and Beryl fight constantly, especially when Beryl announces that she is pregnant again. They have no money for an abortion and pills don't work. Luckily the generous Christie tells the desperate Beryl that he knows how to perform abortions and will do one for free. Reluctantly, Tim agrees and heads off to work.

Christie kills Beryl and when Tim returns, Christie threatens to report Tim to the police as the killer unless he flees. Christie promises to give baby Geraldine to a couple he knows. Christie manipulates the dim and distraught Tim with ease. Tim heads off for Wales and Christie kills the baby. Eventually, Tim goes to the police, who find the bodies of both Beryl and Geraldine. Devastated by the terrible news that his little girl is dead, Tim unaccountably confesses to both murders. He is not pressured to do so and the confession is not coerced.

Tim's trial, conducted by the usual bewigged barristers and judges, is fair, but there is little his counsel can do to help him. Tim tells the truth, but Christie denies any involvement. The circumstantial evidence against Tim is powerful and Christie's low-key and bumbling manner makes his denial persuasive to the jury. Tim cannot explain why he confessed to crimes he did not commit, nor why Christie would have killed anyone.

Tim is sentenced to death. The medical board finds Tim mentally competent to be executed, and probably wishes it could censure Christie for performing abortions without ordering the patient to fill out ten forms. Tim goes to the gallows. Several years later, Christie is caught. He has continued to kill more women, including his wife Ethel, who knew Tim was innocent. Christie is tried and hanged. All the authorities can do for Tim is to dig him up and rebury him in consecrated ground.

Legal Analysis

Tim's case is a lawyer's worst nightmare—a seemingly fair trial which leads to the conviction and execution of an innocent person. The second worst nightmare would be the development of "Trial Lite," which provides all the justice with only half the number of lawyers.

Fair process cannot guarantee a correct outcome. But we can learn from our mistakes, and in retrospect Tim's confession was the cause of his unjust conviction. His attorney should share the blame for not emphasizing strongly that the language of the confession suggested it was more a product of police imagination than Tim's recollection. Also he should have more thoroughly probed the psychological pressures the police put on Tim. An expert witness describing the effect of all that had happened on a person of Tim's mental status might have been persuasive. All this is a reminder that a vigorous and thorough defense is as essential to justice as any other component of a fair trial.

At the end of the day, Tim's confession would still have been powerful evidence of guilt. Most people probably believe that innocent people don't confess—especially to murder. And it is difficult to understand why Tim confessed to crimes of which he was totally innocent, even taking into account his intelligence, feelings of guilt, and terror.

Perhaps because of a confession's persuasiveness, a variety of legal rules circumscribe their use. One such rule is the "corpus delicti" rule, which is often mistaken as referring to a dead body or to a stale corned beef sandwich. Actually, the rule provides that a person cannot be convicted solely on the basis of a confession—the prosecution has to offer independent evidence that a crime was committed. Other rules indicative of the legal system's skeptical attitude toward confessions are the *Miranda* rule (requiring police officers to warn suspects of their right to free counsel before interrogating them), and a rule requiring a judge to determine that a confession is voluntary before a jury can consider it.

At trial, Tim's counsel tries to discredit Christie with Christie's prior convictions of a variety of crimes of both theft and violence. It is permissible to impeach the credibility of a witness for any conviction of a crime carrying more than a one-year prison sentence or any crime involving dishonesty (see *Character Evidence,* p. 259). Unfortunately, the last of Christie's convictions occurred seventeen years before the trial. The convictions were so stale that the trial judge should have excluded all reference to them. And even if they were admissible, the only permissible use the jury could make of them was to consider the effect on Christie's credibility as a witness. They could not be used as evidence that he was the real killer.

A strong argument against capital punishment is that it is irrevocable. When a mistake is made, as in this movie, there is no way to bring an innocent victim back to life. To many people, this alone is a convincing argument against the death penalty. After all the inconclusive arguments about deterrence are put aside, the nasty truth remains: An innocent person can be given a completely fair trial and executed. It's a reality that must give pause to any capital punishment enthusiast.

Trial Brief: The Evans Case

10 Rillington Place is the actual story of another of our century's storied monsters. Christie makes the Psychopath Hall of Fame along with Jeffrey Dahmer, Charles Manson, and Mrs. Fields's Cookies. Tim's IQ was only 68, giving him the intelligence of a ten-year-old child. Despite the film's depiction, Tim's confession may have been coerced.

The police kept him isolated for an extensive period, then grilled him all night long. Tim was totally devastated by the news that Geraldine was dead and blamed himself for the deaths of both Beryl and Geraldine. Much of the wording of his confession is legalistic; these words could have come only from the police, not from Tim. He ultimately signed the confession out of sheer exhaustion and fear that he would be beaten. Inadequate attention was given at Tim's trial to the dubious nature of his confession.

Tim was convicted and hanged in 1950. He was tried only for the murder of baby Geraldine, not for Beryl's murder. Christie was hanged in 1953. The case was a huge cause célèbre in Britain and it, along with the events, dramatized in *Let Him Have It,* led ultimately to the abolition of capital punishment in 1965. Tim was officially pardoned in 1966—far too late to make any difference to him.

The movie's gritty authenticity comes from the fact that it was shot in the flat right next to the real 10 Rillington Place where the murders occurred. After the movie was made, Rillington Place was demolished to build public housing. Nobody except perhaps tour guides misses it.

The Thin Blue Line

Synopsis: A documentary exposé that ultimately freed an innocent Texas drifter who had been sentenced to death for murdering a police officer.

BFI/Third Floor/American Playhouse (Mark Lipson). 1988. Color. Running time: 101 min.

Director: Errol Morris.

Rating: —▮ —▮ —▮

The Story

Around midnight on November 27, 1976, Dallas police officers Robert Wood and Teresa Turko pull over a blue compact car. As Wood approaches the car, the driver shoots and kills Wood. David Harris, a teenager, admits that he was in the car and fingers a drifter named Randall Adams as the killer. The police arrest Adams and interrogate him the old-fashioned way—without counsel and at gunpoint. Adams eventually signs a statement admitting that he was in the car with Harris, but claims that he does not recall what took place.

District Attorney Douglas Mulder wants the death penalty, and thus files murder charges only against Adams because the teenaged Harris is too young to execute. To cement Harris's cooperation, Mulder does not even charge Harris with theft, even though Harris admitted to stealing the car and the gun used to kill Wood. Mulder probably would have nominated Harris for the Nobel Peace Prize to help persuade him to testify against Adams.

At Adams's murder trial, Harris testifies that he met Adams on the morning of Wood's death. They hung out and went to the movies. He claims that Adams was driving as they left the movies. Adams shot Wood with the stolen gun that was stowed under the seat while Harris hunched down in the passenger seat. In addition to Harris's testimony, three eyewitnesses identify Adams as Wood's killer. Mulder keeps the identity of the eyewitnesses a secret from Adams's attorneys, Edith James and Dennis White. Then, to prevent James and White from asking the eyewitnesses about inconsistent statements thay had made to police officers, Mulder lies and says that the eyewitnesses had left the state.

Testifying in his own behalf, Adams agrees that he met Harris on the morning of Wood's death and went to the movies with Harris. But according to Adams, Harris dropped him off in his hotel room around 9:30 P.M.; he didn't see Harris again, and was not in the car when Wood was killed.

The jury convicts Adams, and after a separate hearing sentences him to death. The jurors hear expert testimony from Dr. Grigson that Adams is a Charles Manson–like deviant who will surely kill again if he's ever released. Dr. Grigson also testifies that Adams lacks remorse for killing Wood, which is hardly surprising, since Adams denies committing the crime.

James and White ask the trial judge, Judge Metcalfe, to set aside Adams's conviction and penalty based on "newly discovered evidence." They found a witness who says that Emily Miller, one of the eyewitnesses, is a lifelong liar who provided evidence against Adams to collect a reward and in exchange for Mulder's dismissal of robbery charges against her daughter. (Mulder was single-handedly emptying Texas prisons of robbers.) But Judge Metcalfe denies the request.

The Texas Court of Criminal Appeals upholds Adams's conviction and death sentence. But three days before he is scheduled to die, Adams lucks out. U.S. Supreme Court Justice Lewis Powell sets aside the death sentence. Powell rules that some potential jurors opposed to the death penalty were wrongly excluded from the panel. The governor of Texas then commutes Adams's sentence to life in prison, which avoids any need for a new trial or sentencing hearing.

The Documentary

After Adams's sentence was commuted to life, Errol Morris made a documentary film about the case. Morris became interested in Adams's story while researching a documentary on Dr. Grigson, the so-called

"Dr. Death" whose expert testimony supported imposition of the death penalty on Adams. Dr. Grigson is a physician who makes "louse" calls, regularly showing up in various states to provide expert testimony that defendants ought to be sentenced to death.

Morris's film repeatedly reenacts the fatal shooting of Wood from different angles, showing how difficult it would have been for anyone to identify the killer. In the film, Harris admits that his testimony against Adams was false and that Adams was innocent. By this time, Harris has fulfilled his youthful potential by making it to death row for an entirely separate murder. The eyewitnesses also admit to giving false testimony, telling Morris that they couldn't really see who killed Wood.

Morris's documentary riveted national attention on the Adams case. Based on it, Adams petitioned for a new trial; Judge Larry Baraka held a hearing and granted Adams's request. In the hearing, Harris testified that Adams was innocent and that he committed perjury in exchange for Mulder's dropping of all charges against him. Judge Baraka ruled that Mulder violated both federal and state law by not disclosing the identity of the eyewitnesses to the defense before they testified and by lying when he said they had left the state. At this point, the line of people leaving Texas should have been headed by Mulder.

The state appealed Judge Baraka's new trial order to the Texas Court of Criminal Appeals. In view of the evidence, this was an amazing display of chutzpah, something like the Big Bad Wolf appealing for mercy because grandma's nightgown didn't fit properly. This time the Court of Criminal Appeals was a little nicer to Adams; in 1989 it upheld Judge Baraka's new trial order. But Adams never was retried; the Dallas D.A. dropped all charges and he was freed.

Legal Analysis

As you've seen throughout this book, filmmakers routinely disregard legal rules for the sake of entertainment. But in a perverse example of life imitating art, the state of Texas also rode roughshod over the rules in its quest to convict a cop-killer. Adams could have been excused for thinking that he was watching a film instead of a real trial.

Like *10 Rillington Place,* the film recounts the tragic sentencing of an innocent man to death. Unlike the hapless victim in that movie, Adams lived to tell about it. But the two films certainly form the basis of strong arguments by those opposing the death penalty that the complex procedures called "due process" are no guarantee against the making of fatal mistakes.

Adams's trial was a litany of errors. Like other states, Texas trial rules required Mulder to disclose the identities of his eyewitnesses and their expected testimony to the defense attorneys before they testified. Because Mulder violated this rule, Judge Metcalfe should not have allowed the eyewitnesses to testify. At the very least, he should have delayed the trial to give the defense attorneys a chance to talk to the eyewitnesses or otherwise investigate their claims.

Unlike civil attorneys, who can use depositions to compel unwilling witnesses to tell what they know, criminal defense attorneys often lack the power to force witnesses to speak to them before trial. But James and White were entitled at least to a chance to talk to the eyewitnesses. And even if the eyewitnesses refused to cooperate, Adams's attorneys had the right to examine their statements and prepare to counteract their testimony.

Similarly, federal constitutional law obligated Mulder to disclose to James and White any information tending to exculpate Adams (*Brady v. Maryland,* 1963). Yet Mulder failed to reveal that the eyewitnesses had given inconsistent statements to the police. At trial they identified Adams as the killer, yet they first told the police that Wood's killer was black or Mexican (Adams is Caucasian). That information might have caused the jury to doubt Adams's guilt, and Mulder's failure to disclose it should have been reversible error.

As a prosecutor, Mulder's duty is to seek justice, not to win at all costs by taking unfair advantage of his powerful position. However, to prevent White and James from attacking the eyewitnesses' credibility when the defense attorneys belatedly find out about the inconsistent statements to the police, Mulder falsely said that the eyewitnesses had left Texas after they testified. Perhaps they should have, but they were actually in a nearby Dallas motel. Mulder should have been disciplined by the Texas State Bar for his deceit.

Judge Metcalfe himself committed a serious error by improperly limiting White and James's cross-examination of Harris. In the days and hours leading up to Wood's murder, Harris was in the midst of a robbery spree. His crimes included stealing the car that Wood and Turko pulled over and stealing the gun used to kill Wood. Judge Metcalfe erroneously refused to allow White and James to ask Harris about these crimes.

Perhaps the defense couldn't offer evidence of Harris's crime spree just to show that he's a rotter who couldn't be trusted. But Harris's crimes are relevant for another purpose: They show that he had a strong motive to shoot Officer Wood. When Wood pulled the car over, Harris might well have thought that he was about to be arrested for auto theft, and shot the officer in order to escape. By contrast, Adams had not been involved in any other crimes and had no motive to shoot Wood. Moreover, the crimes are relevant to suggest that Harris might have been offered immunity for his crimes, even though he denied that any deal had been offered. The Court of Criminal Appeals should also have reversed based on this error.

After Adams was convicted, and before the Court of Criminal Appeals first considered the case, White and James asked Judge Metcalfe to order a new trial based on "newly discovered evidence." The new evidence was that robbery charges had been dismissed against the Millers' daughter in exchange for their eyewitness testimony, and that Mrs. Miller was a habitual liar who had been fired from a job for stealing and who decided to testify against Adams only to claim the reward. Judge Metcalfe refused to grant a new trial, conveniently ruling that White and James were too late.

Judge Metcalfe was wrong about their being too late. He didn't need a watch to tell the correct time, a calendar would have done it. Typically, a defendant has two years to request a new trial based on newly discovered evidence. And even if White and James had missed this deadline, Judge Metcalfe could still have considered their claims by treating the new trial request as a motion for habeas corpus or some other procedural way out of a bad mess.

Had Judge Metcalfe properly considered the new trial request, he should have granted it. Judges tend not to favor these requests, believing that defendants will claim to discover new evidence with the same rapid frequency that Hollywood discovers new ingenues. But courts have ruled that a new trial should be granted when the defense discovers that a prosecutor failed to reveal an eyewitness's inconsistent statements and that the prosecutor has promised leniency in exchange for favorable testimony. Both of these factors were present in Adams's case.

Mulder's closing argument movingly tells the jury that society needs its "thin blue line" of police to save it from anarchy. But only a large dose of good luck and a dedicated filmmaker saved Adams from an overzealous prosecutor.

Trial Brief

1. Morris worked on the documentary for about three years and interviewed two hundred people, twenty-four of whom appear in the film. The film left him in debt, but he still plans to complete a documentary about Dr. Death.

2. Unlike some other states, Texas law does not permit a wrongfully

convicted person to seek compensation from the State. Adams and his attorneys are seeking to change the law. Nor can Adams sue Mulder for damages for prosecutorial misconduct. Mulder is absolutely immune from such claims, though he could be disciplined by the Texas State Bar.

3. Morris and Adams had their own legal squabble. When Adams was still in prison, Morris paid him $10 for the rights to his story, and promised to pay him $60,000 if his story was used in a dramatic production rather than a documentary. After his release, Adams wanted the $60,000. They settled in 1989; Adams got no more money, but did get the rights to his own story. In 1991, Adams and two coauthors wrote a book on the case, *Adams v. Texas*.

Men in Uniform

The system of military justice faces an eternal dilemma: Soldiers and sailors deserve a fair trial when they are accused of wrongdoing. But their offenses often occur in time of combat when the need for discipline is paramount. As a result, the niceties of due process often give way to the need for speedy punishment. In addition, the specter of command influence lingers over every court-martial. What's to keep the big brass from telling the military judges how the trial should come out, as they did in *Paths of Glory* or *Breaker Morant?* Can we expect the judges to forget that a verdict of innocent will mightily displease their superiors? They didn't forget in *The Court-Martial of Billy Mitchell.*

Billy Budd

Synopsis: The law of war is harsh and the captain insists on the death penalty. When law and justice split, tragedy is inevitable.

Anglo-Allied (A. Ronald Lubin, Peter Ustinov). 1962. British. Black and white. Running time: 125 min.

Screenplay: Peter Ustinov and Robert Rossen. Novella: Herman Melville. Director: Peter Ustinov.

Starring: Peter Ustinov (Cptn. Edward Fairfax Vere), Robert Ryan (Master of Arms Claggart), Terence Stamp (Billy Budd), Melvyn Douglas (Dansker), Paul Rogers (Lt. Seymour), David McCallum (Lt. Wyatt).

Billy Budd: The members of the court-martial put Billy Budd (Terence Stamp) on trial for killing an officer.

Academy Award nomination: Best Actor (Terence Stamp).
Rating: —■ —■ —■

The Story

It's 1797 and, as usual, Britain and France are at war. Billy Budd is a simple British merchant seaman aboard the ironically named *Rights of Man*. Budd is impressed into naval service aboard HMS *Avenger.* Its captain, Edward Fairfax Vere, is competent but somewhat indecisive. The master of arms (the officer in charge of discipline) is a sadistic monster named Claggart. The Vere/Claggart administrative model is now widely used by high school principals and vice principals.

Budd's sweet personality and nautical skills as foretopman win him the friendship of the crew and the respect of the officers, particularly Captain Vere. During an engagement with the French, Claggart orders Jenkins, a sick crewman, to a post in the rigging. As Jenkins begins to slip, Budd leaves his post to help, but Jenkins falls to his death. During an inquiry, Budd contradicts Claggart's account of what happened. After that, Claggart is determined to have his revenge.

Claggart accuses Budd of organizing a mutiny. When Vere asks Budd for his defense, Budd becomes tongue-tied and cannot speak. In frustration he strikes Claggart and kills him with a single blow. Vere convenes an immediate court-martial proceeding before Lieutenants Ratcliffe, Wyatt, and Seymour. As a witness to the altercation, Vere cannot serve as a member of the court-martial.

Vere and the court-martial judges believe Claggart falsely accused Budd of mutiny. They also are certain that Budd did not intend to kill Claggart. The members of the court-martial wish to acquit Budd, but Vere intervenes. He explains that the Articles of War require the death penalty when an impressed crew member even strikes, much less kills, an officer. No mitigating circumstances can be considered. They are public men and must do their duty regardless of conscience.

Calling out "God bless Captain Vere," Budd is hanged from the yardarm. Vere falls to pieces and cannot command the ship. The crew mutinies, and amid the uproar, a French vessel approaches and fires upon *Avenger*. The vessel is set aflame and Vere is killed. Defeating a mutinous and crippled *Avenger* probably won't make the highlight film as one of "France's Ten Greatest Naval Triumphs."

Legal Analysis

Life aboard the *Avenger* was cruel. The crew were given garbage to eat and were treated like animals. Crewmen were brutally flogged without knowing the offense for which they were being punished. The British class structure was played out aboard ship in all of its full glory. In effect, the crew were prisoners of war without ever being captured by the foe.

In such circumstances, there was concern that crew members (especially impressed seamen) might mutiny. As a result, punishments were extremely severe. The Articles of War permitted no exception to the rule that a crew member who strikes an officer must be executed. Even though Budd was a valued and respected crewman, even though he was falsely accused and terribly provoked, even though he killed Claggart through a freak accident, the law required that he be hanged. Justice, in other words, became separated from law. That is a recipe for tragedy.

The captain and the officers are well aware that this outrageous decision could trigger a mutiny, but they still feel bound to do their duty. After debating the issues, the officers yield to the captain's will. War, after all, is pitiless and wartime military discipline must be the same. Suppose they acquitted Budd and there was a mutiny, Vere asks. Wouldn't they be blamed for being too lenient? Following Vere on this point proves to be a major boo-boo.

Vere was right in his statement of military law (the death penalty was mandatory for striking an officer), but terribly wrong about the appropriate procedure. Most significantly, Budd should not have been tried by a "drumhead" court-martial, but should have been clapped into the brig and turned over to the admiral once *Avenger* rejoined the fleet. Captain Vere had authority only to mete out relatively trivial punishments, such as flogging or banning gum-chewing, not serious ones like the death penalty. Furthermore, the penalty should not have been carried out without a review at higher levels, and the court-martial should have been public, not held in secret. If the decision had been delayed, it is very likely that Budd would not have been executed at all, for the articles were not always carried out strictly.

Of course, by our present-day standards, Billy Budd's court-martial was a farce. He had no defense lawyer to point out Vere's gross procedural errors or to argue for leniency. He was not allowed to call witnesses or to cross-examine the witnesses against him. His trial was held in secret and the decision was not reviewed. The officers wanted to acquit Budd, but their commander forced them to convict. In modern military law, none of this is permitted.

But what about the mandatory minimum death sentence for striking an officer? Is that a relic of the primitive past? Today, American law abounds with extremely harsh mandatory minimum sentences, especially for drug-related offenses. Public fear of crime results in three-strikes-and-you're-out laws, under which three-time offenders get life in prison, often a grossly excessive penalty. The concern about fairly linking the punishment to the crime is as real now as in Billy Budd's day.

Billy Budd shows that fair procedures as well as fair laws are essential to doing justice. It also shows why in a criminal case judges and jurors are permitted to follow their conscience, even if that means not following the letter of the law. It's a lesson that must never be forgotten.

Breaker Morant

Synopsis: The Boer War was brutal. So were the court-martials of Australian officers who took no prisoners. An antiwar, antimilitary justice, and anticolonial movie.

South Australian Film Corp. (Matthew Carroll). Australia, 1980. Color. Running time: 107 min.

Screenplay: Jonathan Hardy, Bruce Beresford, and David Stevens. Play: Kenneth Ross. Director: Bruce Beresford.

Starring: Edward Woodward (Lt. Harry Morant), Jack Thompson (Maj. J.F. Thomas), Bryan Brown (Lt. Peter Handcock), Lewis Fitzgerald (Lt. George Witton), John Waters (Capt. Alfred Taylor), Rod Mullinar (Maj. Charles Bolton), Charles Tingwell (Lt. Col. Denny).

Academy Award nomination: Best Screenplay.
Rating: —▮ —▮ —▮ —▮

The Story

The Boer War of 1899–1902 was a struggle by the Boers (we now call them Afrikaaners) for independence from Britain. The war, and this movie, are anything but boring. Lt. Harry "Breaker" Morant was an officer in the Bushveldt Carabineers, an elite British unit consisting of Australians. Morant was a poet and the best horse breaker in Australia. Luckily the latter skill, not the former, gave rise to his nickname. "Wordsworth" Morant would not have been a great image to carry into battle.

The Carabineers fight the Boers in the Northern Transvaal where the warfare is brutal and unconventional. The Boers draw a platoon of the Carabineers into an ambush and their commanding officer, Captain Hunt, is captured and then killed by the Boers. Morant, who was engaged to be married to Hunt's sister, vows revenge and his men chase the fleeing Boers. They find Hunt's mutilated body. They capture a prisoner named Visser who is wearing Hunt's jacket. Morant orders him shot, perhaps because the jacket didn't go well with Visser's pants.

Later, Morant orders the execution of more prisoners who surrendered under a white flag. His sidekick, Lieutenant Handcock, kills Rev. Hesse, a German missionary who talked to the prisoners against Morant's orders and was thought to be carrying messages for the Boers. Perhaps he even set up the fatal ambush. A third officer, the naive Lieutenant Witton, executed nobody except one prisoner who attacked him.

British general Lord Kitchener decides it's time to make a gesture to the Boers in order to end the war. He also wants to placate the Germans, who are thinking about entering the war, perhaps as a warm-up exercise. Thus, scapegoats are needed and Morant, Handcock, and Witton are elected to take the fall.

Lieutenant Colonel Denny presides over the five-man general court-martial and the fix is in. Major Bolton is the prosecutor. The trial occurs in a grim courtroom at Petersburg, the remote headquarters of the Carabineers. Major J.F. Thomas defends the three. He is a small-town solicitor from Australia who never tried a case before. He has only a few hours to prepare. Witnesses who might have testified for the defense have been shipped to India. Although he bumbles at first, Thomas does a great job of defending his clients in a hopeless case.

Captain John Robinson commanded the Carabineers before Hunt. Like several of the other prosecution witnesses, Robinson obviously hated Morant and Handcock. He testified that it was impossible to discipline the Carabineers. For example, over Robinson's objection, Handcock insisted on placing Boer prisoners in open freight cars where they would be killed if Boer guerrillas blew up the trains, and where they were far away from the dining car. On cross, Robinson admits that this strategy forced the guerrillas to stop blowing up trains. Thomas asks Robinson whether he ever shot prisoners, but Denny sustains Bolton's objections since the answer might incriminate Robinson. Denny was very skillful at finding legal technicalities when they aided the prosecution.

Captain Taylor is an intelligence officer assigned by Kitchener to the Carabineers. He testifies that Kitchener had already ordered Boer prisoners wearing British khakis to be shot. The key point in Morant's trial was whether Kitchener had ever issued orders that permitted other Boer prisoners to be shot. Morant and other witnesses testify that they understood there were unwritten orders to shoot Boer prisoners. Indeed, plenty of prisoners were executed, but Kitchener never put it in writing. The court rules that questions about the unwritten orders are irrelevant since military law prohibits the shooting of prisoners whether or not under order. And it rules that evidence that others may have shot prisoners is irrelevant to the guilt of these defendants.

Thomas asks the court to compel Kitchener to testify. The judges are shocked, but regulations permit the defendants to call anyone as a witness. Kitchener refuses to attend but sends Colonel Hamilton. Hamilton denies that there were ever any orders to shoot Boer prisoners, even if they were wearing British underwear. It's obvious that he's committing perjury, but there is no way to impeach him. And even if there were no such orders, Hunt told Morant that such orders existed and Morant believed him. But none of this is of any interest to the court, which rules that the unwritten order defense has collapsed.

Handcock denies shooting Rev. Hesse. He presents evidence that he spent the afternoon with two different Boer ladies whose husbands were off at war, hence his given name. In fact, Handcock has already admitted to Morant that he killed Hesse before visiting the women. However, he doesn't tell his lawyer the truth; thus Thomas can ethically argue Handcock's innocence.

In his stirring summation, Thomas argues that this was a new kind of war, for the new century, involving nonuniformed combatants and women, children, and missionaries as soldiers. The Boers did not hesitate to use unconventional tactics and the British had to fight them the same way. Officers have wide discretion as to how to treat the enemy; their instructions were hazy and vague. It is unfair to punish men under strict rules of war when the war is fought unconventionally.

As the court-martial deliberates, Taylor offers Morant a chance to escape, but Morant declines. Handcock and Morant are acquitted on the charges of killing Hesse, but convicted on the other charges and sentenced to death. Witton is sentenced to life at penal servitude. We are told that the court split three to two, Denny voting with the majority. Considering the pressure on the court, it's surprising there were any votes against the death sentences.

Thomas tries to find Kitchener, but he's away and no longer wants to be bothered with the case. Morant and Handcock are shot at sunrise, which comes early in the Transvaal. Morant cries, "Shoot straight, you bastards! Don't make a mess of it." Witton is released after three years.

Legal Analysis

The overriding issue in *Breaker Morant* is command influence over a court-martial tribunal. Kitchener has ordered the members of the court to offer up scapegoats to appease the Boers and the Germans. And so Morant and Handcock are the sacrificial lambs (to use a second barnyard metaphor). Their trial is a sham. The judges are doing as they were told, Denny's evidence rulings are absurd, journalists are excluded from the trial, there is no appeal of the sentence (yet no need for haste in shooting the prisoners), and favorable witnesses have been shipped away. Nothing Thomas might have done would have made any difference.

Modern American military justice has gone to great lengths to prevent command influence. Military law is professionalized and the lawyers and judges are not subject to evaluation except by others in the justice system. The Uniform Code of Military Justice offers the same protections to an accused that civilians enjoy. Movies like *Breaker Morant, Paths of Glory, Billy Budd,* and *The Court-Martial of Billy Mitchell* remind us how vital such protections are, because otherwise military personnel are vulnerable to being punished to satisfy some political objective of their superiors. As we see in *A Few Good Men* and *The Caine Mutiny,* due process protection for military defendants makes all the difference.

Breaker Morant raises the issue so dramatically developed in *Judgment at Nuremberg* and *A Few Good Men*. Even if Kitchener issued orders to shoot prisoners or civilians, doing so violates the law of war. It's up to military officers to refuse to carry out unlawful orders. Thus it was legally correct to convict and execute Morant and Handcock—even if they were acting under orders.

But something's wrong with this picture. First, there's selective prosecution. Why are these men, of all of the British who engaged in reprisal killings, being punished? Part of the story is that they were mere colonials themselves—Australian, not British, and thus expendable. Taylor was also accused of shooting prisoners but he was let off, being British. Even the Australians weren't interested in saving Morant and Handcock, since that newly independent country wanted to get rid of its frontier reputation.

Second, consider the circumstances of guerrilla war in the Transvaal. These are the same kinds of conditions that led to American atrocities in Vietnam. Very few of the perpetrators of Vietnam war crimes were ever punished and none by the death penalty. Same thing in the Boer War. The British herded masses of women and children into concentration camps. Many Boers died in the camps, but rarely was punishment meted out.

As in Vietnam, the Carabineers can't tell who is the enemy and who is a civilian. The enemy doesn't wear uniforms and melts back into the populace. They're far out in the bush with no ability to feed and care for prisoners. And these are the people who just wiped out their buddies in a sneaky ambush and tortured their commander to death after he was taken prisoner. Hesse was thought to be carrying messages to combatants and to have set up the ambush. These factors might not excuse shooting prisoners, but they certainly must be considered when deciding the severity of the penalty.

Third, we have Kitchener's hazy oral orders to shoot prisoners. How convenient not to put such orders in writing so they can be plausibly denied later. Clearly, the wrong people are being punished here, but politically it isn't possible to punish the right ones.

Many of the evidence rulings by the court are extremely dubious. The court repeatedly refuses to hear evidence on whether other prisoners had been shot, ruling the evidence irrelevant to the guilt of Morant and Handcock. But, of course, it is not irrelevant. If other officers have ordered the execution of prisoners under similar battle conditions, surely this is relevant at least to the issue of punishment.

The devastating executions in the closing moments of *Breaker Morant* are unforgettable. Movies like *Breaker Morant* teach us better than any dry text on military law that command influence is incompatible with justice and that drumhead trials are no trials at all.

Trial Brief: The True Story of Breaker Morant

Morant and Handcock were really court-martialed and shot toward the end of the Boer War, and Morant is an Australian folk hero. But historians of the Boer War tell a different story from the anti-British line taken by the movie. According to historians, there were no orders, written or unwritten, to shoot prisoners. Kitchener ordered the court-martial because he was disgusted by the lack of discipline of the Carabineers. Morant was fairly tried and was clearly guilty of violating orders and the laws of war.

The Caine Mutiny

Synopsis: Can naval officers seize control of a ship from a deranged captain without being hung as mutineers? The dilemma is played out in a superbly executed court-martial drama.

Columbia (Stanley Kramer). 1954. Color. Running time: 125 min.

Screenplay: Stanley Roberts. Novel: Herman Wouk. Director: Edward Dmytryk.

Starring: Humphrey Bogart (Capt. Queeg), José Ferrer (Barney Greenwald), Van Johnson (Lt. Steve Maryk), Fred MacMurray (Lt. Tom Keefer), Robert Francis (Ensign Willie Keith), E.G. Marshall (Lt. Comm. Challee), Tom Tully (Capt. DeVriess), Lee Marvin (Meatball), May Wynn (May).

Academy Award nominations: Best Picture, Best Actor (Humphrey Bogart), Best Supporting Actor (Tom Tully), Best Editing, Best Screenplay, Best Musical Score (Max Steiner).

Rating: 

The Story

The dramatic events of a World War II naval mutiny are seen through the eyes of Willie Keith, a young ensign from Princeton who figured he would be assigned to a battleship. Instead, he finds himself on the *Caine,* a grubby minesweeper that has yet to be asked to sweep a single mine. As one swabbie remarks, it's a mistake to scrape the rust since it's keeping the water out. The communications officer, Lieutenant Tom Keefer, is trying to write a novel in his spare moments. Keefer remarks that the *Caine* is "an outcast ship, manned by outcasts, and named after the greatest outcast of all time." Keefer has apparently discovered that the real name of the ship is *The Pete Rose.*

Life aboard the *Caine* gets tense when Lieutenant Commander Philip Queeg takes command. Queeg is a stern disciplinarian who makes a big deal about haircuts and shirttails. Never has the phrase "run a tight ship" been taken so literally. Signs of mental problems are quick to appear. While the *Caine* is towing a target, Queeg gets so involved in chewing out a sailor whose shirttail is out that the ship sails in a circle and cuts the towline. When he gets tense, Queeg rolls a couple of little steel balls in his hand; nobody who sees this movie ever forgets the clicking of the steel balls.

The Caine Mutiny: Captain Queeg (Humphrey Bogart) rolls the steel balls.

The executive officer, Lieutenant Steve Maryk, tries to be loyal to his captain. His friend Keefer points out that Queeg is obviously paranoid. He predicts that the time will come when the officers will have to relieve Queeg under Naval Regulation 184. This provision permits such action but only under extraordinary circumstances. Maryk at first denies the problem, but then starts keeping a medical log on Queeg.

There is plenty to write in the log. Because someone forgot to notify him about a movie, Queeg cancels all movies for the crew. Not even great trial movies can be shown. After a few sailors fail to wear helmets and life jackets during a drill, he cancels liberty for the entire crew. Much more seriously, the *Caine* is assigned to lead some marine landing craft in an amphibious assault. The *Caine* is supposed to get within 1,500 yards of the beach before turning back. Disregarding his senior officers, Queeg leaves the marines unescorted. He orders the *Caine* to turn back well before reaching the assigned spot and orders a yellow dye marker to be dropped. At this point, the crew dubs Queeg "Old Yellowstain" and he becomes an object of ridicule.

After this fiasco, Queeg tries to reach out to his officers in a critical meeting in the wardroom. Pathetically, he points out that his family and his dog love him. The officers are stone-faced and they give him no support. Morale plunges and everyone tries to get by doing the least possible to stay out of trouble.

Queeg loses it big-time when someone pilfers leftover strawberries from the officer's mess. Queeg's theory is that somebody made a wax key to the padlock, because years before, he had cracked a similar case of missing cheese. He orders every man stripped and all keys on board brought to him. But Officer Harding had seen the mess stewards eating the strawberries and had told Queeg about it. The entire key search was a complete waste of time, and Queeg knew it all along. Sensing disaster, Maryk, Keefer, and Keith decide to seek Queeg's relief under Article 184 by complaining to Admiral Halsey. At the last moment, however, Keefer loses his nerve and the other two back off.

Disaster strikes during a typhoon. Communications with the fleet are broken. As immense waves break over the little ship, Queeg is immobilized. He refuses to change headings and overrides Maryk's commands to the helmsman. The *Caine* is in imminent danger of sinking with all hands. Finally, Maryk seizes command with Keith's support. The ship is saved.

Then comes the court-martial of Maryk and Keith for mutiny. Their defense is Article 184. After numerous other naval lawyers turn down the case, Barney Greenwald agrees to represent them. A real expert at boosting his clients' confidence, Greenwald tells them that he would rather be prosecuting them.

Maryk is prosecuted first and the defense doesn't go well. The prosecutor, Lieutenant Commander Challee, has it all his own way. Maryk admits he knows nothing about psychiatric problems and that Queeg's eccentric behavior could be compatible with running a tight ship. Maryk concedes that if the psychiatrists are right that Queeg is perfectly sane, he is guilty of mutiny.

Keefer's testimony is so damaging to the defense that Greenwald does not even try to cross-examine. Keefer claims that seizing command from Queeg was an error and that he always was against it. Keefer seems to be trying to save his own neck, since it was he that first told Maryk about Article 184 and planted the idea of Queeg's mental illness. Thus Keefer might be prosecuted for attempted mutiny or failure to suppress a mutiny if he is not careful.

A naval psychiatrist testifies that Queeg was mentally fit to be captain. Greenwald's cross-examination uses the old country bumpkin approach. He gets the shrink to help him by listing Queeg's various personality quirks. At the end, the shrink has to concede that there is a name for this sort of personality—paranoia. The shrink is probably wondering why lawyers are always out to get him.

The prosecution's case comes apart when Queeg is cross-examined. The tribunal turns aside Challee's attempts to shield Queeg from damaging lines of questioning. Queeg's composure crumbles when Greenwald threatens to call Harding to testify about the strawberry incident. Suddenly Queeg's madness erupts. Frantically rolling the steel balls, he blames everyone else for the problems on the *Caine*. Maryk and Keith are acquitted.

As the officers celebrate, Greenwald enters. Already drunk, he reminds everyone that while they had enjoyed life in peacetime, Queeg was doing the navy's dirty work. Greenwald asks whether the disasters on the *Caine* would have occurred if the officers had been loyal to Queeg and responded to his plea for help, rather than trying to undercut and ridicule him. Labeling Keefer as the true author of the *Caine* mutiny, Greenwald hurls a drink in Keefer's face. The other officers thus learn for the first time that Keefer bailed out on Maryk at the court-martial. They all file out, leaving Keefer alone.

Legal Analysis

The Caine Mutiny is about the fateful dilemma confronted by military officers when their commanding officer becomes mentally disabled. Must they obey the captain's orders, even if that means catastrophe, or should they disobey the orders, risking a prosecution for mutiny? Under naval law, the captain is an absolute monarch of his ship; he must be obeyed, right or wrong. In combat or in an emergency at sea, there can be no other way.

Yet, what if the captain is crazy and endangers the ship, especially in an emergency when superior authority cannot be consulted? Article 184 provides the escape valve from the captain's absolute authority. Even the United States Constitution provides a way that the vice president can relieve the president (the commander-in-chief of the armed forces) when the president is disabled and refuses to step aside voluntarily. Only a Girl Scout troop leader has absolute authority.

Under Article 184, Maryk did the right thing by relieving Queeg of command during the typhoon. Otherwise the ship might well have gone down with all hands aboard. Yet naval justice cannot permit officers to seize command except upon the clearest possible showing that a captain has become unfit to command. Otherwise, military discipline would be undermined. Captains would be afraid to treat officers harshly, lest the officers mutiny. And captains might hesitate to make difficult and dangerous decisions under combat conditions if their officers could override those decisions.

Thus Article 184 is very carefully hedged. When it is raised as a defense in a mutiny case, the normal burden of proof is inverted. The defendants must prove their innocence beyond a reasonable doubt. In *The Caine Mutiny,* the prosecutor and the tribunal make every effort to protect the captain. Greenwald is admonished to protect Queeg's reputation and avoid any hint that Queeg might be a coward. Indeed, had Queeg not cracked on the stand, Maryk and Keith would surely have been convicted of mutiny and hanged from the highest yardarm.

A mutiny case cuts very close to the quick. In such a case, it is problematic whether the military justice system can provide justice. There is always a possibility of command influence over the tribunal or over defense counsel. This is not supposed to occur, but it is difficult to prevent or detect. Who knows, for example, whether Greenwald's military career could be jeopardized by poor performance evaluations from superiors who disapprove of his vigorous defense? It's been known to happen: In one case the Court of Military Appeals severely chastised all concerned for such an incident.

Defending a mutiny charge puts a military defense lawyer like Greenwald in a terrible position. No wonder Greenwald wishes he were prosecuting and that numerous other military lawyers turned down the defense. By attacking a captain, Greenwald is himself taking part in violating the taboo that a captain's authority must never be challenged.

When Greenwald admits he would rather be prosecuting, he casts doubt on whether he can discharge his responsibility to defend his clients. Both military and civilian defense lawyers owe exactly the same obligation to defend their clients with the utmost zeal that ethical rules will permit. Maryk and Keith must have lacked confidence in their defender, but he was all they had. They were indeed fortunate that Greenwald put aside his scruples and concern about his career and made an all-out effort on their behalf. But afterward he hated himself for having done it.

The Caine Mutiny shows that despite all of its shortcomings, military justice can work, even in a mutiny case. But how often would a military defense counsel have the courage to attack a ship captain in court as Greenwald did? How often would a tribunal of naval officers take the side of alleged mutineers against one of their own?

Trial Brief: Mutiny

Mutiny is defined by the *Uniform Code of Military Justice* as a refusal to obey orders by two or more persons acting in concert with intent to usurp lawful military authority. It is among the gravest of military offenses and is punishable by death.

At the outset, the movie tells us that there has never been an American naval mutiny. This probably made the navy feel better about the movie, but unfortunately it is not true. In 1842, several crew members and one officer of the vessel *Somers* were hanged as mutineers after being convicted in a hasty and somewhat dubious court-martial of trying to seize the ship to launch a new career as pirates.

Article 184 is still part of the navy regulations (it's now section 1088). It provides that in "most unusual and extraordinary circumstances," a subordinate can relieve a commanding officer by placing him under arrest or on the sick list. Such action is normally taken only with the approval of the chief of naval personnel, except when this is "undoubtedly impracticable." The situation must be "obvious and clear and must admit of the single conclusion that the retention of command will seriously and irretrievably prejudice the public interests." And an officer who takes such action, or counsels it, "must bear the legitimate responsibility for, and must be prepared to justify, such action."

The Court-Martial of Billy Mitchell

Synopsis: A stubborn soldier gets himself court-martialed to make a political statement about the need to develop air power. The brass think he's full of hot air.

United States Pictures/Warner Bros. (Milton Sperling). 1955. Color. Running time: 100 min.

Screenplay: Milton Sperling and Emmet Lavery. Director: Otto Preminger.

Starring: Gary Cooper (Gen. Billy Mitchell), Rod Steiger (Maj. Allan Gullion), Charles Bickford (Gen. Guthrie), Ralph Bellamy (Congr. Frank Reed), Elizabeth Montgomery (Margaret Lansdowne), Jack Lord (Cmdr. Zachary Lansdowne), Fred Clark (Col. Moreland).

Academy Award nomination: Best Screenplay.

Rating: —▮ —▮ —▮

The Story

It's 1925. War is out of style, so nobody wants to waste money on the military and the army and navy are cut to the bone. These services aren't anxious to share what little they have with the new kid on the block, military aviation. Thus, the few planes left over from World War I are death traps for their military pilots.

General Billy Mitchell is a visionary who sees clearly the role of air power in future warfare. But Mitchell is stymied at every turn. When he wants to prove that planes can sink a battleship, the brass creates an unpassable test: They have to say "Simon says" before the pilots can drop bombs. Mitchell breaks the rules by using heavier bombs

Still photo courtesy of Republic Entertainment Inc.

The Court-Martial of Billy Mitchell: General Mitchell (Gary Cooper) and his lawyer Frank Reed (Ralph Bellamy) use lung power in support of air power.

and flying lower. As a result, he's busted to colonel and shipped off to exile in Texas.

Zack Lansdowne, Mitchell's close friend, dies when the poorly maintained dirigible *Shenandoah* is lost in a storm. Then six of Mitchell's flyboys are killed when their wretched planes crash. Mitchell finally gets fed up and calls a press conference. He accuses the big shots of criminal negligence and treasonable conduct. Mitchell is court-martialed, which is exactly what he wants—a forum in which the brass and the public will have to listen to his views.

Mitchell is represented by his friend, Congressman Frank Reed. The presiding judge is Gen. James Guthrie. Guthrie and the other judges are clearly out to convict Mitchell as quickly as possible and to hush up the whole mess. For that reason, they schedule the court-martial in a beat-up old warehouse in hopes that the press won't be able to find it. Luckily, the press has access to the "AAA Guide to Decrepit Warehouses" and they find it right away.

Mitchell is prosecuted under a section of the Articles of War that prohibits conduct bringing discredit on the armed forces. Since he admits making the statement, the primary issue is justification—why he spoke out and whether his statements are true. At first, Guthrie rules that evidence of justification is irrelevant, since the brass wants to prevent Mitchell from using the trial to publicize his views.

The court can't bring itself to exclude the testimony of Margaret Lansdowne, Zack's widow, who testifies about the conditions that made the *Shenandoah* a death trap. Now the judges are intrigued and they permit testimony from a string of witnesses about the truth of Mitchell's statement. The air service has practically no planes and the ones they have are in terrible shape. Seatbacks cannot even be returned to their full and upright position. No way are they ready to fight.

Finally Mitchell testifies and tells his story. The prosecutor, Colonel Moreland, is in over his head. So Mitchell is cross-examined by a special prosecutor, the icy Major Gullion (reminiscent of George C. Scott as Dancer in *Anatomy of a Murder*). But Mitchell is up to the challenge. Yes, he says, if being a good soldier means being complacent, he's glad to be a bad soldier. He goes on to predict the course of warfare in the air, right down to explaining how the Japanese are going to attack Pearl Harbor. In retrospect, the brass should have been suspicious when only the emperor of Japan sent away for a transcript of Mitchell's court-martial testimony.

Mitchell is convicted and suspended from rank and pay for five years. But the closing scene shows military jets wheeling in the sky. While Mitchell may have lost the dogfight, he won the air power war.

Legal Analysis

Many elements of military justice depicted in this movie seem strange to viewers steeped in ordinary criminal procedure. For example, the *Uniform Code of Military Justice* contains extremely vague articles. Article 133 punishes conduct unbecoming an officer and a gentleman. Article 134 punishes conduct that discredits the armed forces or prejudices good order and discipline; this was the section in the Articles of War under which Mitchell was prosecuted.

This sort of vague language would be unacceptable in civilian criminal law, but it has been upheld in military law. These articles traditionally applied to insubordination, which was Mitchell's basic crime—taking his criticism of the general staff outside the chain of command and to the public. That's a military no-no.

Similarly, the right of freedom of speech under the First Amendment would normally protect Mitchell's statement to the press, but even today the First Amendment applies to members of the armed forces only in limited form. In *Parker v. Levy* (1974), the Supreme Court observed that the First Amendment in the military must be tempered by concern for obedience and discipline. The military, it remarked, is a specialized society separate from civilian society, since the military's main business is to fight. Therefore, the Court upheld the court-martial convictions of a military doctor who made a public statement advising army personnel to refuse to go to Vietnam and called special forces personnel murderers.

Thus Mitchell was properly court-martialed for making a public statement impugning the competence and patriotism of the general staff. Nevertheless, he should have been permitted to introduce evidence about his justification for making the statements at some point during the trial. The judges thought the evidence was not relevant to the charge of insubordination. This seems questionable: Even for insubordinate statements, there must be an exception for necessity—Mitchell had tried for years to make his protests within the chain of command but he had been regarded as an annoying pest. Even if the evidence was not relevant on the question of whether insubordination occurred, it was relevant in extenuation of the penalty. If Mitchell's conduct was justified because his statements were true and vital to national security, surely his penalty should be reduced.

As in some of the other military justice movies (such as *Paths of Glory* and *Breaker Morant*), the court-martial judges were subject to command influence. The general staff—right up to President Coolidge—were determined to shut Mitchell up, and that's what the members of the court-martial did. During the era of military justice preceding adoption of the Uniform Code in 1950, command influence was taken for granted.

Today, the problem of command influence has been greatly alleviated. A professional military judge presides at the court-martial and makes evidentiary rulings. That judge is part of a separate command structure. The Uniform Code firmly prohibits command influence. If any is detected, the Court of Military Appeals will set the convictions aside, and has done so on several occasions.

Yet command influence remains a pervasive problem, since military justice is an uneasy compromise between a system of discipline and a system of justice. The "convening authority" (the defendant's superior officer) makes the decision to prosecute, supervises the investigation, decides whether to treat the matter as a major or minor offense, picks the jurors, and ultimately reviews the sentence.

The Court-Martial of Billy Mitchell shows that trials have many functions besides dispensing justice. Trials can be valuable for clearing one's name (and court-martials have often been used for this purpose) or for making a political statement to the public. But the movie also reminds us that military justice has often been military injustice.

Great vigilance is needed to protect the rights of people in the service who offend their superiors.

Trial Brief

Billy Mitchell (1879–1936) was a hero of World War I. He looked quite a bit like Gary Cooper, who plays him in the movie. Mitchell commanded the air service, led huge bombing raids, and was the first to fly over enemy lines. His efforts to get additional resources for the air service, and to give it greater independence from the army, were thwarted by the brass.

After the crash of the *Shenandoah,* Mitchell held a press conference and accused his superiors of "incompetency, criminal negligence, and almost treasonable administration of the national defense" and was court-martialed. Mitchell actually did predict the future of air warfare, including the Japanese attack on Pearl Harbor.

According to Mitchell's biographers, the court-martial occurred in an old warehouse. Proceedings lasted seven weeks and were extensively covered by the press. One member of the court-martial was General Douglas MacArthur, a longtime family friend of Mitchell's—who said not a word during the proceedings (but according to the biographers voted against Mitchell's conviction). Most of the members of the court knew nothing about military aviation.

The biographers state that Mitchell was allowed to introduce evidence about the truthfulness of his charges. Thus Eddie Rickenbacker, Hap Arnold, Carl Spaatz, and even Fiorello LaGuardia testified on his behalf. Margaret Lansdowne testified about the *Shenandoah* disaster near the end of the trial. She stated that the brass had tried to script her testimony, but she had torn up the script. Moreland's objections to her testimony were overruled. The sarcastic Gullion tried everything to discredit Mitchell's testimony, but got nowhere.

As in the movie, however, the fix was in and there was no way Mitchell was going to be acquitted. He was suspended from rank and pay for five years. This made his situation a bit unusual—he remained subject to military orders but wasn't getting paid.

President Coolidge confirmed the judgment in 1926 and Mitchell immediately resigned from the army and became a stock farmer in Virginia. He continued his crusade for airpower. After his death, he was raised posthumously to the rank of major general and in 1948 received the Congressional Medal of Honor. In 1958, the secretary of the air force refused to reverse the court-martial decision because Mitchell had attacked his superiors in public. Of course, all of his prophecies about air power were precisely fulfilled during World War II.

A Few Good Men

Synopsis: A brash young lawyer develops from lazy plea bargainer to master courtroom tactician in his first trial, a court-martial of two marines charged with murder.

Columbia TriStar/Castle Rock (David Brown, Rob Reiner, and Andrew Scheinman). 1992. Color. Running time: 138 min.

Screenplay: Aaron Sorkin. Stage play: Aaron Sorkin. Director: Rob Reiner.

Starring: Tom Cruise (Lt. J.G. Daniel Kaffee), Jack Nicholson (Col. Nathan Jessep), Demi Moore (Lt. Cmdr. JoAnne Galloway), Kevin Bacon (Capt. Jack Ross), Kiefer Sutherland (Lt. Jonathan Kendrick), Wolfgang Bodison (Lance Cpl. Harold Dawson), Kevin Pollak (Lt. Sam Weinberg), James Marshall (Pfc. Louden Downey), J.T. Walsh (Lt. Col. Matthew Markinson).

Academy Award nominations: Best Picture, Best Supporting Actor (Nicholson), Best Editing.

Rating: —▮ —▮ —▮

The Story

Private Willie Santiago was a desperately unhappy marine stationed at Guantanamo Bay, Cuba. To get a transfer, he offered to snitch on a fellow marine who had fired a shot over the fenceline into Cuba. Corporal Dawson (who had fired the shot) and Private First Class Downey carry out a Code Red on Santiago (marine lingo for severe hazing). They shove a rag down Santiago's throat and tape his mouth closed. Before they can continue the fun, Santiago dies. Dawson and Downey are charged with murder.

Lieutenant Kaffee is a brash young navy lawyer. He has plea-bargained forty-four cases in a row and has yet to try one. The brass assign the defense of Dawson and Downey to Kaffee, apparently figuring he'll plea-bargain it and avoid a lot of nastiness. Lieutenant Commander JoAnne Galloway desperately wants to defend. But as she once took nine weeks to try a disorderly conduct case, the brass have no intention of letting her near this one. Nevertheless, Galloway weasels her way into the case by convincing Downey's aunt to appoint her as Downey's counsel. Lieutenant Weinberg is the third member of the defense team.

Journeying to Cuba, the trio meet the notorious Colonel Nathan Jessep, the base commander. Jessep is one of the marine's "few good men." Jessep claims that he ordered Lieutenant Kendrick to protect Santiago and that he ordered Santiago transferred to the United States on the next available flight to Andrews AFB at 6:00 A.M. the next

A Few Good Men: Col. Nathan Jessep (Jack Nicholson) lacks a few good answers.

morning. Jessep even produces the transfer order. Unfortunately, Santiago was killed the night before the flight.

Lieutenant Colonel Markinson and Kendrick confirm Jessep's account, but it is totally false. In fact, Jessep had decided not to transfer Santiago and he ordered Kendrick to run a Code Red on him. Kendrick in turn ordered Dawson and Downey to carry out the job. Dawson and Downey had nobody to give orders to, so they carried out the attack. Markinson then vanishes and Kendrick denies everything. The prosecutor, Captain Ross, offers a generous plea bargain—six months in prison and dishonorable discharge. Kaffee loves the deal since he has no case, but Dawson rejects it contemptuously.

At the court-martial, the issue is whether Dawson and Downey acted on their own. Things go badly for Kaffee. Downey testifies that Kendrick came to their room at 4:20 P.M. and ordered them to Code Red Santiago, but Ross shows that Downey was walking back to his room from a distant post at that very moment, so could not possibly state that Kendrick gave this order.

Markinson surfaces as suddenly as he vanished. He tells Kaffee that Jessep never issued a transfer order. The transfer order document that Jessep showed Kaffee was fake. Moreover, Jessep could have put Santiago on a flight leaving Guantanamo for Andrews AFB at one A.M. which would have saved his life. However, Jessep has removed all evidence of the flight from the Guantanamo and Andrews logs. But Markinson is Code Blue over his role in the coverup, and he kills himself before Kaffee can call him as a witness.

Short of defense witnesses, Kaffee subpoenas Jessep, despite Ross's warning that Kaffee will be in big trouble if he accuses Jessep of wrongdoing without being able to prove it. Jessep has nothing but contempt for Kaffee, Galloway, and the whole trial process. Kaffee infuriates Jessep by asking him why he needed to transfer Santiago if he had given orders not to harm him. And he casts doubt on Jessep's account by suggesting that Santiago would have phoned his family and packed his gear if he thought he was leaving Guantanamo the next morning.

Jessep loses it completely when Weinberg walks in with two officials from Andrews AFB. Jessep assumes that they will testify that there really was a 1 A.M. flight from Guantanamo that Santiago could have made. In fact, they couldn't remember whether there was or not. When he sees them, Jessep turns Code Purple with rage. He admits proudly that goddamn right, he ordered Kendrick to run a Code Red on Santiago, who wasn't a real marine. He is given the appropriate warnings and is dragged off by the bailiffs, screaming at Kaffee that he's weakened the country.

The court-martial acquits Dawson and Downey of murder but convicts them of conduct unbecoming a marine and sentences them to dishonorable discharge—the result Dawson feared most.

But at least Kaffee has established himself as a primo trial lawyer in his very first case, and his daddy, a famous trial lawyer, would sure have been proud of him. Nothing like a "few good genes."

Legal Analysis

A recurring theme in this movie is that the military justice system protects Jessep against being accused of any sort of wrongdoing without solid proof. Horrible things will happen to Kaffee's career if he tries to blame it all on Jessep but fails to prove it.

But there's no such principle of military law. Kaffee is a member of the staff of the Judge Advocate General (JAG). In theory, JAG lawyers are independent and are free to conduct the defense of their clients as they see fit without concern for being blamed if they anger their superiors. Like civilian criminal defense lawyers, their ethical responsibility is to defend their clients—and if that means putting others on trial for the crime, so be it.

In practice, however, Kaffee and the rest of the defense team were right to be concerned about going after Jessep and probably never would have called him. First, it is unlikely that the high-ranking officers on the court-martial panel would disbelieve Jessep, who was a highly regarded and often decorated officer on the fast track to becoming a general. The defense attorneys would have to assume that Jessep would never get so rattled that he would confess to having ordered the Code Red or to having lied about the transfer. He certainly would not have been bluffed out by the presence of the Andrews airmen, especially since his opponent was a novice like Kaffee.

Second, the Marine Corps and Naval JAGs are small clubs and it would not pay for defense lawyers to be disrespectful to superior officers anywhere in the service. Somehow, an unfavorable performance rating might show up in the files. This was a much greater concern for Galloway and Weinberg, who were career officers, than for Kaffee, who apparently was in the service only for the short term.

The movie treats Galloway in a patronizing way. She doesn't know how to try a case, she outranks Kaffee but can't win his respect, she doesn't examine any witnesses, her judgment stinks, and she makes foolish objections to evidence. Her superiors explicitly decided not to assign her the Santiago case—then she goes out and unethically solicits Downey's aunt to get on the case. Obviously, the moviemakers are telling us, it takes a real man to try a case like this. Female lawyers have good reason to be offended by Galloway's treatment in this film (see *Women Trial Lawyers in the Movies*, p. 90).

Dawson and Downey were sentenced to be dishonorably discharged from the corps. Was this fair? After all, Dawson and Downey followed Kendrick's order. But it was established at the Nuremberg trials that military personnel cannot rely on illegal orders as a defense to wrongdoing (see *Judgment at Nuremberg*). Kendrick's order to impose a Code Red on Santiago was an illegal order and Dawson and Downey should have refused to carry it out. As Dawson says to Downey when the sentence was handed down, "We didn't protect Willie."

But let's get real—how can you expect marines, so schooled in the iron discipline of the corps, to disobey such an order? This is particularly true since Dawson had gotten in trouble for disobeying a similar order from Kendrick in the past. Military law seems to put people like Dawson and Downey in an impossible position—damned if you do, damned if you don't.

This picture is a lot of fun to watch and the acting is great, but it falls short on courtroom realism and on fairness to female attorneys.

Trial Brief: The Real Story

A Few Good Men is loosely based on a case that arose at Guantanamo in 1986. As in the movie, Private First Class Willie A was miserable at Guantanamo and pleaded for a transfer. He threatened to report a fence line shooting. Willie A was the subject of a "blanket party" in which ten marines woke him up, shoved a rolled-up pillowcase down his throat, and gave him a severe haircut. Willie A went into a coma but survived.

The colonel in charge of Guantanamo allegedly refused to transfer Willie A and said, "Let's keep him over the weekend and let him sweat." The colonel was later transferred to another base. Although the company commander told the men not to touch Willie A, a lieutenant figured out who the snitch was and supposedly told his men: "I don't want you to touch him. I don't want you to take him to the third deck and throw him off. But if he falls down the steps in the middle of the night, oh well."

Kaffee might be based on Don Marcari, a navy lawyer who represented one of the ten marines who administered the Code Red. It was Marcari's first trial. Ultimately, seven of the ten accused marines took other than honorable discharges. Three, including Marcari's client, refused to accept the discharges, went to trial, and were convicted of assault and sentenced to time already served. Those three were not discharged from the marines and continued to serve.

Alternatively, Lieutenant Kaffee might be based on Major Walter Bansley, a career lawyer in the marines who defended the lieutenant. Bansley was called in by a navy admiral to investigate and after a two-day investigation, recommended that all the men involved go to trial. The lieutenant who allegedly encouraged the hazing incident requested that Bansley represent him. The lieutenant's case was dismissed for missing the statutory requirement of a speedy trial by one day.

Deborah Sorkin was one of the lawyers for the ten accused marines; her brother, Aaron Sorkin, wrote the theatrical play and then the screenplay of *A Few Good Men*. Five of the ten marines involved in the original incident sued the filmmaker, Castle Rock, claiming libel, invasion of privacy, and invasion of the right of publicity. The case is still pending in Texas.

Paths of Glory

Synopsis: A French World War I court-martial presents the recipe for "le scapegoat."

UA/Bryna (James B. Harris). 1957. Black and white. Running time: 86 min.

Screenplay: Stanley Kubrick, Calder Willingham, and Jim Thompson. Novel: Humphrey Cobb. Director: Stanley Kubrick.

Starring: Kirk Douglas (Col. Dax), Adolphe Menjou (Gen. Broulard), George Macready (Gen. Mireau), Ralph Meeker (Cpl. Paris), Joseph Turkel (Pvt. Arnaud), Timothy Carey (Pvt. Ferol), Wayne Morris (Lt. Roget).

Rating:

The Story

It's 1916, the middle of World War I. The Germans and French are bogged down in deadly trench warfare. The polished but evil General Broulard wants to seize the Ant Hill, a fortified German position. To persuade a reluctant General Mireau to commit his battered troops to the hopeless assault, Broulard offers Mireau another star. Such promotions are the "paths of glory" in the film's ironic title. Mireau orders Colonel Dax to lead the assault. Mireau estimates that only half the men will be killed, so the Ant Hill will be well worth the price. You know which half he'll be in.

The attack on the Ant Hill is led by Colonel Dax, but it is a catastrophic failure. Many men are killed, few get beyond their own wire, and some refuse to leave the trenches at all. Mireau calls down artillery fire on his own men, but the officer in charge refuses to fire without a written order. Mireau has to back down.

Mireau decides that the attack failed because of cowardice and orders three men, chosen by lot, to be court-martialed as an example to the others. Lieutenant Roget chooses Corporal Paris to stand trial, as a handy way to get rid of a witness to his earlier cowardice under fire. The other two are Private Arnaud, who is chosen at random, and Private Ferol, chosen because he is considered a social misfit. Dax, a criminal lawyer in civilian life, volunteers to defend them.

The general court-martial is conducted in a gorgeous chateau, quite a contrast to the ghastly conditions in the trenches. It's a shabby business. The prosecution puts on no witnesses. The indictment isn't read and no record is maintained. The officers believe that it is wholly appropriate to select men by lot for execution when an entire unit is guilty of cowardice. As to the three unfortunate defendants, their prior records of bravery are irrelevant, as is the fact that one of them was knocked unconscious and could not even leave the trench. The prosecutor asserts that the conduct of all of the men is a blot on the honor of the French nation. Apparently, the nation's honor can handle the kangaroo court-martial.

Dax is eloquent in defense, pleading that the trial is a mockery of justice. But it is all for naught. In hopes of sparing the men, Dax interrupts General Broulard at a ball, handing him evidence that Mireau called down fire on his own troops, but it's in vain. All three are executed the next morning; Arnaud is unconscious and has to be propped up on a stretcher.

After the executions, Broulard removes Mireau from command and offers the job to Dax. Dax denounces Broulard, who regards Dax as a village idiot. According to Broulard, troops crave discipline, and a good way to maintain discipline is to shoot a man every now and then.

The film ends in a barroom as the soldiers hum along to a song sung by a captured German woman. A few weep as they contemplate the ghastly tragedy in which they are all engulfed. They are about to return to the front.

Legal Analysis

The court-martial in *Paths of Glory* is conducted strictly as a matter of military protocol. It is an annoying formality that a trial must take place before the men are killed. There is nothing even faintly resembling a fair hearing. Mireau sits on a comfortable sofa, benignly observing the proceedings. It is obvious to all that the three unlucky victims must be found guilty as quickly as possible so they can be shot in the morning. Indeed, the trial resembles nothing more than a primitive ritual in which a tribe purges its troubles by casting some poor scapegoat into the wilderness.

There is nothing Dax can do and it is unclear why he even tries. His eloquence is wasted. The tribunal's evidence rulings are consistent with the basic purpose of the proceedings. It's cowardice in the face of the enemy not to reach the German lines or die trying. The unit did not reach the German lines and some of them did not die trying. Therefore, the entire unit is guilty of cowardice; since they cannot all be shot, a few randomly chosen victims must be sacrificed. No other evidence has any relevance.

Paths of Glory was banned in France for many years. The film is an unsparing indictment of militarism and the evil of unchecked power. It vividly reveals the despair of men waiting to die a useless death—whether in battle or before a firing squad. The trial is conducted by polite men in an elegant setting, but it is no less savage than the massacres in the nearby trenches.

Trial Brief: French Military Justice during World War I

During World War I, the military justice system in the French army was governed by a code adopted in 1857. As a matter of practice, the only capital offense was abandonment of a post in the presence of the enemy. Cowardice, the offense punished in *Paths of Glory,* was not a violation of military law at all.

The events pictured in the movie are fictitious. They do resemble some cases that occurred during 1914 and 1915. In one case, a shell-shocked soldier who abandoned his unit was convicted and shot on the same afternoon in front of his entire unit.

By 1916, however, the military justice system had become less ferocious. There was an appeal from a court-martial conviction to a tribunal that included civilians. Death sentences had to be approved by the president of the Republic. Various protections were in place to prevent command influence over court-martials. The effect of this was that the military justice system was not an effective deterrent to desertion in the deadly conditions of military stalemate prevailing in 1916.

Prisoners of the Sun

(Alternate Title: *Blood Oath*)

Synopsis: A War Crimes Tribunal prosecutes Japanese officers who slaughtered Australian POWs on Ambon Island during World War II. Think of it as "The Nurambon Trials."

Village Roadshow Pictures/Charles Waterstreet and Siege/Skouras Pictures. 1990. Color. Running Time: 109 minutes.

Screenplay: Denis Whitburn and Brian A. Williams. Director: Stephen Wallace.

Starring: Bryan Brown (Capt. Robert Cooper); George Takei (Vice Admiral Baron Takahashi); Terry O'Quinn (Major Beckett); Toshi Shioya (Lt. Tanaka); Tetsu Watanabe (Capt. Ikeuchi); Sokyu Fujita (Shinji Matsugae)

Rating: —▮ —▮ —▮

The Story

A World War II Japanese POW camp on Ambon Island, Indonesia (then the Dutch East Indies), held approximately 1,000 Australian prisoners. By the time of the Japanese surrender in 1945, only 300 are left alive. The Japanese cannot account for the missing POWs, nor for the whereabouts of four Aussie airmen whose unarmed reconnaissance plane was shot down near Ambon. Then the Australians find the remains of many of the missing POWs in a mass grave, bayoneted or shot in the back. Before an Australian war crimes tribunal, ninety-one Japanese officers and soldiers who served on Ambon are charged with war crimes. The big fish are Vice Admiral Baron Takahashi, Ambon's Oxford-educated commanding officer, and Captain Ikeuchi, who ran the prison camp.

It's not easy for Australian prosecutor Captain Cooper to prove that Takahashi and Ikeuchi were responsible for the killings. The Japanese won't talk, and the surviving POWs are so battered and weak that they can't testify. In addition, all camp records have mysteriously disappeared, suggesting that the Japanese record keepers would have fit in nicely as civil servants in U.S. government agencies. Captain Cooper also has political problems: U.S. officer Major Beckett wants the tribunal to set Takahashi free, as the Allies have already decided to give him a sensitive postwar job in Tokyo. Cooper does get one break—as a legal officer, he doesn't have to wear the funny-looking, one-curled-brim hats that many of the Australian soldiers wear.

Watch carefully, and you'll notice that the film portrays three separate trials. The defendant in Trial No. 1 is Takahashi. Called as a witness by Cooper, he stoically denies everything. He doesn't know how the POWs died, what happened to the missing airmen, or the tune to "Waltzing Matilda." He falls back on the old defense of "passing the yen," saying that the POW camp was entirely Ikeuchi's responsibility. Takahashi shows no emotion; under his uniform he probably wears a T-shirt reading, "Emperor Hirohito sent me to Oxford and all I got was command of this lousy island." Cooper then confronts Takahashi with a written statement in which a surviving POW says that he overheard Takahashi order executions. But defense attorney Matsugae objects on the ground that he can't cross-examine the POW, and the tribunal bars Cooper from using the POW's statement. The tribunal's ruling leaves Cooper with no evidence against Takahashi. Despite Cooper's argument that Takahashi should be held responsible for the executions as Ambon's commanding officer, the tribunal sets Takahashi free.

In Trial No. 2, the defendant is Ikeuchi. Ikeuchi apparently went to the same memory training military school as Takahashi, for he too remembers nothing about executions. But with Cooper's urging, Fenton, a gravely ill POW, uses his last breaths to testify that he saw Ikeuchi beat and torture POWs. In a startling revelation, Fenton also testifies that he saw Ikeuchi supervise the killings of the missing airmen, one of whom was Fenton's brother.

The night after Fenton testifies, an enraged Cooper batters and bloodies Ikeuchi, turning him into "Icky-ouchy." A dazed Ikeuchi finally names Lt. Tanaka as an officer who was given the "honor" of executing an airman. Thus begins Trial No. 3, against Ikeuchi and Tanaka for murdering the airman.

The truth emerges during Trial No. 3. Tanaka admits that he killed an airman, but only after he was told that Takahashi had properly court-martialed the airman. Had the court-martial been held, the killing would have been legal. But another Japanese officer, Shimura, testifies that no court-martial took place; Shimura admits lying to Tanaka about the court-martial on orders of Takahashi. Shimura also states that both Takahashi and Ikeuchi participated in the mass executions of POWs on Ambon.

After Shimura's testimony, Cooper asks for mercy for Tanaka, who had been misled by Shimura and cooperative with Cooper. But the tribunal finds Tanaka guilty and sentences him to death; he's executed by firing squad. Ikeuchi commits hara-kiri, taking his own life before he can be executed. Takahashi's fate proves that life is better at the top. Though he masterminded the dirty deeds, he takes up high office in postwar Tokyo.

Legal Analysis

Some of the most notorious defendants who were charged with war crimes after World War II were broadly charged with "crimes against humanity" (see *Judgment at Nuremberg*). The Ambon defendants, by contrast, were charged with the narrower and more traditional crimes of murdering and mistreating prisoners of war.

In what Genghis Khan would have regarded as the good old days, prisoners of war had about the same life expectancy as mayflies. It was not until a 1785 Treaty of Friendship between the United States and Prussia that nations first formally agreed that prisoners of war should be held in captivity rather than killed or enslaved. Eventually, the Geneva Convention of 1929 provided for humane treatment of prisoners of war. Japan did not sign the Geneva Convention. But the Australian Tribunal had the power to try Japanese officers for killing and mistreating POWs pursuant to the Instrument of Surrender signed by Japan in September 1945, which provided for Allied prosecution of war criminals.

Cooper tries to hold Takahashi responsible for the execution of POWs on Ambon on two theories. Cooper's first theory is that Takahashi personally ordered the executions. He calls Takahashi as a witness and tries to force him to admit his personal involvement. Cooper's tactic is improper. Even in a war crimes trial, Takahashi had the same right as all defendants under the Anglo-American system of justice not to be called as a witness against himself. Thus, the tribunal should not have allowed Cooper to put Takahashi on the stand.

When Takahashi denies guilt, Cooper tries to use a POW's written statement that Takahashi personally ordered executions as evidence against Takahashi. Cooper's evidence actually consists of two statements: Takahashi's ("kill POWs") and the POW's ("I heard Takahashi give an order to kill POWs"). Cooper has to get both over the hurdle of the hearsay rule (see *The Hearsay Rule* p. 163). There's no hearsay problem with respect to Takahashi's order, both because he's the defendant and because the very giving of the order makes him a murderer. The hearsay problem arises with the POW's statement. The tribunal can conclude that Takahashi gave the order only if it believes the POW, and the POW is not present in the courtroom for cross-examination. Thus, the tribunal properly rules that the statement is hearsay and excludes it.

Cooper's second theory is that the tribunal should hold Takahashi responsible for the execution of POWs because as Ambon's commanding officer, Takahashi was legally responsible for war crimes committed on Ambon regardless of whether he authorized them. But under war crimes law, Cooper at least has to prove that Takahashi knew that POWs were being executed and did nothing to stop them. Since Cooper has no direct evidence of this, the tribunal's acquittal of Takahashi at first glance seems legally correct.

But the tribunal needn't have insisted on direct evidence of Takahashi's guilt. After all, "Ambon" was not a Dutch word meaning "huge, busy island." Mass executions undeniably took place at a time when Takahashi was on Ambon. And even if he had been a YMCA camp counselor instead of a commanding officer, Takahashi would have had to notice that the POW camp had lots of empty space. Based on this circumstantial evidence, the tribunal could have properly concluded that Takahashi knew about the executions and convicted him. As we've seen in the films *Breaker Morant* and *Paths of Glory*, Takahashi's acquittal suggests that the tribunal's verdict was more a product of politics than legal reasoning.

Shimura eventually testifies that Takahashi did authorize the executions. But by then there's nothing that Cooper can do; double jeopardy rules forbid him from trying Takahashi twice for the same war crime. Tactically, Cooper probably made a mistake by prosecuting Takahashi first. If he had gone after the inferior officers first, he would have given himself more time to find evidence of Takahashi's guilt. For example, some of the other officers might have implicated Takahashi in exchange for a light sentence. This is why U.S. prosecutors often go after illegal drug syndicates by charging the little guys first. By making deals, the prosecutors get them to provide evidence against the ringleaders.

A picture of the unfortunate Tanaka should appear under the dictionary definition of the phrase, "damned if you do, damned if you don't." Tanaka is ordered to carry out the judgment of a court-martial. If he refuses, there's a good chance he'll wind up on the wrong end of Ikeuchi's bayonet. He agrees, and winds up sentenced to death when it turns out that no court-martial was held.

Under international law, the tribunal can legally convict Tanaka of murder even though he was "just following orders" if he had reason to know that the orders were illegal. The tribunal says that Tanaka should have demanded confirmation that a court-martial had been held. But it's hard to imagine Takahashi and Ikeuchi putting Tanaka up for a promotion for seeking confirmation; even the request may have been hazardous to Tanaka's health. Besides, if Tanaka's superiors can lie about whether a court-martial took place, surely phonying up a confirmation would have been a snap.

But even conceding that Tanaka's conviction was proper, the Tribunal wrongly states that the only legally possible punishment is death. When a lawyer says, "my hands are tied," be careful. The lawyer often means, "I want my hands where you can't see them." The tribunal had the power under war crimes law to give Tanaka a lighter sentence. Tanaka's having been ordered to carry out the killing of the airman is a factor that the tribunal should have considered in mitigation of punishment. Tanaka's death sentence was unduly harsh and not required by law. Perhaps with Takahashi already acquitted and Ikeuchi far beyond its jurisdiction, the tribunal simply spent all its anger on Tanaka.

Cooper's beating of Ikeuchi is probably meant to suggest that the Australians were as capable of mistreating prisoners as the Japanese. From a legal standpoint, however, Cooper's conduct was unwise. Under a rule known as the "fruit of the poisonous tree," a prosecutor can't use information gained illegally. The rule is meant to deter misconduct by taking away the rewards. Cooper learned about Tanaka (the "fruit") through his beating of Ikeuchi (the "poisonous tree"). Thus, Cooper really went out on a limb by placing both his case against Tanaka and his legal career in jeopardy.

As in other war crimes trials, the outcomes of the Ambon trials were a product of law and politics. Despite the trappings of due process, Takahashi was acquitted and Tanaka was executed for reasons that had little to do with their moral responsibility. The trial of

Ikeuchi reached a just result, but only because he literally took matters into his own hands.

Trial Briefs

1. The events depicted in *Prisoners of the Sun* are based on the war crimes trials that were held on Ambon after World War II. Brian Williams, one of the film's coauthors, is the son of John Williams, the actual prosecutor of many of the Ambon defendants.

2. Baron Takahashi was not a single historical figure, but rather an amalgam of different people. Also, the pressure by the United States suggested by the character of Major Beckett is entirely fictional. The trials were conducted by the Australian government, and there was neither direct nor indirect U.S. involvement in their outcome.

The Lighter Side of Lawsuits

To plaintiffs and defendants who are unfortunate enough to be involved in trials, there's usually nothing funny about the proceedings. But satirists have poked fun at lawyers, judges, and trial practice as long as trials have existed. We guarantee that you'll chuckle as Amanda Bonner deflates her pompous husband Adam in *Adam's Rib* or Richard Courtois defends a pig accused of murder in *The Advocate*. You'll laugh out loud as Fielding Mellish in *Bananas* destroys a witness on cross-examination even though he's bound and gagged. And nobody can keep a straight face when expert witness Mona Lisa Vito discourses on Positraction and tire tracks in *My Cousin Vinny*. So if you're ever on the stand yourself, think back to these funny trial films and smile—it's one thing your lawyer can't bill you for.

Adam's Rib

Synopsis: Husband and wife square off in court in a comic commentary on the battle of the sexes.

MGM (Lawrence Weingarten). 1949. Black and white. Running time: 101 min.

Screenplay: Ruth Gordon and Garson Kanin. Director: George Cukor.

Starring: Spencer Tracy (Adam Bonner), Katharine Hepburn (Amanda Bonner), David Wayne (Kip Lurie), Judy Holliday (Doris Attinger), Tom Ewell (Warren Attinger), Jean Hagen (Beryl Caighn).

Adam's Rib: Doris Attinger's (Judy Holliday) hat is not the only thing standing between Adam and Amanda Bonner (Spencer Tracy and Katharine Hepburn).

Academy Award nomination: Best Screenplay.
Rating: —▮ —▮ —▮

The Story

Doris Attinger follows her wayward husband Warren to the home of his sweetie, Beryl Caighn. Doris pulls a gun and, after consulting the instruction manual, fires away, wounding him. She's up for attempted murder. The prosecutor is Adam Bonner. Adam, who reveres each law as if it were written on a stone tablet, is highly displeased when his wife Amanda takes on Doris's defense. The only time he wanted to be together with Amanda in front of a judge was when they said "I do." He is even less amused when their friendly neighbor and Amanda's client Kip Lurie composes the hit song "Goodbye Amanda" in her honor.

Adam is downright indignant at Amanda's defense. She asserts that Doris should have the same right as a man to rely on the "unwritten law" that it's okay to shoot one's spouse caught in, as the lawyers say, flagrante delicto. Betraying a teeny bit of insecurity, Adam says, "Contempt for the Law, that's what you've got. It's a disease, a spreading disease . . . the Law is the Law. . . . You start with one law then pretty soon it's all laws, pretty soon it's everything; then it's me." This is an example of a favorite lawyer argument: the "slippery slope." If we take one little misstep, the result is chaos. Adam goes beyond the slippery slope; he produces an avalanche.

At the trial, Beryl testifies that Warren was at her apartment only to sell her a new health and accident policy. In light of what happened, that showed remarkable foresight. Warren had never touched her, Beryl claims, except they shook hands quite a lot. Warren admits that he had hit Doris a couple of times, but claims that she hit him too, especially after he fell asleep. She never stayed out all night, he concedes, though he wishes she had, so he could get a decent night's sleep.

Doris testifies that she only meant to frighten Warren and didn't mean to hurt him or Beryl. She has three kids and was just trying to save her marriage. Amanda calls three highly successful women (a chemist, a foreman, and a circus performer) as witnesses to show that men and women are equal. The circus performer illustrates her act by hoisting Adam above her head, which makes it difficult for Adam to cross-examine her.

Adam and Amanda discuss the case at home each evening. He urges her to drop it, and criticizes her for shaking the law by the tail. She complains that he never sees her point of view and breaks down in tears. Their relationship deteriorates steadily throughout the trial. Adam complains that he wants a wife, not a competitor. Finally, after the circus incident, Adam moves out.

Adam's closing argument does not go well. Amanda interrupts him by objecting to his reference to Doris as a criminal and he completely loses his composure. He snatches Doris's hat off her head, complaining that he had given that very hat to Amanda. He even introduces the purchase receipt into evidence.

Needless to say, the jury acquits Doris. In the ensuing media frenzy, it looks like Doris and Warren may get back together but Amanda and Adam remain cool. Kip tries to take advantage of the situation by romancing Amanda in her apartment, and Adam charges in with a gun. He claims that he can use the "unwritten law" too. Luckily, it's a licorice gun, but Amanda is not amused. The next day, at their accountant's office, in the midst of a discussion about the deductibility of interest payments, they make up and head for the farm together. This proves once more that discussion of tax law can be a potent aphrodisiac. Adam mentions that he might be the Republican candidate for judge. Amanda asks if the Democrats have picked their candidate yet.

Legal Analysis

Adam's Rib is a marvelous comedy, so it isn't fair to take the courtroom high jinks too seriously. Still, the picture raises a few concerns. Most important, it is completely inappropriate for a husband and wife (or two lovers, for that matter) to be opposing each other in court, even with the full knowledge and consent of their clients. The district attorney's office would surely have reassigned the case to another prosecutor once Amanda appeared for the defense. Adam and Amanda's personal relationship could have interfered with their ability to represent their respective clients. It would have been easy for Amanda to give in to Adam's wishes in order to improve the atmosphere at home. This didn't happen in the movie, but it could have. Actually, the harm went the other way—Amanda succeeded in rattling Adam in a way that no other defense lawyer could have. Under ethics rules, a lawyer should not represent a client when that representation may be adversely affected by the lawyer's responsibilities to a third person or to the lawyer's own interests.

It isn't clear how Amanda got Doris's case. Apparently Amanda called up Legal Aid and volunteered to take it. Since she wasn't getting paid, this seems appropriate. There is a long and noble tradition of lawyers handling criminal defenses for free, even though the public defender is also available to do the job.

More troubling is the fact that Amanda used Doris's case to make a point about equality of the sexes. It is always dangerous for a lawyer to use a client for the purpose of making a political statement. The client's interests may play second fiddle to the lawyer's agenda. Here, Amanda's political agenda and Doris's best interests seemed to coincide—Doris was acquitted. However, it is easy to imagine male jurors being turned off by the equal rights defense. Or Amanda might counsel Doris to turn down a favorable plea bargain just so that Amanda will be able to make her novel "unwritten law" defense in front of the media.

Amanda's use of the three successful women as witnesses to show that men and women are equal was funny but wholly irrelevant. The fact that women can be successful in business or the circus tells us absolutely nothing about any issue in Doris's case. But perhaps we have to allow comedy writers to take a few liberties with the rules of evidence. The same is true of Adam's snatching Doris's hat during his closing argument and demanding to introduce the purchase receipt into evidence. Who paid for the hat has no bearing on the case and the closing argument is too late to introduce evidence. At least, Amanda could have objected that the hat was "im-material."

Amanda's "unwritten law" defense in *Adam's Rib* is entirely bogus. There is no "unwritten law" that allows men to kill their wives when they catch them in bed with a lover. Something like this was recognized on the frontier a hundred years ago or so, but it is not recognized any more and never was in New York. At most, the passionate-lover defense gets you a reduction from murder to manslaughter (or, in this case, attempted murder to attempted manslaughter). The judge should have stricken all argument and testimony designed to establish the "unwritten law" defense, not to mention Amanda's theory that women are as entitled to it as men.

The true meaning of the "unwritten law" is that jurors may ignore the judge's instruction and acquit a spouse who kills after finding his or her wife in bed with a lover. Jurors, after all, can always free a defendant whom they think is unjustly accused. In this day and age, however, it seems doubtful that jurors are really going to be that forgiving. Adultery no longer seems to most of us sufficient provocation to excuse murder.

The most important and the best part of *Adam's Rib* is Amanda. In 1949, there were very few female lawyers at the bar. Law school classes contained only a handful of women, if there were any at all, and the general sense was that the profession was not suitable for women. Thus Amanda was a wonderful role model for women who were considering possible careers in the law (see *Women Trial Lawyers in the Movies,* below). Amanda is loving and committed to her marriage, but equally committed to her politics and to her client, even when it jeopardizes her marriage. The sexual politics so humorously dramatized in *Adam's Rib* remain as fresh today as the day the film was written.

Sidebar: Women Trial Lawyers in the Movies

Would you want to hire a woman trial lawyer for your law firm or to represent you in a criminal case? Would you want to fall in love with one? Definitely not, if you base your decision on what you've seen in the movies. Almost without exception, trial movies present women lawyers in viciously stereotypical terms. It's almost as if filmmakers are scared stiff of powerful, successful women.

What do we learn about women lawyers from the movies? For one thing, they're looking for love in all the wrong places.

- Carolyn Polhemus in *Presumed Innocent* slept her way to the top. Before her untimely death, she had affairs with her college professor, the lawyer who hired her into the D.A.'s office, the supervising deputy, and the D.A. himself.

•Teddy Barnes in *Jagged Edge* leaps into bed with her client. As a result, she loses all objectivity about the case.

•Maggie Ward in *Class Action* is carrying on a secret affair with her law firm supervisor.

•Gail Packer in . . . *And Justice for All* is on the ethics panel—and sleeping with a lawyer who is being investigated by the panel.

•Laura Fischer in *The Verdict* allows herself to be used by her law firm as a sexual spy on the opposition.

For another thing, women are just lousy lawyers. They have no judgment or common sense, their personal lives are a mess, they don't understand trial tactics and their ethics are in the toilet.

•Maggie Ward in *Class Action* conspires with the opposing side in a lawsuit to do in her client. Maggie is boiling over with neurotic hatred for her father, pointlessly bullies a witness during a deposition, and drinks herself into oblivion every night because her work is so distasteful.

•JoAnne Galloway in *A Few Good Men* took nine weeks to try a drunk and disorderly case and has no common sense about how to handle herself in trial. A male twerp who's never tried a case in his life does the heavy lifting.

•Ann Talbot in *The Music Box* represents her father in a denaturalization proceeding. She loses all objectivity about the case, first suffering from an inability to even consider the possibility of her father's guilt and then overreacting violently when she is convinced of it.

•Jennifer Haines in *Guilty As Sin* plants incriminating evidence so that her guilty client won't get away with it. Although she's a competent lawyer, she uses terrible judgment in accepting this creep as a client. Framing him with fake evidence is the only way she can figure out to save her own neck. She's also shaky on evidence law.

•Kathleen Riley in *Suspect* allows a juror to be her investigator in a murder case.

•Gareth Peirce in *In the Name of the Father* tenaciously digs up the evidence of police misconduct that frees the Guildford Four. But she loses her cool during the critical hearing, shouting unprofessionally at the key police witness.

•Kathryn Murphy in *The Accused* plea-bargains away a pretty good gang rape case—then bullheadedly insists on prosecuting the onlookers, against the sensible orders of her boss (of course, she does manage to win the case).

•Belinda Conine in *Philadelphia* makes a horrible blunder when she cross-examines the plaintiff who is dying of AIDS. She hands him a mirror and asks whether he can see any visible lesions on his face. Otherwise, however, Conine does a decent job of representing her detestable client, even though she hates doing it.

•Jennifer Hudson in *Physical Evidence* just barely manages to avoid getting into bed with her client before he's acquitted. She works hard in his defense, but she calls a key witness over his vehement objection because "we have to."

•Stand up T.K. Katwuller. Your performance in *Defenseless* (an absolute turkey) gets you the worst ethics award. T.K. defends a client in a murder trial without telling the client and the police the embarrassing facts that she was a material witness to the murder and even left behind the clue that implicated her client.

Of course, it wasn't always this way. Women lawyers got off to a wonderful start in 1949 in *Adam's Rib*. Amanda Bonner took a criminal case pro bono because she saw that it raised an important issue of women's rights. She did a great job representing her client, even though it infuriated her husband Adam who was prosecuting the case. She was a loving wife, yet a dedicated and skillful lawyer. This movie must have made armies of little girls want to go to law school.

Of course, there were very few female lawyers at

the bar in 1949 and only a handful of women in law school. Today, women lawyers fill every professional role with distinction. The gender balance in law school is close to 50–50. The same proportion of men and women have bad judgment and lousy ethics. Filmmakers—get a life! Stop picking on female attorneys.

The Advocate

Synopsis: A bawdy comedy-mystery about a medieval lawyer whose plans for a sedate practice in rural France are dashed when he finds himself representing an alleged witch and a murderous pig. Both a "whodunnit" and a "whatdunnit."

Miramax Films (David Thompson). 1994. Color. Running time: 102 min.

Screenplay: Leslie Megahey. Director: Leslie Megahey.

Starring: Colin Firth (Richard Courtois), Donald Pleasence (Pincheon), Nicol Williamson (The Seigneur), Ian Holm (Albertus the Priest), Jim Carter (The Clerk), Lysette Anthony (Filette), Amira Annabi (Samira).

Rating: —▮ —▮ —▮

Surprise ending warning: Reading this analysis may be harmful to your enjoyment of the film!

The Story

In 1452, Richard Courtois moves his law practice and his clerk from crowded Paris to the rural village of Abbeville. He plans to escape the Black Plague and to enjoy a calm lifestyle helping grateful villagers with their mundane legal problems. Pincheon, the only other lawyer in Abbeville, prosecutes cases on behalf of the Seigneur, who controls village life. Thus Courtois gains an instant law practice representing everybody else.

Courtois soon finds that rural life is not as bucolic as he expected. As he arrives in town, a man and a donkey are about to be hanged for sodomy. (In the Middle Ages, animals were often held equally accountable with people for crimes.) Sanity seems to prevail when a villager rushes forward at the last minute with a petition to spare an innocent life. However, the petition is on behalf of the donkey, which is released. The man is hanged.

Courtois's first client is a peasant charged with murdering his wife's lover. Courtois bests Pincheon when the jury votes "not guilty." Courtois ascribes the verdict to his eloquence. But he soon learns that the jury acquitted the peasant not because he was innocent, but because the victim was a gigolo who had slept with many of the jurors' wives.

Big city life looks even better after Courtois meets his next client, a woman accused of being a witch. Pincheon's evidence of witchery is that the woman cast a spell over some village rats. Courtois insists that the Seigneur's law requires the rats to appear in court and testify. When the rats fail to show up, the charge is dismissed. At this point, Courtois must be thinking that "Abbeville" is an old Latin term meaning "easy victory." But in the end it is Pincheon who triumphs. The woman had been tortured into confessing that she was a witch. Pincheon successfully argues that the court must apply church law separately from the Seigneur's law. And under church law, people who confess to being witches are witches. An unbelieving Courtois sees his client pronounced guilty of witchcraft, then hanged and burned.

Although he normally would not play "Ace Ventura, Pet Attorney," Courtois reluctantly agrees to represent a pig charged with murdering a young Jewish boy. Courtois accepts the inane assignment because he's hot for the pig's owner, Samira, who is a member of a small and despised band of gypsies traveling through Abbeville. For once at least it's the client and not the lawyer who's a swine.

The Seigneur refuses Courtois's request to drop the charges, ruling with the support of Albertus the Priest that the devil can inhabit any body, animal or human. Courtois tries to save the pig by arguing to the Seigneur that the unearthing of the skeleton of another Jewish boy killed before the gypsies arrived in Abbeville shows that a human killer is on the loose. But the Seigneur insists on trying Samira's pig for murder, and to make sure things come out right the Seigneur himself is the judge.

Courtois's investigation reveals that the real killer is the Seigneur's son. The Seigneur needs Courtois's client to serve as a "scapepig" and satisfy the villagers that the case has been solved. Courtois cleverly cooks up a plan to save the pig's life and the Seigneur's face and son. The peasant, who had promised Courtois a favor after being acquitted of murder, appears in court with a pig that, by virtue of a quick dying, resembles Courtois's client. It's a cheap rush job that wouldn't even fool an infomercial audience, but everyone is happy to agree that the peasant's pig was the actual murderer. Courtois's client is deemed as innocent as a lamb—or as a pig. The relieved Seigneur sets Samira's pig free, at least until the winter, when it is destined to become the gypsies' chief source of food. The peasant's porker, unfortunately, is prematurely reduced to ham-on-croissant sandwiches.

Courtois can stand no more of village lunacy, and returns to Paris where he has a long and prosperous legal career. His timing is perfect: as he leaves, the Black Plague enters Abbeville.

Legal Analysis

Despite its occasional mistakes, most of us take comfort in our adversary system of justice. The rationality of the legal system and the formality of the proof process—as well as the presence of flags in all courtrooms—seem to offer assurance that for the most part our laws are fair and just. Though ribald and often funny, *The Advocate* is a sobering reminder that no matter how rational a legal system or how formal its courtroom processes, it can carry out laws that are silly and even monstrous.

For example, take the medieval rule making witchcraft a capital offense. The legal system of Courtois's day was as capable of enforcing this law rationally and formally as our modern court system is of deciding whether a driver was negligent or a defendant robbed a bank. Just as today's court rules would require, Pincheon had to offer evidence of witchcraft. And he had some: rats behaved in a strange manner after the witch went by, and she confessed with the help of a few thumbscrews.

Is this evidence "rational"? Sure. Rationality is rooted in a culture's experience; evidence is rational as long as people in a culture perceive a connection between a piece of information and the fact it is offered to prove. Given their belief in witchcraft, it was perfectly rational for the good citizens of Abbeville to infer from Pincheon's evidence that Courtois's client was a witch. And even though by today's standards her trial was a turkey, it had many of today's due process trimmings: she was represented by counsel, and had a chance to testify in her own defense. All of which suggests that despite our legal system's claim to objective rationality and fairness, our truths are just as much a reflection of our cultural beliefs as Abbeville's truths were of theirs. For example, in "wrongful death" cases we pretend that we can rationally place a dollar value on the worth of people negligently killed. And in "toxic tort" cases we pretend that science enables us to determine with certainty which of potentially thousands of environmental factors have contributed to disease.

Courtois's ability to represent the pig successfully suffers an initial setback when the Seigneur rules that Courtois's expert witness, a surgeon prepared to testify that the boy was killed by a knife and not by an animal, cannot testify because he's Jewish. Nor could Samira testify that her pig was always tethered and couldn't have killed the boy, because she was a gypsy. These rules seem silly now, but until the twentieth century many classes of people were disqualified from testifying. Ex-felons, parties to a case, lunatics, agnostics, and spouses were just some of the people who were deemed incompetent to testify. For example, assume an old civil suit for damages growing out of a barroom brawl. One potential witness, the bartender, has suffered an embezzlement conviction; a second hasn't been to church in years; a third is the village idiot; a fourth is the plaintiff's wife; and the fifth is the plaintiff himself. Who could testify? Nobody. Actually, maybe these incompetency rules weren't so silly; what a great way to cut down on crowded court calendars.

The fifteenth-century notion of trying an animal for a crime seems initially preposterous. But you could forgive animals for thinking that the medieval legal system was more enlightened than is ours. Think of today's rogue elephant who runs wild through an Indian village, or the bear or coyote who comes down from the hills and chases suburban families into their houses. Assume that they are given a choice: "We'll shoot you right here and have it over with, or, like those fools in the fifteenth century, we'll cart you away, appoint a lawyer for you, and give you a trial." Surely the world of *The Advocate* is looking pretty welcome to our animal friends right about now.

Like Courtois, lawyers today often have to represent people who are legally incapable of speaking for themselves. For instance, assume an all-too-prevalent modern happening: A young child is physically abused by the mother's boyfriend, who was living in the child's home. A social welfare agency seeks to remove the child from the mother's home. One lawyer will represent the agency, another will represent the mother, and a third is likely to be appointed to advocate on behalf of the best interests of the child. Anybody wandering into the courtroom to get out of the rain had best be careful, lest the judge immediately appoint lawyers for them too.

Lawyer No. 3 is in much the same position as Courtois: Neither the pig nor the young child can participate in the proceedings. Representing the pig's best interests is pretty easy: The pig would surely rather live than die, even if it knew that come wintertime it would play the starring role in a barbecue. But what might be best for the child is more problematic. Is the child better off in a foster home, or with a mother who kicks out the abusive boyfriend and agrees to take parenting classes? Such a decision can put a lawyer in a difficult ethical spot. Lawyers' supposed expertise is in representing others. Yet lawyers who represent legal incompetents like a small child, a comatose patient, or a regular watcher of TV talk shows inevitably substitute their own prejudices for those of their clients.

It's too bad for modern lawyers that Courtois didn't author current ethical rules. Then the way to resolve such ethical pressures would be one that lawyers could understand and follow: run away to Paris.

Trial Brief

The character of Richard Courtois is based on Bartholomew Chassenee, a French lawyer who wrote a treatise defending animal trials in 1531. Chassenee thought that animals knew right from wrong, and therefore could be prosecuted. During a celebrated career, Chassenee represented a variety of animals, including dogs, rats, and even a swarm of locusts.

One trial (not involving Chassenee) took place in Saint Julien, France, in 1575. Weevils were charged with destroying wine vineyards. The villagers offered a deal. Land outside the vineyards would be set aside for the weevils. The weevils' attorney objected to the deal because the land that was offered was not suitable for the weevils' needs. Ironically, the outcome of the case is unknown. Insects (perhaps unhappy weevils) ate the last page of the trial record!

Bananas

Synopsis: A gag-a-minute Woody Allen comedy about a nerd who becomes the leader of a small South American country. The film culminates in a classic send-up of the trial process.

United Artists (Jack Rollins and Charles Joffe). 1971. Color. Running time: 82 min.

Screenplay: Woody Allen and Mickey Rose. Director: Woody Allen.

Starring: Woody Allen (Fielding Mellish), Louise Lasser (Nancy), Howard Cosell (Himself), Sylvester Stallone (Subway Thug).

Rating: —▮ —▮ —▮

The Story

Fielding Mellish is a college dropout who has a humdrum existence working as a product tester. He meets Nancy, a radical college student who agrees to a date, provided she isn't scheduled to blow up a building. They begin a relationship, consisting primarily of joint appearances at antiwar demonstrations. When Mellish tells Nancy that he loves her, she breaks off the relationship.

The dejected Mellish goes to the tiny South American country of San Marcos, where he and Nancy had planned to write about a group of rebels trying to overthrow the latest in a long line of dictators. The rebels save him from being killed by the dictator and hide him in their camp. He soon becomes one of their leaders, feeding the hungry troops by ordering hundreds of sandwiches from a tiny village deli and taking

Bananas: Fielding Mellish (Woody Allen) finds little difference between a courtroom and a jungle.

them without paying. The revolution succeeds when the dictator mistakenly requests assistance from the UJA (United Jewish Appeal) instead of the CIA, and Mellish becomes the president of San Marcos.

Returning to New York to seek financial aid for his country, Mellish is put on trial for treason when the police recognize him as an antiwar protester. The witnesses against him include Miss America, who testifies that Mellish is a traitor, and J. Edgar Hoover, the director of the FBI, disguised as a black woman. (Only in later years did it become generally known that the real-life J. Edgar was a cross-dresser.) During the trial, an anguished man runs in and confesses to murder, only to realize that he has run into the wrong courtroom. One witness testifies in a way that helps Mellish, but when the court reporter reads back the testimony it condemns him. Mellish tries to testify in his own behalf, but the judge orders him bound and gagged when he runs back and forth between the witness box and counsel table. The pot-smoking jury convicts Mellish of treason, but the judge grants him probation on the condition that Mellish not move into the judge's neighborhood. Mellish and Nancy finally marry, and Howard Cosell (a sports announcer) announces the proceedings as Mellish battles to consummate the marriage.

Legal Analysis

The film's trial scene is a satirical classic, poking fun not only at courtroom procedures, but also at such American cultural icons as Miss America and J. Edgar Hoover.

One of the funniest moments occurs when Mellish, reduced to unintelligible mumblings by the judge who has ordered him tied to his chair and gagged, successfully cross-examines a witness who claims that she heard him utter treasonous statements. With each bit of muffled sound from Mellish, the witness becomes increasingly nervous and finally collapses, admitting that she lied. The scene is a wonderful parody of the celluloid cross-examiner who by force of personality and verbal dexterity is able to bend any witness to his will. Real-life lawyers, of course, rarely experience this kind of heady success. They are typically grateful if an adverse witness doesn't suddenly remember that their client committed war crimes.

Miss America is a parody of beauty pageant contestants. She testifies by singing an opera excerpt, and then mechanically reciting a belief that Mellish is a traitor because his views are different from those of the president. The absurdity of her testimony underlines two important limitations on parties' rights to present evidence. One limitation is that only witnesses who have personal knowledge of relevant events are allowed to testify. So even if the "talent" that won Miss America the crown was "Encyclopedic Knowledge of All Human Learning," it wouldn't matter. If Miss America knew nothing about what Mellish did or said pertaining to the charge of treason, she couldn't testify.

The second limitation is the "opinion" rule. Miss America states her belief that Mellish is a traitor. Also, a police officer testifies that Mellish is "a bad apple—a New York Jewish intellectual Communist crackpot." But a judge is not interested in a witness's opinion. In an actual trial, Miss America and the policeman would be limited to what they saw Mellish say or do. An opinion as to whether those acts or words are treasonous is strictly for the judge or jury.

These limitations are important. Without them, trials would drag on even longer than they do now. Every plaintiff and defendant could call on numerous relatives and friends to come forward and testify to their opinions about what wonderful people they are. Every plaintiff and defendant who isn't a lawyer, anyway.

Before he is bound and gagged, Mellish is allowed to testify in his own defense. He does so comically, by standing in front of the witness box, posing questions, and then running into the box to answer them. But with it becoming increasingly common for people to represent themselves in court, this raises the question of how people are supposed to testify when they represent themselves. Do they run back and forth while testifying? If so, do they have to do ten push-ups before taking the oath, and will judges have to become licensed aerobics instructors? Luckily, no. People representing themselves generally testify in a narrative format; they just go into the witness box and tell their stories. Of course, they may be asked questions by the judge or the adversary.

The judge puts Mellish on probation, on the condition that Mellish not move into the judge's neighborhood. Probation is a form of leniency which allows a person found guilty of a crime to carry on normal life. In exchange for leniency, judges can impose conditions on probationers related to their crimes. For example, a person convicted of improper behavior with young children may not be allowed to be within 100 feet of a day-care center. Similarly, had Wile E. Coyote been convicted of assault on the Roadrunner, he might have been placed on probation on the condition that he not seek future employment in animated cartoons. The condition of Mellish's probation is improper not only because it involves the judge personally, but because it bears no relationship to the crime of treason. Though the condition of Mellish's probation is meant to be comical, the NIMBY ("Not in My Back Yard") phenomenon is increasingly common when people find out that a convicted felon is about to be paroled into their community.

Actually, Mellish should not have been put on probation because he was not guilty of treason in the first place. Under the Constitution, "treason" consists of levying war against the United States or giving "aid and comfort" to an enemy. An "enemy" is a country against which the United States has declared war. Since the United States never declared war on North Vietnam (or San Marcos, for that matter), Mellish did not commit treason.

Thus, *Bananas* screws up both legal rules and trial procedures. Real cases are nothing like this. Too bad.

Mr. Deeds Goes to Town

Synopsis: A hick inherits $20 million and wants to give it all away. He protects the money in an incompetency hearing that is even daffier than he is.

Columbia (Frank Capra). 1936. Black and white. Running time: 118 min.

Screenplay: Robert Riskin. Original story: Clarence Budington. Director: Frank Capra.

Mr. Deeds Goes to Town: Babe Bennett (Jean Arthur) speaks up on behalf of Longfellow Deeds (Gary Cooper) with Dr. Von Haller's chart in the background.

Starring: Gary Cooper (Longfellow Deeds), Jean Arthur (Babe Bennett), Douglass Dumbrille (John Cedar).

Academy Award: Best Director.

Academy Award nominations: Best Picture, Best Actor (Gary Cooper), Best Screenplay (Robert Riskin).

Rating: —▮ —▮ —▮

The Story

Longfellow Deeds is an eccentric resident of Mandrake Falls, Vermont, whose first love is the tuba. He makes a modest living composing poems for greeting cards. His uncle, a playboy named Martin Semple, dies and leaves him $20 million. This was real money in 1936!

The happy news is delivered in person by oily lawyer John Cedar of the firm of Cedar, Cedar, Cedar and Budington. The firm managed Martin's affairs so creatively that the Cedar firm owes Deeds about half a million dollars. Cedar tries get Deeds to sign a power of attorney, but the shrewd Deeds never gets around to signing it.

Cedar brings Deeds to New York, where he experiences extreme culture shock. The poets he meets make fun of him. They're probably jealous because Deeds can rhyme more words with "sugar" than they can. Everybody from the head of the opera association on down tries to get their hooks into Deeds's money. He even gets drunk for the first time in his life and feeds doughnuts to a horse. But he hangs on to the money.

Hard-boiled reporter Babe Bennett pretends that she's a damsel in distress and wins Deeds's grateful friendship. Deeds, who only reads rhymed couplets, doesn't realize that she's reporting every detail for the paper, even dubbing him "Cinderella Man." Ultimately, of course, Deeds falls in love with Bennett—only to learn her true identity. He also finds out that the poor people in New York despise him because Bennett's stories make him out to be a jerk. So Deeds decides to give all the money away. He plans to buy a huge farm, split it up into pieces and give a plot and a horse to every unemployed person willing to farm it.

Cedar has a different kind of plot in mind. Cedar joins with Semple's other nephew and his shrewish wife to get control of the bucks. They go to court to have Deeds declared incompetent and the nephew named as conservator. That way they can get the money without standing behind a horse. Meanwhile Deeds has sunk into such a deep depression that he refuses to defend himself. He is probably thinking about a poem for a new condolence card starting "So you've inherited $20 million . . . "

The competency hearing is chaotic. Numerous witnesses testify to Deeds's erratic behavior, and nobody pays any attention to the judge. The Faulkner sisters, two old biddies from Mandrake Falls, testify that Deeds was always "pixillated," which seems to mean that he acted like a pixie. A famous German psychiatrist, Dr. Von Haller, just happens to be in town. Making good use of a silly chart with lots of wavy lines, Von Haller testifies that Deeds is a manic-depressive. Cedar declares that society will collapse if Deeds is allowed to give his fortune to the poor. The horse owner complains that his horse now refuses to eat anything except doughnuts.

Babe Bennett, by now in love with Deeds, rises to his defense. This happy news revives Deeds, who asks to take the stand. Deeds acknowledges that he's a bit peculiar. He plays the tuba a lot because it helps him concentrate. But he's no crazier than anybody else in the courtroom. Greedy cousin Semple is a nose twitcher, his ghastly wife a knuckle cracker, Von Haller a doodler, and even the judge fills in the "o's" on his papers. With that, the Faulkner sisters declare that everybody in Mandrake Falls is pixillated and probably the judge is too.

Now in rare form, Deeds demands to know what's wrong with giving his money away to the poor. Isn't it better to give money to people who are drowning than to people like his cousin and Cedar who are in the lifeboat but are just tired of rowing? He discredits Cedar, revealing that Cedar offered to dismiss the competency hearing in exchange for a handsome sum. When Cedar rises to protest, Deeds slugs him.

The judge rules that Deeds is a bit strange but obviously sane. Deeds is carried out on the shoulders of the crowd, who are already having visions of their new farming careers. Deeds returns, sweeps Bennett into his arms, and the two lovers go off together, perhaps to Mandrake Falls. A big-city girl, Bennett may not fit in too well there. In fact, she will probably be regarded by the locals as hopelessly pixillated.

Legal Analysis

Most early trial movies treated lawyers generously, sometimes heroically. *Mr. Deeds Goes to Town* is most definitely an exception. The movie is well ahead of its time in portraying the sleazy underside of the legal profession. Cedar and his partners are thoroughly loathsome. They are frantically trying to steal Deeds's money to cover up what they've already stolen from Semple. And the lawyers are well aware that the competency proceeding against Deeds is completely baseless.

It's Deeds who seems heroic when he hauls off and slugs Cedar in court. Perhaps he had heard of "cross-examination," and thought it meant "right cross" examination. We, however, do not recommend punching out your least favorite lawyer. Trust us, you'll regret it.

In a competency proceeding, a judge is asked to appoint a conservator to manage the property of a person who is no longer competent to manage it for him or herself. This often occurs when children decide that their aged parents have become unable to deal with their money and are wasting it. Of course, the children always know what's best for mom or dad—especially when the parent is wasting the money on a new sweetheart. Conservatorships can indeed be a way for greedy relatives or lawyers to pry an eccentric or an elderly person loose from his or her money.

Conservatorship proceedings tend to be expensive, unpleasant, and public. All of the family's dirty laundry is hung out for everyone to see on court TV. There are far better ways for aging parents to turn over management of their affairs to the next generation. For example, parents can execute a durable power of attorney that shifts management of the assets to a relative or friend in case a physician certifies that the elderly person is incompetent. But a durable power wouldn't have been much use to Deeds, since his relatives were slime and his friends were pixillated.

In a notorious case in California, Groucho Marx's family was alarmed because he was supporting a lady named Erin Fleming. Groucho said that if somebody was going to manage his money, he wanted Erin to do it. The family managed to get a court to declare Groucho incompetent, splashing the elderly Groucho's physical and mental limitations all over the papers.

In Deeds's competency hearing, the court should have appointed an attorney to represent Deeds, even though he didn't want one. He would have difficulty representing himself against big trees like Cedar, Cedar, Cedar and Budington. Of course, Deeds did a great job of representing himself once he snapped out of his depression, but real life would seldom have such a happy ending.

In addition, the court should have been much more skeptical about whether Deeds's cousin Semple would be a suitable conservator. After all, this deadbeat and his wife were desperate for money and bitter about being disinherited. Even though a conservator must render an annual accounting, no doubt they'd have found a way to steal most of it.

Everybody loves a story about the country cousin getting rich and outsmarting the city slickers, including the venal lawyers. The legendary Frank Capra is at the top of his game. The courtroom scene is hilarious and the movie is enormous fun.

My Cousin Vinny

Synopsis: A brash, profane, and inexperienced New York lawyer and his fiancée come to a small Alabama town to defend his nephew and a friend, who are wrongfully accused of killing a store clerk.

20th Century Fox (Dale Launer and Paul Schiff). 1992. Color. Running time: 120 min.

Screenplay: Dale Launer. Director: Jonathan Lynn.

Starring: Joe Pesci (Vincent Gambini), Marisa Tomei (Mona Lisa Vito), Ralph Macchio (Bill Gambini), Mitchell Whitfield (Stan Rothenstein), Fred Gwynne (Judge Chamberlain Haller), Lane Smith (Jim Trotter).

Academy Award: Marisa Tomei (Best Supporting Actress).

Rating:

The Story

Bill and Stan, driving through Alabama on their way to college, stop to pick up a few snacks at a convenience market. They soon find more trouble than the earlier team of Ollie and Stan. The market is held up and the clerk killed by two people who look a bit like Bill and Stan and whose metallic green convertible is similar to Bill and Stan's.

My Cousin Vinny: Vinny Gambini (Joe Pesci) elicits expert testimony from Mona Lisa Vito (Marisa Tomei).

Bill and Stan are arrested and charged with the crime. Stan opts to be represented by the public defender; Bill sends for the only lawyer he knows, his cousin Vinny. Little does Bill know that Vinny, an ex-auto mechanic who only recently became a lawyer after flunking the bar examination six times, has never appeared in court.

Vinny and his fiancée, Mona Lisa Vito, could not look any more out of place in Alabama than if they had come from Mars. Vinny wears leather and chains and speaks with an accent that the Dead End Kids would have regarded as uncouth. Mona Lisa matches him diphthong for diphthong and probably needed a second car to carry her makeup and clothes. Life for them in Alabama is living hell: train and factory whistles shriek before daylight, breakfast consists of fried grits, and there's no Chinese take-out.

But it is the stern Judge Haller who brings true misery to Vinny. Vinny's lounge-lizard courtroom attire, his vocabulary and a few minor procedural missteps (such as Vinny's lack of knowledge of how to plead a client "not guilty") provoke increasing hostility in the judge. Finally, an exasperated Judge Haller holds Vinny in contempt of court. Vinny ends up in the same jail as Bill, generally a no-no for a lawyer seeking to bolster a client's confidence.

When the trial finally gets under way, D.A. Trotter produces three eyewitnesses who identify Bill and Stan as the perpetrators of the crime. To the amazement of all, Vinny cross-examines them effectively and demonstrates that their identifications are very probably mistaken. But it appears that Vinny's luck has run out when Trotter produces a surprise witness, an FBI agent who is an expert on automobile tires. The expert testifies that he compared tire marks made by the murderers' car as it sped away from the convenience store and bits of rubber left on the ground with the tires of Bill and Stan's Chevrolet. The expert's opinion is that the marks and bits of rubber were left by their car.

Just as matters seem bleak, Vinny realizes that a photo which Mona Lisa had taken of the tire marks in front of the convenience store proves that the FBI agent is wrong. He calls Mona Lisa, like him an ex-mechanic, to testify as an expert on general automotive mechanics. Mona Lisa, however, is very upset at Vinny for refusing her earlier offers of help, and does not want to do anything to help him. Thus, Vinny has to drag her kicking and screaming into the courtroom. Only after Judge Haller orders her to answer questions does she convince an astounded Trotter that she really is an expert on general automotive mechanics. Then, closely examining her photo of the tire marks for the first time, she testifies that Bill and Stan's Chevrolet could not possibly have made those marks. Her expert opinion is that the tire marks could only have been left by a car with Positraction, a feature not available on Bill and Stan's Chevrolet. She also says that a Pontiac would be the only other make and model car that did have Positraction and a similar body style to Bill and Stan's Chevrolet.

Mona Lisa's testimony unravels Trotter's case. First, Trotter's FBI agent admits that Mona Lisa is right and that he was wrong; the defendants' car could not have made the tire marks. Then, the sheriff testifies that a Pontiac of the type described by Mona Lisa was recently found stolen by two lads resembling Bill and Stan, with the murder weapon inside. Trotter dismisses all charges, and it's hugs and kisses all around for the defense team. Trotter, the sheriff, and Judge Haller stand outside the courthouse waving good-bye to Vinny and Mona Lisa as if a joyous family reunion had just come to a close. Meanwhile, Vinny and Mona Lisa beat a hasty retreat out of Alabama before Judge Haller finds out that Vinny lied about his extensive New York trial experience.

Legal Analysis

The film succeeds by playing the trial process for laughs without reducing it to a farce. Judge Haller and Trotter are like the Washington Generals, the basketball team doomed to forever lose to the Harlem

Globetrotters. Like the Generals, Judge Haller and Trotter attempt to play by the rules, but their efforts are constantly thwarted by Vinny's antics. The difference is that unlike the Globetrotters, the inexperienced Vinny often has no clue as to the rules he's breaking.

The legal highlight of the trial consists of Mona Lisa's expert testimony. Despite the fact that she is currently an unemployed hairdresser, her testimony about the unavailability of a certain size of engine on a particular model of car convinces Trotter that she is qualified as an expert in automobile mechanics. Of course, half the cast turns out to be expert mechanics. Vinny, Mona Lisa, the FBI agent, and Trotter all sound like they should be maintaining the Starship *Enterprise* rather than doing hair or trying cases. This may explain why it's so difficult to get a decent tune-up these days; the qualified mechanics are writing movies or practicing law.

The term "expert witness" conjures up for many people the image of people trained in science who wear white jackets and carry stethoscopes in their pockets; other people think of doctors. But at trial an expert is simply a person with specialized knowledge, and it doesn't matter whether the knowledge is a product of advanced education or on-the-job experience. Thus, though her background is a bit unusual, Mona Lisa's experience as a mechanic could qualify her to give expert testimony.

Vinny takes a real chance with Mona Lisa, showing her the photo with the tire marks for the first time on the witness stand and hoping that she will see the same thing that he saw. A real-life Vinny would have secured a favorable opinion long before trial. Indeed, if Expert No. 1 had not confirmed Vinny's Positraction theory, he might have gone to Expert Nos. 2, 3, and so on until he found one with a favorable opinion. This is a major reason that the role of experts at trial is currently under attack: An attorney with enough money can find an expert to say almost anything.

Confronted unexpectedly by the FBI agent's expert testimony, Vinny first asks for a delay in the trial so that he can try to counter it. Judge Haller refuses his request, a refusal that probably would have been a reversible error had Bill and Stan been convicted. Thus, if Vinny's fiancée hadn't miraculously turned out to be an expert in auto mechanics, Vinny might have been forced to testify himself. Perhaps surprisingly, evidence rules do not bar attorneys from testifying in cases in which they appear as counsel. Attorneys' ethical rules generally forbid them from representing clients in cases in which they anticipate having to testify. But as Vinny had no idea when the trial started that his expertise in auto mechanics would be relevant, he could testify without violating any ethical rules. Indeed, since Trotter too is an automotive expert, Vinny might have tried calling him as a witness. (There is some precedent for this. In the case of *Tennessee v. Scopes,* dramatized in *Inherit the Wind,* defense attorney Clarence Darrow called the prosecutor, William Jennings Bryan, as an expert witness on the Bible.)

The film's tongue-in-cheek approach conceals a troubling issue—the fallibility of eyewitness testimony. Trotter brings forth three ordinary citizens with no ax to grind, each of whom swears that Bill and Stan are the ones who sped off just after the store clerk was shot. It does not take much for Vinny to poke holes in their stories, because the only way the prosecution could have produced weaker eyewitnesses is if all of them had blindly stumbled into each other trying to find the witness stand. One eyewitness saw the lads through thick shrubbery and screens so encrusted with filth that the evolutionary process could have been starting all over again in them. The second eyewitness wears glasses as thick as binoculars and still can't see from one side of the courtroom to the other. And the third says that the whole robbery incident lasted five minutes, just long enough for him to cook his morning grits. Vinny, an expert on grits preparation after a week in Alabama, forces him to admit that decent grits cannot be cooked in under twenty minutes.

In actual cases, eyewitness testimony is not so obviously improbable, and it tends to be very persuasive. In fact, defense attorneys often attack prosecution cases as untrustworthy whenever eyewitness testimony is absent. Yet, studies repeatedly cast doubt on the credibility of eyewitness identification. For example, research shows that stress reduces most people's abilities to observe events accurately; jurors are likely to think that just the opposite is true. This is why defendants like Bill and Stan typically have to rely on diligent police officers and prosecutors to weed out identifications that are too shaky to support guilty verdicts. Therefore, though he seems a very fair-minded prosecutor, perhaps we can legitimately fault Trotter for basing a murder prosecution on such highly improbable eyewitness testimony.

Cousin Vinny has the same reverence for trial procedures that the Marx Brothers had for classic opera and that James Bond had for martinis that were stirred. The result is a marvelously funny and entertaining film.

Heroic Lawyers and Clients

Today, lawyers are often viewed about as favorably as the criminals they defend. The general perception is that lawyers are dishonest, greedy, and responsible for most of society's problems. And that perception is reflected in the movies, where some pretty sleazy lawyers ply their trade on film.

Nevertheless, in real life and the movies, heroic lawyers abound. Many lawyers toil in obscurity for the underdog, or put everything on the line to defend an unpopular client. Who can forget Atticus Finch in *To Kill a Mockingbird,* endangering his small-town southern practice and his family by defending Tom Robinson, a black man charged with rape? Or Gareth Peirce, tenaciously fighting to clear the Guildford Four in *In the Name of the Father?* Or even Clarence Darrow, appealing desperately for the court to spare the lives of Leopold and Loeb in *Compulsion?*

The movies in this chapter just may raise your opinion of lawyers a bit. Or maybe not.

. . . And Justice For All

Synopsis: A criminal defense attorney loses it when he defends a judge he's always loathed against a rape charge.

Columbia/Malton (Joe Wizan). 1979. Color. Running time: 119 min.

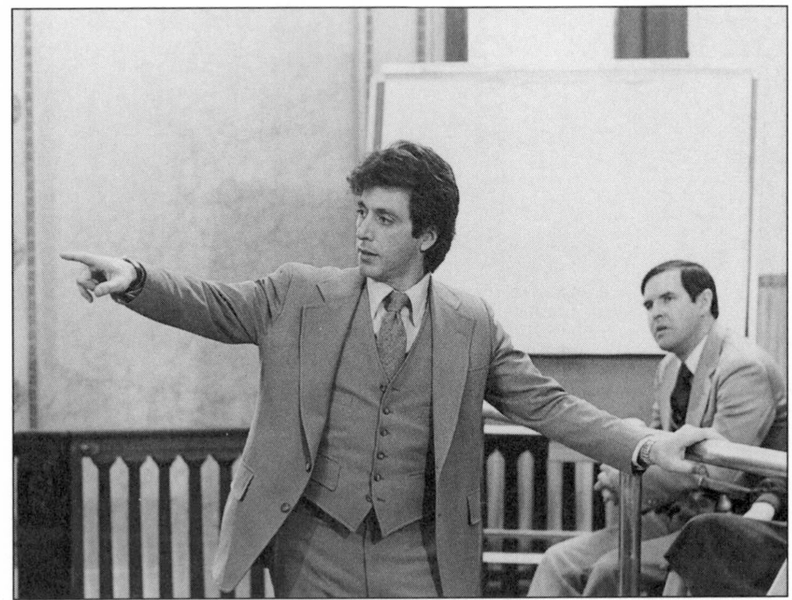

. . . And Justice For All: Arthur Kirkland (Al Pacino) makes a pointed opening statement.

Screenplay: Valerie Curtin and Barry Levinson. Director: Norman Jewison.
Starring: Al Pacino (Arthur Kirkland), Jack Warden (Judge Rayford), John Forsythe (Judge Fleming), Lee Strasberg (Grandpa Sam), Christine Lahti (Gail Packer), Sam Levene (Arnie).
Academy Award nominations: Best Actor (Al Pacino), Best Screenplay.
Rating: —▮

The Story

Arthur Kirkland is a small-time Baltimore criminal defense attorney, Judge Fleming his harsh and arrogant nemesis. The film opens with Kirkland in jail on contempt charges. Kirkland had taken a swing at Fleming for refusing to reopen the criminal conviction of his client McCullough, who had been wrongly convicted of a crime. Because Kirkland filed his motion to reopen McCullough's case three days late, Fleming refused to consider it.

Kirkland should probably have stayed in the nice quiet jail, because upon release his life takes on the surreal quality of a Salvador Dali painting. Fighting with Fleming lands him in front of the ethics committee, which is looking into his fitness to practice law. The boxing commission has to meet separately. But Kirkland keeps swinging, this time romantically with Gale Packer, a member of the ethics committee.

Meanwhile, Kirkland and his partner Jay represent a variety of unsavory or unfortunate clients. Jay gets a murderer off on a technicality, following which the client murders two children. This causes Jay to have a nervous breakdown.

Kirkland represents a transvestite who participated in an armed robbery. The transvestite is understandably terrified of going to prison. One of Kirkland's partners appears at the transvestite's sentencing hearing but forgets to correct errors in the probation report. The transvestite is sentenced to three years in prison. One hour later, he kills himself.

Proving that law is as capable of producing strange bedfellows as politics, Kirkland finds himself representing Judge Fleming, who is charged with rape. Fleming forces Kirkland to take his case by threatening to disclose a serious ethics violation. Years ago, Kirkland had ratted on a particularly despicable client. Why Fleming would want a lawyer who hates his guts to defend him isn't made clear.

Fleming promises to reopen McCullough's case, but he stalls. Meanwhile, McCullough, who is helpless to protect himself in prison, is brutally raped. He snaps, getting a gun and taking hostages. Despite Kirkland's attempts to cool him off, McCullough is killed by guards. At least, after the debacles with McCullough and the transvestite, Kirkland can advertise that his clients don't spend a lot of time in jail.

Although Fleming at first denies the rape charge, he privately confesses his guilt to Kirkland. Nevertheless, Fleming somehow manages to pass a polygraph test. Taking no chances, he also pays a witness to testify that he saw someone else enter the victim's apartment. Kirkland's opening statement is remarkable: He admits his client's guilt. The courtroom erupts in turmoil and the movie ends with Kirkland sitting on the courthouse steps wondering whether he should shift to a new career and how he's going to collect his fee from Fleming.

Legal Analysis

. . . And Justice For All effectively lampoons the criminal justice system, but the price tag for satire is unreality. The climactic scene in which Kirkland declares his client guilty during the opening statement could never happen. Kirkland is washed up as an attorney after this impulsive decision to shoot his mouth off and betray his client. Kirkland must provide Fleming the best possible defense. It doesn't matter whether Fleming is guilty, or whether Kirkland loathes Fleming, or whether Fleming blackmailed him into taking the case. Of course, Kirkland could not put on testimony that he knew to be perjured, such as the phony witness or Judge Fleming's denial of having

committed the crime. But declaring his client guilty in front of the jury is a colossal no-no. Kirkland urgently needs a career counselor.

While we can predict that Kirkland will have to turn to boxing to make a living, what about the unlovable Judge Fleming? Fleming would hire a new attorney who would promptly be granted a mistrial. This means a whole new trial with a new jury. The rule against double jeopardy would not preclude the state from retrying Judge Fleming, since Fleming would be requesting it. Fleming will not confess guilt to his new lawyer, so the new lawyer can ethically call the witness and even Judge Fleming to the stand to give testimony that we and Kirkland know to be perjured.

Before he makes the fateful decision to announce Fleming's guilt, Kirkland twice tells the jury in his opening statement that Fleming passed a polygraph test. Polygraph tests are not generally admissible as evidence because they are considered unreliable. Mentioning the test results in his opening statement was, therefore, extremely improper. If Kirkland weren't already in hot water with the ethics committee, this gaffe would have landed him there.

There are numerous scenes in the movie involving plea-bargaining in which harried defenders and prosecutors agree to sentences if clients will plead guilty. To the uninitiated, plea-bargaining seems repulsive, an affront to the rights of the crime victim, as well as to the rights of the people of the state and of defendants. Yet it is inevitable. The criminal justice system could not possibly try every criminal case. As a result, defendants have considerable leverage to bargain for a reduced sentence or a lesser offense. But the picture isn't pretty.

The scenes involving the transvestite client are dramatically powerful but misleading. The transvestite had evidently participated in the armed robbery of a taxi driver, although he claimed it was not his idea. Kirkland's promise that he'd get probation was unrealistic. Attorneys never make promises to their clients about what will happen in court, and this one was silly. Even a charter member bleeding-heart judge would require at least some jail time for an armed robbery, first offense or not.

Kirkland's involvement with the ethics committee is equally unconvincing. The committee members seem befuddled about why they called Kirkland to testify. And it's highly unlikely that Packer would start an affair with Kirkland when she is probably going to judge his case before the committee. Packer should have immediately disqualified herself from any further matters involving Kirkland once she began a relationship with him. She becomes just another caricature of a female lawyer (see *Women Trial Lawyers in the Movies,* p. 90).

The old ethics charge hanging over Kirkland—that he abused a client's confidence by tipping off the police—is quite serious. A lawyer must guard a client's confidence. This is true even where it is obvious the client has committed a serious crime and only the lawyer could help the police solve it. A lawyer can go to the police if a client tells the lawyer about a crime he's going to commit in the future, but the lawyer cannot disclose a confidential communication that would help the police solve a crime that has already occurred.

. . . *And Justice for All* provides a few good yuks at the expense of the criminal justice system and the ethics of the people who make their living from it. But it's grossly exaggerated and as informative about the criminal justice system as *Gilligan's Island* is about ocean navigation.

Compulsion

Synopsis: Two brilliant law students kidnap and kill a child for thrills. Their attorney's eloquent argument saves them from the gallows.

Twentieth Century Fox (Richard D. Zanuck). 1959. Black and white. Running time: 103 min.

Screenplay: Richard Murphy. Novel: Meyer Levin. Director: Richard Fleischer.

Starring: Orson Welles (Jonathan Wilk), Dean Stockwell (Judd Steiner), Bradford Dillman (Artie Strauss), E.G. Marshall (Henry Horn), Diane Varsi (Ruth Evans), Martin Milner (Sid Brooks).

Rating: —▮ —▮ —▮

The Story

Judd Steiner and Artie Strauss are rich, spoiled, and brilliant law students at the University of Chicago in 1924. They are much younger than their classmates, having graduated from college in their early teens. They believe they qualify as Nietzschean supermen who aren't bound by the same laws as normal human beings. They are the sort of snotty superior kids whose necks you'd love to wring. Just to experience the thrill of committing a perfect crime, they kidnap little Paulie Kessler. When Paulie acts up, they kill him. But they make a fatal error. Steiner loses his glasses at the scene.

As the police search for the killer, Strauss and Steiner plan further criminal exploits. They're sure that the bumbling police can't find them. Strauss challenges Steiner to rape Ruth Evans. Steiner takes her out birdwatching, but is physically incapable of raping her.

Strauss has a fine old time misleading the police and the press, but

Compulsion: Henry Horn (E.G. Marshall) and Jonathan Wilk (Orson Welles) argue the fate of two thrill-killers.

the party ends when the tough district attorney, Henry Horn, traces the glasses back to Steiner. At that point, their contrived alibi collapses and they confess, each blaming the other for killing Paulie.

Their parents hire the legendary socialist lawyer Jonathan Wilk to defend them. This isn't an easy decision, since Wilk has spent his career hounding the ruling class, of which the parents are charter members. Wilk doesn't mind getting paid a huge fee to defend a couple of rich kids. After all, he says, the rich are entitled to a good defense too. And Wilk could use the money. By the time he arrives and tells his clients to shut up, they have already made a detailed confession. Horn even allows them to be interviewed by the media. By this time, the locals are out for blood.

After Horn's opening statement, Wilk changes his clients' plea to guilty. It isn't clear whether Steiner and Strauss agree, but their parents are horrified. Wilk's reasoning is that the jury is certain to sentence them to death, but the trial judge might be more merciful. Once the client pleads guilty, the judge, not the jury, decides the penalty.

Then follow ten days in which Wilk offers evidence of mitigating circumstances. This consists largely of psychiatric testimony about how desperately ill the two youths were. Horn keeps objecting that this is evidence of insanity, which should have gone to the jury. But the judge allows it. Ruth Evans, who has seen Steiner's gentler side, has the courage to stand against her friends and testify as a character witness in his favor.

The dramatic climax of the movie is Wilk's eloquent closing argument. It is a stirring diatribe against capital punishment that would soften the heart of Genghis Khan. If killing Steiner and Strauss would bring little Paulie back to life, Wilk argues, then execute them; but it won't and the state should not engage in premeditated murder just because the defendants did. He graphically describes every detail of their hanging. He's spent his life struggling against hatred and barbarism, he argues, and capital punishment is the embodiment of hatred. The world is already a huge slaughterhouse and one more execution won't change that.

Wilk's eloquence works. The judge spares the defendants but gives them life plus ninety-nine years. Strauss and Steiner are contemptuous of Wilk. They show no remorse. Perhaps, Wilk tells them, it was the hand of God that made Steiner drop his glasses.

Legal Analysis

Although Strauss and Steiner were mentally ill, they were not legally insane. Legal insanity, under the McNaghten test, means an inability to distinguish right from wrong. The two defendants thought they were smarter than everyone else, and as superhumans not even bound by the same laws, but they knew perfectly well that kidnapping and killing Paulie Kessler was wrong.

Therefore, Wilk's strategy is shrewd. He gets in the psychiatric evidence in mitigation of the penalty, but not for the purpose of showing insanity, since the jury would never have bought that approach. The judge realizes that the two men are terribly sick and spares their lives.

Without the defendants' confessions, Horn would not have had sufficient evidence to bring them to trial. True, Steiner's glasses were found at the scene, but by itself this would not have been enough to charge Steiner and certainly not Strauss. After all, Steiner claims that he'd been bird-watching in the area and dropped his glasses accidentally. If Wilk had arrived in time, he would have shushed them, and the case might never have gone to trial.

Today, Horn would be required to give the defendants Miranda warnings at the time they were taken into custody. They would have been told that they had a right to keep silent and had a right to an attorney. But despite Miranda, a great many defendants go right on talking to the police. Probably Steiner and Strauss were so arrogant that they would have kept blabbing despite receiving a warning. They were sure their alibi story would fool the police (they claimed they had been out that afternoon in Steiner's Stutz Bearcat picking up a couple of chippies). But once a hole opened up (their chauffeur told the police that the Stutz was in the garage that day), they fell apart and told all.

It is unclear whether Strauss and Steiner agreed with Wilk's decision to plead them guilty. Certainly, their parents, who were paying the bills, objected violently. Regardless of who is paying, however, the clients—not the parents and not the attorney—are entitled to make the call about a fundamental decision like the plea.

Many fine trial movies focus on capital punishment. Innocent men are executed in *10 Rillington Place* and *Sommersby*. In the military, the executions in *Billy Budd* and *Paths of Glory* are monstrously unjust. The ghastliness of the gas chamber is dramatized in *I Want to Live!* *Compulsion* takes its place with these pictures as one more eloquent and emotional statement against the death penalty.

Trial Brief

Compulsion is based quite literally on the notorious case of Richard Loeb and Nathan Leopold. These eighteen-year-olds were University of Chicago law students who killed fourteen-year-old Robert Franks for thrills in 1924. Clarence Darrow defended them. Darrow's closing argument in the movie lasts fifteen minutes; in real life, it lasted two days. It was later released as a phonograph record.

The movie only hints at the sexual relationship between Leopold and Loeb—this was 1959, after all. In fact, they had a master-slave relationship in which Loeb gave the orders and Leopold, who was deeply in love, carried them out. Darrow made much of the erotic relationship in arguing that the defendants were too sick to be executed. In fact, he tried to get Sigmund Freud to testify at the trial, but Freud begged off.

Loeb died in a knife fight in prison at the age of thirty. Leopold was finally paroled in 1958 after serving thirty-three years in prison. He married in 1961 and moved to Puerto Rico, where he taught high school math, and died in 1971.

Meyer Levin, who wrote the book on which the film was based, was a contemporary of Leopold and Loeb at Chicago and, like Sid Brooks in the movie, was a journalist who followed the case firsthand. After he wrote the novel *Compulsion,* Nathan Leopold sued him for $1.5 million for invasion of privacy, but the case was dismissed under the First Amendment.

In the Name of the Father

Synopsis: The IRA bombs an English pub during a wave of anti-British violence. The police concoct a case against the "Guildford Four," who serve fifteen years in prison before the truth emerges.

Universal Pictures/Hells' Kitchen–Gabriel Byrne (Jim Sheridan). 1993. Color. Running time: 127 min.

Screenplay: Terry George and Jim Sheridan. Book: Gerry Conlon, *Proved Innocent.* Director: Jim Sheridan.

Starring: Daniel Day-Lewis (Gerald Conlon), Pete Postlethwaite (Giuseppe Conlon), Emma Thompson (Gareth Peirce), Corin Redgrave (Robert Dixon), Don Baker (Joe McAndrew), Britta Smith (Annie Maguire), John Lynch (Paul Hill).

Academy Award nominations: Best Picture, Best Director, Best Adapted Screenplay, Best Editing (Gerry Hambling), Best Actor (Daniel Day-Lewis), Best Supporting Actor (Pete Postlethwaite), Best Supporting Actress (Emma Thompson).

Rating: ⚖ ⚖ ⚖

The Story

Belfast, Northern Ireland, 1974: heady economic times for bomb component manufacturers and street sweepers. A petty thief named Gerry Conlon accidentally triggers an anti-British riot. The IRA (Irish Republican Army) threatens to shoot him in the knees when the British nearly find an IRA weapons cache while suppressing the riot. Conlon's dad Giuseppe always admired his son's knees, and so sends Conlon to London to keep him out of trouble. Conlon can live either with Aunt Annie Maguire or in a commune devoted to free love and drugs; Aunt Annie is lucky to finish as high as second.

During a spate of IRA attacks on English targets, two bombs go off in a Guildford pub. Five persons are killed; many more are seriously wounded. At the time, Conlon is nowhere near Guildford. Already moving up the social ladder, Conlon and his friend Paul Hill are in London stealing money from a prostitute's flat and talking to Charlie Burke, a homeless wino. Nevertheless, the police suspect Conlon and Hill of being part of the IRA Active Service Unit that bombed the pub. They are arrested under a law that allows the police to detain suspected terrorists without charges for seven days.

Chief Inspector Dixon and his henchmen use the tactics they learned in Coerced Confessions 101. If the IRA is making bombs, the cops can make evidence. Using a combination of threats, lies, physical abuse, and cold fish and chips, they induce Conlon and Hill to confess to the bombing. To allow them to go down in history as the

In the Name of the Father: The Guildford Four (Mark Sheppard, Beatie Edney, John Lynch, and Daniel Day-Lewis) in the dock.

Guildford Four, Carol Richardson and Paddy Armstrong, two other members of the commune, also confess. All four are charged with murder. Seven more defendants (the Maguire Seven, who include Giuseppe, Aunt Annie, and fourteen-year-old Patrick Maguire), are charged with using Annie's house to make bombs and shelter terrorists. Police technicians had searched Annie's house for traces of nitroglycerin, an ingredient favored by most terrorists for making bombs and dentists for preventing tooth decay. Their reports were negative, but nothing that creative police perjury couldn't overcome.

The trial of the Guildford Four and the Maguire Seven adds up to eleven guilty verdicts. The only evidence against the Guildford Four is their confessions, and Dixon denies pressuring the defendants into signing them. He also testifies that he was unable to locate the wino, Charlie Burke. Conlon and Hill testify to their innocence and describe how they were tortured into confessing, but as admitted thieves and drug users their words carry little weight. The Guildford Four are given life sentences; the sentences of the Maguire Seven run between twelve and fifteen years.

Conlon and Giuseppe share the same cell in a maximum-security prison, an unusual father-son bonding technique. They are soon joined by Joe McAndrew, a real IRA terrorist. He was the mastermind of the Guildford bombing and told the police that innocent people were behind bars, but the police ignored him. To Giuseppe's disgust, Conlon hangs around with McAndrew. But when McAndrew torches a prison guard and Giuseppe's lungs start giving out, Conlon joins his father's campaign for freedom.

Gareth Peirce, a civil rights lawyer, takes up the Conlons' cause. She searches for Charlie Burke, and receives permission to examine the Conlon files stored in police archives. Peirce gets a break one day when a substitute file keeper who knows nothing about the case mistakenly allows Peirce access to a file she's not supposed to see. She sees a document marked, "not to be shown to the defense." Probably wondering if it's a "Guide to Old Bailey Restrooms," Peirce dramatically finds that it's a record of Dixon's interview of Charlie Burke, made shortly after the arrest of the Guildford Four. The cops knew all along that Conlon had an alibi.

Fifteen years after the convictions, Peirce has the matter back in court. She calls Dixon as a witness, and berates him for lying and concealing evidence. The judge angrily tries to quiet her, then reads through the Dixon-Burke interview while Dixon sweats nitroglycerin. The judge immediately dismisses all charges against the Guildford Four and Maguire Seven and sets them free. The latter dismissals come too late. Six finished serving their sentences, and Giuseppe died in prison.

A postscript adds that no IRA member was charged with bombing the Guildford pub, and that the police officers who interrogated the Guildford Four were acquitted of conspiracy to subvert justice.

Legal Analysis

The scenario is all too familiar. Needing to calm a terrified public, the police hastily make arrests based on sketchy information. When new information suggests that the wrong people are in jail, the police conceal it rather than add to the public panic by revealing their mistake. The plight of the Guildford-Maguire defendants is a reminder that even the elaborate set of Anglo-American procedures known as "due process" can be subverted when public hysteria goads police officers into overzealousness.

Of course, all that Conlon and Co. got was the process that Parliament decided was due to terrorists. And under the Prevention of Terrorism Act, that wasn't much. Normally, a suspect who's in jail has to be speedily charged and brought before a judge or magistrate, and in most cases has a right to reasonable bail. If the police want to interrogate a suspect, they must inform him of his right to have counsel present. In the United States, a court would undoubtedly strike down a law that didn't have these protections as unconstitutional (*United States v. Salerno,* 1987).

By contrast, Great Britain has no written constitution. Therefore, even if he had wanted to, the British judge had no power to invalidate the Prevention of Terrorism Act on the ground that it was unconstitutional. Under that act, the police had Conlon and the others to themselves for a week. The prisoners were not eligible for bail, they could not talk to a lawyer, no charges had to be filed, and they did not have to be brought before a judge. Instead of thoroughly investigating and trying to find the real bombers, the police concentrated on extracting confessions from the first suspects they could lay their hands on. The short-term losers here were the Guildford Four. The long-term loser is society, which instead of a vigorous police force able to search out criminals gets a bunch of nasty couch potatoes who try to intimidate convenient suspects into confessing. And many countries have responded to the threat of terrorism by enacting preventive detention laws.

Currently, attempts are under way in the United States to overturn the *Miranda* case, the 1966 Supreme Court decision that requires police officers to inform suspects of their right to have an attorney present during any interrogation, and forbids prosecutors from offering confessions into evidence when the police don't comply. Watering down or eliminating the *Miranda* rule would make it easier for police officers to extract confessions. Because *Miranda* is an interpretation of the Constitution, Congress cannnot overturn the case simply by passing a piece of legislation. The outcome can be changed only by an amendment to the Constitution or by a Supreme Court abandonment of *Miranda*. However, the fate of the Guildford Four at least raises cautionary flags as to the wisdom of a change.

Most of us would like to think that when they come together as a jury, ordinary people acquire mystical powers that allow them to detect perjury and live on $5 a day. However, Dixon was a decorated veteran officer, and the jurors could not bring themselves to believe that everything he said was a lie. Yet the clues were there. The confessions followed days of secret interrogations, and as brought out by defense counsel, contained inconsistent accounts of how the pub bombing was carried out. Moreover, if they hadn't been able to gather independent evidence of the guilt of the Guildford Four before they confessed, surely the confessions, if true, should have pointed the police to such evidence. Thus, the jury should have regarded the inability of the prosecution to offer any evidence against the Guildford Four other than their confessions as highly suspicious. However, the jurors were probably just as caught up as the police in the desire to punish someone for the horrific IRA bombings, and perhaps overlooked signs pointing towards reasonable doubt.

In the United States, Dixon's concealment of his interview with Charlie Burke would have violated the rule of *Brady v. Maryland* (1963), which requires the prosecution to turn over potentially exculpatory information to the defense. Of course, the Crown attorney who prosecuted the Guildford Four may not have known about Dixon's interview with Burke; Dixon may have concealed it from everyone, including the prosecutor. But the failure to inform the defense of the interview would still constitute error. Otherwise, prosecutors could avoid their duty to turn over helpful information simply by instructing police officers not to reveal it to anyone, even the prosecution.

A policeman like Dixon who is willing to torture defendants into confessing is unlikely to obey a silly procedural rule requiring him to turn over exculpatory information. Just as in the film, it's often hard for the defense to find out about information that's been wrongfully withheld. A prosecutor is hardly likely to approach a defense attorney after trial and say, "Here's the information that would have helped you out. We knew about it all along; we sure pulled a fast one on you." When the defense learns about a *Brady* violation, it's often through a blunder such as the one that enabled Peirce to find the secret Dixon-Burke memorandum.

Peirce's anger at Dixon is understandable. But the way she carried on in the courtroom was unprofessional. The judge should have told her to "put a lid on it," by which he would have meant, "You should be wearing a wig in my courtroom." Peirce's yelling and screaming would have earned her a contempt of court citation. Many judges would have quickly sent her to the Old Bailey Jailey.

Yet Peirce is an admirable figure. Against the odds, she believes in her clients and won't give up, and she lucks out when the police goof up. Despite the negative public images of lawyers, many devote their careers to protecting the civil rights of the weak and poor. If you're ever wrongfully accused of blowing up a pub, supply your own wig and hope that someone like Gareth Peirce is nearby.

Trial Brief

The film combines fact with fiction. As depicted, the Guildford Four were convicted in 1975 of two Guildford pub bombings. The only evidence against them was their coerced confessions. The police failed to disclose evidence that Charlie Burke had been with Conlon in London on the night of the bombing. They also failed to follow up on information they had concerning the identity of the real Guildford bombers. The Guildford Four were released after a Court of Appeal decision in 1989, and the police were later acquitted of conspiracy to obstruct justice.

The Maguire Seven were also convicted (although at a separate trial) of making bombs and providing safe houses for bombers. Giuseppe was in the wrong place at the wrong time; he was in London to hire a lawyer for his son and was staying at the Maguires' house when they were arrested. He died after five years in prison. The Maguire Seven were apparently convicted on falsified forensic evidence. Their convictions were also reversed in 1989, but they had already served their time.

Though the basic facts seem dramatic enough, the filmmakers added a few fictitious flourishes. Conlon and Hill were not arrested at random. The police focused on them because intelligence reports predating the Guildford bombing had identified them as IRA bombers. Conlon's burglary of the prostitute's apartment occurred ten days after the Guildford bombings, and thus was not part of his alibi. Conlon and Giuseppe did not spend their prison years in the same cell; in fact, they were often not in the same prison. There was no Inspector Dixon and no Joe McAndrew.

Solicitor Gareth Peirce (a well known fighter for wrongly accused prisoners) got more credit in the film than she deserved; she was involved in the case only at the end. She did not argue the case to the Court of Appeal; she was a solicitor, and only a barrister is allowed to do that. (This explains why Peirce is not wearing a wig in court. Only barristers can wear wigs, at least to court.) The fiery courtroom speech in the film never occurred. The truly heroic lawyer was Alastair Logan, a humble family lawyer, who fought for the Guildford-Maguire defendants for the whole fifteen years of their imprisonment and continued fighting to clear their names after the charges were dismissed. He was airbrushed out of the story.

The British home secretary referred the case to the Court of Appeal in 1989, and the government did not oppose the release of the prisoners. As a result, there was no testimony concerning defense allegations of coerced confessions and suppressed evidence. In fact, the Court of Appeal proceeding was not triggered by Gareth Peirce's discovery of hidden evidence in police archives, but by evidence unearthed by the police themselves of irregularities in the notes of the original interrogations. These irregularities, not the suppression of Conlon's alibi evidence, were the basis of the Court of Appeal's decision freeing the Guildford Four.

In 1993, Paul Hill, one of the Guildford Four defendants, married

Courtney Kennedy, daughter of Robert and Ethyl Kennedy. At the time of the marriage, Hill was appealing a separate conviction for murdering a British soldier in Belfast. The conviction was overturned in April, 1995.

The Life of Emile Zola

Synopsis: The great French writer and social critic abandons a life of ease to fight for the pardon of Alfred Dreyfus, a French military officer who had been wrongfully convicted of treason.

Warner Bros. (Alfred Blanke). 1937. Black and white. Running time: 116 min.

Screenplay: Norman Reilly Raine. Original story: Heinz Herald and Geza Herczeg. Director: William Dieterle.

Starring: Paul Muni (Emile Zola), Joseph Schildkraut (Alfred Dreyfus), Gale Sondergaard (Lucie Dreyfus), Gloria Holden (Alexandrine Zola), Henry O'Niell (Cptn. Picquart), Louis Calhern (Maj. Dort), Vladimir Sokoloff (Paul Cézanne), Harry Davenport (Chief of Staff), Filbert Emery (Minister of War), Robert Barrat (Maj. Esterhazy), Donald Crisp (Maitre Labori).

Academy Awards: Best Picture, Best Script, Best Supporting Actor (Joseph Schildkraut).

Academy Award nominations: Best Actor (Paul Muni), Best Director, Best Original Story, Best Musical Score.

Rating: —▮ —▮ —▮ —▮

The Story

In 1862, Emile Zola is a poor writer in his early twenties, sharing a Paris loft with an equally poor artist, Paul Cézanne. State censors threaten to punish Zola for his antiestablishment writings, but he finds fame with *Nana,* a novel focusing on a Paris prostitute. Over the years Zola produces a string of successful books, enabling him and wife Alexandrine to move into an elegant mansion and fill it with pricey objets d'art. But he is hurt when Cézanne, who has managed to stay poor, criticizes him for abandoning his social activism.

In the mid-1890s, Count Esterhazy, a French major, secretly sends "the bordereau," a letter describing French military secrets, to the German ambassador. The Germans probably needed these secrets like they needed another sausage factory, as they had recently defeated France in battle for the umpteenth time. However, after being mysteriously removed from the ambassador's office, the bordereau makes its way back to the French army's general staff. The commanders are upset, and comb their roster for a suspect. These geniuses pass over Esterhazy, apparently finding nothing suspicious in the fact that he's German. Instead, they fix on Captain Alfred Dreyfus, a Jew they consider unworthy of being an officer. Dreyfus is charged with treason, quickly court-martialed, and exiled to a slow and torturous death on Devil's Island.

Colonel Picquart, the new chief of intelligence, discovers that Esterhazy, not Dreyfus, was the traitor. The army rewards Picquart by making him a former chief of intelligence and transferring him to Africa, where the croissants are not nearly as fresh. The army cannot admit a mistake, lest the populace lose faith in its army's honor. What honor the army has in mind isn't clear. But for good measure another court-martial formally declares that Esterhazy is innocent.

Lucie Dreyfus pleads with Zola to help clear her husband's name. Zola is reluctant, as he's enjoying the good life and is about to be inducted into the prestigious French Academy. But after reviewing Dreyfus's file and glancing at Cézanne's self-portrait, it's no more Mr. Nice (south of France kind) Guy. Zola publishes the famous "I Accuse" letter, accusing the army's general staff of falsely convicting Dreyfus and covering up Esterhazy's guilt. As a result, Zola is charged with criminal libel.

At trial, Zola gets not "due" but "rue" process, as street mobs have already pronounced him guilty. The advocate general in charge of the proceedings forbids Labori, Zola's attorney, from offering any evidence about the Dreyfus case. Colonel Picquart, back from Africa, tries to testify to the truth, but he's silenced by the spectators and an army officer. Labori calls Esterhazy as a witness, but the advocate general doesn't let Labori question him.

Suddenly it becomes okay to talk about Dreyfus's guilt—so long as it's the army doing the talking. The advocate general allows the army's chief of staff to testify that a new document has come to light proving Dreyfus's guilt. Labori uselessly demands to see it; the chief refuses for reasons of national security. The last witness is Picquart, who returns to testify that the army won't produce the document because it's a forgery. Despite an emotional personal appeal by Zola, he's convicted and sentenced to a year in prison.

Friends convince a reluctant Zola to flee to England rather than go to jail, so he can continue fighting for Dreyfus's release. His writings keep the pressure on the French, and finally a new war minister frees Dreyfus and sacks those who took part in the scandal. Dreyfus is promoted to commandant and made a member of the Legion of Honor in a massive public ceremony. Zola is not present; he died the previous night when carbon monoxide gas leaked into his study from a faulty stovepipe.

Legal Analysis

Military history is replete with kangaroo court-martials; they have been dramatized in such movies as *Billy Budd, Breaker Morant,* and *Paths of Glory* (featuring another deplorable performance by the French army). What is especially distressing about the trial of Emile Zola is that he was a civilian. He was prosecuted in a civilian court rather than in a court-martial. Nevertheless, the influence of the army was so pervasive that Zola's trial was a farce. It demonstrates that the right to trial is an empty formality unless the state guarantees a fair process.

The trial opens with Labori trying laboriously to prove that what Zola said in "I Accuse" was accurate. Ordinarily, you would expect the state as the prosecutor to go first, offering evidence that Zola's claims were false. But libel law has always been something of an oddity. Traditionally, all that a prosecutor has to show is that a defendant made libelous remarks—that is, made remarks that are likely to bring a person into disrepute. After that, it's up to the defendant to prove that the statements are true or go to jail. Since there's no dispute that Zola wrote "I Accuse," it's Labori calling all the witnesses.

Normally, libel cases are private civil actions for damages, not criminal cases. (The film *Libel* is an example of such a civil action.) Criminal prosecutions for libel are unusual in the United States, though permissible on the theory that a libelous statement may provoke its victim into a breach of the peace.

However, the First Amendment's guarantee of free speech blocks many civil and criminal libel actions. As interpreted in *New York Times v. Sullivan* (1964), the First Amendment would protect Zola against a libel conviction by giving him nearly an absolute right to criticize public figures such as army generals and government officials. In order to convict Zola or hold him liable for damages, the government would have to prove not only that the statements in "I Accuse" were false, but also that Zola knew they were false. Practically speaking, the latter requirement wipes out most libel claims by public figures. Assume for the sake of argument that Zola was wrong; the government proved at his trial that Dreyfus really was passing French military secrets to the Germans. Nevertheless, since Zola looked at documents that gave him reason to believe that what he said was accurate, the First Amendment would prevent his conviction.

Zola's trial was a farce from beginning to end. The courtroom was packed with spectators who jeered every defense effort. Defense witnesses were silenced, and army officers interrupted the trial to address the jury spontaneously and to offer evidence that the defense was not permitted to see. But perhaps the most repugnant aspect of the trial was preventing Zola and Labori from presenting evidence about the Dreyfus case. It was impossible to separate Zola's attack on the court-martial verdict acquitting Esterhazy from the issue of Dreyfus's innocence. Thus, the state charged Zola with a crime and never gave him an opportunity to prove his innocence. The court might just as well have demanded that Zola eat a grapefruit without breaking through the peel.

Trial Briefs

1. The film accurately depicts the hysteria surrounding the trial of Zola, which took place over the course of two weeks in February 1898. The courtroom was crammed to the windowsills; outside the courtroom, mobs cheered the army and denounced Zola and Dreyfus as traitors. However, Zola did not make a final address to the jury; his speech in the film is taken from "I Accuse." The jury took barely a half hour to decide that Zola and his codefendant Alexandre Perrenx (an editor of *L'Aurore,* which published "I Accuse") were guilty.

2. Zola's conviction was overturned on appeal, on the technical ground that the prosecution had been instituted by the wrong party. Zola was prosecuted by the minister of war, and the appeals court decided that the minister was incompetent to prosecute. Since Zola's defamation was directed at the members of the court-martial who had acquitted Esterhazy of being the author of the bordereau, only they could prosecute. Labori did not contest the retrial, as evidence of Dreyfus's innocence would have remained inadmissible and Zola had already fled to London. Zola never did go to jail. He returned to Paris after eighteen months in exile in England, and accidentally died of carbon monoxide poisoning in 1902.

3. Dreyfus was returned to France in 1899, old and white-haired after his ordeal on Devil's Island, though still only thirty-nine. Upon his return, he was shocked to learn that he had to face a second court-martial. Unlike Dreyfus's first court-martial, which was conducted secretly, the second was covered by over three hundred journalists from all around the world. Perhaps the most amazing witness to testify against Dreyfus was Bertillon, who claimed to have developed a system for determining whether someone was a criminal according to measurements of his body parts. Bertillon also fancied himself a handwriting expert, and testified that discrepancies between the handwriting on the bordereau and Dreyfus's handwriting indicated that Dreyfus was the bordereau's author! By a vote of five to two, Dreyfus was again convicted and sentenced to ten years in prison.

Zola and Theodore Roosevelt were among the world leaders who loudly protested the conviction. Ten days after the conviction, the president of the French Republic pardoned Dreyfus, and in 1906 he was restored to his army rank. Dreyfus was shot and slightly wounded in 1908 during a ceremony transferring Zola's remains to the Pantheon. Dreyfus served in the French army during World War I and was promoted to lieutenant-colonel. He then led a quiet life and died in his bed in Paris at the age of seventy-five in 1935.

Murder in the First

Synopsis: A fledgling lawyer defending a prisoner charged with murder puts Alcatraz on trial.

Warner Bros. (Marc Frydman and Mark Wolper). 1994. Color. Running time: 122 min.

Screenplay: Dan Gordon. Director: Marc Rocco.

Starring: Kevin Bacon (Henri Young), Gary Oldman (Assoc. Warden Glenn), Christian Slater (James Stamphill), R. Lee Ermey (Judge Clawson), William H. Macy (William McNeil).

Rating: —▮ —▮

The Story

As an orphaned teenager, Henri Young stole $5 from a hardware store. Unfortunately, it was also a post office, which turned the offense into a federal crime. Young is sent to Alcatraz, a rocky island only a mile from San Francisco reserved for the most incorrigible prisoners. In 1938, Young takes part in an escape attempt that is foiled because fellow escapee Rufus McCain snitches to the guards.

The escape attempt brings Young to the attention of the sadistic Associate Warden Glenn who runs the prison. Glenn maims Young with a razor and throws him into solitary confinement. Solitary at Alcatraz is truly the pits—the cells are icy dungeons and are totally dark. Although prison regulations limit solitary confinement to nineteen days, Young is kept there for three years. His only breaks are for half an hour and take place once a year.

Within an hour after finally being released from solitary in 1941, Young kills Rufus McCain with a spoon in the mess hall. The feds prosecute him for first-degree murder, which carries the death penalty. This hopeless case is assigned to public defender and recent Harvard Law grad James Stamphill, on the theory that a monkey could try the case without making it any worse. It's Stamphill's first trial.

Stamphill's biggest problem is to get his catatonic client to even talk to him. Ultimately, Stamphill establishes empathy with Young, although Young cannot explain anything about the killing. Actually, Young fully expects to be executed, but he is happy to have someone to discuss Joe DiMaggio's batting streak with. This requires Stamphill (who's a bit of a nerd) to find out who DiMaggio is.

To everyone's amazement, the stern Judge Clawson allows Stamphill to put Alcatraz on trial for crimes against humanity. Stamphill runs into some serious problems, however, since the prisoners are understandably afraid to testify about conditions in Alcatraz. He also encounters heavy political pressure not to embarrass the power structure. In fact, he's fired from the public defender's office. Somehow he gets back on the case (apparently because Young won't cooperate with anyone else) and he perseveres.

Stamphill gets a former guard, Derek Simpson, to testify about how Young was brutalized. However, prosecutor McNeil effectively impeaches Simpson, since Glenn fired him for drunkenness. Judge Clawson instructs the jury to disregard Simpson's testimony.

Stamphill is more successful calling Glenn to the stand. Although Glenn denies any wrongdoing toward Young or anyone else, he's hard put to explain why thirty-two prisoners were taken from Alcatraz in straitjackets and placed in mental institutions during his tenure.

Stamphill also calls the warden, James Humson. Humson had to supervise several prisons, so he seldom visited Alcatraz and had no idea what Glenn was up to. Confronted with evidence about Young's treatment, Humson could say little more than that Young had tried to escape.

Realizing he might be convicted only of a lesser crime and sent back to Alcatraz, Young demands that Stamphill plead him guilty. Stamphill refuses, but calls Young to the stand so he can plead guilty himself if he wants to. In tearful testimony, Young does not plead guilty. He explains why he is literally more afraid of Alcatraz and Warden Glenn than of going to the gas chamber. He declares that he was the weapon, but they are the killers.

The jury returns a verdict of involuntary manslaughter and petitions the judge to investigate Alcatraz and its management for crimes against humanity. Young is sent back to Alcatraz, thrown into solitary confinement, and is found dead in his cell seven months later.

However, Glenn is sacked as the warden and Alcatraz is finally closed down (largely for economic reasons) in 1963, glutting the market with excess strait jackets. Today it is northern California's leading tourist attraction.

Legal Analysis

Stamphill never explains precisely why he thinks that the evidence about prison conditions at Alcatraz is relevant to the charge of first-degree murder. However, his defense that "Alcatraz made him do it" is similar to the I-am-a-victim defense, which has become quite common in contemporary criminal law. Thus Stamphill was ahead of his time.

Several possibilities come to mind. Young might have been legally insane. This requires proof that he did not know the difference between right and wrong. Another possibility is the defense of "irresistible impulse," which requires a showing that because of a mental disease the defendant could not control his conduct. However, Stamphill did not plead insanity.

Perhaps Young killed McCain in the heat of passion and thus qualified for voluntary manslaughter. This is a lesser degree of homicide, often used for killings that occur during fights or when someone catches his or her spouse in bed with somebody else. But Young had three years to think about McCain in a dark and icy cell, which normally qualifies as sufficient cooling-off time. Moreover, Stamphill did not present any evidence about McCain being the snitch, so the jury had no way of coming to this conclusion.

Another possibility is that Young was not legally insane but suffered diminished mental capacity as a result of three years in solitary. This might have the effect of reducing first-degree murder to second-degree murder, since the mental defect would make premeditation impossible. In a few states, diminished mental capacity can even reduce a charge of murder to voluntary manslaughter.

However, it is difficult to understand how the jury came up with involuntary manslaughter, which is an unintentional killing that occurs through reckless conduct. If you kill a pedestrian while driving your car 100 miles an hour through a parking garage, that's involuntary manslaughter. It seems unlikely that the jury would have been told about involuntary manslaughter in the Young case since the facts do not seem to fit that crime at all.

Judge Clawson was generous to the defense in allowing it to present evidence about conditions at Alcatraz, but he was wrong in instructing the jury to disregard Simpson's testimony. Just because the cross-examination suggested Simpson had a motive to lie about Glenn, it is for the jury, not the judge, to decide whether Simpson was telling the truth.

Viewers may wonder why Clawson sent Young back to Alcatraz when it was so obvious that this placed him in mortal danger. The answer seems to be that the judge has no control over what prison a convict is sent to. That's for the Bureau of Prisons to decide.

The film raises broader questions about what, if anything, courts can do about prison brutality. Such brutality is surely cruel and unusual punishment. Today, courts have the power to literally take over a prison and decree improvements in conditions. But that was unheard-of in 1941. Today, prisoners can sue their jailers for damages, and they do by the thousands. Again, that remedy was unknown in 1941. Moreover, prisons like Alcatraz were sealed off from the outside world. Convicts had no access to lawyers and the warden controlled all communications in and out. Literally, convicts like Young were totally at the mercy of the warden and the guards. And the people running Alcatraz had no mercy at all.

Trial Brief: The Real Henri Young

Murder in the First purports to be based on a true story but it is more fiction than fact.

It is true that Young tried to escape from Alcatraz and later killed McCain. He was put on trial in federal district court in San Francisco for first-degree murder in 1941. He was allowed to put on evidence of brutal conditions at Alcatraz, and was convicted of involuntary manslaughter. The jury did petition the judge to investigate Alcatraz. Stamphill is an amalgam of several lawyers who represented him.

Just about everything else is pure make-believe. Far from being an orphan sent to Alcatraz for stealing $5, Young was a hardened criminal who was convicted of bank robbery and sent to Leavenworth. Considered incorrigible, he was then shipped to Alcatraz. Young had previously served time in state prisons for burglary and robbery. After the escape attempt, Young was placed in solitary. The Bureau of Prisons claims he was there only for three weeks. The moviemakers stick to their story that it was three years. No trial transcript exists, so it is difficult to resolve this difference. Young was not maimed with a razor.

Young killed McCain long after he was released from solitary (not one hour after). He did it with a knife in the laundry, not with a spoon in the mess hall, or a candlestick in the conservatory. One witness, a former guard and later a tour guide at Alcatraz, claims the killing was a lovers' quarrel.

Young did not die at Alcatraz. He was transferred from Alcatraz to Springfield and finished his federal sentence in 1954. Then he was transferred to state prison in Washington to serve more time for a killing that occurred during one of his robberies. He was released in 1972, jumped parole, and disappeared. It is unknown whether he is still alive.

Philadelphia

Synopsis: A wrongful termination trial is the vehicle for a dramatic appeal for the civil rights of persons infected with AIDS.

Tristar Pictures/Clinica Estetica Productions (Edward Saxon and Jonathan Demme). 1992. Color. Running time: 125 min.

Screenplay: Ron Nyswaner. Director: Jonathan Demme.

Starring: Tom Hanks (Andrew Beckett), Denzel Washington (Joe Miller), Jason Robards (Charles Wheeler), Mary Steenburgen (Belinda Conine), Antonio Banderas (Miguel Alvarez).

Academy Awards: Best Actor (Tom Hanks), Best Original Song: "Streets of Philadelphia" (Bruce Springsteen).

Rating: —▮ —▮

The Story

Andrew Beckett is a young, highly successful senior associate in one of Philadelphia's most prestigious law firms, and the fair-haired boy of the firm's senior partner, Charles Wheeler. When the firm takes on the represention of a high-tech company called High-Line in a massive copyright infringement lawsuit, Wheeler and his partners put Beckett in charge of it.

A couple of days later, Wheeler unceremoniously gives Beckett the sack, supposedly because of sloppy work and a bad attitude. The last straw was Beckett's misplacement of the High-Line complaint, which almost caused the firm to miss a critical filing deadline. Beckett, however, is convinced that the partners recognized a lesion on his face as a symptom of AIDS, and fired him because he was gay and had AIDS.

Beckett searches all over Philadelphia for a lawyer to represent him against the firm in a wrongful termination case. He finally ends up in the offices of Joe Miller, who had been an opposing counsel in an earlier case. Miller, not particularly sympathetic with gay rights and fearful of AIDS, turns Beckett down. But two weeks later, when he sees a law librarian trying to separate the visibly ill Beckett from other library patrons, Miller decides to represent him.

Beckett's health is much worse seven months later, when the trial begins. Miller has to prove that the firm was aware that Beckett had AIDS, and that he was fired because of it. Miller offers evidence that Beckett was an excellent attorney who the firm trusted to take on one of its biggest cases, and tries to show that the partners intentionally hid the High-Line complaint to create an excuse to fire Beckett once they learned that he had AIDS. In addition, Miller offers evidence that one of the firm's partners, Walter Kenton, knew that a

Philadelphia: All things considered, Andrew Beckett (Tom Hanks) and Joe Miller (Denzel Washington) prefer trial in Philadelphia.

lesion on Beckett's face that Beckett tried to pass off as a racketball injury was a symptom of AIDS. Wheeler and Kenton testify that they knew nothing about Beckett's lifestyle or illness. Wheeler testifies that Beckett was given important assignments only because the firm was hoping to cash in on all the money that had been spent training him, but finally had to let him go when his work became increasingly sloppy.

By the time the trial concludes, Beckett is in the hospital, near death. In his absence, the jury concludes that Beckett was fired because he had AIDS, and awards him millions of dollars in compensatory and punitive damages. Wheeler and the other partners vow to appeal, as Beckett dies after saying good-bye to Miller, Miguel, his longtime companion, and his family and friends.

Legal Analysis

Philadelphia dramatically portrays both the human tragedy of AIDS as well as the dilemma confronting not only Beckett and Miller, but many other plaintiffs: How do you prove the reasons for someone else's actions? Beckett and Miller have to prove that Wheeler fired Beckett because he had AIDS. But Wheeler is too smart to have a firm policy stating, "We will fire anyone with AIDS and lie to make it look like they screwed up big-time." So Miller must show that the stated and lawful reason for the firing is a pretext, hoping the jury will conclude that Beckett was fired for the unstated and unlawful reason.

Although it is often difficult to prove that an employer's stated reasons (such as an employee's misdeeds or a bad economy) are a pretext, Wheeler's story verges on the absurd. He testifies that even though he had just entrusted Beckett with one of the biggest cases in the history of the firm, he had pretty much concluded that Beckett was an incompetent fool. Wheeler expects the jurors to believe that it was purely a coincidence that Beckett's firing came just around the time he developed AIDS! Surely Wheeler, supposedly the sharpest and most creative lawyer in Philadelphia, could have come up with a more plausible reason. For example, Wheeler might have told Beckett, "We're thinking of suing the ozone layer to stop it from getting bigger. We're transferring you to Antarctica for a couple of years to keep track of it." As it is, if Wheeler can't come up with a legally sounder idea than firing Beckett for misplacing the High-Line complaint, maybe Philadelphians seeking legal advice should in the future try Pittsburgh.

Philadelphia manages to illustrate some good trial strategies. Belinda Conine, representing the Wheeler firm, is low-key and nonconfrontational. This is an effective manner for a lawyer representing a large corporate law firm against a terminally ill plaintiff. And cross-examining Beckett, Conine elicits evidence that Beckett went to great lengths to conceal both his lifestyle and his illness from the firm. Beckett blames this on the partners' antigay attitudes. Nevertheless, Conine pursues a very effective trial strategy by eliciting this evidence. The steps that Beckett took to conceal his lifestyle and illness, for whatever reason, support the partners' testimony that they did not know that he had AIDS. In an unguarded moment, Conine admits that she hates what she's doing. Like many attorneys, she has to set aside her personal values to provide professional representation.

For his part, Miller effectively offers evidence that Beckett was a highly competent lawyer, thus undermining the believability of Wheeler's explanation for firing him. Miller locates a former firm client who admits that he was greatly impressed with Beckett's work. When the client, apparently trying to keep in Wheeler's good graces, tries to downplay Beckett's role, Miller forces him to admit that it was Beckett who won the case. Miller also elicits testimony from some of the firm's employees who worked closely with Beckett. They testify that he was an effective supervisor and that he had never previously misplaced any documents. (A reality that the movie neglects to point out is that these employees were probably putting their jobs on the line by testifying against Wheeler, and that Miller might have had great difficulty convincing them to testify truthfully.)

For the most part, however, these glimmerings of effective trial strategies are masked by a host of irrelevant evidence and improper trial procedures. For example, one of the trial's dramatic moments occurs when Conine cross-examines Beckett. She holds a mirror up to his face, and asks him whether he has any visible lesions. Beckett answers honestly that he does not, suggesting that Wheeler and Kenton could not possibly have known when they fired him that Beckett had AIDS. But Miller recaptures the initiative when Beckett testifies that he has lesions on his chest that resemble the one he had on his face at the time he was fired. As everyone in the courtroom and movie audience winces, Miller has Beckett unbutton his shirt to reveal a chest full of ugly lesions. Beckett then looks again into Conine's mirror and testifies that he has no trouble seeing these lesions.

Despite its power, this scene could not have occurred in an actual trial. Conine's initial question to Beckett is improper, because whether or not Beckett has lesions on his face at the time of trial is irrelevant. The only thing that matters is what Beckett's face looked like at the time he was fired, and the fact that the facial lesion disappeared after he was fired is irrelevant.

Miller's clever response is equally improper. Certainly, Miller is entitled to show the jury what Beckett's facial lesion looked like at the time he was fired. It's relevant because the more apparent the lesion, the more likely that Wheeler and Co. knew that Beckett had AIDS. So Miller could properly have offered into evidence a photo of Beckett taken around the time that he was fired, or even a photograph of a lesion that looked like the one on Beckett's face at the time he was fired. But the sight of Beckett's lesion-filled chest creates an emotional impact on the jury that goes far beyond what is necessary to illustrate the appearance of Beckett's facial lesion. The judge should have forbidden Miller's grandstand play. It is amazing that Conine, especially after seeing how Wheeler treated Beckett, would sit idly by as it unfolds. Perhaps she's always had a yen to spend a year or two in Antarctica.

Compared to some of the other trial sequences in *Philadelphia,* however, the "Mirror Mirror on the Chest" scene comes across as a Supreme Court Guide to Proper Trial Techniques. One of the most misleading sequences occurs during Conine's cross-examination of

Beckett. She elicits testimony that on a number of occasions, Beckett had visited a gay porno movie house known as the Stallion Cinema. Not only that, while inside the cinema Beckett had sex with a stranger, even though he was living with Miguel at the time. Conine's cross-examination is utterly irrelevant, except perhaps to Miguel. The only issue in the case is whether Wheeler fired Beckett because he had AIDS, and Conine has no right to try to poison the jury's attitude toward Beckett with irrelevant questions about Beckett's occasional forays into a gay cinema.

Further legal improprieties emerge during the direct and cross-examination of Ms. Burton, a paralegal who worked closely with Beckett at the firm. The judge leads the parade of errors by failing to uphold a perfectly proper objection made by Conine during Miller's direct examination of Burton. Burton testifies that Beckett looked so ill just before he was fired that Wheeler and the others must have known that Beckett had AIDS. Conine properly objects, because while Burton can certainly describe Beckett's appearance, it's not for her to speculate about what other people knew. Rather than striking Burton's testimony as improper, the judge follows the fine tradition of movie judges by simply growling at Burton to "just answer the questions."

But Miller does not let the judge wallow alone in legal error. He asks Burton, who is black, whether Wheeler's firm ever discriminated against her. Burton responds that Wheeler's secretary once criticized Burton for wearing earrings that were "too ethnic." This testimony is amazing: it simultaneously tars the entire firm with a chance remark made by Wheeler's secretary and introduces the highly prejudicial and completely irrelevant subject of racial discrimination. Perhaps Miller figures that since he's already got a jury, he might as well try to win two job discrimination cases at once. But all he does is give a higher court a good reason to void the jury's verdict on appeal.

In truth, a higher court might have trouble deciding which of Miller's actions gets the most credit for wiping out the jury's verdict. At one point, Miller loads a question with every deplorable epithet that gay people have ever been called, adding at least one new word to the vocabulary list of every teenager in the country. When the judge asks for an explanation, Miller erupts into a speech castigating the public for its fear and loathing of homosexuals. And later, after Wheeler testifies with great sincerity to Beckett's sloppy work habits, Miller applauds his performance, in effect improperly testifying that Wheeler's direct testimony was all an act. With a hollow jury verdict and no client, Miller better not be spending any legal fees.

A "Philadelphia lawyer" has traditionally signified an attorney who is shrewd and suave. That image will probably survive this movie, but one can't help but notice the look of worry on the face of the William Penn statue high atop the State Building.

Trial Briefs

1. Many states and cities have enacted laws protecting the job rights of persons with AIDS. For example, both California law and the federal Americans with Disabilities Act provide that the results of a blood test for AIDS cannot be used to determine a person's suitability for employment.

2. *Philadelphia* is based on an actual AIDS discrimination case filed by a New York City lawyer named Geoffrey Bowers against the law firm of Baker and McKenzie. Bowers was eventually awarded the sum of $500,000 by the New York State Department of Human Relations in 1994, seven years after his death in 1987 at the age of thirty-three. Baker and McKenzie have appealed the decision. Meanwhile, Bowers's relatives have sued the makers of *Philadelphia,* claiming that the filmmakers reneged on their promise to compensate family members for providing details about Bowers's life. "Lawsuit-itis" may be the only disease growing faster than AIDS, and we are even further away from a cure.

Sommersby

Synopsis: Is he really Sommersby or a clever impostor? It all comes down to a murder trial in which the defendant insists he's Sommersby, even though he could beat the rap if he was someone else.

Warner Bros. (Arnon Milchan and Steven Reuther). 1991. Color. Running time: 110 min.

Screenplay: Nicholas Meyer and Sarah Kernochan. Based on *The Return of Martin Guerre,* a 1982 French movie. Director: Jon Amiel.

Starring: Richard Gere (Jack Sommersby), Jodie Foster (Laurel Sommersby), James Earl Jones (Judge Isaacs), Bill Pullman (Orrin Meecham), William Windom (Rev. Powell).

Rating: —▮

The Story

The Civil War ends and Jack Sommersby returns to his wife Laurel and son in Tennessee after a six-year absence. Trouble is, he may not be Sommersby at all. The dog doesn't know him and the shoe size is wrong. Whoever he is, he wins back Laurel's love, since he is far nicer than the roughneck who had gone off to war years before. Laurel gladly ditches a local bumpkin named Orrin, who she had decided to take into her bed.

Sommersby owns a large farm, but it's heavily mortgaged. He realizes that not growing tobacco is hazardous to his wealth, so he proposes that they plant tobacco instead of cotton. He sells shares of the land to the sharecroppers, including the black ones. The hardy bunch confronts every known hazard to interracial tobacco farming, including the hornworm and the Ku Klux Klan, but they persevere and finally harvest a great crop.

Suddenly, a federal marshal arrives and arrests Sommersby for the murder of Charles Conklin. Prosecutor Dawson offers evidence that Sommersby checked into a hotel, cheated at poker, and got caught. Conklin challenged him and a fight ensued. Conklin punched Sommersby in the stomach and knocked him down. Sommersby pulled a gun and killed Conklin. Witnesses identify Sommersby as the killer and his handwriting on a hotel register matches that of a prewar mortgage he's taken out.

The defense contention is that the man on trial is not Sommersby and therefore not the killer. Defense lawyer Webb calls Laurel to the stand to testify that the defendant isn't Sommersby. She knew all along but liked the impostor a great deal better than the original model. A second defense witness, Folsom, identifies the defendant as Horace Townsend, a con artist who cheated a town out of $1,200.

The defendant decides he'd rather go down as a killer than a cheat. He fires Webb and takes over his own defense. He cross-examines Laurel, bullying her verbally until she admits that he is really Sommersby and that she had testified falsely to save his neck. He also cross-examines Folsom successfully, accusing him of being one of the Ku Klux Klan riders who tried to prevent sale of the farm to black sharecroppers. Folsom tells Judge Isaacs, who is black, that he'll soon be back picking cotton. Perhaps, the judge replies, but meanwhile Folsom can serve sixty days for contempt. Sommersby offers no defense to the charge of murdering Conklin. Thanks to his masterful defense, the defendant is convicted and sentenced to death.

Talking to Laurel in his cell before the execution, the defendant admits that he is Townsend, not Sommersby. He'd shared a cell in a Union army POW camp with Sommersby for years and learned all about his life and family. Still, he'd rather die as Sommersby than live as the despised Townsend. In addition, if he's Townsend, his new daughter Rachel is illegitimate, Laurel is disgraced, and the deeds transferring ownership of Sommersby's land to the sharecroppers would be invalid.

And so both Sommersby and Townsend go to the gallows, although only one rope is needed. But all is not lost: The local church builds a new steeple with the profits from the tobacco harvest.

Legal Analysis

Sending Sommersby to the gallows for killing Conklin in the midst of a fight seems a tad severe. At most, the killing was second-degree murder, which would not carry the death penalty. To qualify as first-degree murder, the act must be premeditated (planned in advance). Sommersby didn't plan to kill Conklin; he acted on the spur of the moment. It doesn't matter that the trial took place in the 1860s; the distinctions between degrees of homicide were defined by then. So Sommersby could have had his case and eaten it too; he didn't have to hang.

In fact, Sommersby probably should have been convicted of manslaughter, not second-degree murder. Manslaughter is a killing in the heat of passion. After all, the killing happened in the midst of a vicious fight after Sommersby had been knocked down. Even though Sommersby started the fight by cheating at cards, he might have pulled a short jail term instead of a rope.

Webb, Sommersby's counsel, was obligated to respect his client's wishes about how the defense should be conducted. The big decisions about defense strategy are for the defendant, not for his lawyer. Webb should not, therefore, have undertaken his mistaken identity strategy after consulting with Laurel but without his client's consent.

Dawson, the prosecutor, thinks Laurel and Folsom are lying and he makes outraged speeches about it. But it's improper for the prosecutor to make speeches about the evidence, especially in a jury trial. There was nothing objectionable about Laurel's and Folsom's testimony, and Dawson should have kept quiet. If he thought they were lying, he could cross-examine them. Of course, he didn't have to since Sommersby did it for him.

This movie has a clever plot, but ultimately rings hollow. The trial scenes are gimmicky and no more convincing than the movie as a whole.

Trial Brief: Black Judges in the South

It is possible, though unlikely, that Sommersby would have been tried by a black judge. Right after the Civil War, there were numerous black officials throughout the South, placed in office by the occupying Union army, including a few justices of the peace. These were probably "carpetbaggers" imported from the North since few southern blacks had any legal education (or any education at all, for that matter).

Starting in the 1870s, the Union army was withdrawn from the South and it was left to its own devices. The various black public officials were all driven from office or killed by white violence and anarchy. As Folsom predicted, Judge Isaacs probably returned to picking cotton or moved to the North. It was more than one hundred years before blacks in the South, with the aid of voting rights legislation and militant federal law enforcement, started to reclaim the power they enjoyed in 1866.

To Kill a Mockingbird

Synopsis: A classic trial movie, one of the most inspiring pictures about law ever made. Unflinchingly defending a despised innocent black man in a hopeless rape case, Atticus Finch sets a standard to which all lawyers should aspire.

U-I (Alan Pakula). 1962. Black and white. Running time: 129 min.

Screenplay: Horton Foote. Original book: Harper Lee. Director: Robert Mulligan.

Starring: Gregory Peck (Atticus Finch), Mary Badham (Scout), Brock Peters (Tom Robinson), Robert Duvall (Boo Radley). Duvall makes his screen debut as Boo Radley. He utters not a word, but his portrayal of this brave, gentle, and terrified young man is unforgettable.

Academy Awards: Best Screenplay, Best Actor (Gregory Peck).

Academy Award nominations: Best Picture, Best Director, Best Cinematography, Best Musical Score, Best Supporting Actress (Mary Badham), Best Art Direction.

Rating: —▮ —▮ —▮ —▮

The Story

The story is told through the eyes of Scout Finch, a young girl who lives with her brother, Jem, and father, Atticus, in Maycomb, Alabama, during the Depression. In a neighboring house lives a mysterious and thus terrifying recluse, Boo Radley.

Atticus is a widower and a respected lawyer who is struggling to make a living during hard times. A local judge asks Atticus to represent Tom Robinson, a black man accused of beating and raping Mayella Ewell, a young white woman. With the timely assistance of his children, Atticus faces down a lynch mob bent on snatching Robinson from the jail.

At the trial, Mayella testifies that she invited Tom into her house to do chores when he attacked her. Mayella's father, Bob, is a racist and alcoholic redneck. Bob testifies that he came home, found Robinson

To Kill a Mockingbird: Atticus Finch (Gregory Peck) and Tom Robinson (Brock Peters) get the bad news from the jury.

on top of his daughter, and chased him from the house. Nobody called a doctor. Atticus's cross-examination of both witnesses leaves little doubt that they are lying through their remaining teeth.

Robinson testifies that Mayella had often invited him in to do chores. He did them for free because he felt sorry for her—definitely not a smart thing to say to an all-white Southern jury. On the critical day, she grabbed and kissed him. Her father came home and saw it happen. Atticus demonstrates that Mayella's facial injuries were caused by a left-handed person. Bob was left-handed. Robinson could only use his right hand; his left arm was useless.

Atticus's closing argument is powerful. He argues that Mayella lied out of guilt for breaking a code that prohibits white women from being attracted sexually to black men. He asks them not to assume that whites tell the truth and that black people lie.

Nevertheless, the jury convicts Robinson. Shortly thereafter, Robinson tries to flee and is killed by a deputy. When Atticus goes to tell the news to Robinson's family, Bob Ewell shows up and spits in his face.

In a stunning conclusion, Bob Ewell attacks Scout and Jem as they walk home from a school pageant. The mysterious Boo appears and kills Ewell. The sheriff tries to atone for his terrible mistake in having believed the Ewells' false story. He asserts that Ewell fell on his own knife, sparing the reclusive Boo further torment. Atticus at first thinks the truth should be told, but finally agrees with the wisdom of the sheriff's plan.

Legal Analysis

When he is asked to defend Robinson, Atticus Finch never hesitates. To his children, Atticus explains that if he refused this task, he could never hold up his head in town again. His defense of Robinson challenged the comfortable myths of rural southern life and placed him and his family in considerable danger. Thus Atticus defines the ideal to which all lawyers should aspire but which few ever achieve: to accept and vigorously defend even the most hated and despised person in society, regardless of the consequences.

The film is surely on the money in its portrayal of a rural southern courtroom in which whites sat downstairs and blacks sat upstairs. Of course, the jury was all white. It would have been unthinkable to have blacks on the jury, even though the U.S. Supreme Court had long ago held in *Strauder v. West Virginia* (1880) that blacks could not be legally barred from being eligible to serve on juries. Needless to say, a black man suspected of raping a white woman had no chance whatsoever in 1930s Maycomb, Alabama, before such a jury. Atticus's defense was hopeless from the start.

After Robinson's death, Atticus muses that he had a strong case on appeal, but it is not clear why. The trial simply came down to the word of a black man against two white people, and it is hard to imagine an appellate court reversing the jury's factual conclusion. Similarly, the all-white jury panel was taken for granted and it seems unlikely that Atticus could have won a reversal on that score, even had he petitioned the U.S. Supreme Court. By the 1930s, many states had subtle means of excluding blacks from juries that escaped legal review.

Not long before Robinson's trial, the U.S. Supreme Court had held in the famous case of the Scottsboro boys, *Powell v. Alabama* (1932), that impoverished defendants in capital cases are entitled to the effective assistance of counsel. Robinson certainly got the benefit of dedicated and effective defense counsel. Indeed, it is not very likely that the judge who appointed Atticus expected him to mount such a vigorous defense. After all, Atticus accused a white woman of the unspeakable offense of trying to seduce a black man, then falsely accusing him of rape when her seduction was unsuccessful.

A famous legal scholar named John Wigmore wrote long ago that "cross-examination is the greatest engine for the discovery of truth ever invented." Despite the guilty verdict, the film bears out the wisdom of

Wigmore's statement. Questioned by Atticus, Mayella quickly loses her composure. It's apparent to everyone except the jury that her injuries came from a beating by her father. Our legal system relies on cross-examination to test the credibility of witnesses. However, few attorneys display Atticus's skill or get to question witnesses as naive as Mayella.

The conclusion of the movie uncovers a difficult moral dilemma and reveals Atticus's humanity. Atticus has sacrificed a great deal to reveal the truth about Tom Robinson. Can he take part in covering up the truth that Boo Radley killed Bob Ewell?

At first, when he thought that Jem had killed Ewell, Atticus refused to agree to any cover-up. But when Atticus realized that Boo was the killer, he reluctantly agreed to hush up the truth. Had Boo been prosecuted, he could have asserted the defense that he killed Bob Ewell in the reasonable belief that it was necessary to protect the lives of the children. But it is not clear that he would have been successful. Ewell's family and friends would have demanded a trial. The pitiful Boo, who never utters a word, would have been destroyed by becoming a public figure—this would "kill the mockingbird." Atticus concurs in the cover-up. Even to him, some values are of greater importance than the truth.

Trial Brief

The Maycomb courtroom in *To Kill a Mockingbird* is an almost perfect copy of one in Monroeville, Alabama, where author Harper Lee grew up. Scout is certainly the author herself and Atticus Finch is modeled on her father, A.C. Lee, a lawyer in Monroeville. Jem and Scout's peculiar friend Dill is based on author Truman Capote, who was a childhood friend and neighbor of Harper Lee's. Harper Lee attended law school at the University of Alabama, but did not graduate. The story is fictional, although A.C. Lee once represented two blacks who killed a merchant and were hanged in the Monroeville jail.

Trial

Synopsis: A law professor tries to save his job by defending a racially charged felony murder case and overcomes inexperience, bigots, and Communists.

MGM (Charles Schnee). 1955. Black and white. Running time: 105 min.

Screenplay: Don Mankiewicz. Novel: Don Mankiewicz. Director: Mark Robson.

Starring: Glenn Ford (David Blake), Dorothy McGuire (Abbe Nyle), Arthur Kennedy (Barney Castle), Katy Jurado (Consuela Chavez), Rafael Campos (Angel Chavez), Juano Hernandez (Judge Motley).

Trial: David Blake (Glenn Ford) points to Angel Chavez's (Rafael Campos) innocence.

Academy Award nomination: Best Supporting Actor (Arthur Kennedy).

Rating: —▮ —▮ —▮

The Story

David Blake is a law school professor who is about to get fired because he has no trial experience. Fortunately, this standard is not generally applied or about half the law professors in America would get the sack. The dean agrees that if Blake can get some trial work over the summer, he can keep the job. So Blake knocks on doors until he finally hooks up with Barney Castle, who agrees to let Blake try a case.

Angel Chavez, a Mexican American high school student, is making out with Marie Willsey on a private beach in San Juno. When cops arrive to clear the beach, they find Marie dead of heart failure. The cops figure Chavez was attempting statutory rape when Marie died, and they charge him with first-degree murder.

Castle bribes his way past sleazy sheriff Fats Sanders and gets into Chavez's cell. Although his client skills seem somewhat lacking (he slaps Angel when Angel says he was making love to Willsey), Castle talks Chavez and his mother Consuela into retaining him. Meanwhile, the town bigots are baying for blood. A lynch mob storms the jail, but Sanders stops them by promising to resign if Angel isn't hanged.

Blake prepares for Angel's trial. Since he knows nothing, he's fortunate to have Castle's super-competent secretary Abbe Nyle to hold his hand, and, eventually, other parts of his anatomy. Meanwhile, Castle heads to New York to raise money for the defense. He does everything he can to turn Angel's case into a major political cause célèbre. Castle stages a giant fund-raising rally put on by the All Peoples Party, which turns out to be a Communist front. Castle summons Blake to speak to the rally, but shuts off the mike when Blake starts to denounce the Communists. The rally is a rousing success in raising funds, with Castle using the tried-and-true "sea of green" technique (the dupes wave one-dollar bills and the ushers come around and snatch them).

Meanwhile, back in San Juno, the trial begins before Judge Motley who, surprisingly, is black. Blake manages to disqualify a juror who was part of the lynch mob; then he gets the whole jury panel dismissed because the cops visited the jurors in their homes before the trial. Finally, after three weeks the jury is chosen. In the middle of it all, Blake gets a subpoena from the state Un-American Activities Committee, because of his appearance at the rally. He manages to delay his appearance until the end of the trial.

All-American district attorney Jack Armstrong's first witness is Dr. Shacter, who had treated Marie since childhood for rheumatic fever. He testifies that she died from a heart attack because of violent exertion. On cross-examination, Blake gets Shacter to admit that Marie could have dropped dead at any moment just from crossing the street. They must have really wide streets in San Juno.

Another witness testifies that he heard cries for help and shined his car spotlight on the beach. He immediately picked out Angel clutching at Marie. Blake counters with a terrific demonstration. He gives the witness a spotlight like the one on the car. Nyle cuts the lights and starts screaming. When the witness turns on the spotlight it wanders all over the courtroom and he can't pick out the screamer.

Blake, who turns out to be a pretty mean cross-examiner for a novice trial lawyer, plans not to put on a defense. He will try to persuade the jury that Armstrong failed to meet his burden to prove that Angel was trying to commit statutory rape at the time Marie died. But Castle shows up and demands that Angel take the stand. When Blake disagrees, Castle persuades Consuela to fire Blake and Castle takes over the defense.

Called by Castle as a witness, Angel admits he kissed Marie on the beach but claims it was all her idea and that was as far as it went. He's slaughtered on cross-examination. He can't explain why Marie's dress was ripped or why he was trying to leave the beach. Worst of all, he claims he doesn't know what seduction means or how to do it. Armstrong presents Angel with proof that he completed a high school course on "hygiene," apparently a euphemism for sex education. Although high school hygiene classes probably were less informative than army training films in 1947, the jury finds Angel totally untrustworthy and convicts him.

Castle is thrilled. His evil communist cause needed a martyr, so he deliberately threw Angel to the sharks. He's also keeping a big cut of the $320,000 raised for Angel's defense. Castle figured Blake would be so inept that he'd blow the defense.

Blake shows up at Angel's sentencing hearing. Despite Castle's hysterical objection, Motley lets Blake explain Castle's game. Motley thinks the death penalty is mandatory, but Blake digs up a code section allowing the judge to sentence a juvenile offender to reform school. With Armstrong's support, Motley accepts this sentence and Angel miraculously goes from the gas chamber to the class chamber. Motley also sentences Castle to thirty days for contempt. After Blake's boffo performance, next semester's law students had better be prepared when he calls on them in class.

Legal Analysis

Trial walks an interesting political line. The story was set in 1947 but the film came out in 1955. This was a time of ferocious anticommunism, especially in Hollywood where the studios were blacklisting anybody who refused to cooperate with the Un-American Activities Committee. The script for *Trial* is so anticommunist that it could have been written by J. Edgar Hoover. On the other hand, the state Un-American Activities Committee is treated with contempt. Its chair, Senator Battle, is portrayed as a cheap headline hunter. By 1955, Senator McCarthy had fallen and it was politically possible for a film to denounce legislative red-baiting while simultaneously condemning the Red Menace.

Angel is being prosecuted for felony murder. Traditionally, one whose conduct brings about an unintended death in the commission or attempted commission of a felony is guilty of murder. The typical case is a robbery in which the defendant accidentally kills a victim or a cop. Prosecutors love felony murder because they only have to prove that the defendant committed a felony; they don't have to bother with proving premeditation and the other elements of homicide.

Here the felony murder rule comes into play because Angel supposedly was attempting to commit the felony of statutory rape when Marie died of a heart attack. Statutory rape means intercourse with a female under the age of consent (usually sixteen or eighteen years). It doesn't matter whether the "victim" is an enthusiastic participant in the fun. Thus statutory rape occurs even though the victim consents; regular rape, by contrast, requires that the victim not consent.

This case illustrates the extreme harshness of the traditional felony murder rule: Marie's death was purely accidental and statutory rape (as distinguished from regular rape) is not a crime of violence. Indeed, it's seldom prosecuted at all. Based on what he learned in hygiene, Angel could not possibly have imagined that Marie would die as the result of consensual sex. Yet because death occurred, the incident was suddenly transformed into a capital case.

Because the felony murder rule can have such harsh effects, most states have sharply limited the crime. Typically, felony murder only applies to felonies that are dangerous to life. In a state that followed that rule, Angel could not have been charged with felony murder. And he probably would not have been charged with it in San Juno either, except that he was Mexican and the deceased girl was an Anglo.

It is not clear why Angel was prosecuted as an adult. In all states, juveniles (usually defined as those below the age of eighteen) are tried in juvenile courts, not in the regular criminal courts. In some states, a juvenile can be tried as an adult, based on the juvenile's prior criminal record, his age and maturity, his potential for rehabilitation, and the severity of the crime. Under these factors, Angel would certainly have been tried in juvenile, not adult court. Ultimately Angel was given a penalty appropriate for juvenile court, but he should have been there in the first place.

Early in the case, Blake suggested a change of venue. The judge would probably have granted this motion, since the townspeople had already tried to lynch Angel and the sheriff had staked his job on convicting him. But Castle absolutely refused to seek the change. Only later do we learn the reason—Castle wanted a conviction.

Blake has the good sense not to put Angel on the stand and subject him to cross-examination. In the majority of criminal cases, the defendant does not testify and this movie graphically shows why. Most defendants are in fact guilty of the crimes with which they have been charged—and Angel may very well have been guilty of attempted statutory rape. The defense usually does better by attacking the prosecution's case and arguing reasonable doubt than by exposing the defendant to prosecutorial cross-examination and impeachment by prior crimes.

Castle commits numerous grave breaches of legal ethics. He rejects Armstrong's plea bargain without discussing it with his client. He assigns the trial of a capital case to an attorney who never tried a case before. He cheats the members of the All Peoples Party out of their contributions. Worst of all, he breaches his duty of loyalty by trying to sacrifice his client to a political cause. Thus Castle was guilty of a terrible conflict of interest and should be subjected to much harsher punishment than thirty days in the slammer. At the least, he should be disbarred.

Blake has saved his law school teaching job, rehabilitated himself politically, slain the Red dragon, earned the gratitude of Angel and Consuela, become a primo trial lawyer, and won Nyle's heart. He proved the legal cliché that he lived by: Where there's a right, there's a remedy. But the Hollywood happy ending is implausible. It's unlikely that a defendant about to be sentenced to death would be saved by a statute unearthed at the last moment that sends him to reform school.

Young Mr. Lincoln

Synopsis: Putting precedent before president, Abe Lincoln defends two brothers accused of murder.

Twentieth Century Fox (Kenneth MacGowan). 1939. Black and white. Running time: 100 min.

Screenplay: Lamar Trotti. Director: John Ford.

Starring: Henry Fonda (Lincoln), Alice Brady (Mrs. Clay), Richard Cromwell (Matt Clay), Eddie Quillan (Adam Clay), Eddie Collins (Scrub White), Ward Bond (J. Palmer Cass).

Academy Award nomination: Best Screenplay.

Rating: ⚖ ⚖ ⚖

Surprise ending warning: Reading this summary may be hazardous to your enjoyment of the movie!

The Story

Recently elected to the Illinois legislature, Lincoln has started a small law practice in Springfield. He is respected by rich and poor alike. No wonder. At a county fair, Lincoln judges a pie-tasting contest, wins a log-splitting contest, and takes part in a tug-of-war, all without submitting a bill.

Young Mr. Lincoln: Abe Lincoln (Henry Fonda) tries to save the lives of the Clay brothers (Richard Cromwell and Eddie Quillen).

Trouble intrudes when two local toughs, Scrub White and J. Palmer Cass, pester a young woman at the fair. Confronted by her husband Matt and brother-in-law Adam, the toughs leave. That night, however, White pulls a gun on Matt and Adam. A struggle ensues, the gun goes off, and White is left lying on the ground. Cass comes running up, checks on White, and holds up a bloody knife that he has pulled from White's dead body. Cass accuses Adam and Matt of murder.

Matt and Adam are promptly arrested, each claiming to be the murderer to protect the other. Their mother, Mrs. Clay, saw the fight but says nothing.

From the community's angry reaction to White's death, one would think that he had been on the verge of discovering the cure for dusty sidewalks. A lynch mob immediately forms and descends on the jail. In a scene reminiscent of a later one in *To Kill a Mockingbird,* Lincoln disperses the angry crowd with a powerful and emotional speech. He might have begun with "twoscore and seven years ago," since this was long before Gettysburg and the grubby mob would probably have been subdued by vainly trying to add twoscore to seven.

Prosecutor Felder calls Cass to the witness stand twice at the brothers' trial. First, Cass testifies that he came running into a clearing about 11:30 P.M. after hearing a gunshot, and found White lying dead with a knife in his heart and the brothers standing nearby. Then, after Mrs. Clay refuses Felder's offer to save the life of one of her sons by naming which one killed White, Cass returns with a change of heart and story. Testifying that he is unwilling to see both brothers hang, Cass says that it was Matt who killed White. Though he was one hundred yards away at night, he saw Matt commit murder by moonlight.

Lincoln immediately begins to earn the nickname "The Great Emancipator," and perhaps "The Jail Splitter," as his devastating cross-examination of Cass springs Matt and Adam from jail. Dramatically, Lincoln produces a farmer's almanac to prove Cass a liar. The almanac shows that the Moon had set nearly an hour before White was killed, so Cass could not have seen the killing. Lincoln then browbeats Cass into admitting that it was he who killed White. When Cass ran to White after hearing the gunshot, he realized that White was unhurt. Cass was angry with White over an earlier argument, and so picked up the brothers' knife lying nearby and stabbed White.

As the grateful Clay family leaves Springfield, Mrs. Clay pays Lincoln "what little we have" for the successful defense, a few coins. We have to assume that none of the coins were Lincoln pennies.

Legal Analysis

The late comedian Lenny Bruce once said that "in the halls of justice, the only justice is in the halls." *Young Mr. Lincoln* suggests that when it came to frontier justice, the only justice was on the frontier. Felder knows that only one of the brothers could have killed White, yet charges both with murder. Perhaps a case like this led to Lincoln's lucrative career as a lawyer for the railroad industry. He figured that as long as he was going to work on cases in which defendants were railroaded, he might as well be paid handsomely for it.

One of the trial's most dramatic moments occurs when Felder calls Mrs. Clay as a witness and asks her to save the life of one of her sons by identifying which one killed White. She refuses to choose between her children and leaves the witness stand. While we can all sympathize with Mrs. Clay's plight, under the law she had no right to refuse to answer Felder's question. As an eyewitness, she has to answer truthfully if called as a witness. Judge Bell could have held her in contempt of court and put her in jail until she agreed to testify. Then, with Mom, Adam, and Matt in custody, Springfield could have bragged that it had the country's only jail made entirely of Clay.

Cass's reason for retaking the stand and testifying that he saw Matt do the stabbing is unclear. As the actual murderer, Cass would not want to go anywhere near the courtroom or leave Adam around to implicate him in the murder. At any rate, Lincoln makes the most of the opportunity by using the almanac to demolish Cass's story. Lincoln's tactic is quite proper. Modern "judicial notice" laws assume the accuracy of authoritative publications like telephone books, stock market tables, almanacs, and books about courtroom movies, and allow attorneys simply to offer their contents into evidence without proving their accuracy. Unfortunately, we don't learn whether the almanac considered the night of the killing a good time to harvest the rutabagas.

By contrast, Lincoln's badgering of Cass until he confesses to the murder is highly improper. Borrowing a page from a book that Lieutenant Columbo had not yet written, Lincoln states that he wants to ask Cass "just one more question" as Cass is about to leave the courtroom. Lincoln then continues his cross-examination as Cass stands amongst the spectators. (Here the film takes the term "witness stand" too literally!) As is most attorneys' wont, the "one question" turns into a lengthy series of questions, most of which are improperly "argumentative." Even on cross-examination, an attorney has no right to shout repeated accusations at a witness. Judge Bell should have terminated the questioning long before Cass confessed, and might even have imposed a fine on Lincoln for his improper conduct.

Moreover, like any other witness, Cass has a constitutional right under the Fifth Amendment not to provide evidence that could be used against him in a criminal proceeding. Once it became clear that Lincoln was accusing Cass of the murder, Judge Bell should have warned Cass of his right not to incriminate himself, and given Cass an immediate opportunity to consult with an attorney. Any attorney would doubtlessly have advised Cass to respond to Lincoln's questions by saying something like, "I decline to answer the question based on my Fifth Amendment right not to incriminate myself." This answer would save Cass from confessing to murder, and enhance his chances of becoming president of the Teamsters Union. But it would also mean that Lincoln has no opportunity to cross-examine Cass. As a result, Judge Bell could strike all of Cass's testimony from the record, leaving Felder with no way to pin the murder on Matt.

Young Mr. Lincoln is one of the few courtroom movies to devote time to jury selection, and the jury selection scenes provide some of the film's lighter moments. Lincoln questions four potential jurors, disqualifying one who's ready to hang Matt and Adam and another who personally knows Felder. (Lincoln comically explains that he's trying to help Felder by excusing jurors who know him.) But Lincoln accepts the other two, one an honest drunk who says he enjoys hangings and the other a man who dislikes Matt and Adam, but who is the son of a man Lincoln respects.

This jury selection scene effectively captures the difficult judgments attorneys have to make when selecting jurors. Lincoln has valid reasons for wanting to disqualify the two jurors he accepts. But he can disqualify only a few jurors (five to ten in criminal cases in most states), so he has to rely on intuition to decide that these two jurors can overcome their inherent prejudices and render a fair verdict.

Even so, Lincoln might have trouble recognizing today's jury selection process. He'd be shocked (pleasantly, we assume) to see women jurors; in his time and for years afterward, only men were eligible to serve as jurors. Clients who have a lot more money than Matt and Adam often pay large sums of money to professional jury research firms to poll a community in order to ascertain the background characteristics of people who react favorably to the client's position. At the same time, many judges would not allow Lincoln's personal banter with the prospective jurors. Because it's sometimes taken longer to select a jury than to try a case, many judges now do most of the questioning. Finally, no matter what an attorney's intuition about a juror's biases, attorneys can't disqualify potential jurors based on their race or gender alone.

Young Mr. Lincoln presents a romantic account of traditional American values: the Lone Hero; award-winning apple pie without a fat-free crust; and an angry lynch mob. But had Lincoln conducted his cross-examination of Cass as argumentatively as depicted in the film, Judge Bell might well have disciplined him. The ensuing blemish on his record might have prevented him from being elected president. The consequences would have been disastrous: Ford's Theater would not be a tourist attraction, we'd be spending Douglas pennies, and Presidents' Day might not be a three-day weekend.

Trial Briefs

1. As depicted in the film, Lincoln became a lawyer through the apprenticeship system, which is how people became lawyers before a group of sadists developed law schools. A few states, California among them, still authorize apprenticeships. However, like law school graduates, apprentices must pass a bar examination before they can practice law.

2. Lincoln was generally regarded as one of the finest lawyers of his day, often handling complex railroad matters. Before becoming

president he handled about five thousand cases, of which less than 10 percent were criminal cases.

3. The murder trial featured in the movie is a combination of two actual trials. One was an 1857 Illinois trial in which Lincoln represented a defendant named Armstrong. In that trial, Lincoln used an almanac to undermine the believability of a prosecution witness who testified that the light of the Moon enabled him to see who committed a crime. To this day, some scholars still feel compelled to deny the persistent rumors that the real "Honest Abe" used a phony almanac. The second actual trial that served as the basis of the movie took place in Georgia early in the twentieth century, and resulted in the hanging of two brothers who allegedly committed a murder to which their mother was the only witness.

Don't Become Too Attached to Your Client

A good lawyer must empathize with a client but must never get too close. Without objectivity about the client and a healthy skepticism for what the client says really happened, a lawyer cannot do a competent job. In the movies, as in real life, lawyers often forget this and make serious personal and professional blunders.

Lawyers and clients can get too close because the lawyer becomes romantically involved with the client, as in *Jagged Edge*. A daughter can trust her father too much, as in *The Music Box*. Friendship can lead the lawyer astray, as in *The Letter*. Or a lawyer can believe too wholeheartedly in the client's innocence, as in *The Paradine Case*. Warning to lawyers: keep your distance.

Guilty As Sin

Synopsis: A beautiful trial attorney is fascinated and repulsed by a client charged with murder. Uncertain whether to help free or convict him, she does both.

Martin Ransohoff Prod. 1993. Color. Running time: 107 min.

Screenplay: Larry Cohen. Director: Sidney Lumet.

Starring: Rebecca DeMornay (Jennifer Haines), Don Johnson (David Greenhill), Jack Warden (Moe).

Rating:

© Hollywood Pictures.

Guilty As Sin: Jennifer Haines (Rebecca DeMornay) examines David Greenhill (Don Johnson) at close range.

Surprise ending warning: Reading this analysis may be hazardous to your enjoyment of the movie.

The Story

Jennifer Haines is a very successful criminal defense attorney whose clients run the gamut from mobsters to hitmen. David Greenhill is an interested courtroom spectator as charges are dismissed against one of Haines's gangland clients.

Greenhill visits Haines's plush law offices the next day. He tells her that he's been charged with murdering Rita, his wealthy wife; that he's innocent; and that he wants her to represent him. Haines realizes that Greenhill is an egotistical womanizer, but decides to represent him because she believes that he is innocent. With such a keenly questioning mind, it's easy to see why Haines has made it to the top of her profession.

Before long, Greenhill has insinuated himself into all aspects of Haines's life. He repreatedly phones her at home, visits Haines's boyfriend, and delivers dry cleaning to Haines's office without asking for a tip, insinuating that he and Haines have been intimate. Haines tries to withdraw as Greenhill's counsel. But despite his bizarre behavior, the only excuse that Haines gives to the judge for wanting to withdraw is that Greenhill hasn't paid her legal fees. This is like describing the sinking of the *Titanic* as a "boating mishap," or the German bombing of London during World War II as a "violation of noise restrictions." Understandably, the judge orders Haines to fulfill her obligations to Greenhill.

At trial, the prosecutor's primary evidence of Greenhill's guilt consists of a couple of phone calls made by Rita to the police shortly before her death describing her fear of Greenhill, and a letter supposedly written by Rita on the day of her death. The letter states that she is no longer able to fight back against Greenhill, and that she hopes that Greenhill will be punished for her death. However, the letter becomes worthless as evidence when the prosecution agrees with a defense handwriting expert that the letter was not written by Rita.

Outside the courtroom, Greenhill continues to harass Haines, who is alternately fascinated and repulsed by him. When he talks about other women he's murdered, she fears for her own safety. Guessing that Greenhill himself undercut the prosecution by writing the phony letter, Haines figures out how Greenhill committed the murder. His apartment building was in the midst of extensive renovation at the time Rita was killed, and Greenhill escaped the doorman's detection by walking up the back stairway to his apartment dressed as a construction worker. Haines then plants incriminating evidence in his building, and anonymously tips off the police. Realizing the evidence might convict him, Greenhill produces a surprise witness, a woman who testifies that she and Greenhill were having sex at the time of his wife's murder. The trial concludes with the jury unable to reach a verdict.

That night, Moe, Haines's investigator, shows her evidence that he's gathered of Greenhill's prior crimes. Haines decides to turn the information over to the police, even though she might be disbarred for violating her client's confidences. But Greenhill shoots Moe and burns the evidence. He then tries to kill Haines by his preferred method—shoving her over a balcony. However, they both pitch over the side. Greenhill is killed by the fall; Haines lands on him and is hurt, but she lives. Greenhill thus pays dearly for ignoring the social etiquette of "ladies first."

Legal Analysis

If you can only see one trial movie your whole life, consider making it *Guilty As Sin*. This will enable you to see plot devices that you'd otherwise have to rent a number of courtroom films to see. For example:

• A high-powered female trial attorney suddenly loses all objectivity when representing a sexually-charged male scoundrel, a theme in *Jagged Edge*.

• A defendant's chance for acquittal soars when it is discovered that the highly incriminating letter he created is a phony, a plot twist in *Witness for the Prosecution.*

• An attorney violates ethical principles by secretly planting evidence implicating her own client, a technique found in *Class Action.*

Despite these derivative plot elements, *Guilty as Sin* offers up an interesting variety of evidentiary and ethical issues for analysis. Consider first the prosecutor's most damning evidence that Greenhill killed Rita: Rita's statements shortly before her death that she was terrified of Greenhill and believed that he was going to kill her. Despite her past success as a trial attorney, Haines fails to recognize that Rita's statements are not admissible in evidence. She should have objected to the police officer's testimony as to what Rita said about her fear of Greenhill, as well as to the letter supposedly written by Rita. Without this evidence, the prosecutor has no way of connecting Greenhill to his wife's death, and the charges would have been dropped.

Rita's oral and written statements are inadmissible under the hearsay rule, which generally prohibits the introduction into evidence of out-of-court statements offered for their truth (see *The Hearsay Rule,* p. 163). In essence, Rita tells the police, "My husband is going to kill me." If Rita's statements are true, they constitute strong evidence of Greenhill's guilt. But because those statements have to be true to connect Greenhill to her death, they are hearsay. Haines should never have allowed them to be offered into evidence. Given Haines's knowledge of evidence law, perhaps Greenhill was perfectly justified in not paying her legal fees!

Along with her shifting attitudes towards her client, Haines's devotion to legal ethics meanders throughout the movie. Before the trial starts, Greenhill asks Haines what will happen if he confesses other crimes to her. Haines properly describes the "attorney-client privilege." She tells Greenhill that whatever he tells her about past crimes is confidential, though she is obliged to reveal any information he discloses about future crimes he's planning to commit. The existence of this privilege shows that our legal system places a higher value on full disclosure between attorneys and clients than on revealing past crimes.

But Haines disregards her ethical obligations when she plants the evidence that incriminates Greenhill. It is the prosecutor's duty to convict Greenhill, and Haines's duty to be loyal to him. Nevertheless, Haines buys work clothes like those worn by Greenhill when he murdered Rita, sneaks into his apartment and presses plaster debris from the stairway into a pair of his shoes, and anonymously tips the police to where to find them. Apparently Haines figures that if she's going to commit an ethical violation, she might as well commit a doozy.

Haines is confronted with another ethical dilemma when Greenhill introduces her to Kathleen Bigelow, who comes forward at the last minute to say that she was in bed with Greenhill when Rita was killed. Bigelow conveniently accounts for Greenhill's possession of work clothes: he had worn them a week before Rita's murder, when he helped Bigelow redecorate her apartment. Bigelow tells Haines that she didn't come forward earlier because she is a married woman, but she now wants to testify to protect the innocent Greenhill.

Haines knows for sure that the work clothes portion of this story is a lie. Thus, Haines correctly warns Greenhill and Bigelow that she cannot knowingly put on perjured testimony. But when Bigelow insists that she's telling the truth, Haines caves in and calls Bigelow as a witness. Her motive for doing so is unclear. Perhaps she wants to balance her ethical books. Earlier she broke one ethical rule to try to convict Greenhill; this time she breaks a different ethical rule to help him. But whatever the reason, Haines knows that Bigelow is lying, and she violates her ethical obligations by offering her testimony.

Before the trial starts, Haines makes a half-hearted attempt to withdraw as Greenhill's attorney. By complaining to the judge only about her unpaid legal fees, and concealing Greenhill's bizarre behavior, Haines gives the judge little reason to grant her request. But once she can reasonably infer from Greenhill's words and conduct that he intends her to be his next victim, Haines could have sought additional protection without violating her ethical obligations to him. An attorney is allowed to disclose confidences to prevent a criminal act that is likely to result in imminent death—especially the death of the attorney! Thus, Haines should have renewed her motion to withdraw as counsel and divulged everything to the judge. In addition to allowing Haines to withdraw as Greenhill's counsel, the judge might have given Haines additional protection by revoking Greenhill's bail and putting him back in jail. (As a defendant in a capital murder case, Greenhill probably wouldn't be out on bail in the first place. But no bail, no movie.) Ethically, this is a much better course of action than planting evidence around Greenhill's apartment building that could get him convicted.

Before Haines agrees to represent Greenhill, her boyfriend Phil tells her, "The guy's bad news; don't take his case." She also speaks with her law partners, who tell her, "The guy's bad news, don't take his case." Thus, when Haines gets out of the hospital she can look forward to getting back to the mobsters and hitmen who constitute the good news of her practice.

Jagged Edge

Synopsis: A prosecutor with political ambitions is matched against a defense attorney who falls in love with her socialite client. It's the client who produces the best evidence.

Columbia Pictures (Marvin Ransohoff). 1985. Color. Running time: 108 min.

Screenplay: Joe Eszterhas. Director: Richard Marquand.

Starring: Jeff Bridges (Jack Forrester), Glenn Close (Teddy Barnes), Peter Coyote (Tom Krasny), Robert Loggia (Sam Ransom), John Dehner (Judge Carrigan), Leigh Taylor-Young (Virginia Howell), Marshall Colt (Bobby Slade).

Academy Award nomination: Best Supporting Actor (Robert Loggia).

Rating:

Suprise ending warning: Reading this summary may be hazardous to your enjoyment of the movie!

The Story

Jack Forrester and his wife Page are a wealthy San Francisco couple. Forrester runs the couple's publishing empire, though the company assets are all in Mrs. Forrester's name. One night a hooded attacker enters the couple's home wielding a large knife with a jagged edge. The attacker sexually maims and kills Mrs. Forrester. The police find Jack Forrester alive but wounded. Forrester is soon charged with his wife's murder. Teddy Barnes, a former prosecutor turned civil litigator, reluctantly agrees to defend him. Barely before Barnes can plead Forrester "not guilty," they start a torrid love affair.

At trial, District Attorney Krasny offers evidence that Forrester and his wife were unfaithful to each other and that she intended to divorce him. Forrester told his lover that if his wife divorced him, he'd lose everything. However, Krasny's case is far from airtight. Virginia Howell testifies to Mrs. Forrester's intention to divorce Forrester, but admits that she herself tried to bed Forrester. Fabrizi, a locker room attendant who works at Forrester's posh tennis club, testifies that he saw a knife similar to the one that killed Mrs. Forrester in Forrester's locker. However, Fabrizi's knife testimony dulls when another tennis club member testifies for the defense that he had a jagged-edged knife in his gym locker, which was near Forrester's locker. If nothing else, we know that the tennis club had one of the best-armed locker rooms in San Francisco. And Bobby Slade, the tennis pro having an affair with Mrs. Forrester, incriminates Forrester but in open court refers to Barnes as a "bitch," the same word that was scrawled in blood on the Foresters' bedroom wall the night of the attack.

Jagged Edge: Teddy Barnes (Glenn Close) and D.A. Tom Krasny (Peter Coyote) debate the admissibility of evidence.

Finally, clued in by an anonymous note, Barnes calls Julie Jensen as a surprise defense witness. Jensen tearfully testifies that she was attacked in the same way as Mrs. Forrester, eighteen months earlier. Barnes argues that the same person carried out both attacks; since Forrester did not attack Jensen, Forrester did not attack his wife.

Forrester is found not guilty. After he is freed, Forrester and Barnes spend the night together. The next day, Barnes finds an old typewriter stashed away in Forrester's closet. Using the "hunt and peck" typing method, she types enough to realize that Forrester sent her the anonymous note about Julie Jensen. Barnes concludes that Forrester carried out both attacks, attacking Jensen first to set up evidence that he didn't kill his wife. Barnes speaks on the phone with Forrester and tells him what she suspects; he asserts his innocence. But soon a hooded figure enters Barnes's bedroom wielding a jagged-edged knife. It looks bad for Barnes until she pulls a gun out from under her nightgown and kills him. She pulls off the hood, revealing Forrester as the attacker.

Legal Analysis

Forrester's murder trial becomes a sideshow to two sets of personal relationships—a romantic affair between him and Barnes, and a bitter feud between Barnes and Krasny, the prosecutor for whom she once worked. It is no wonder that improper lawyer behavior abounds. For example:

• As Teddy Barnes listens to Krasny's examination of Ilene Avery, who had an earlier sexual liaison with Forrester, Barnes becomes jealous and angry with her client. She immediately turns from a self-assured professional into an emotionally-unbalanced stereotype of a betrayed woman. She refuses even to proceed with the defense case until she is goaded into doing so. By letting her personal feelings interfere with her professional responsibility, Barnes behaves in a highly unethical but not unsurprising way (see *Women Trial Lawyers in the Movies,* p. 90). At the very least she ought to advise Forrester of her attitude and give him the option of changing attorneys. But what the heck—it's only a capital punishment case.

• In front of the judge, Barnes vehemently accuses Krasny of withholding evidence. The only basis for this serious charge is that years earlier, Krasny had concealed evidence in a case called the Styles case. Barnes will probably next charge Krasny with failing to brush his teeth before coming to court, based on a cleanliness citation Krasny received as a first-grader. But Barnes's charge is foolish. First, she has no evidence that Krasny is withholding evidence in Forrester's case. Second, as she and Krasny coprosecuted the Styles case and jointly participated in the withholding of information, she puts her own career in jeopardy by talking about the case in front of a judge.

• Later events prove that Barnes was right; Krasny did try to hamper the defense by removing the police report on Julie Jensen from his file. This is a plain and obvious violation of *Brady v. Maryland* (1963), which requires a prosecutor to turn over to the defense any information which might be exculpatory, even if it turns out to be neither helpful nor admissible.

• Given his sorry record, Krasny goes for the Chutzpah of the Decade award by objecting that Barnes should not be allowed to call Jensen as a witness because she did not notify the prosecution in advance of her intention to do so. Krasny is hardly in a position to complain, since he already knew about and tried to conceal Jensen. Anyway, Krasny probably has no right to demand that Barnes disclose her defense strategy. Growing out of a defendant's privilege against self-incrimination, the general rule is that the defense has no obligation to notify the prosecution of the evidence or witnesses it intends to present. Pretrial exchange of information has traditionally been a one-way street: the prosecution has to disclose information to the defense, but the defense does not have to disclose anything in return. However, this traditional rule is changing, and some jurisdictions now require that the defense disclose its witnesses to the prosecution prior to trial.

Forrester may have been desperate to get rid of his wife, but the financial consequences of a divorce would probably not have been nearly as dire as he predicted. Under California community property law, half of the money that the couple earned but didn't spend would belong to Forrester. Also, he'd be entitled to half the increase in the value of the publishing empire, since he ran the paper. Finally, at least half the wealthy women of San Francisco were anxious to read Forrester's fine print. Thus, he might be out as a newspaper publisher, but he'd have plenty of money for tennis lessons.

Julie Jensen's testimony is a clever variation on the usual situation in which a separate crime is offered into evidence. Usually, it's the prosecution that offers evidence of a separate similar crime committed by the defendant to prove that the defendant committed the charged crime (see *Character Evidence,* p. 259). Here, it's the defense offering evidence of a separate crime to prove Forrester's innocence.

For all its dramatic effect, Jensen's testimony was probably irrelevant. Jensen testifies that she was sexually attacked in the same way as Mrs. Forrester, eighteen months earlier. Krasny objects twice that the evidence is irrelevant; each time Barnes responds, "It is too." Instead of lawyers, they sound like two five-year-olds arguing over a cookie: "It's mine!" "Is not."

Instead of summarily overruling Krasny's objection, Judge Carrigan should have insisted that Barnes approach the bench and tell him how the evidence is relevant. That way, the jury wouldn't hear testimony that the judge may later rule improper. As lawyers and Quasimodo are fond of saying, "You can't unring a bell." Lawyers mean by this that jurors are likely to be influenced by what they hear, even if a judge tells them to disregard it. Of course, "You can't unstretch elastic socks" either, but lawyers haven't figured out the legal significance of this saying.

In reply to Judge Carrigan, Barnes would have said something like, "Your Honor, Ms. Jensen was attacked in almost the exact and repulsive same way as Mrs. Forrester. That means that it's very likely that the same person committed both attacks. Since my client didn't attack Ms. Jensen, the evidence is relevant to show that he didn't attack his wife."

"Aha," Judge Carrigan would have responded. "I suppose that you have evidence that Forrester wasn't the one who attacked Ms. Jensen?"

Here, Barnes is in trouble, because Jensen has no idea of who attacked her. She makes two stabs (pun intended) at proving that Forrester had nothing to do with the Jensen attack. First, Jensen testifies that Krasny's assistant told her that the two attacks were unrelated. But the assistant's statement to Jensen is inadmissible hearsay and a baseless opinion, so Judge Carrigan wouldn't have paid any attention to it. Second, Barnes tries to suggest that Bobby Slade, the tennis club pro, attacked both Jensen and Mrs. Forrester. Slade helps Barnes by calling her a "bitch." Of course, if he'd really been trying to help, he could have directed the remark at Julie Jensen. Barnes also offers evidence that when they were attacked, both women were having an affair with Slade. This testimony may cause some people not to take tennis lessons, but it is a questionable basis for arguing that Slade committed a double fault by attacking both women. They were both serving well, and Slade had a good racket going. Thus, Barnes's evidence doesn't exonerate Forrester of the Jensen attack, and a judge may not have allowed the jury to hear Jensen's testimony.

In a scene which is almost obligatory in trial movies, a nervous Barnes has a private conference with Judge Carrigan. She describes the problems she is having defending Forrester, and seeks his guidance. This is highly unethical; a lawyer cannot talk to a judge about a case unless the other side knows about it and has a chance to be present. It was also unnecessary. As a member of a well-known local law firm, surely Barnes could turn to her law partners or another judge for advice!

Much of Krasny's evidence consists of people's conversations, and potentially runs afoul of the hearsay rule (see *The Hearsay Rule,* p. 163). Judge Carrigan correctly admits the statements to show Mrs. Forrester's "state of mind." For example, Mrs. Forrester tells Virginia Howell that Forrester no longer loves her (Mrs. Forrester) and that she's planning to dump him. Despite Barnes's hearsay objection, Mrs. Forrester's statements are not barred by the hearsay rule. They indicate her intent to seek a divorce, which Krasny can argue furnishes Forrester with a motive to kill her. Even Mrs. Forrester's statement to Slade that Forrester takes women on horseback rides as a form of foreplay is probably admissible to show her anger at and resentment of Forrester.

After Forrester is acquitted of his wife's murder, Barnes tells him that she's found the typewriter and knows that he is guilty. Forrester then tries to kill Barnes. But why? He had little motive to do so. The "double jeopardy clause" of the U.S. Constitution provides that a person cannot be tried twice for the same crime. This means that once Forrester has been found "not guilty," he cannot be retried for his wife's murder even if new evidence suggests that he is guilty. Surely someone as cold and calculating as Forrester would know this, and laugh in Barnes's face when she mentions the typewriter.

Of course, Forrester might fear that Barnes will report the new information to Krasny, leading him to charge Forrester with the attack on Jensen. The double jeopardy clause would not prevent this, since Forrester has never been charged with that crime. However, it is probably too late to try Forrester for the Jensen attack, because the statute of limitations would have run out. Thus, Forrester's motive for trying to kill Barnes is very weak.

In fact, a nasty sort such as Forrester had a far safer alternative to trying to kill Barnes. He could threaten to reveal their sexual relationship to Barnes's staid corporate law firm, which is bound to take a dim view of her conduct. Under current rules Barnes might even face disciplinary sanctions from the state bar, since many states now forbid attorney-client sexual relationships that exploit the client or affect the quality of legal representation. So Forrester could respond to Barnes's threat by making a quite credible one of his own. This game of threat and counterthreat might have been entertaining to moral philosophers, but moviegoers were probably much happier to see Forrester lying dead at the foot of Barnes's bed.

Sidebar: The Hearsay Rule

Most people assume that the hearsay rule bars witnesses from testifying to any statements made outside the courtroom. But if the hearsay rule were so broad, trials in their present form could not exist. What people say is often at least as important as what they do, and witnesses have to be allowed to testify to statements and conversations if a judge or juror is to have any chance of figuring out how events took place.

More narrowly, then, what the hearsay rule says is that an "out-of-court statement" is inadmissible only if it is offered for "the truth of the matter asserted." An "out-of-court statement" is any statement not made on the witness stand, under oath, whether the statement is oral or written. (Don't be fooled by the "hear-say" label; the rule does apply to the contents of documents.) For example, assume that Laurel was involved in a traffic accident with Hardy, and is trying to prove that Hardy caused the accident by running a red light. Laurel testifies: "After the accident,

I spoke to a fellow named Costello. Costello told me that he saw Hardy's car run the red light." Laurel's testimony is hearsay. He's testifying to Costello's out-of-court statement, and offering it for the truth of what it asserts—that Hardy's car ran the red light. (Laurel would also be offering hearsay if he offers into evidence a letter from Costello stating that Hardy's car ran the red light.)

The general rule is that hearsay is not admissible in evidence. The primary reason for barring hearsay is to protect the right to cross-examination. If the party whose case is damaged by hearsay is unable to cross-examine the maker of the statement, the party loses an important opportunity to show that the statement is false or in some way untrustworthy.

However, evidence is often admissible even though it is hearsay. The reason is that the hearsay rule is riddled with exceptions. There are around thirty to forty known exceptions, none threatening to go on the endangered species list. Generally, hearsay exceptions arise when the circumstances under which an out-of-court statement is made are such that the statement is likely to be trustworthy. For instance, here are some of the popular hearsay exceptions and their rationales:

- *Dying Declarations.* This exception makes admissible a statement made by a person who thinks he's about to die (even if he in fact lives!). To be admissible, the statement has to pertain to the reason he thinks he's dying. The rationale is that people would not want to meet their Maker with a lie on their lips. So assume that Binder has been shot. Binder tells Moore with what he thinks are his last words, "Boland did it." Moore can testify to what Binder said; his words qualify as a dying declaration. But what if Binder told Moore, "Boland owes me $25,000?" Binder's statement would be inadmissible hearsay, not a dying declaration, because the statement doesn't pertain to the reason he thinks he's dying.
- *Excited Utterances.* This exception makes admissible statements made under the stress of excitement of seeing an unusual event. The rationale is

that people don't lie in stressful situations. Example, Houston sees a robbery and immediately shouts, "Oh my God, the robber has a tattoo of the Magna Carta on his left arm." Houston's statement would be admissible hearsay. What if in another case Houston had said, "Gee, my sock has a hole in it." This would not be an excited utterance; most people wouldn't be stressed out by a hole in a sock.

• *Business Records.* This exception makes admissible all sorts of business documents such as receipts, invoices, shipping orders, and reports. The rationale is that such documents are likely to be trustworthy because businesses prepare them routinely and need them to be accurate to stay in business.

• *Assertions of State of Mind.* This exception makes admissible what people say about their physical condition, feelings, beliefs, intentions, and the like. The rationale is that people are very capable of assessing their own state of mind, and are likely to report it accurately. For example, assume that Resnik claims that Even was speeding on Main Street. Even offers evidence that a week before the accident, he told a friend, "I'm really afraid of the traffic on Main Street." Even's statement is admissible circumstantial evidence that he was driving carefully a week later, on the theory that people don't speed on streets they're afraid to drive on.

You may be dubious about some of these rationales. For instance, you might think that someone about to die would take advantage of the situation to settle old scores and libel everyone he could think of. Nevertheless, the exceptions are well established. And the broadest exception doesn't even have a trustworthiness rationale! This is the exception for *admissions.* This exception allows one party to a civil or criminal lawsuit to offer into evidence anything ever said by the opposing party, as long as it's relevant. The circumstances under which the statement was made are largely irrelevant; an "admission" doesn't have to be trustworthy to be admissible. The real rationale for this broad exception is that ours is an adversary system of trial. If Party A makes a statement and Party B offers it into evidence, it's up to Party A to explain to the jury why the statement was inaccurate or incomplete. (As you can see, a "confession" in a criminal case is simply a type of admission that qualifies as a hearsay exception.)

Now you can see why "out-of-court statements" are so often admissible in evidence. Even if they're hearsay, very often an exception applies. But you've only seen the half of it. In many situations, statements are offered for purposes other than their truth. Then a hearsay exception isn't necessary to make the statements admissible, because the statements are not hearsay in the first place. Remember, a statement is hearsay only if it is "offered for the truth of the matter asserted."

Here's a simple example of how a statement can be offered for something other than its truth. Assume that Jones is trying to prove that she was not at fault in an automobile accident. Jones testifies that a minute or so before the accident, her passenger Smith said, "People drive like maniacs along this stretch of highway." Jones could testify to Smith's statement without violating the hearsay rule. Regardless of whether Smith's statement is true, Jones can claim that hearing what Smith said made her drive especially carefully. Jones is not offering Smith's statement "for the truth of the matter asserted," so it's not hearsay.

Like their real-life counterparts, movie trials are typically filled with testimony about statements and conversations that escape the ban of the hearsay rule. A few examples:

- In *They Won't Believe Me,* John Ballentine is charged with murdering his wife Greta. Explaining their relationship, Ballentine testifies that when he told Greta of his intention to run away with a woman by the name of Janice, Greta told him that she had bought a house in Beverly Hills and made him a partner in an investment firm. Ballentine's testimony is not hearsay. Even if Ballentine does not really intend to run off with Janice, his saying that he intends to do this indicates that not all was well in their relationship. And even if Greta lied about what she had done, her statement to Ballentine is relevant to explain why he dumped Janice and moved to Beverly Hills.

• In *Anatomy of a Murder,* Lieutenant Manion is on trial for murdering Barney Quill. Manion's defense is that he believed that Quill raped his wife Laura, and that the killing was excusable as the result of an irresistible impulse. Manion's and Laura's testimony that Laura told Manion that Quill had raped her is not barred by the hearsay rule. Even if Laura is not telling the truth, hearing her statement may help Manion to form a reasonable belief that Quill did rape her and thus give rise to an irresistible impulse to retaliate.

• In *Physical Evidence,* prosecutor Nicks seeks to prove that Joe Paris murdered Jake Farley. Nicks offers into evidence a tape of Paris threatening Farley with physical harm. Paris's statement is an admission, and thus admissible as an exception to the hearsay rule.

The hearsay rule is complex, and some of the blame for it can be laid at the feet of Sir Walter Raleigh. The rule developed in England in the late sixteenth to the early seventeenth century as a result of popular dissatisfaction with the conviction and eventual beheading of Sir Walter for treason. He was convicted of plotting the overthrow of Queen Elizabeth I, based largely on testimony from witnesses who described what other people had told them that Sir Walter said.

After his conviction, Sir Walter languished in the Tower of London for many years, long enough to write a history of the world. He was freed in order to lead a military expedition against Spain. Sir Walter's forces were defeated, and he lost a son in the battle. In the sporting manner of the British nobility, Sir Walter returned to England, was reimprisoned in the Tower, and later beheaded. Law students forced to study the hearsay rule often think that beheading was far too lenient a punishment for Sir Walter.

The Letter

Synopsis: A Malay plantation wife charged with murder claims she was defending her honor, but an incriminating letter turns up showing she'd already given it away. Her defense lawyer must either buy the letter or let her hang.

Warner Bros. (Robert Lord). 1940. Black and white. Running time: 95 min.

Screenplay: Howard Koch. Original Story: W. Somerset Maugham. Director: William Wyler.

Starring: Bette Davis (Leslie Crosbie), Herbert Marshall (Robert Crosbie), James Stephenson (Howard Joyce), Frieda Inescort (Dorothy Joyce), Gale Sondergaard (Mrs. Hammond), Sen Yung (Ong Chi Seng), Tetsu Kumai (Head Boy).

Academy Award nominations: Best Picture, Best Director (Wyler), Best Actress (Davis), Best Supporting Actor (Stephenson), Best Cinematography (Tony Gaudio), Best Musical Score, Best Editing.

Rating: —▮ —▮ —▮

The Story

Robert Crosbie manages a Malayan rubber plantation. One night when he's away, his wife Leslie empties a gun into Hammond, another rubber farmer. Robert rushes back home with a police officer and solicitor-friend Howard Joyce in tow. Leslie explains that Hammond, a local acquaintance married to a Eurasian woman, showed up unexpectedly and tried to rape her. She shot him in self-defense with Robert's pistol. Everyone sympathizes with Leslie, but she must stand trial in Singapore for murder.

Joyce is confident of a not guilty verdict. Leslie's self-defense story is compelling, and the all-white jury will undoubtedly detest Hammond for marrying a Eurasian. Ong, Joyce's upwardly mobile clerk, then shows Joyce a copy of a letter written by Leslie to Hammond on the day of the shooting, saying how she was desperate to see him. The Crosbies' head boy found the incriminating letter after Hammond was killed and delivered it to Mrs. Hammond. The helpful Ong says that for a price, Mrs. Hammond might sell the letter to Joyce. Of course, Ong gets to keep part of the price as his commission.

Joyce confronts Leslie in jail with the letter. She at first claims it's a forgery, then tearfully admits her affair with Hammond and her fury at finding out that he had dumped her for a heathen foreigner. She implores Joyce to buy the letter. Joyce reluctantly gives in when Leslie convinces him that the truth would destroy Robert. The letter's price is $10,000, almost all of Robert's savings, a steep price for a cross-

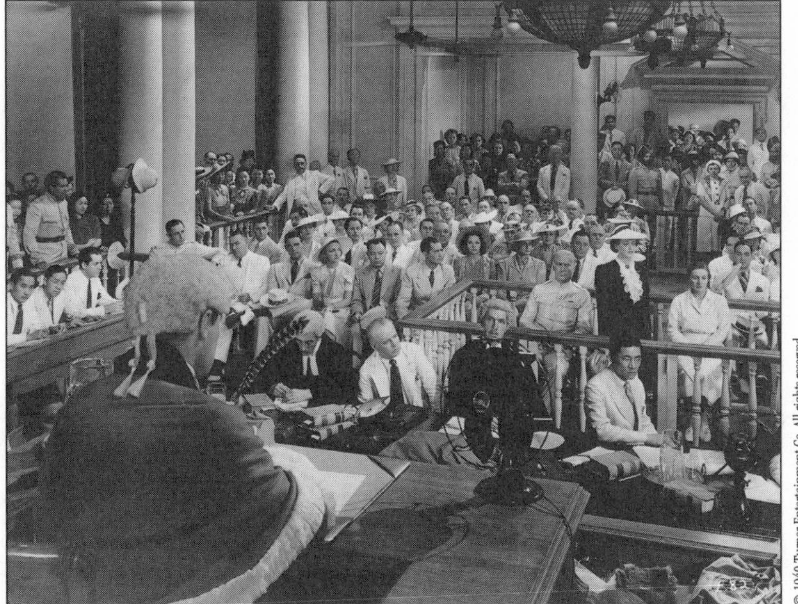

The Letter: Leslie Crosbie (Bette Davis) is protected by the letter of the law.

town delivery. Joyce has Leslie released to his personal custody, thereby enabling her to comply with the mysterious Mrs. Hammond's demand that she personally hand over the money to her in Chinatown.

With the letter out of the way, the defense goes smoothly. Leslie testifies that she shot Hammond in self-defense, and Joyce argues that the prosecution has no evidence to contradict her. The jury speedily finds Leslie not guilty.

The night of the acquittal, the Crosbies are given a gala victory party. Robert announces his plan to buy a plantation on Sumatra with the $10,000 he thinks is still in the bank. Time to check those bank statements more carefully, Robert! Probably realizing that the seller won't accept the letter in lieu of cash, Leslie is forced to tell Robert about Hammond. Though Robert promises to stick by her, the sight of sap bleeding from trees no longer excites Leslie. She can't face life without Hammond. She wanders outside, sensing that even though Mrs. Hammond was not on the guest list, she's waiting with a knife. Sure enough, Mrs. Hammond kills Leslie. Thus, Leslie wanted both Hammond and the evidence, but she winds up with neither the farmer nor the letter.

Legal Analysis

Two hallmarks of our adversary system of justice are trials that are supposed to produce the whole truth, and lawyers who are supposed to zealously fight for their clients. The ethical dilemma in the body of *The Letter* comes about because, as is often the case, these objectives are in conflict. The jurors can't know the whole truth unless they hear about Leslie's letter. But Joyce cannot give the prosecution his copy of the letter, or even tell the prosecution that the letter exists. In the adversary system, defense counsel does not have to turn over incriminating evidence to the prosecution. If the prosecution doesn't find out about the letter on its own, too bad for truth. As Joyce says, his feelings about Leslie are irrelevant. He clearly disapproves of her, but he owes her a duty of loyalty and can't help bring about her conviction.

Joyce exceeds his duty of loyalty when he buys the letter and he knows it. It's one thing for Joyce to keep quiet about the letter, and quite another for him to prevent the prosecution from learning of its existence. Joyce actively conceals the evidence, which is not only unethical but a crime all by itself. And it's a crime that might well have come to light—after Leslie's acquittal, either the vengeful Mrs. Hammond or the unctuous Ong could go to the police. Joyce clearly makes the wrong choice, but he acted out of a desire to protect Robert. Many people in Joyce's position would be tempted to do the same thing.

What should Joyce have done if Ong had given him not a copy of the letter, but the letter itself? Could Joyce have kept the letter buried in his file and said nothing about it to the prosecution, claiming that he's done nothing wrong since he didn't actively seek out the letter? This would be a more difficult issue than hiding a copy, because the prosecution would have practically no chance of ever finding out the truth. However, the answer would probably still be the same: Joyce should not turn the letter over to the prosecution. As long as he played no part in finding it, his obligation to his client outweighs the legal system's interest in the truth.

The balance swings the other way if Joyce is handed an "instrumentality" of the crime; then he'd have to hand it over. For example, assume that Leslie came running into Joyce's law office and threw the murder weapon on his desk, saying, "Here's the gun I used to blow away that jerk Hammond." If Leslie were charged with murder, Joyce would have to turn the gun over to the prosecution because it's an "instrumentality," the means by which the crime was committed. But he would not have to inform the prosecution that Leslie gave him the gun, because that's a confidential attorney-client communication.

After Joyce arranges for Leslie to purchase the letter from Mrs. Hammond, he compounds his ethical fall from grace during the trial. First, he has Leslie testify that she shot Hammond in self-defense. But Joyce knows that Leslie is testifying falsely. Even though he's entitled to keep silent about the letter, as an officer of the court Joyce cannot present testimony which he knows to be perjured. Joyce should not have called Leslie as a witness.

Second, during his final summation to the jury Joyce argues that the prosecution has not contradicted Leslie's self-defense claim, and that no contradictory evidence could exist. Here again Joyce violates his responsibilities as an officer of the court. He's entitled to point out the weaknesses in the prosecution's case, though he knows that Leslie is guilty. Even the guilty are entitled to the benefit of reasonable doubt. But Joyce cannot assert the nonexistence of evidence which he knows does exist.

Concealment of the letter aside, one reason that Joyce is so confident of a not-guilty verdict is that he knows that the jury will despise Hammond for violating the ultimate colonial taboo—marrying a "native." Shrewdly, Joyce tells Robert that it won't be necessary to ask the jury to condemn Hammond for his indiscretion. He'll simply make sure that the jury knows who Hammond married, and trust the jury to rely on its prejudices.

Joyce's strategy reflects an unfortunate reality of trial. Attorneys often offer evidence in the hope that biased jurors will draw improper inferences on their own. But for this strategy to work, the evidence has to have some proper relevance in the first place. Here, the fact that Hammond was married might be relevant to Leslie's defense, but the fact that his wife was Eurasian is not. The judge at least should have warned the jury not to consider the ethnicity of Hammond's spouse during deliberations.

In a rudimentary effort to conceal her identity, Leslie might at least have signed the letter in Pig Latin. It would have read "Eslie-Lay." Of course, that would have had its own negative connotations.

Trial Brief

In the original Maugham story on which the picture is based, Leslie and Robert resume a happy married life after the trial. This was a morally improper ending under the Hays Code, which was then in effect. To satisfy the code, in the film Leslie had to pay for her indiscretion with her life.

Knock on Any Door

Synopsis: A lawyer who feels partly responsible for his client's life of crime defends him against a murder charge, but fails to make a crucial objection.

Columbia/Santana (Robert Lord). 1949. Black and white. Running time: 100 min.

Screenplay: Daniel Taradash and John Monks Jr. Original story: Willard Motley. Director: Nicholas Ray.

Starring: Humphrey Bogart (Andrew Morton), John Derek (Nick "Pretty Boy" Romano), George Macready (District Attorney Kerman), Allene Roberts (Emma), Barry Kelly (Judge Drake).

Rating: —▮ —▮ —▮

Warning: Reading this summary may be hazardous to your enjoyment of the movie!

The Story

A robber holds up the 380 Bar and kills Officer Hawkins in an alley while trying to get away. The police round up the usual suspects and charge Nick Romano with the crimes. With a nickname like "Pretty Boy" and a rap sheet like "Pretty Long," Romano is definitely in deep trouble. Andrew Morton, an attorney who had left criminal defense work for a cushy property practice, reluctantly agrees to defend Romano.

District Attorney Kerman's opening statement is to the point: Romano has the black heart of a murderer and should be executed. Trying to gain the jury's sympathy, Morton's opening is a long story suggesting that Morton himself is partly to blame for Romano having a tougher time growing up than Odysseus had returning to Penelope. Lucky for Morton the story is told in flashbacks, so he can save his voice for the rest of the trial.

Morton's opening tells the jurors that years earlier, Morton's small law firm defended Romano's father. Morton was busy and assigned the defense to an associate, who muffed it. Romano's father went to prison, where he died before Morton could get him out. As a result, Romano's family had to move to the slums. Posters reading "Violent street gang has immediate opening for a 'pretty boy'; must have gun and sneer," must have abounded, because Romano quickly joined a gang and embarked on a life of crime. He occasionally tried to go straight, aided by the guilt-ridden Morton and Emma, whom he has married. But when Emma became pregnant, Romano ran off. They showed the strain of the breakup in different ways: Emma killed her-

Knock On Any Door: Andrew Morton (Humphrey Bogart) observes that the hat fits himself as well as Pretty Boy Romano (John Derek).

self, Romano held up a train station. Morton concludes his opening by insisting that Romano did not rob the 380 Bar or kill Officer Hawkins. It's a good thing that Romano was still a young man, or there's no telling how long Morton's opening would have been.

When it's finally his turn again, Kerman calls a number of eyewitnesses who finger Romano as the culprit. But Morton effectively casts doubt on their credibility. For example, Swanson, the owner of the 380 Bar, claims that Romano was the robber, but cannot recognize Morton as the person who interviewed him at length before trial. Kid Fingers claims that he saw Romano running out of the alley just after Officer Hawkins was shot. But handling Kid Fingers with kid gloves, Morton forces him to concede that he's a homeless bum who's been convicted of numerous crimes. Kerman reads a statement given by Juan Rodriguez to the police in which Rodriguez stated that he had seen Romano in the alley when Hawkins was shot. Morton elicits Rodriguez's testimony that Romano was not in the alley, and that he implicated Romano only after the police threatened to deport him.

To further bolster Romano's defense, Morton calls two alibi witnesses who claim they were drinking beer with Romano at the time of the crime. Kerman does little more than bring out a conflict as to what kind of beer they were drinking. Butch thinks it "tasted great"; Sunshine thinks it was "less filling."

Morton advises Romano about the risks of taking the stand, but Romano rashly decides to do it and proclaims his innocence. Kerman's cross-examination suggests what Attila the Hun would have been like as a prosecutor. Over and over, he screams murder accusations at Romano. As Morton sits by silently, Kerman's lowest and most objectionable blows accuse Romano of causing Emma's suicide. Romano finally collapses and confesses to the robbery and the murder.

In a last-ditch effort to save Romano's life, Morton dismisses the jury and pleads Romano guilty. He makes an emotional plea to Judge Drake, attributing Romano's actions to his father's death, life in the slums, brutal treatment in reform school, his wife's suicide, and so on. If he's guilty, Morton argues, so are we. "Knock on any door" in the slums and you'll find another Nick Romano just waiting to commit crimes. The plea for mercy fails. Judge Drake sentences Romano to death and he goes to the chair.

Given the results of the defense of father and son, future Romanos needing legal advice will probably "knock on any door" but Morton's.

Legal Analysis

Morton's final plea for mercy is a stirring effort to show that criminals are made, not born. But that plea probably would have been unnecessary had Romano not fallen apart on the witness stand, one of the worst places to confess to murder. Kerman's witnesses were far from convincing, and the jury might well have had a reasonable doubt as to Romano's guilt.

Romano should not have testified. The jury would have been instructed not to draw a negative inference from Romano's failure to testify. And if the prosecution's case is weak, a defendant usually does more harm than good by taking the stand and exposing himself to cross-examination. Ethically, attorneys must advise clients about risks and benefits of possible alternatives, such as whether or not to take the stand. However, the final decision is for the client, not the attorney. Of course, Romano thought he could help himself by taking the stand and claiming innocence. As an experienced, hardened criminal, it was implausible that he would break down on cross-examination and confess that he killed Hawkins.

Having done a good job of representing Romano to this point, it is inexplicable that Morton falls asleep at the objection switch during Kerman's cross-examination of Romano. Kerman doesn't simply "badger" Romano, he rains down a whole zoo of creatures on him. He screams "murderer" at Romano, waves the murder weapon around, and accuses him of causing Emma to commit suicide, all the while standing in Romano's face. For a while, Romano gamely counterpunches, maintaining his innocence. Finally distraught and exhausted, Romano breaks down when Kerman again plays the "Emma" card.

Kerman's tactics are more than improper. Morton could have tossed a book of evidence rules to Judge Drake, asked the judge to close his eyes, open the book and point to a rule, and then successfully objected based on whatever rule the judge had pointed to. Kerman's questions are argumentative, repetitive, and irrelevant. Whether Romano caused Emma to commit suicide has nothing to do with the crimes with which he's charged. Morton's failure to object, especially to the critical question about Emma's suicide, was a disastrous and inexplicable error.

Before Romano's confession, Morton does a capable job of attacking Kerman's case. Perhaps Morton's cleverest ploy emerges during his cross-examination of Swanson, the bar owner, when Swanson admits that he does not recognize Morton. When Morton concluded his interview of Swanson in the 380 Bar prior to trial, he accidentally-on-purpose spilled a drink on him. Morton's purpose isn't clear at the time of the interview, though it probably makes Soupy Sales fans anxious to see Morton interview a baker in a cream pie factory. This clever gambit severely undercuts the believability of Swanson's identification of Romano. If Swanson can't identify a man who spilled a drink on him during the calm of an interview, how can he possibly identify an armed robber?

Morton's ploy was tactically risky and legally questionable. The tactical risk is that by spilling the drink on Swanson, Morton makes it more likely that Swanson will be able to recognize him in court. The legal impropriety is that Swanson's inability to recognize Morton as his interviewer tells us little about his ability to recognize Romano as the robber. The conditions under which he saw the men are too dissimilar to permit an inference that if he can't recognize Morton he's mistaken about Romano. Morton's questions should have been ruled irrelevant.

Even more improper were Kerman's and Morton's opening statements. An opening statement is supposed to be a preview of evidence, a road map to help jurors follow testimony. But Kerman sounds more like a lynch mob leader than a prosecutor when he calls Romano a hoodlum and a black-hearted murderer. Such remarks appeal to jurors' passions rather than their reasoning, and are grossly improper. And listening to Morton's opening is like being handed an atlas of the world when you want to know the way to the closest grocery store. Romano's life history has nothing to do with whether he committed the crime he's charged with. Moreover, by revealing the tawdry facts of Romano's past crimes, Morton's opening may lead the jurors to think that Romano is just the sort of person who would have robbed the bar and killed the officer.

Both Kerman and Morton have a field day attacking each other's witnesses with their past crimes. But trial rules prevent attorneys from embarrassing witnesses with a litany of their misdeeds. In general, unless a witness has been convicted of a felony, or of a lesser crime if it involves dishonesty, an attorney cannot offer evidence of a witness's past crimes. Moreover, juvenile offenses often can't be used at all (see *Character Evidence,* p. 259). These rules would have taken the teeth out of much of Kerman's and Morton's cross-examinations.

For instance, Morton attacks Kid Fingers's credibility by showing that he's been convicted of begging and selling pornographic literature to children. But these are probably misdemeanors, not felonies. Likewise, Kerman asks Sunshine, one of Romano's alibi witnesses, if he's ever been in jail or reform school. This evidence may be proper in a supermarket tabloid, but not in trial.

Judge Drake, who sits idly by while the attorneys make these evidentiary blunders, is called upon to rule on a number of critical objections. Perhaps not wanting to show up Kerman or Morton, he almost always gets it wrong. For instance, Judge Drake rules that Morton can't ask Kid Fingers whether Kerman's office paid Fingers's flophouse rent or bought Fingers the new clothes that he wears to court. But this evidence is highly relevant. If Kerman is shelling out support money, Fingers's testimony is likely to be biased in his favor.

Similarly, Judge Drake improperly prevents Morton from asking Swanson whether the police had told him that Romano was guilty before asking him if he recognized Romano as the robber. Such police suggestiveness goes directly to the credibility of Swanson's identification. Indeed, under present constitutional standards the police remark may have poisoned Swanson as a witness and prevented him from testifying at all.

Finally, the examination of Juan Rodriguez raises a subtle issue of evidence procedure. When Kerman calls him as a witness, Rodriguez testifies that he can remember nothing about the shooting of Officer Hawkins. Kerman then reads Rodriguez's statement implicating Romano in the killing to the jury. But Rodriguez's statement to the police is hearsay, and admissible only if it is inconsistent with his courtroom testimony (see *The Hearsay Rule,* p. 163). And the courts have determined that it's not inconsistent for a witness to remember something at an earlier time (that is, when Rodriguez spoke to the police), but not at a later time (that is, at trial). Thus, Judge Drake probably should not have allowed Kerman to read Rodriguez's statement to the jury.

On the other hand, Rodriguez's loss of memory is certainly a convenient break for Romano. In this situation, some judges might rule that Rodriguez is only feigning his lack of memory, and treat it as though Rodriguez had testified that Romano had nothing to do with the killing. Under that approach, they would permit Kerman to read Rodriguez's prior inconsistent statement to the jury. Of course, Morton could still elicit Rodriguez's explanation that the police coerced him into implicating Romano.

The film is an intense but error-filled courtroom drama. Morton's speech about how we're all responsible for Romano's life of crime because we haven't cleaned up the slums was the best that Morton could do under the circumstances. But it doesn't work with Judge Drake and it doesn't work with us either. Like Morton (who also grew up in the slums), Romano could have overcome his circumstances. He had every opportunity to lead a respectable life. He richly deserved the harshest penalty that the law could administer.

The Music Box

Synopsis: The feds seek to strip a kindly old man's U.S. citizenship because he's a war criminal. His daughter represents him—and learns more than she ever wanted to know.

Guild/Carolco (Irwin Winkler). 1989. Color. Running time: 126 min.

Screenwriter: Joe Eszterhas. Director: Costa-Gavras.

Starring: Jessica Lange (Ann Talbot), Armin Mueller-Stahl (Mike Laszlo), Frederic Forrest (Jack Burke), Donald Moffat (Perry Talbot), Lukas Haas (Mikey Talbot), Michael Rooker (Kartchy Laszlo), J.S. Block (Judge Silver).

Academy Award nominations: Best Actress (Jessica Lange).

Rating: ⚖ ⚖

Surprise ending warning: Reading this summary may be hazardous to your enjoyment of the movie.

The Story

Mike Laszlo is a twinkly old Hungarian American. He's very close to his daughter Ann Talbot, and Ann's little boy Mikey. Laszlo is also a fa-

The Music Box: Ann Talbot (Jessica Lange) argues that her father is not a war criminal.

natic anticommunist. It's quite a surprise when Laszlo learns that the government plans to strip him of his U.S. citizenship and deport him to Hungary to stand trial for war crimes. The feds claim that Laszlo lied on his citizenship application by failing to disclose that he was a member of Arrow Cross, a notorious police terrorist organization responsible for brutal war crimes and jaywalking tickets.

Talbot is a tough criminal lawyer, and pappa wants her to fight the feds for him. Certain that it's an unfortunate case of mistaken identity, Talbot agrees and takes a leave from her firm. Jack Burke, prosecuting the case for the government, seems harsh and driven, determined to deport Laszlo. Talbot's defense strategy is that the whole case was concocted by the communist government in Budapest in retribution for her father's fanaticism.

The trial opens in federal court in Chicago before Judge Irwin Silver. Burke introduces a photostat of an Arrow Cross ID card with a photo of a youthful Laszlo and his signature. The photo matches one on Laszlo's visa application. Burke's document examiner opines that the card is genuine. Talbot thinks the Reds forged it.

A procession of witnesses follows, describing horrible atrocities and identifying Laszlo (then called Mishka) and his superior (who had a facial scar). They shot a man and then his child. They tortured prisoners, raped women. They massacred Jews by shooting them and dumping them in the Danube.

Talbot raises a few doubts with effective cross-examination. One witness admits that his son is a Communist party official in Budapest, and another admits to having rehearsed his testimony with a previous witness. And she calls a KGB defector, to testify that Moscow frequently concocted war crimes accusations and documents.

The judge and the lawyers fly to Budapest to examine one last witness who is too ill to travel. He identifies Laszlo as Mishka, but Talbot destroys him on cross-examination with some documents given to her by a mysterious stranger. The documents show that the witness had previously denounced two other men as the notorious Mishka.

Judge Silver dismisses the government's case—even before Laszlo testifies. But Talbot goes to visit the sister of Tibor Zola, a mysterious man to whom Laszlo had written numerous checks. There she sees photos of her father with Tibor—who had a big facial scar. The sister also gives Talbot a pawn ticket for a music box that Tibor had hocked before his death. She redeems the music box and finds photos showing Laszlo committing the war crimes described in the trial. He'd been lying all along.

Talbot denounces her father, refusing ever to speak to him or let him see little Mikey. Then she sends the damning photos to Burke, who passes them on to the press.

Legal Analysis

Though technically civil cases, denaturalization and deportation are very severe sanctions. They are much worse than most criminal penalties, especially when a war crimes trial is waiting for you back in friendly Hungary. As a result, the government has to satisfy a stronger burden of proof than it normally has in a civil case. Instead of merely proving fraud in a citizenship application by a "preponderance of the evidence," it must prove this fact by clear and convincing evidence. This is close to the "beyond a reasonable doubt" standard used in criminal cases. And it isn't easy to prove that someone committed war crimes forty or fifty years ago. Mistaken identity is a definite risk.

Judge Silver dismissed the proceeding by ruling that Burke failed to prove his case. This ruling is dubious. Burke put on more than enough evidence back in Chicago to establish his case by clear and convincing evidence. Evidently, the judge was irritated at having to travel to Budapest, especially coach class. The discredited witness there probably was the key to the judge's ruling. Talbot originally speculated that a Jewish judge might lean over backwards to be fair. This seems to be exactly what happened.

Some of Judge Silver's evidence rulings were also questionable. For example, he should not have allowed Talbot to ask the document examiner whether he was Jewish. Normally it is improper to attack a witness's credibility by asking about his religion, at least without some other indication that the witness might be biased. Silver evidently wanted to err on the side of the defense. After all, it wasn't a jury trial and it is safer for the judge to let in all defense evidence for what it's worth than risk being reversed on appeal.

The main theme that emerges from this film is that it was a great mistake for Ann Talbot to represent her father in such a case. She could not maintain the necessary objectivity and distance from the case.

For example, on the eve of the trial Talbot invites Burke to dinner to try to establish a good working relationship; it's a complete fiasco. She can't resist taunting him about a car accident in which he was driving and his wife was killed. He stalks out. Her ability to represent her client suffered because of her personal involvement with the case.

Similarly, Talbot just can't face the likely truth as it emerges at the trial. She practices personal denial straight through. Thus when she is finally confronted with the proof of guilt, she overreacts, denouncing her father and cutting herself and little Mikey off from the rest of her family.

Even though the photos establish Laszlo's guilt, he cannot be subjected to another denaturalization trial. The rules of "res judicata" establish that a fact established in one case cannot be reexamined in a second case.

Thus Talbot's release of the photos to Burke and the press served no purpose except to destroy Laszlo's reputation. It was a terrible lapse of judgment and grossly unethical. The most fundamental of all canons of legal ethics is that you must place your client's interest first. Once more, Talbot's lack of distance from her case has unfortunate consequences.

In Talbot we see a skilled trial lawyer, but a person whose loyalty to her father led her down the perilous path to personal and ethical disaster. It's said that the lawyer who represents himself has a fool for a client. The same holds true for getting your kids to do the job.

Trial Brief

Joe Eszterhas, author of the screenplay of *The Music Box* was born in Hungary and lived in refugee camps before moving to the United

States. Eszterhas, who is not Jewish, was well aware of Arrow Cross, a Hungarian political party that collaborated with the Nazis and was deeply implicated in the sort of atrocities depicted in the film. He got the idea for the film after a harrowing visit from an older woman who had witnessed many atrocities.

The character of Mike Laszlo was inspired by John Demjanjuk, whom the United States also sought to denaturalize and deport for war crimes committed as a concentration camp guard. Eszterhas sat through Demjanjuk's trial and was repelled by the defendant. Eszterhas felt that Demjanjuk had walled off his terrible past, thus presenting a friendly, twinkly eyed demeanor. Demjanjuk was later extradited to Israel, but was acquitted by the Israeli courts of war crimes. The courts ruled that he was misidentified by witnesses, although he may have been guilty of atrocities at a different camp.

The Paradine Case

Synopsis: A beautiful young wife is accused of poisoning her elderly husband. The case poisons her barrister's marriage.

United Artists (David O. Selznick). 1947. Black and white. Running time: 115 min.

Screenplay: David O. Selznick. Original novel: Robert Hitchens. Director: Alfred Hitchcock.

Starring: Gregory Peck (Anthony Keane), Alida Valli (Maddalena Paradine), Louis Jourdan (Andre Latour), Charles Laughton (Lord Horfield), Charles Coburn (Sir Simon Flaquer), Ethel Barrymore (Lady Sophie Horfield), Ann Todd (Gay Keane).

Academy Award nomination: Best Supporting Actress (Ethel Barrymore).

Rating: ⚖ ⚖

Surprise ending warning: Reading this summary may be hazardous to your enjoyment of the movie!

The Story

Maddalena Paradine is an attractive woman with a checkered past. She is accused of poisoning her husband, Colonel Paradine, who was blind and many years her senior. The colonel might have killed himself or might have been murdered. His death may have been a joint project of himself and his wife or his valet, Andre Latour. Amazingly, nobody suggests that the colonel's butler, Lakin, might have been the guilty one, possibly because it would make the movie too long.

Anthony Keane, a successful London barrister, is engaged to defend Mrs. Paradine. Keane is fascinated by Mrs. Paradine and soon becomes the latest to fall under her spell. He loses interest in his wife Gay and his objectivity about the case. Mrs. Paradine instructs him not to try to pin the blame on Latour. Latour, on the other hand, is deeply hostile to Mrs. Paradine, whom he considers "bad to the bone." Possibly Latour was an X-ray technician before becoming the colonel's valet.

Judge Horfield presides over the trial with a marvelous blend of sarcasm and silkiness. Horfield is a repellent character who comes on to Mrs. Keane and bullies his meek wife, Lady Horfield. Meanwhile, he looks forward with delight to sending Mrs. Paradine to the gallows, apparently forgetting that he needs a conviction first.

At the trial, Keane ignores his client's wishes and tries to pin the murder on Latour, who strongly denies it. Yet Keane's cross-examination leaves a strong impression that Latour was having an affair with Mrs. Paradine and that Latour assisted the colonel to do away with himself. After his damning testimony, Latour kills himself. Professional valet to the end, he manages it without messing up his clothes.

News of Latour's suicide coaxes the truth from Mrs. Paradine, whom Keane has called as a witness. Mrs. Paradine testifies that she had seduced Latour, but that he felt deeply conflicted because of his loyalty to Colonel Paradine. The colonel discovered the affair and discharged Latour. Mrs. Paradine then poisoned the colonel, perhaps to free herself to run off with Latour. Having confessed to the crime, Mrs. Paradine denounces Keane. Crushed, Keane apologizes and staggers from the courtroom, his strategy and reputation in ruins.

Legal Analysis

A trial lawyer must maintain cool objectivity about a client in order to make appropriate strategic decisions. Certainly, the worst thing a criminal lawyer can do is to fall in love with his client, thus losing the ability to view the situation objectively. Keane makes this critical blunder, simply refusing to believe that the woman with whom he is infatuated could possibly have killed anyone. He is also extremely jealous of Latour, which again affects his trial strategy.

Keane ignores his client's instructions and tries to pin the murder on Latour. His cross-examination of Latour is withering and would probably have caused the jury to believe that Latour killed the colonel rather than Mrs. Paradine. Though an effective strategy, Keane improperly disregarded Mrs. Paradine's instructions. Major questions of trial strategy are supposed to be made by the client, not the lawyer. However devastating the consequences to Mrs. Paradine, she is entitled to make the major decisions about her own case. If Keane cannot abide by her instructions, he has to withdraw.

Keane makes a fatal error in calling his client to the stand. There was no reason to do this, since he did not know what she would say and since his cross-examination of Latour had probably raised a reasonable doubt in the mind of the jury. His strategy turns into a calamity when she confesses to the crime and denounces him.

Several times, Keane assures his client that they will win the case. This is a bad idea. Competent counsel never promise victory in any type of litigation, and certainly this holds true for criminal defense. Despite a fine cast and the great director Alfred Hitchcock at the helm, this film never catches fire. Instead of seeing it, you're better off watching *Witness for the Prosecution* twice.

Witness for the Prosecution

Synopsis: A man is accused of murdering an elderly woman in order to inherit her property. His wife's damning testimony appears to sink his defense, until surprise impeachment turns up.

UA/Theme/Edward Small (Arthur Hornblow Jr.). 1957. Black and white. Running time: 114 min.

Screenplay: Billy Wilder and Harry Kurnitz. Original theatrical play: Agatha Christie. Director: Billy Wilder.

Starring: Charles Laughton (Sir Wilfrid Robarts), Tyrone Power (Leonard Vole), Marlene Dietrich (Christine Vole), Elsa Lanchester (Miss Plimsoll).

Academy Award nominations: Best Picture, Best Director, Best Actor (Charles Laughton), Best Supporting Actress (Elsa Lanchester), Best Editor.

Rating: —▮ —▮ —▮ —▮

Surprise ending warning: Reading this summary may be hazardous to your enjoyment of the movie!

The Story

Sir Wilfrid Robarts is a curmudgeonly barrister who is convalescing from a heart attack. Against the orders of his despairing nurse, Miss Plimsoll, he sneaks the occasional cigar and also agrees to defend Leonard Vole. Vole is accused of murdering Emily French, a woman many years his senior who had befriended him. Vole tells Robarts that he wanted French to give him money to promote an invention. He admits to Robarts that he was at her home the night she was murdered, but claims to have left before the murder and returned home to his wife Christine at 9:25. Things look a bit fishy when it is disclosed that French's will left Vole £80,000, although he claims he didn't know the terms of her will.

At the trial, the prosecution puts on a drop-dead circumstantial ev-

Witness for the Prosecution: Sir Wilfrid Robarts (Charles Laughton) examines Leonard Vole (Tyrone Power).

idence case against Vole. French had Type O blood, which matches stains on Vole's jacket. French's housekeeper, Janet Mackenzie, testifies that she heard Vole and French talking through a door when she returned home around the time the murder was committed. Also damaging is evidence that Vole, accompanied by an affectionate brunette, had inquired at a travel agency about expensive cruises.

The final straw is Christine Vole, unexpectedly called as a "witness for the prosecution." She testifies that she and Leonard were never legally married. She also testifies that Leonard confessed the murder to her and that he returned home after 10:00 with blood on his sleeve. Vole protests loudly that she's lying, but the only way he could have looked worse is if Christine had testified that Vole never took out the trash.

Courtroom genius though he is, Robarts's case looks worse than his EKG. The night before a hopeless closing argument, Robarts is contacted by a mysterious woman. He meets her in a train station, and she gives him letters that destroy Christine's credibility. The letters were written by Christine to "Max," who is evidently her lover. Christine writes of her intention to testify falsely against Vole to get rid of him so that she and Max can run off together. Robarts calls

Christine to the stand, reads one of the shocking letters, and destroys the prosecution's case. Vole is acquitted.

Rapidly, things turn from trial to tribulation as Robarts realizes he's been had. Christine brags to Robarts that in fact she was the mysterious woman in the train station, and that she cooked up the letters in order to get Vole acquitted. She knew that the jury would never believe her if she merely supported his alibi. Only by being a totally discredited prosecution witness could she persuade the jury of his innocence. In fact, Christine admits, Vole was guilty all along, but she was willing to take a perjury rap to get him off. Vole returns, thanks Christine politely, and embraces the brunette. This sweetie is indeed Vole's lover and he is planning to use French's money to disappear with her—just as had been testified to at the trial. This is all a bit much for the faithful Christine, who grabs a knife and does in Vole on the spot. To Miss Plimsoll's despair, Sir Wilfrid immediately volunteers to represent her.

Legal Analysis

You may be unfamiliar with the English legal profession, in which the work of lawyers is divided between two groups—solicitors and barristers. Most legal work is done by solicitors, but litigation in the Crown Courts is conducted exclusively by barristers. They're the ones who appear in court decked out in funny-looking but expensive wigs. If a client needs representation in court, the client's solicitor must engage a barrister to do the job, as occurs near the beginning of the film. Barristers effectively keep their numbers down by limiting available space in the Inns of Court, where fledglings must apprentice and where practicing barristers have their offices. This system is under attack in Britain and may well be supplanted by the American system in which lawyers' licenses allow them to engage in all legal chores. English wigmakers are certainly hoping that solicitors will be able to go to Crown Court soon.

British practice is different in other interesting ways from American practice. At one point, Robarts moves to reopen the defense after he had rested in order to recall Christine to the stand to ask about the letters. The prosecution objects. To argue the legal point, Robarts brings lawbooks with precedent cases to court and prepares to read the decisions aloud to the judge. This looks quite odd to American lawyers but in fact written briefs are seldom used in either trial or appellate courts in Britain. Instead, counsel bring the books to court and read pertinent sections to the judges. For this reason, a single appeal may consume several days of court time. In an American courtroom, lawyers would file written briefs and, if necessary, supplement them with relatively brief oral arguments. American lawyers who like to give speeches can become commentators on Court TV.

Robarts makes the customary point that the prosecution's evidence is all circumstantial, meaning that nobody testified they actually saw Vole kill French. But there's nothing wrong with a case based on circumstantial evidence (see *Circumstantial Evidence,* p. 193).

Assuming that Vole had survived Christine's assault in the final reel, he could not have been retried for French's murder. He is protected by the rule against double jeopardy, even though he was guilty and had been acquitted only because of Christine's perjury. In a civil case, newly discovered evidence can lead to a new trial, but not in a criminal case after the defendant has been acquitted. In order to protect defendants from being persecuted by multiple trials, we allow them to go free despite the discovery of new evidence that establishes their guilt. Prosecutors get only one shot at a conviction—or in this case, only one stab.

Had Vole been convicted, he would not have been permitted to inherit money from French. Quite sensibly, the law bars a convicted killer from inheriting from the victim. We assume that if the victim had known the circumstances of her death, she probably would have wanted to leave the goodies to someone else.

A key evidentiary point in the case is that Christine could be compelled to testify for the prosecution. Had she and Vole been married, her testimony would have been privileged and she could not be compelled to give evidence against him (or in many states he could have successfully objected to her testimony even if she wanted to testify). However, because of her prior marriage, Christine and Vole were not legally married. Yet he thought they were married. A person who believes wrongly but sincerely that he or she is married is a "putative" spouse. Putative spouses are given the same property rights as real spouses. The rules relating to marital privilege should be the same for real spouses and putative spouses, at least from the point of view of the spouse who was deceived. Thus, Vole might have been allowed to prevent Christine from testifying. Then the film would have been called *Why the Spousal Privilege Prevented Testimony from a Witness for the Prosecution.*

Robarts was quite effective in cross-examining the prosecution's witnesses. For example, he showed that Mackenzie had applied for a hearing aid from the National Health. Also, she could not hear him when he spoke in a low tone. Thus, how could she be sure it was Vole's voice she heard through a door? Moreover, Robarts was able to impeach Mackenzie effectively by showing that she had been disinherited by French. This gave her a motive to hate Vole, which suggested that she might be lying.

A basic rule for cross-examination is not to ask a question to which you do not know the answer. Sir Wilfrid breaks the rule and pays the price. Seeking to undermine Mackenzie's testimony that she heard French and Vole talking, Robarts asks her if she might not have heard male and female voices on television. Impossible, Mackenzie replied. Why? Because the television was being repaired that week. Whoops.

When Sir Wilfrid recalls Christine to the stand and springs the letters on her, he pulls off a superb bluff. He first holds up a letter which in fact was an invoice for his new bermuda shorts and pretends to read from it. Christine immediately says that is not her stationery. This adds dramatic impact when he pulls out the actual letter. The ethics of this sort of chicanery are dubious, but even if it were ethically acceptable, Robarts probably couldn't have pulled it off. He would have had to show whatever he was reading to the prosecutor, who would have objected to his trying to mislead the witness.

When Robarts represents Christine in her murder case, as he promises to do at the end of the movie, what defense can he offer? He can try to have the charge reduced from murder to manslaughter on the theory that she was in the heat of passion when she stabbed Vole after learning he had been unfaithful and was planning to ditch her for the brunette. Even better, though, Robarts might appeal to the sympathy of the jury. The jury can always acquit a defendant who it believes is unjustly accused of a crime, regardless of the absence of any legal justifications for the deed. Who could argue that the creep Leonard Vole did not have it coming?

Laughton's immortal performance, together with the truly elegant plot twists, make this picture an absolute must-see for trial movie fans.

It's Nothing but a Bunch of Circumstantial Evidence

Circumstantial evidence is an inescapable part of nearly every actual trial and courtroom movie (see *Circumstantial Evidence,* p. 193). But many of the films in this chapter portray circumstantial evidence as a powerful force that obscures rather than develops truth. The protagonists are as helpless in the face of circumstantial evidence as a twig in a whirlpool. For instance, Lawrence Ballentine in *They Won't Believe Me* and Robert Hale in *They Won't Forget* appear to be wrongly accused murderers faced with trying to explain away powerful circumstantial evidence of guilt.

Despite its menacing portrayal in these films, most evidence other than an eyewitness identification is circumstantial evidence. To say that evidence is circumstantial is simply to say that a judge or juror must draw an inference to connect the evidence to the point it's offered to prove. Thus, if Bill is charged with murder, and the prosecutor offers evidence that Bill ran away from the murder scene, that's circumstantial evidence. The prosecutor would be asking a judge or juror to infer that Bill was running away because he committed the crime. Of course, inferences consistent with innocence are possible—maybe Bill was running away because he didn't want to be the next victim. And the ever-present possibility of an innocent explanation supplies the dramatic underpinnings to this chapter's films.

An Act of Murder

(Alternate Title: *Live Today for Tomorrow*)

Synopsis: A harsh judge's trial for the mercy killing of his wife gives him a new slant on the meaning of justice.

Universal-International (Jerry Bresler). 1948. Black and white. Running time: 90 min. Not released on videotape.

Screenplay: Michael Blankfort and Robert Thoeren. Original book: Ernst Lothar. Director: Michael Gordon.

Starring: Fredric March (Calvin Cooke), Florence Eldridge (Cathy Cooke), Edmond O'Brien (David Douglas), Geraldine Brooks (Ellie Cooke).

Rating: —▮ —▮

Surprise ending warning: Reading this analysis may be hazardous to your enjoyment of the movie!

The Story

Calvin Cooke is a judge whose strict view of the law has earned him a reputation as "Old Man Maximum." He nearly holds defense attorney David Douglas in contempt for trying to argue that the emotional condition of a defendant named Novak is relevant to the question of whether Novak committed a violent act. And before the jury has reached a verdict, Cooke has already penciled in a twenty-year sentence for Novak. Of course, Cooke could show that even he has a soft spot by reducing the sentence to ten years if the jury finds Novak not guilty.

When not wearing a robe, Cooke is a pussycat. He's devoted to wife Cathy and daughter Ellie, a law student. However, Cooke is upset to learn that Douglas and Ellie are secretly engaged, and probably wants to hold Douglas in "contempt of courting."

However, Cooke's real concern soon becomes Cathy. Cathy has kept her headaches and blurred vision a secret from Cooke. She visits Walter, the family physician. Walter realizes that Cathy has a fatal brain tumor, but keeps it a secret from her. Instead, Walter tells Cooke that Cathy will soon die, and convinces him to keep her condition a secret.

Cathy is thrilled when Cooke takes her on a second honeymoon. But Cathy finds a prescription for powerful pain pills and Walter's description of her illness hidden in Cook's suitcase. This horrible discovery returns the family's "keep a secret" ball to her court; she doesn't tell Cooke that she knows she is dying. As Cooke and Cathy drive

An Act of Murder: David Douglas (Edmond O'Brien) withdraws the guilty plea of Calvin Cooke (Fredric March).

home, they stop at a diner. Afterward, Cooke's car suddenly veers off the road and crashes. Cathy is killed.

After recovering from his own injuries, Cooke insists that the D.A. indict him for murdering Cathy. He pleads guilty because he intentionally drove off the road to kill Cathy and spare her further suffering. But over Cooke's protest, Judge Ogden appoints Douglas to represent Cooke at the sentencing hearing. Douglas requests an autopsy, which reveals that Cathy died of an overdose of pain medication before the crash. Douglas also produces a witness who saw Cathy fill the pain medication prescription and another who saw her swallow pills inside the diner.

Judge Ogden dismisses the charges. Cooke promises to become a reformed judge who will consider people's emotions when judging their behavior. Cooke's nickname will probably have to be changed to "Old Man Minimum," and the first defendant to appear before him will probably be sentenced to five years on the Love Boat.

Legal Analysis

This film raises the important issue of the legal consequences of "mercy killing," or euthanasia. (Question: Why is an act primarily affecting older people called "youth"-anasia?) At present, a very few countries, such as Holland, treat mercy killings as noncriminal acts. But laws in the United States tend to be far more restrictive. In most states, doctors may legally withhold life-prolonging treatment from patients with irreversible last illnesses, but they may not actively hasten death. Thus, Dr. Jack Kevorkian, who has developed a "suicide machine" to assist terminally ill patients who want to end their suffering, has found himself in continuous legal turmoil.

Trying to steer a middle course, this film has ties to both camps. Antieuthanasia enthusiasts will find support in the opinions of Walter, Judge Ogden, and Cooke himself, all of whom say that Cooke's actions were morally wrong. Yet the film portrays Cooke as a sympathetic, almost heroic character. A scene in which a police officer mercifully shoots a wounded, suffering dog arouses empathy for Cooke's plight. Luckily for Judge Ogden and the filmmakers, the coroner's surprise evidence that Cathy died of an overdose before Cooke could kill her eliminates the need for a ruling on the legality of Cooke's act.

But Cooke may not be totally out of the criminal woods. An unsuccessful attempt to commit a crime is itself a crime. For example, if you try to hit your worst enemy with a rock, but bungle the effort by imitating an L.A. Dodger pitcher by firing high and wide and hitting nothing, you might be found guilty of "attempted battery." The law punishes dangerous acts that don't succeed because you might succeed next time. So, since Cooke readily admits that he tried to kill Cathy, should Judge Ogden have convicted him of attempted murder? No. A person cannot be convicted of an attempt to commit a crime that was impossible to commit. Since at the moment Cooke tried to kill Cathy she was already dead, it was impossible for him to have murdered her. Therefore, he could not be convicted of attempted murder.

Judge Ogden appoints Douglas to represent Cooke at the sentencing hearing even though Cooke insists that he wants to represent himself. Douglas gets the appointment by citing a California case supposedly establishing a rule that a judge must appoint counsel for a defendant in a murder case. However, no such rule currently exists. In the mid-1970s, the U.S. Supreme Court decided *Faretta v. California,* which established that people have a constitutional right to represent themselves, even in murder cases. Most judges will discourage defendants facing serious charges from representing themselves, but if they are knowledgeable and understand what they're doing (and Cooke certainly fits into this category), judges have no choice but to allow self-representation.

Even though Cooke had already pleaded guilty, Judge Ogden had the power to find Cooke not guilty. Hoping only to convince Ogden to impose a minimum sentence on the maximum man, Douglas instead proved that Cooke was innocent. And in a criminal case, it's never too late for a judge to decide that a defendant is not guilty.

Before Cooke's transformation, Ellie and Douglas portray him as an uncaring judge who applies legal rules mechanically and harshly. But the evidence does not support the charge. Defending Novak against a charge of attempted murder, Douglas asks a witness whether in the witness's opinion Novak acted like a man who was about to commit a murder. Cooke sustains the D.A.'s objection to this question, which leads Douglas to angrily accuse Cooke of improperly looking only at Novak's actions and disregarding Novak's state of mind.

However, Cooke's ruling was proper. The general rule is that a witness cannot give an opinion about another person's state of mind. Witnesses have to testify from personal knowledge, and nobody can know what thoughts are running through someone else's mind. Since Douglas asked his witness for an opinion about what Novak intended to do, his question was improper.

Cooke's ruling that Douglas's question is improper does not prevent Douglas from offering evidence about Novak's mental state. The witness could have testified to Novak's statements, his tone of voice, and body language. From that evidence, the jury could have drawn its own conclusions about whether Novak acted like someone about to commit a violent act. For example, Douglas might have elicited evidence that at the time he was supposedly attempting a murder, Novak was dressed as a clown and was saying, "Time to try out my new squirt gun." Douglas would then ask the judge or jury to infer from this evidence that Novak did not attempt to kill someone. Thus, Cooke's ruling does not mean that he regards Novak's mental state as legally irrelevant. After Cooke's ruling, it was up to Douglas to offer proper evidence concerning Novak's lack of intent.

Some of the film's legal portrayals are as charmingly naive as the cigarette that Walter, a respected physician, gives Cooke when delivering the bad news about Cathy. For example, Douglas appears marvelously creative by thinking of requesting an autopsy to establish the true cause of Cathy's death. But when a person dies under unusual circumstances or with no physician present, and especially with murder charges in the offing, an autopsy would automatically be performed.

And when Cooke rules that Douglas's question about Novak's state of mind is improper, Douglas retorts, "I take exception to that ruling." Many years ago, trial attorneys had to take "exception" to evidence rulings that they disagreed with in order to preserve for appeal their right to argue that the trial judge's ruling was incorrect. The "exception" rule was probably designed to discourage attorneys from raising evidence issues on appeal, because by "taking exception" an attorney in effect had to say, "Not only do I think that ruling stinks, but I'm going to let the appeals court judges know just how badly it stinks. You'll be a lowly trial judge for the rest of your life." Now, attorneys no longer have to "take exception" to raise issues on appeal; it is presumed that they think that all adverse evidence rulings stink.

After his narrow brush with prison, Cooke decides to remain a judge. Too bad. Given his family's history of refusing to discuss problems with each other, he probably could have made a fortune by inventing the old TV game show, *I've Got a Secret.*

Sidebar: Circumstantial Evidence

Many trial films rely heavily on "circumstantial evidence." The very term has an unpleasant connotation, undoubtedly the result of generations of movie and TV lawyers deriding their opponents' cases as "nothing but a bunch of circumstantial evidence." You might almost think that circumstantial evidence is something to wipe off the bottom of your shoe while holding your nose.

Circumstantial evidence is simply evidence whose probative value depends on an inference. An inference is a mental link between an item of evidence and the point it's offered to prove. Its counterpart is direct evidence, for which no inference is necessary. To illustrate, assume that in a prosecution of Moe for murder, the prosecution offers two pieces of evidence: Curly's testimony that he saw Moe fire the fatal shot, and Larry's testimony that a few seconds after he heard a shot he saw Moe running away from the scene of the crime. Curly's testimony is direct evidence; it establishes Moe's identity as the shooter without the need for the jury to draw an inference. Larry's testimony is circumstantial evidence; the jury must infer that Moe committed a crime from the evidence that he was running away.

Despite its negative image, circumstantial evidence is a perfectly honorable form of proof, accepted in fine courtrooms everywhere. In fact we draw inferences all the time in everyday life. For example, if you see someone crying, you may infer that he is sad. If the person behind you honks her horn as soon as a light turns green, you may infer that she is in a hurry, is a cabdriver, or saw your "Honk If You Love the Beatles" bumper strip. Judges and jurors draw these same kinds of inferences in trial.

Thus, there's nothing unusual about circumstantial evidence. It can even be more convincing than direct evidence. To paraphrase a wise legal sage, "Everyone would accept dog tracks in the snow as evidence that a dog had passed by against the word of a hundred onlookers who swore that it hadn't."

Circumstantial evidence plays a central role in movie trials because rarely is a single piece of circumstantial evidence conclusive. Thus, moviemakers can create tension by developing some evidence that is indicative of guilt, but balancing it with other evidence indicative of innocence. Some examples:

- In *Jagged Edge,* Jack Forrester is charged with the murder of his wife, Page. Prosecutor Krasny's evidence that the couple was having marital difficulties and that a divorce would cause Forrester to lose his extravagant lifestyle is circumstantial evidence that Forrester killed his wife. But the defense evidence that Forrester was wounded in the same attack and that a Manson-like killer may have carried out this and other attacks tends to support his innocence.
- In *Suspect,* Carl Wayne Anderson is charged with killing Elizabeth Quinn. Prosecutor Stella's evidence that Anderson was found with Quinn's purse near the place where her body was found is circumstantial evidence that Anderson killed Quinn. But defense evidence that a person named Michael was seen lurking around Quinn's body before Anderson got there suggests his innocence.
- In *Beyond a Reasonable Doubt,* Tom Garrett is charged with killing Patty Gray. Prosecutor Robinson's evidence that Garrett withdrew $3,000 from his bank account just before Patty was killed and replaced almost all of it right afterwards, along with evidence that Patty was seen waving around $3,000 just

before she died, is circumstantial evidence suggesting that Garrett had a financial motive to kill Gray. Garrett's explanation that he withdrew the money to buy an engagement ring and replaced it when he broke up with his fiancée tends to negate the inference of motive.

Because our legal system leaves the strength of inferences largely up to jurors, a miscarriage of justice can result if jurors give circumstantial evidence more weight than it is logically entitled to. A good example of this is the film, *They Won't Forget.* Robert Hale is charged with killing Mary Clay. District Attorney Griffin's proof is remarkably thin: Hale's coat had a spot of blood on it, and Hale was planning to leave town. Despite the weak evidence, and Hale's innocent explanations for both, he is convicted by jurors who are out to make an example of a northern infidel. In such situations, we have to depend on judges to keep the inference process in check, and ensure that jurors' inferences are reasonable.

Beyond a Reasonable Doubt

Synopsis: A writer plants clues implicating himself in an unsolved murder as a protest against capital punishment, only to become trapped in his own web of lies. It's not nice to fool around with Mother Circumstantial Evidence.

RKO/Bert Friedlob Productions. 1956. Black and white. Running time: 80 min.

Screenplay: Douglas Morrow. Director: Fritz Lang.

Starring: Dana Andrews (Tom Garrett), Joan Fontaine (Susan Spencer), Sidney Blackmer (Austin Spencer), Arthur Franz (Bob Hale), Barbara Nichols (Dolly), Philip Bourneuf (Roy Thompson), Sheppard Strudwick (Jonathan Wilson).

Rating: —▪ —▪ —▪

Surprise ending warning: Reading this analysis could be hazardous to your enjoyment of the movie!

The Story

Tom Garrett is a successful writer who will soon marry Susan Spencer. Susan's father Austin is a newspaper publisher who rails against District Attorney Thompson's penchant to seek executions of murderers convicted by circumstantial evidence. To whip up hostility to capital

Beyond a Reasonable Doubt: The D.A. (Philip Bourneout) reaps what Tom Garrett has sewn.

punishment, Austin develops a scheme to plant clues implicating an innocent person in an unsolved murder. When the person is convicted and sentenced to death, along will come Austin to reveal his innocence. A chastened public will then renounce capital punishment and properly dispose of litter.

Garrett volunteers to become the fall guy in Austin's plan, figuring to turn the experience into another best-seller. Soon the right kind of case comes along, the unsolved murder of nightclub dancer Patty Gray. Photographing their every step, Garrett and Austin spread traces of Patty's body powder inside Garrett's car and toss his cigarette lighter into the bushes near where Patty's body was found. Garrett also dresses like the man who was seen picking up Patty on the night she died, and starts dating Patty's friend Dolly. Dolly becomes fearful, and alerts the police to Garrett's attentions. When Garrett takes Dolly on a ride and begins attacking her, Lieutenant Kennedy arrests him for murdering Patty.

With the planted evidence, Thompson easily builds a strong case against Garrett. Wilson, Garrett's attorney, must have a sense that the trial is being run by the gamblers who fixed the 1919 World Series. Garrett is even hoist on an unplanted petard. Thompson proves that

Patty suddenly came into possession of $3,000 around the time that Garrett withdrew this same amount from his bank account. Garrett explains that he withdrew the money to buy an engagement ring for Susan, but the coincidence further connects Garrett to Patty.

Garrett wins by losing; he is probably the calmest person ever sentenced to death. But panic sets in when Austin dies in a fiery automobile accident that also destroys all the photographs. Garrett hurriedly reveals the secret scheme to Susan and Wilson, who appeal to Thompson for mercy. He's not interested, having already planned a party around the execution. And to prevent the governor from granting Garrett a pardon, Thompson instructs assistant D.A. Bob Hale, Susan's old flame, to look for even more evidence connecting Garrett to Patty. But Hale strikes out, learning only that Patty's former name was Emma.

On the eve of the execution, Austin's executor finds a letter written by Austin detailing the secret plot to implicate Garrett. Thompson finally agrees that he's been had, and asks the governor to pardon Garrett. But before the governor can act, Garrett carelessly refers to Patty as "Emma" in a conversation with Susan. Susan realizes from Garrett's slip of the tongue that he really did kill Patty.

Garrett confesses to Susan that he killed Patty out of love for Susan. Patty (Emma) was supposed to have gotten a divorce to end her loveless marriage to Garrett, but she never did. Austin's scheme provided him with a fool-proof way of clearing a path for his marriage to Susan. Shocked by hearing all this, a distraught Susan tells Hale of Garrett's guilt. Hale calls the governor, who is moments away from signing Garrett's pardon. The governor slowly returns his pen to its holder and Garrett to death row. Thompson, we assume, returns to his caterer; the execution party is on again.

Legal Analysis

This marvelously entertaining film provides an unexpected twist. Its focus is the ambiguity of circumstantial evidence, about as easy a target for screenwriters as Nazis and mustachioed landlords. But as we have stressed, there's nothing wrong with the stuff (see *Circumstantial Evidence,* p. 193). Austin might just as well have directed his anger at the unfairness of convictions based upon uncertain eyewitness identifications, which is direct evidence. Austin may have a valid complaint against capital punishment, but tying his opposition to circumstantial evidence is silly.

Moreover, Austin makes it sound like all of us are in imminent danger of being plucked off the street at any moment and sentenced to death. But the plan that he and Garrett have to concoct belies this risk. The chances of an innocent person (a) dating one of Patty's best friends; (b) having traces of Patty's body powder in his car; and (c) losing a personally inscribed cigarette lighter at the scene of Patty's murder have got to be small. A bettor could probably get better odds on a high school debate team winning the Super Bowl.

Austin's scheme provides Garrett with the impetus to kill Patty. But having done the deed, perhaps he should have backed out of the plan. On the plus side, if Austin's plan succeeds, double jeopardy will protect Garrett from further prosecution even if the truth one day comes out. But on the other, Garrett already stands a good chance of getting away with the crime. The police tell Austin that they have no idea who killed Patty. Even if the police were to dig into Patty's past and find that she was married to Garrett, that would hardly prove that he killed her. Besides, the police are probably more likely to find out about the marriage once they arrest Garrett and try to build a case against him. On balance, Garrett should have suggested to Austin that they scrap the original plan and instead blow the lid off the unfair treatment of jaywalkers.

Even if we disregard the plot twists and assume that Garrett is innocent, Austin and Garrett are not as clever as they think. First, having only one set of photos is risky business. Granted, "Bonus Prints" was not yet a popular marketing device. But Austin owned a newspaper; he could have sprung for a spare set of prints as insurance.

Second, even if Garrett escapes the electric chair, he and Austin will face another criminal trial. You might say that Garrett would be going from the frying pan back to the trier. There's a name for activities like lying to the police and planting phony evidence all around town, and it's not "Scavenger Hunt." It's "obstruction of justice," and it's a serious felony. Thompson doesn't appear to have a rich sense of humor. He's unlikely to react by going, "Great coup, boys; you got us good. Let me in on the planning for the phony Russian atomic attack." Garrett and Austin could well have gone to prison, hardly a pleasant thought for a newspaper publisher and a best-selling author.

Observers of the legal system can only marvel at how quickly Garrett goes from death row to nearly being pardoned to returning to death row. A pardon is an important act; it has the same legal effect as a verdict of "not guilty." The governor would undoubtedly have referred Thompson's request to pardon Garrett to a committee, in the meantime delaying Garrett's scheduled execution. Hale's phone call would not have dramatically reversed a pardon decision; that decision would not have been made yet.

Patty Gray's killer was seen smoking a pipe. The cleverest moment of the trial occurs during Garrett's cross-examination, when he tells Thompson that he has never smoked a pipe. Thompson then turns to a pipe smoker on the jury and asks him to light up. After the juror does so, he tamps down the tobacco with his matchbook cover, leaving a small brown circle on the cover. Thompson then triumphantly produces identically marked matchbook covers, which the police had found in Garrett's garage. Garrett lamely explains that they must have been left by pipe-smoking friends of his. Unfortunately for Thompson, his ploy was highly improper and would probably have constituted reversible error. Jurors may often wish that they could "pipe up" in the middle of trial, but an attorney cannot make them into witnesses. Thompson should either have provided expert testimony about the significance of the brown circles on the matchbooks in Garrett's garage, or simply asked the jurors to infer from their own experiences that those circles meant that Garrett smoked a pipe.

If the dramatic turn of events at the end of the film did in Garrett, think what it did to future defendants. Who would want to be the next attorney who goes in to Thompson to complain that the police got the wrong guy?

Boomerang

Synopsis: A prosecutor refuses to give in to public pressure to convict a suspected murderer, and instead proves him innocent. A true story, told in a gritty semi-documentary style.

Twentieth Century Fox (Louis de Rochemont). 1947. Black and white. Running time: 88 min.

Screenplay: Richard Murphy. Original story: Anthony Abbott. Director: Elia Kazan.

Starring: Dana Andrews (Henry Harvey), Lee J. Cobb (Police Chief Robinson), Cara Williams (Madge Harvey), Arthur Kennedy (John Waldron), Sam Levene (Dave Woods), Karl Malden (Lt. White), Ed Begley (Paul Harris), Wryley Birch (Father Lambert).

Rating: [gavel] [gavel] [gavel]

The Story

Father Lambert is a beloved priest in Bridgeport, Connecticut. While taking his regular evening constitutional, he is killed in a walk-by shooting. A number of other people are in the vicinity, but the killer escapes.

As the days pass without an arrest, the old-line politicians who for years had run city affairs for their personal gain whip the public into

Boomerang: Prosecutor Henry Harvey (Dana Andrews), right, tries to free an accused murderer.

a frenzy. The recently elected progressives fear they will be voted out in the upcoming election unless the killer is found. They put pressure on Chief Robinson and Henry Harvey, the prosecutor, to solve the case.

The chief gets a break when Ohio police arrest John Waldron. Waldron fits the general description of Father Lambert's killer and was in Bridgeport on the night of the murder. Waldron is returned to Bridgeport, and the evidence against him mounts. Eyewitnesses identify him as the killer; he left town soon after the killing; and a ballistics report indicates that the fatal bullet came from his gun. After being mercilessly questioned and taunted by the police for two days, Waldron confesses. When Waldron is bound over on a charge of murder after a coroner's inquest (like a preliminary hearing), the citizenry exults. If they had their way, he'd also be charged with spreading the bubonic plague and inventing calories.

But Harvey suspects that Waldron is a victim of mob psychology, and continues to investigate. At the next court hearing, Harvey stuns his political allies by systematically advancing and then destroying the prosecution's case. He demonstrates that some of the eyewitnesses are confused or biased, and then informs the judge of the results of an experiment in which he and seven assistants reenacted the crime seven different times. No one could recognize the killer from the eyewitnesses' locations. He undermines the confession by reading aloud from the transcript of the brutal police interrogation. Harvey submits reports from five ballistics experts who state that Waldron's gun could not have fired the fatal bullet. Finally, Harvey plays a courtroom version of Russian Roulette. He has the judge load Waldron's gun, and then asks an assistant to fire it at the back of his (Harvey's) head at the same angle as the shot that killed Father Lambert. The assistant pulls the trigger, but the gun fails to fire. Harvey explains that the firing pin is broken, and that the gun had failed to fire in sixteen previous attempts.

A relieved Waldron is freed. Though a few cynics remain, most of the citizens are grateful that Harvey has saved them from convicting an innocent man.

Legal Analysis

An important protection in the American system of justice is that prosecutors rather than police officers usually make the decisions about who to prosecute. And if a prosecutor like Harvey believes that evidence is not strong enough to prove a defendant's guilt beyond a reasonable doubt, the prosecutor has a duty not to proceed. Rarely, though, will prosecutors have the time or the inclination to conduct an independent investigation as thorough as Harvey's. Harvey not only had to buck the public clamor for Waldron's blood, but also he had to contradict the politicians, police officers, and scientific technicians he has to work with every day. Harvey was not a team player, and he might be kicked off the team, even though he was right.

Before publicly destroying the case against Waldron, Harvey tells the judge that he is considering dropping the charges. The judge uses this as an opportunity to show off his Latin, angrily responding that he will not permit a "nolle prosequi" (a prosecution decision to abandon a case). Perhaps the judge studied too much Latin and not enough law, for he cannot force Harvey to proceed against his will. To do so would violate our country's fundamental notion of separation of powers: Prosecutors are part of the executive branch of government, and judges are in the judicial branch.

Harvey's public attack on the evidence provides Waldron with far greater protection than a "nolle prosequi" anyway. For one thing, a "nolle prosequi" would not prevent another prosecutor from refiling the same charges. Because Waldron's trial has not yet begun, another prosecutor could start over again without violating the rule forbidding double jeopardy.

But more importantly, the angry townspeople would remain convinced that Waldron was guilty if Harvey quietly dropped the charges. They might decide to lynch Waldron, and save the other end of the rope for Harvey. Harvey's predicament is inherent in the system—charges can be dropped or a defendant can be found "not guilty," but there's no mechanism for pronouncing a defendant innocent. Thus, Harvey's public attack on the evidence is a clever means of persuading the community that Waldron really is innocent.

The police interrogation of Waldron dramatically illustrates the psychological forces that can impel an innocent person to confess. They refuse his request for a lawyer, subject him to rapid-fire questioning, wear him down, and ultimately lead him into confessing. Just in time—the only thing left in their arsenal was repeated playings of Kate Smith singing "God Bless America." The refusal to honor Waldron's request for a lawyer means that Waldron's confession could not be offered into evidence under the rule of *Miranda v. Azizona,* decided in the mid-1960s. But even before *Miranda,* Waldron's confession would have been inadmissible in evidence because he was coerced into giving it. What is astonishing is that the police made a transcript of the interrogation. They obviously didn't think they were doing anything wrong, and may even have been hoping to win a prize from the Committee to Bring Back the Middle Ages.

Waldron is broke and has to settle for whoever the judge appoints, so it's not surprising that O'Shea, the appointed counsel, is inept. The best thing O'Shea does is keep quiet during Harvey's presentation. He's got to realize that Waldron's chances are looking good when Harvey stands in front of Waldron's gun and has it fired.

But before that, O'Shea is incompetent. He plans to show that Waldron was temporarily insane when he killed Father Lambert. A hard defense to prove given Waldron's story that he didn't shoot the priest at all. If O'Shea is unwilling to represent Waldron's interests, he should withdraw. Moreover, O'Shea should have moved for a change of venue. The entire town stands ready to convict Waldron, and there's no way he could have gotten a fair trial in Bridgeport.

The film illustrates how easily overzealousness and emotion can lead to injustice. But it also suggests a way for hard-pressed cities to balance their budgets. With prosecutors like Harvey around, who needs defense attorneys?

Trial Briefs

1. The film is based on the still-unsolved murder of an Episcopal priest in Bridgeport, Connecticut, in 1924. The name of the town is

not identified in the movie, apparently due to the hard feelings that still lingered when the movie was made over twenty years later. The prosecutor was not, as suggested in the movie, a young prosecutor just becoming part of political life. He was Homer E. Cummings, an experienced and well-known prosecutor who became U.S. attorney general in the Franklin Roosevelt administration.

2. Though he could not force Harvey to prosecute Waldron, the judge was not completely toothless. The judge might have written a letter asking the state's attorney general's office to take over the case. Though Harvey's motives are pure and professional, in other situations a dismissal might reflect corruption or ineptness in a local prosecutor's office.

A famous case in which a state took over when a local prosecutor declined to go forward involved Angelo Buono, the notorious Los Angeles "Hillside Strangler." Buono was charged with killing several people in the Los Angeles hillsides. The local district attorney asked the trial judge to drop the charges, on the ground that Kenneth Bianchi, the primary witness against Buono, had changed his story and therefore made a conviction impossible. The judge referred the case to the California attorney general, who took over the case and got a conviction. Buono was sentenced to life in prison.

Fury

Synopsis: A brutal lynch mob burns down the jail to kill an innocent man. But oh boy, does he get his revenge.

MGM (Joseph L. Mankiewicz). 1936. Black and white. Running time: 94 min.

Screenplay: Bartlett Cormack and Fritz Lang. Original story: Norman Krasna. Director: Fritz Lang.

Starring: Spencer Tracy (Joe Wilson), Sylvia Sidney (Katherine Grant), Walter Abel (District Attorney Adams), Edward Ellis (Sheriff), Walter Brennan (Buggs Meyers), Bruce Cabot (Bubbles Dawson).

Academy Award: Best Original Story.

Rating: —▮ —▮ —▮ —▮

The Story

Joe Wilson is an ordinary guy trying to make a living during the depression. Wilson is on his way to marry his fiancée, Katherine Grant, when Deputy Meyers arrests him on suspicion of being part of a kidnapping team. Wilson is totally innocent, but by horrible luck a $5 bill in his pocket matches the serial numbers for the ransom money.

Fury: D.A. Adams (Walter Abel) is not proposing marriage to Katherine Grant (Sylvia Sidney), but instead asking her to identify the fateful ring.

Meyers stupidly lets his wife know that they are holding a kidnap suspect in the local lockup. Immediately, rumors start flying around the peaceful midwestern town of Strand. Rabble-rousers rouse the rabble. The solid citizens of Strand are not about to wait for the niceties of due process. They storm the jail, batter down the door, and set the place afire. A motley collection of town morons hold their babies up to get a better view or munch hotdogs during the fabulous entertainment. All the action is filmed for the newsreels. The governor could have sent in the militia, but decides against it since it might further irritate the locals. He may, however, go slow on Strand's request for a bailout loan for a new jail.

Hearing of Wilson's arrest, Grant arrives in Strand just as fire is consuming the prison. She sees Wilson surrounded by flames, screaming in terror through the prison window, and she faints dead away. In fact, Wilson escapes and rejoins Tom and Charlie, his two dim-witted brothers back in Chicago. He is determined to exact his revenge and sends the brothers to Strand to demand that the lynch mob be tried for murder. State law provides that if death occurs through the actions of a lynch mob, it's first-degree murder. Thus the brothers don't tell the determined D.A., Adams, that Wilson is alive.

Adams indicts twenty-two Strandites for murder. The town closes ranks around the accused. By this time, the real kidnappers have been caught, so everyone realizes Wilson was innocent. It was a shame that an innocent man got burned to death, but hey—forgive and forget. Even the sheriff, who fought the mob heroically, comes down with selective amnesia.

Adams calls several witnesses and each serves up a perjured alibi. Then he screens the newsreel which, inexplicably, seems to catch the defense by surprise. The newsreel provides evidence that all twenty-two were involved. It also clears the way to indict the alibi witnesses for perjury. Unlike the average murder victim, Wilson listens to the trial live on his radio and is delighted by the proceedings. It looks like the mob is going to jail (if only Strand had one) or even to the chair.

Since Wilson's body was never found, there's a big hole in the prosecution's case. Grant (Wilson's fiancée) provides the key testimony that Wilson was in the jail at the time of the fire. But she's starting to suspect that Wilson is alive (one of the brothers is wearing his raincoat). The defense undermines her testimony on cross-examination, and then moves for a dismissal because Adams failed to prove that Wilson or anybody else actually died in the fire.

Seeing his carefully prepared frame-up tottering, Wilson mails the judge his own burned ring together with a phony letter from an anonymous citizen who claims to have found it in the ruins of the jail. Grant testifies that she gave Wilson the ring—but she knows that he wrote the letter (he habitually uses "momentum" when he means "memento"). Her false testimony pretty well seals the fate of the twenty-two defendants.

The brothers and Grant have had enough and want to stop the charade before it's too late. Wilson insists on having his revenge, even if they abandon him. In haunting scenes, he walks the town at night, alone. Bit by bit, he realizes that he has become the lynch mob. Just in time, he strides into the courtroom and 'fesses up. Grant embraces him; all is forgiven. Strand gets its varsity mob back for the upcoming lynch-offs.

Legal Analysis

The lynch mob is a potent symbol of injustice, and it contrasts vividly with the due process provided to the twenty-two accused members of the mob. Lynch mobs appear in several of our films, including *The*

Oxbow Incident and *They Won't Forget.* But none of them are as scary and realistic as the mob in *Fury.*

The crusading Adams refers to seven thousand lynchings taking place in the last forty-nine years, but almost no prosecutions. That may very well have been accurate. Generally, law enforcement personnel and prosecutors, especially in the South, turned a blind eye at lynch mobs and other vigilantes. Even when the members of mobs were prosecuted, juries were reluctant to convict them—especially in cases of whites who lynched blacks. Lynchings have been successfully prosecuted under the federal civil rights laws, which were enacted after the Civil War and brought to life by court decisions one hundred years after their enactment.

Everybody commits perjury at the trial of the twenty-two defendants. As perjury may be much more common than judges and lawyers would like to admit, it's refreshing to see Adams set up the alibi witnesses for a perjury rap. However, it was probably an improper trial tactic. Generally, an attorney cannot put on testimony that he knows is perjured, even for the purpose of discrediting it. In addition, the relevance of the evidence to Adams's case is unclear: these witnesses are lying about the defendant's alibis, therefore . . . what? The fact that some witnesses lied to save the defendants' skins doesn't tell you whether the defendants put them up to lying. Adams should have just shown the newsreel and been done with it.

Wilson commits no crime by failing to come forward and announce that he is alive, though he may have difficulty getting a library card if the killers are convicted. But he crosses the line into criminality by conspiring with his brothers to have the mob prosecuted for lynching him. He and the brothers arrange for Grant to testify (truthfully, she thinks) that Wilson was in the prison. And he even mails in the burned ring to cinch the case.

What crime have Wilson and his brothers conspired to commit? At least, they have conspired to obstruct justice. Even worse, they have probably conspired to commit murder—to cause the death of the twenty-two people. The fact that the twenty-two will be killed through the legal process doesn't matter. If the twenty-two had been executed and the plot was uncovered, Wilson, Tom, and Charlie might well have found themselves on trial for murder.

The criminal trial of the twenty-two defendants has its bumpy spots. Both attorneys feel free to make speeches to the jury in the midst of the trial. Adams commits a serious error by blurting out that one defendant (Bubbles Dawson) has served two years in prison. Such evidence would not have been admissible even if the defendant had testified—and he had not (see *Character Evidence,* p. 259). This statement was serious prosecutorial misconduct and the judge probably should have declared a mistrial. The anonymous letter the judge received along with the ring is inadmissible. The letter is improper hearsay because it's used to prove the truth of its contents (i.e., that the ring was found in the ruins of the jail). (See *The Hearsay Rule,* p. 163.) And since the letter cannot be admitted, neither can the ring, since there's no admissible evidence of where it was found and by whom.

The lynching scene and the trial in *Fury* are absolutely riveting. The story is ingenious and the direction and acting are superb. *Fury* reminds us how thin the veneer of civilization can be and how little it takes to incite mob violence in a peaceful midwestern town.

Trial Brief

The great Viennese director Fritz Lang cowrote and directed *Fury.* Lang also directed another classic four-gaveler, *M,* which was made in Germany in 1931. *Fury* was Lang's first American film after fleeing the Nazis. The harrowing lynch mob scenes in *Fury* must have drawn heavily on his personal experience in Nazi Germany. For example, the sheriff blames the whole fiasco on unknown people from out of town— which sounds quite a bit like Hitler blaming the Jews for Germany's troubles.

The film was first titled *The Mob* and then *Mob Rule* but the Hays Office (the official Hollywood censors) rejected both titles. Supposedly, MGM also softened the hard edges of the script, especially at the end. Louis B. Mayer detested Lang, so MGM released the movie without publicity in hopes it would flop, so they could get rid of Lang. Fortunately the critics found the movie and immediately declared it to be a classic.

The film is based on an incident that occurred in San Jose, California, in 1933. A mob dragged two accused kidnappers from their cells and hanged them in a public park. All the action was captured on newsreels. The governor of California, Sunny Jim Rolfe, refused to send in the militia and later declared that the lynching was the best lesson ever given the country. Nobody was charged with a crime.

I Confess

Synopsis: A Catholic priest's silence about a confession lands him in court for a murder actually committed by the confessor.

Warner Bros. (Alfred Hitchcock). 1953. Black and white. Running time: 95 min.

Screenplay: George Tabori and William Archibald. Director: Alfred Hitchcock.

Cast: Montgomery Clift (Father Michael Logan), Anne Baxter (Ruth Grandfort), Karl Malden (Police Inspector Larrue), Brian Ahearne (Public Prosecutor Willie Robertson), O.E. Hasse (Otto Keller).

Rating: —■ —■

The Story

Father Michael Logan, a Quebec priest, hears the confession of Otto Keller, who works as a church caretaker. Keller tells Father Logan how he (Keller) disguised himself as a priest and attempted to rob Villett, but killed him in the process. Suspicion falls on Father Logan after two young girls report seeing a priest leaving Villett's home around the time of the murder. Also, Father Logan, unwilling to talk to or about anyone, whether they've confessed to him or not, refuses to explain his whereabouts at the time of the murder to Inspector Larrue.

In an effort to clear Logan, Ruth Grandfort, his prewar, precollar flame, explains to the police that Villett was blackmailing her. She's vulnerable because, before Logan became a priest, Villett saw her and Logan spend a night together to escape a storm. (How quaint. Today, Villett's story wouldn't even get the attention of a supermarket tabloid unless he had photos of Grandfort and Logan spending the night together in an alien's spaceship.) However, Inspector Larrue regards Grandfort's story as evidence that Father Logan had a motive to kill Villett. Finally, the police find a bloody priest's cassock stashed away in the bottom of a chest belonging to Father Logan; the blood type matches Villett's.

Father Logan goes on trial for the murder of Villett. He denies killing Villett, but still refuses to say anything about Keller's confession. The jury finds him not guilty anyway. Keller goes berserk, yelling that Father Logan has told the police about his confession. At this point Inspector Larrue finally realizes that Father Logan is innocent. The police corner Keller in a ballroom of a hotel. Father Logan approaches Keller to ask him to give himself up. Keller is about to shoot Father Logan, but before Keller can do so, he is killed by the police.

Legal Analysis

The film's trial sequence is abbreviated; only the public prosecutor asks questions of a police officer and Father Logan. Lest Americans think that due process of law stops at the Canadian border, be assured that Canadian law too allows criminal defendants to present a defense and cross-examine the prosecution's witnesses. Even in Quebec.

The movie's central legal issue revolves around what is known as the "priest-penitent privilege." This privilege had its origins in the sanctity of Catholic confessions. Today, the privilege extends to any religious sect or denomination that authorizes its leaders to receive confidential disclosures, even if those leaders don't wear black robes and funny-looking hats. However, before confessing a serious misdeed to your religious leader or guru, better ask him or her for the latest copy of your state's rules of evidence.

The priest-penitent privilege prevents a clergyperson from revealing statements made in religious confidence. The privilege protects the secrecy of the confessional while protecting clergy from being forced to choose between betrayal of confidences and risking possible jail sentences for refusing to testify. However, the Constitution does not require states to recognize the priest-penitent privilege. Any state is free to enact a law requiring clergypeople to reveal matters told to them in private. One sure consequence is that clergypeople in such states would miss out on a lot of juicy secrets.

Thus, Father Logan properly invokes the priest-penitent privilege to refuse to disclose what Keller told him. In fact, even if Father Logan wanted to testify to Keller's confession, at Keller's request the judge would have to prevent Father Logan from doing so. Keller is the "owner" of the privilege. This means that he can choose to reveal what he said to Father Logan, but Father Logan must remain silent unless Keller authorizes him to speak.

Before the trial begins, Keller tells his wife of his confession to Father Logan. By so doing Keller risks giving up his privilege, because privileges usually end when a person who makes a confidential statement tells somebody else about it. However, a separate privilege exists for statements made by one spouse to another. Therefore, even if Father Logan found out that Keller had revealed his confession to his wife, Keller would still be able to prevent Father Logan from testifying. Keller is either very lucky, or he is really an evidence expert masquerading as a church caretaker.

Nevertheless, Father Logan is not as helpless to defend himself as the movie makes it appear. Looking out of his church window on the night of Villett's death, Father Logan sees a shadowy figure hurry into the church. He realizes that the figure was Keller, who after a brief conversation asks to make his confession. Father Logan could properly testify to all of his observations preceding the confession. The priest-penitent privilege applies only to Keller's confession, not to the activities leading up to it. Had the film not exaggerated the impact of the privilege on Father Logan, probably Keller and not Father Logan would have ended up being tried for Villett's murder.

The jury's "not guilty" verdict and the events following it reinforce an important reality about our criminal justice system. The foreman of the jury is careful to say that the prosecution has not sufficiently overcome the jurors' doubts about whether Father Logan is guilty. This is far different from a statement that Father Logan is innocent. The distinction is well understood by the angry mob that hounds Father Logan as he leaves the courtroom, yelling that he killed Villett and demanding that he leave the church.

The scene is a reminder that even if a judge or jury pronounces a defendant "not guilty," many people continue to believe that the defendant really is guilty. The Scots have found a way around this. Jurors in Scotland have a choice of three verdicts: Guilty, Not Proven, and Not Guilty. A defendant gets off if the jury comes back either "Not Proven" or "Not Guilty." The former verdict means, "You might be guilty, but the government didn't prove it so you're free." The latter verdict means, "We really think you're innocent." So a "Not Guilty" verdict in Scotland really clears a person's name. Of course, a Scottish jury might also come back "Not Kilty." This verdict means, "We don't really know if you're a Scot."

A Place in the Sun

Synopsis: A man takes his fiancée for a boat ride and decides to kill her. He gets cold (and wet) feet, but faces a murder charge when she accidentally drowns.

Paramount (George Stevens). 1951. Black and white. Running time: 122 min.

Novel: An American Tragedy by Theodore Dreiser. Screenplay: Michael Wilson and Harry Brown. Director: George Stevens.

Starring: Montgomery Clift (George Eastman), Elizabeth Taylor (Angela Vickers), Shelley Winters (Alice Tripp), Raymond Burr (Frank Marlowe).

Academy Awards: Best Screenplay, Best Director, Best Musical Score, Best Cinematography, Best Editing.

Academy Award nominations: Best Picture, Best Actor (Montgomery Clift), Best Supporting Actress (Shelley Winters).

Rating: —▮ —▮ —▮

The Story

George Eastman, the poor relation of a wealthy family, is given a job in his uncle's factory. There he begins dating Alice Tripp, a fellow assembly line worker. Later Eastman falls in love with Angela Vickers. Vickers is wealthy and beautiful—giving her two advantages over Tripp. But Tripp is pregnant and unable to arrange for an abortion. (Under the Hays Code prevailing at the time, the word "abortion"

A Place in the Sun: The D.A. (Raymond Burr) prepares to sink George Eastman's (Montgomery Clift) rowboat.

could not be used.) Eastman and Vickers want to marry, but can't figure out how to get rid of Tripp—who is threatening publicity and suicide if Eastman won't tie the knot.

Tripp comes to the Vickers's summer place to confront Eastman. She drags him to the courthouse to get married, but the clerk's office is closed for Labor Day. Eastman takes her for a boat ride on Loon Lake, which sports the spookiest bird calls in movie history. Eastman considers overturning the boat and drowning Tripp (who can't swim), but cannot bring himself to do it. Nevertheless, when Tripp stands up in the boat, it overturns and she is drowned. It is unclear whether Eastman could have saved her.

At Eastman's murder trial, there is overwhelming circumstantial evidence against him. District Attorney Marlowe engages in a brutal cross-examination which effectively destroys Eastman's credibility. The highlight occurs when the rowboat is brought into the courtroom and Eastman has difficulty reconstructing the accident. Hardly surprising, since the designers of the courtroom forgot to include a lake. At the climax, the D.A. accuses Eastman of striking Tripp with an oar and he dramatically smashes the oar across the boat. Eastman is convicted and goes to the electric chair.

Legal Analysis

A perplexing legal issue lies at the heart of *A Place in the Sun*. We know that Eastman is innocent of the charge of overturning the boat to drown Tripp. He planned to do it but he didn't; the boat capsized accidentally. Nevertheless, it is possible that he could have saved Tripp had he tried.

Normally in American criminal or tort law, there is no duty to rescue another person. It is legally permissible (though morally reprehensible) to sit on the beach and watch another drown without even calling for help. However, in many special relationships, there is a duty to rescue. For example, had Eastman and Tripp been married, such a duty would be imposed. It is very possible that a duty would have been imposed in this case based on the fact that Eastman encouraged Tripp to go rowing with him when he knew she could not swim. Moreover, Eastman was the father of their unborn child and had attempted to marry Tripp that very day.

But it is also possible that no such duty would be imposed. Eastman and Tripp were not married, Tripp assumed the risk by going rowing with Eastman and negligently overturning the boat, and it would have been quite risky for Eastman to have tried to save Tripp from drowning in the middle of a deep lake in the dark. Assuming that Eastman had a duty to try to rescue Tripp but consciously decided not to, Eastman's failure could constitute homicide. Probably, however, it would not be first-degree murder but, at most, second-degree murder or involuntary manslaughter. These theories should have been presented to the jury (assuming it were found that Eastman owed a duty to Tripp to rescue her).

Eastman was convicted solely on circumstantial evidence, meaning there was no direct testimony of a witness who had seen him kill Tripp. The circumstantial evidence was, however, quite powerful. It is brought out very effectively in the movie by a series of quick cuts of the testimony of the prosecution's witnesses: the doctor, Tripp's landlady, the boatman to whom Eastman gave a fake name, a witness who had seen Eastman and Tripp quarreling, a camper that Eastman stumbled over after swimming to shore, and several others. Circumstantial evidence can be very reliable as proof, but the inferences it creates can sometimes be incorrect, as they were in this case (see *Circumstantial Evidence,* p. 193).

Eastman's rich uncle pays for his counsel, on the stipulation that Vickers's name will be kept out of the trial. It is not clear whether it would have done Eastman any good to have called Vickers to testify on his behalf; indeed she could have been a prosecution witness whose testimony would have created another link in the chain of circumstantial evidence against Eastman. However, it is troubling that counsel would accept representation in a capital case on the condition that a key witness not be named or called to testify. Such decisions belong to the client, not to the person who is paying the attorney. It is equally troubling that the D.A. would not call Vickers as a witness because of the high social standing of her family.

The D.A. clearly overreaches in his presentation. Breaking the oar over the rowboat was dramatic but improper; it proves nothing but could inflame the passion of the jury by implying that Eastman busted an oar over Tripp's head or shoved her down in the water with the oar. Similarly, the D.A. errs in his questioning of the boatman by giving a speech about how Eastman set things up to avoid witnesses. This sort of prosecutorial overzealousness could easily get the conviction reversed on appeal.

A Place in the Sun is a great picture about class differences. The working-class Eastman had no business mixing with his betters or aspiring to wed the aristocratic Vickers. However, the electric chair seems a bit harsh as a punishment for trying to rise above one's station in life.

Presumed Innocent

Synopsis: A district attorney is charged with the brutal murder of an office colleague with whom he'd been having an affair. But they're model citizens compared to the other D.A.s.

Warner/Mirage (Sydney Pollack and Mark Rosenberg). 1990. Color. Running time: 127 min.

Screenplay: Frank Pierson and Alan J. Pakula. Novel: Scott Turow. Director: Alan J. Pakula.

Starring: Harrison Ford (Rusty Sabich), Brian Dennehy (Raymond Horgan), Raul Julia (Sandy Stern), Bonnie Bedelia (Barbara Sabich), Paul Winfield (Judge Lytle), Greta Scacchi (Carolyn Polhemus).

Rating: —■ —■ —■

Surprise ending warning: Reading this summary may be hazardous to your enjoyment of the movie!

The Story

Rusty Sabich is chief deputy district attorney. His boss, D.A. Raymond Horgan, is facing a tough election challenge from Nicco della Guardia. Sabich learns that another deputy, the glamorous Carolyn Polhemus, has been brutally raped and murdered. Horgan asks Sabich to head up the investigation—an unwelcome assignment since Polhemus had

Presumed Innocent: Sandy Stern (Raul Julia) confers with Rusty Sabich (Harrison Ford) and his wife Barbara (Bonnie Bedelia).

recently ditched Sabich after a torrid affair and taken up with Horgan. Sabich gets his trusted cop friend Lipranzer to do the legwork.

After della Guardia wins the election, Sabich finds himself charged with Polhemus's murder. Della Guardia and his new deputy, Tommy Molto, lead the prosecution team. Things look mighty grim for Sabich fans, including his loyal wife Barbara and his young son. A beer glass with Sabich's prints is found in Polhemus's apartment. There were numerous phone calls from Sabich's house to Polhemus's apartment, including one on the night of the murder. A semen sample taken from Polhemus matches Sabich's blood type. The police, armed with a search warrant for Sabich's home, find clothing stained with Polhemus's blood and traces of her carpet. However, evidently not wanting to run up the score on Sabich, the officers executing the warrant do not search for the murder weapon.

Before his being pulled off the Polhemus investigation, Sabich found that the former D.A., Horgan, had referred a bribery investigation (a "B-file") to Polhemus, though her normal assignment was sex crimes. The B-file was based on an allegation that a D.A. had taken a $1,500 bribe to dismiss a criminal case. Strangely, Polhemus, Horgan, and Molto were all involved in the case. Worst of all, according to a sleazy informant whom Lipranzer and Sabich terrify into talking, the bribe may have been paid to Larren Lytle—the judge who will preside over Sabich's trial. With the law enforcement folks committing so many crimes, the local crooks are probably hard pressed to find jobs to pull.

Sabich retains the crafty Sandy Stern as his lawyer and wisely clams up, taking the Fifth before the grand jury. At the trial, della Guardia and Molto are as inept as they are corrupt. Their case falters badly when the beer glass with Sabich's prints cannot be located. Although the judge admits oral testimony that Sabich's prints were found on the glass, the evidence is much weaker because the glass was lost.

Horgan testifies (falsely) that Sabich volunteered to head up the investigation of the Polhemus case, a chore which would be highly unusual given Sabich's administrative duties. Horgan also testifies that Sabich dragged his feet on the investigation and had ordered only a restricted search for matching prints that would not have turned up his own prints. When Stern asks Horgan about the B-file, everybody gets extremely jumpy—and with good reason, since most of the people in the courtroom were apparently involved in the bribery.

Much worse for della Guardia, Stern's skillful cross-examination annihilates the pathologist who testifies about the semen sample. It seems that the sample included traces of a spermicide normally used with a diaphragm, but Polhemus was not wearing a diaphragm. The case collapses when the coroner is confronted with the fact that Polhemus's tubes were tied. Therefore, she would not have been using a spermicide, so the semen sample must have come from someone else. Judge Lytle grants Stern's motion to dismiss and discharges Sabich.

Then follow a series of stunning plot twists. First, Stern reveals that he threatened Judge Lytle with disclosure of the B-file. Could this have been the reason that Lytle dismissed Sabich's case? Stern assures us that Lytle would have dismissed it anyway. Not likely in view of the strong prosecution case.

Then we find that Lipranzer had kept the beer glass when he was kicked off the case. Since nobody asked him for it, he just never turned it over to della Guardia. He assumed that his friend Sabich was guilty and wanted to obstruct the prosecution. Besides, he'd be prepared if he worked on a case involving stolen beer.

Finally, Sabich accidentally discovers the murder weapon in his own toolbox. It's a small hammer obviously soaked with blood and blond hair. As he washes the weapon, Barbara enters. She is the killer. She phoned Polhemus from home, went to her apartment, and bashed her head in with the hammer. She left the murder weapon, covered with blood and hair, in Sabich's toolbox where she figured the police would find it. She planted the beer glass with Sabich's fingerprints in the apartment and she injected Sabich's semen (which she had thoughtfully bagged and frozen for the occasion) into Polhemus's vagina. Barbara's ability to create such a skillful frame-up shows that she was paying attention at D.A. office parties.

Barbara claims that she would have spoken up in time to save Sabich from the gas chamber. Not so certain, Sabich sits in the empty courtroom, forever afraid to look in his toolbox and his freezer.

Legal Analysis

Although the trial scenes are well done and the story's climax surprising, the plot of *Presumed Innocent* defies belief. For example, Stern would never have privately threatened Judge Lytle with disclosure that he had once taken a bribe. If this ploy had backfired, Stern would be through practicing law. Making an ex parte contact with a judge is unethical, and extortion is downright criminal. As criminal lawyers like to say, "Sometimes somebody has to go to jail—make sure it's the client."

Also, the police would surely have found the bloody hammer in Sabich's toolbox when they executed the warrant, and there would have been no chance of a dismissal. To explain the police failure to find the hammer, Sabich explains that they did not search for the murder weapon, because failure to find it could be used as evidence that Sabich was innocent. This is hogwash. Failure to find the murder weapon hurts della Guardia's case whether the police have searched for it or not. Similarly, Lipranzer would not want to jeopardize his police career by holding on to the beer glass. Between Lipranzer and the beer in the glass, the latter had a better head.

On cross-examination of Horgan, Stern is allowed to introduce the B-file into evidence. The apparent rationale is that it gives the jury a reason to distrust Horgan, because Horgan had the B-file in his desk and didn't turn it over to Sabich until Sabich demanded it. That suggests that Horgan, not Sabich, dragged his feet in investigating Polhemus's death. But Judge Lytle should have ruled evidence of the B-file inadmissible, since its probative value (if any) is outweighed by the probability that its admission would consume a lot of time and confuse the issues in the minds of the jury. Of course, in a criminal case, a judge often errs in favor of admitting defense evidence, since this error cannot be appealed (while an evidence ruling against the defense can be the subject of a successful appeal).

Judge Lytle should not have granted Stern's motion to dismiss. Della Guardia's case against Sabich was strong enough to go to the jury despite the fiasco with the semen sample. There was still the evidence of the phone calls and the prints on the beer glass, plus the clothing contaminated with Polhemus's blood, hair, and carpet fiber. And there was Horgan's testimony that Sabich had acted quite suspiciously in investigating the Polhemus affair. All this is more than enough to get to the jury. Thus Lytle's action can only be explained by Stern's attempt to blackmail him.

Polhemus's character is viciously stereotypical. Her entire career was based on sleeping her way to the top. She was sleeping with Lytle at the time of the bribery incident, and in return he got her appointed as a D.A. straight out of law school. Her affair with Sabich was designed to get her appointed chief deputy, because she was hoping that Horgan would resign and appoint Sabich D.A. When this didn't work out, she dumped Sabich and invited Horgan into her bed. Professional women don't need another glamorous movie character who gets ahead by adroitly selecting the right sex partners (see *Women Trial Lawyers in the Movies,* p. 90).

There are some realistic scenes of Sabich conferring with Stern about trial strategy. At one point, Sabich says he is innocent. Stern says nothing. He probably doesn't believe Sabich and he doesn't want to know. His job is to defend Sabich, and whether Sabich did it or not just doesn't matter. This is the way criminal defense attorneys look at their jobs, although it is a difficult role for the general public to accept. Under our system, the prosecution must prove guilt, for every defendant is "presumed innocent." The defense lawyer's job is to make the state prove it, and the defendant's actual guilt or innocence is a question for the jury, not the defense lawyer, to resolve.

As things stand, Sabich can't really turn Barbara in, since there's no evidence against her. Because of the spousal privilege, he cannot testify to her confession to him. Della Guardia probably doesn't even want to hear more about the Polhemus case anyway.

The movie leaves unclear the critical and fascinating question of whether Barbara would have really spoken up to save Sabich if he had been convicted. Her frame-up job against him was overwhelmingly effective. The combination of the blood, semen, carpet, fingerprints, phone calls, and hammer should certainly have resulted in Sabich being convicted and probably sentenced to death had the plan not gone astray. Barbara claims she would have saved him by confessing her own guilt in time. But would she really have done so? And, if she had, would anyone have believed her?

They Won't Believe Me

Synopsis: A philandering husband is on trial for murdering his wife. He admits trying to kill her, but claims that she died from a fall before he could do the deed.

RKO Radio Pictures (Joan Harrison). 1947. Black and white. Running time: 80 min.

Screenplay: Jonathan Latimer. Director: Irving Pichel.

Starring: Robert Young (Lawrence Ballentine), Susan Hayward (Verna Carlson), Jane Greer (Greta Ballentine).

Rating: —■ —■ —■

Surprise ending warning: Reading this summary may be hazardous to your enjoyment of the movie!

The Story

Lawrence Ballentine is on trial for the murder of his wife Greta. Ballentine's attorney opens the defense by telling the jurors that all of the state's witnesses, whose testimony we do not see, were accurate and truthful. These are not exactly words that bolster Ballentine's confidence. But the attorney then explains that even if the state's witnesses were truthful, Ballentine is innocent. Ballentine is the only defense witness, and his story unfolds in flashbacks.

Ballentine admits that he is a scoundrel who was in love only with Greta's fortune. When he threatens to leave her for a girlfriend named Janice, Greta proves that the quickest way to Ballentine's heart is through her wallet. Greta coolly wins him back by purchasing a big house in far-off Beverly Hills and buying him a partnership in a stock brokerage.

But Ballentine didn't sell his loyalty to Greta; he just leased it to her for a few months. He's soon snared by the temptations of Verna Carlson, and again prepares to walk out on Greta. Greta sells back his partnership interest and moves to a remote mountain ranch, leaving him an unhappy choice between earning his own living and moving with her. True to form, Ballentine decides that the mountains are lovely at that time of year.

Ballentine is soon as restless as a politician with unspent campaign funds. Deciding to finally play straight, he leaves Greta and her money forever to begin a new life with Verna. Ballentine and Verna are driving towards a quick Reno divorce when a truck collides with their car. Ballentine survives, but Verna dies, burned beyond recognition.

Recuperating from his injuries, Ballentine realizes that everyone assumes that the dead woman was Greta. Immediately burning the new leaf he just turned over, Ballentine hatches a scheme to inherit Greta's fortune. He'll play along with the story that Greta died in the accident, kill her, hide the body, and inherit her money as the surviving spouse. Ballentine hurries back to the ranch, and searches it with gun in hand. He's surprised to find Greta already dead, sprawled at the bottom of a cliff. To avoid questions about who died in the car wreck, he hides her body even though he didn't kill her, and starts living the good life. But the police find Greta's body and charge Ballentine with murder.

His story concluded, Ballentine watches the jurors file in to report their verdict. Fearing conviction, he suddenly tries to escape through an open window, but is shot and killed. The foreman of the jury then reads the ironic verdict: not guilty.

Legal Analysis

Ballentine's (and the film's) plot depends on nobody figuring out that it was Verna who died in the accident. Even if he collided with an asteroid instead of a truck, Ballentine is taking a big risk. For instance, through a comparison of the remains with Verna's dental records or Verna having told a friend, "I'm off to Reno with Ballentine," the authorities are likely to figure out who died in the accident. Ballentine would have been far safer finding out about the careless truck driver's upcoming routes, and taking Greta for a spin.

Since the film consists almost entirely of flashbacks, it is easy to forget that the story represents Ballentine's courtroom testimony. Therefore, because witnesses can only testify based on their personal knowledge, legally we must see and hear only what Ballentine personally saw and heard. And the movie gets high marks for being true to legal principles and making its star earn every penny of his salary. Ballentine is in every scene, and all the flashbacks consist of information he could provide based on his personal knowledge.

Trial attorneys, many of whom already secretly think of themselves as entertainers, would dearly love to present their witnesses' testimony the way this film tells Ballentine's story. How much more interesting for a judge or a juror to see events reenacted than to have lawyers and witnesses drone on orally! Well, witnesses anyway. If it's true that "a picture is worth a thousand words," a videotape should be worth at least ten thousand, or enough to silence a lawyer for about five minutes.

Unfortunately, the rules of trial were not written to satisfy the whims of dramatists. Ballentine would have to give an oral account of what happened. And to make sure that his evidence is as dull as possible, trial rules would prevent him from telling a complete story, the way a camp counselor might when sitting before a campfire. Instead, Ballentine would have to tell what happened bit by bit in response to his lawyer's specific questions. The reason is that both judges and lawyers have primordial fears of people who have not gone to law school. Judges fear that witnesses asked to "tell the story in your own words" might digress into irrelevancies or say something not allowed by the rules of evidence. Lawyers have a worse fear—witnesses asked to "tell the story in your own words" might actually do so, instead of using the words fed to them by the lawyers.

In the essentially oral world of the courtroom, lawyers look for opportunities to visually influence jurors with tangible objects like guns, photographs, and even computer reenactments, depending on how much of their clients' money they can spend. This is a good idea, since studies show that people are primarily visual learners; about 85 percent of what we know is the result of seeing things rather than hearing about them. Ballentine's lawyer, for example, might have produced a photo of the cliff from which Greta fell, and brought in Ballentine's gun to show that he had intended to shoot her, not push her off a cliff. Of course, limits exist; objects can't be so disgusting that they may cause jurors to throw up. Greta's spleen wouldn't make it into evidence. Nor could Ballentine's lawyer hand him a plastic baggie of Verna's ashes and ask him, "Do you recognize who that is?"

The flashbacks are filled with conversations—Ballentine is talking to Greta, Verna, and others, and they are talking to each other and to him. None of this evidence violates the hearsay rule, because that rule prevents a witness from testifying to what a person said only if what the person said has to be true to be relevant (see *The Hearsay Rule,* p. 163). And most of the conversations in this film are relevant regardless of the truth of what is said. For instance, Ballentine testifies that he told Greta that he was going to run off with Janice, and Greta responded by telling him that she bought him a fancy Beverly Hills house and a partnership. Neither of these statements is barred by the hearsay rule because they don't have to be true to be relevant. Even if he's not actually planning to run off with Janice, Ballentine's statement displays lack of affection for Greta and explains why Greta lavished more money on him. Similarly, Greta's response explains why Ballentine decided to abandon Janice and remain with Greta. Another example is when Ballentine testifies that Verna said, "I love you and I'll marry you." Regardless of whether Verna told him the truth, Verna's statement shows why Ballentine left Greta.

Ballentine's fear that the jury will convict him of murdering Greta is understandable. Not only is he a bounder, but the state has powerful circumstantial evidence that he killed Greta. He had a passion for other women and Greta's money; he lied about who had died in the car crash; he tried to prevent Greta's body from being discovered; and he has an annoying habit of dissolving into flashbacks while testifying. Nevertheless the jury, evidently a gullible group that any defense attorney would want to hire, concludes that he's not guilty. One reason might be that the state has no eyewitnesses. And the jury's verdict may prove the old adage about honesty being the best policy. Perhaps the jurors were so impressed by Ballentine's admissions that he hungered after his wife's money and set off to kill her that they believed his story that Greta's death was caused by a fall off a cliff—or was suicide.

Nevertheless, the end of the film is ambiguous. Was Ballentine's attempted escape out the courtroom window the desperate act of an innocent man who believed himself trapped in a web of circumstantial evidence, or his subconscious admission of guilt? Of course, Ballentine claims to be testifying to "what really happened." But Ballentine testifies that when he awoke the morning after finding Greta dead, he was in a daze and did not realize what had happened. Thus, it is quite possible that Ballentine found Greta standing at the edge of the cliff and decided on the spot to push her rather than shoot her. He then subconsciously makes up the "fall" story to protect himself from feeling guilty. Though he thinks that his testimony is truthful, all it may represent is what he wishes had happened. So—does the jury get it right, or does Ballentine's desperate act correct what would have been a miscarriage of justice? You'll have to make this judgment yourself.

They Won't Forget

Synopsis: Southerners don't care much for Yankees. A northern business school teacher on trial for murder is in very deep trouble.

Warner (Mervyn LeRoy). 1937. Black and white. Running time: 94 min.

Screenplay: Robert Rossen and Aben Kandel. Novel: *Death in the Deep South* by Ward Greene. Director: Mervyn LeRoy.

Starring: Claude Rains (Andy Griffin), Edward Norris (Robert Hale), Allyn Joslyn (William Brock), Elisha Cook Jr. (Joe Turner), Clinton Rosemond (Tump Redwine), Lana Turner (Mary Clay), Gloria Dickson (Sybil Hale), Otto Kruger (Michael Gleason).

Rating: —■ —■ —■

They Won't Forget: Prosecutor Andy Griffin (Claude Rains) argues with defense attorney Michael Gleason (Otto Kruger).

The Story

It's the 1920s in the small town of Flodden, Georgia. A few creaky Civil War veterans are preparing to march in the annual Confederate Memorial Day parade. They vow that "they won't forget" the sacrifices made by the Confederacy, though several have forgotten how to zip their fly.

The adorable Mary Clay, a student at Buxton Business College, has a date with her sweetheart, Joe Turner, to watch the parade. Mary returns to school to pick up her vanity. Later, Tump Redwine, a black janitor, finds Mary's murdered body in the basement. Robert Hale, Mary's shorthand teacher, is in the building grading papers at the time Mary is killed. Hale is a northerner who recently moved to Flodden. Mr. Buxton, the crusty old dean, and Tump Redwine, are there as well.

The press, led by the cynical Bill Brock, goes wild. To ambitious D.A. Andy Griffin, this is the perfect case to carry him all the way to the U.S. Senate. Griffin can play Dial-a-Defendant, choosing the one who is most unpopular. The hands-down winner is Hale, a hated Yankee who should have been watching the parade. Redwine finishes a distant second, since nobody would give Griffin much credit for convicting a black man. Buxton comes in last—social connections protect him.

Reporters invade Hale's apartment, rifle the drawers, and make off with his pictures. A sweet old scribe tricks Hale's loyal wife Sybil into giving an unwise interview in which she admits that Robert never felt welcome in Flodden. To the locals, this is like spitting on the statue of Robert E. Lee. Mary's redneck brothers make it clear that if Griffin won't prosecute Hale, they'll deal with him, thus positioning themselves for their own political careers.

The northern press gets wind of this tasty story and hires a hotshot detective (Pindar) to investigate the case and a prominent attorney (Michael Gleason) to defend Hale. This outside interference just makes the citizenry angrier. Upon arriving in Flodden, Pindar and Gleason are promptly set upon by mobs, getting "Southern hospitals" instead of "Southern hospitality." In particular, Gleason seems intimidated, since his performance in court is pathetic.

The trial consists of Griffin's arm-waving oratory in his opening and closing statements with presentation of questionable circumstantial evidence in between. There is an interesting Battle of the Mothers, with Mary's and Hale's mothers trying to out-anguish each other at critical moments.

Imogene Mayfield, Mary's friend, testifies that Mary had a huge crush on Hale, but admits that she never saw Hale make any advances to Mary or even talk to her outside of class. On redirect examination, Griffith asks Mayfield to identify the bloody outfit that Mary was wearing when she was killed. This elicits the predictable howl of anguish from Mother Clay.

Joe Turner, Mary's boyfriend, came looking for her and ran into Hale, who was leaving the building at 3:00. He told Turner that none of the girls were there and barred Turner from the building. There was a spot of blood on Hale's coat. Hale claims that the blood came from a shaving cut, but the barber denies that he cut Hale. Worst of all, Hale was making plans to quit his job and leave town when he was arrested.

Tump Redwine testifies that he saw Hale at 1:00 and again at 3:00 and heard some suspicious noises from Hale's classroom before that. On cross-examination, Redwine retracts the testimony about the noise and claims he slept the whole time. He is petrified, and says over and over "I didn't do it."

Hale is permitted to make a statement to the jury denying that he killed anyone and is not cross-examined. Gleason's closing is short and lame. Staring into the stony eyes of the jury, he argues that any of the witnesses could have done it and that the real witnesses against Hale were hatred, fear, and prejudice. The worthies on the jury probably wonder why Gleason is confused about the witnesses' names.

In the jury room, one juror holds out briefly against guilt but is swept away by the others and the guilty verdict is inevitable. The state supreme court affirms. Governor Monson's political career is on the line. He courageously commutes Hale's death sentence to life imprisonment. A mob, led by Mary's brothers, stops the train carrying Hale to prison, pulls Hale off, and lynches him.

It looks like Griffin's a shoo-in for the Senate now. Sybil tells Griffin and Brock that they will have to live with Hale's death for the rest of their life. After she leaves, Brock says: "Now that it's over, Andy, I wonder if he really did it." Griffin gazes out the window and murmurs, "I wonder."

Legal Analysis

Hale's conviction was based on an accumulation of circumstantial evidence. But there's nothing wrong with that (see *Circumstantial Evidence,* p. 193). The inferences arising from circumstantial evidence can point very convincingly to guilt. Many times, circumstantial evidence can be more reliable than direct, eyewitness evidence.

What were the items of evidence that convicted Hale:

1. He acted suspiciously toward Joe Turner at 3:00 at Buxton Business College. But if he didn't kill Mary, he wouldn't have known she was in the building and his behavior toward Turner was perfectly natural.

2. Hale was planning to leave town in a hurry. This is pretty damaging. But he and Sybil had been unhappy in Flodden and Buxton had humiliated Hale in front of his students on the day of the parade. This gave him reason to quit.

3. There was a blood spot on Hale's coat. But this could have come from a shaving cut, and the barber who denied cutting him wasn't credible. Most important, the jury heard no scientific testimony matching the spot to Mary's blood type.

4. Mary Clay had a crush on Hale. So what? Hale didn't reciprocate.

5. Hale was trembling when arrested. But as the arresting officer admitted, most suspects are terrified when arrested (except for hardened criminals).

This collection of bits and pieces of evidence was not nearly sufficient to meet the prosecution's burden of proof beyond a reasonable doubt. It suggests Hale might be the killer, but it's nowhere near enough to prove that he was. It could have been Redwine (whose changeable testimony is rather suspicious), or Buxton or anybody else who might have followed Mary Clay back into the building.

As Gleason points out, the real witness against Hale was the bitterness toward Yankees left over from the Civil War. Apparently, this was even more poisonous than the hatred of blacks; Redwine was indeed lucky that a Yankee was around to take the fall. The press did a great job of whipping up chauvinistic hysteria. And the jurors were probably intimidated by the Clay brothers and the other local rednecks who didn't care about due process. Indeed, there was heavy-duty intimidation in the jury room. One juror was slipped a note saying "vote guilty if you feel like living." If this came to light, the verdict would be overturned.

Under present-day constitutional standards, the court would be required to take measures to counteract the overpowering pretrial publicity. There's just no way that a fair jury could have been seated in Flodden. This was a kangaroo court that would have convicted a northern kangaroo. If Gleason had not been brain-dead, he would have requested a change of venue to some other town in the state, as far away from Flodden as possible. Although the locals in the new venue would probably have heard about the case, their passion would have been less intense than the hometown crowd.

As noted in the review of *Fury,* the lynch mob was an ever-present reality in the American justice system, especially in the South. Although Griffin promises Sybil Hale that he plans to prosecute the leaders of the mob, we know that this will never happen. Griffin's too politically astute to do any such thing. And even if he did, the chances of convicting anybody would be less than the proverbial snowflake in Hades.

Hale's statement of his innocence to the jury provides a fascinating historical footnote. Hale is not placed under oath and Griffin can't cross-examine him. This procedure was an artifact of the old common law rule that kept criminal defendants from testifying at all. Of course, today a criminal defendant has the choice to testify or not to testify. If he chooses to testify, it must be under oath and subject to cross-examination. If he does not testify, the prosecution cannot ask jurors to draw any adverse inference from his silence. Some states, particularly in the South, came up with an ingenious compromise: The defendant can make a statement without being placed under oath and free from cross-examination. This procedure doesn't exist in criminal cases any more, but it still is available in military courts-martial.

For the most part, the trial scenes in *They Won't Forget* are solidly authentic. But Griffin went overboard in his oratorical denunciation of Hale, because he improperly appealed to the jurors' emotions rather than to the evidence. Probably such histrionics were within the bounds of acceptable courtroom behavior for the time and place. Also the introduction of Mary's dress during Imogene's redirect exam was improper; redirect examination is limited to whatever matters came up on cross-examination.

Such quibbles aside, *They Won't Forget* does a superb job of putting southern justice on trial. Up against a witch's brew of anti-Yankee prejudice, the D.A.'s political ambition, the craving of the Clay boys for revenge, and yellow journalism at its yellowest, Hale had no chance.

Trial Briefs

They Won't Forget is based on a tragic case occurring in Georgia in 1915. Ward Greene, on whose novel the movie is based, was a reporter who covered the case. Leo M. Frank, a Jew from New York, came to Atlanta to manage a pencil factory. He was tried and convicted for the murder of Mary Phagan, an employee of the company. As in the movie, the evidence against Frank was entirely circumstantial and not very strong. A black man was also a suspect.

The ambitious D.A. and a racist newspaper publisher decided to prosecute Frank, because "we can lynch a nigger anytime but when do we get a chance to hang a Yankee Jew?" They formed an organization, "The Knights of Mary Phagan," which later became "The Knights of the Ku Klux Klan." Governor John Slaton courageously commuted Frank's sentence, for which he was hounded out of the state. Frank was then lynched. It is said that the black man later confessed to the crime. Evidently in 1937 Hollywood could handle a story based on prejudice against Yankees, but wasn't ready for hard-core anti-Semitism.

In *They Won't Forget,* Mary Clay walks down the street, looking absolutely sensational in her sweater. Lana Turner's career took off as the result of this scene.

The Wrong Man

Synopsis: Based on mistaken eyewitness identification, the wrong man is charged with robbery, shattering his life. Seen through the eyes of an innocent man, the routine processes of police investigation and criminal trial are terrifying.

Warner (Herbert Coleman). 1956. Black and white. Running time: 105 min.

Screenplay: Maxwell Anderson and Angus MacPhail. Director: Alfred Hitchcock.

Starring: Henry Fonda (Manny Balestrero), Vera Miles (Rose), Anthony Quayle (O'Connor), Harold J. Stone (Lt. Bowers).

Rating: —▮ —▮ —▮

The Wrong Man: Manny Balestrero (Henry Fonda) looks for someone who'll believe he didn't do it.

The Story

Manny Balestrero is the bass player at the Stork Club and a devoted husband and father. The family is short of money and badly in debt. When Rose Balestrero needs $300 for dental work, Manny visits the Associated Life Insurance office to arrange a loan on Rose's policy. The women in the office mistakenly identify him as the man who twice held up the office at gunpoint. Manny is arrested.

The police refuse to let Manny call Rose, leaving her frantic. He passively accepts the authority of the detectives, but denies committing the robberies. The detectives ask him to print the same note that the robber gave to the clerks. The printing looks similar, and Manny prints "draw" instead of "drawer"—the exact mistake that the robber made. The police hold a lineup and two women from Associated pick Manny as the robber. The police also suspect him of other neighborhood robberies, but the clerks in those stores are uncertain and Manny is not charged with those robberies.

The police finally call Rose, and Manny's family bails him out the next morning. Manny hires an attorney, Frank O'Connor, who admits he doesn't have any criminal law experience. At O'Connor's direction, Manny starts trying to establish an alibi. In fact, he and Rose were at a resort hotel during one of the robberies. But the men he played cards with that afternoon are dead or untraceable, and the police don't believe his story about playing in a high-stakes game of "go fish." Just about the only hope at the trial is that Manny's jaw was badly swollen from a toothache at the time one of the robberies was committed, a point that none of the identifying witnesses mention.

Rose goes completely to pieces from stress. Blaming herself for the catastrophe, she falls into a deep depression and has to be institutionalized.

The prosecution puts on powerful evidence of Manny's guilt. O'Connor tries to cross-examine one of the Associated eyewitnesses about the lineup, but seems to be getting nowhere. Nobody in the courtroom is paying attention. They are bored out of their brains.

Finally, a juror stands up and asks whether they really have to listen anymore. The judge grants O'Connor's motion for a mistrial. It looks like Manny is going to have to go through the whole thing all over again.

Then Manny's prayers are answered. The real holdup man is caught and he's a dead ringer for Manny. A police detective remembers Manny and it all clicks when he sees the new suspect who looks just like him. Manny's case is dismissed, but Rose remains sunk in hopeless depression in a mental institution. "That's fine for you," she says, staring blankly into the distance, when he tells her about their good luck. The epilogue tells us that two years later, Rose walked out of the hospital completely cured. The Balestreros move to Florida, where they stay out of insurance offices. In Florida, that's no mean feat.

Legal Analysis

The most unforgettable aspect of *The Wrong Man* is simply the routine functioning of the criminal process. Everything about the arrest, interrogation, incarceration, lineup, arraignment, bail, and trial are routine. Just another humdrum armed robbery case. Each step is accurately presented, documentary style, in gritty detail. Yet to an innocent and rather simple fellow like Manny, these procedures are mystifying and utterly terrifying—a "meatgrinder" in his words.

Manny is arrested by two reasonably fair and competent police officers. "An innocent man has nothing to fear," they assure him repeatedly, but wrongly. In order to achieve dominance over their suspect and increase his anxiety, they refuse to let him tell Rose about the arrest, even though he is taken into custody on his own doorstep. When Manny doesn't come home on time, Rose is terrified and starts her downward spiral. Today, the general practice is to allow a prisoner at least one phone call and Rose's plight shows how humane that practice is.

After experiencing the horrors of claustrophobia in his tiny cell all night, Manny gets bailed out the next morning. Manny's pathetic gratitude when he's allowed to walk out of the drab jail into Rose's arms illustrates the importance of bail pending trial. Bail allows Manny to help prepare his defense, keep his job, and protect his family, during the lengthy period before trial. The Eighth Amendment to the U.S. Constitution protects the right to bail, providing that "excessive bail shall not be required." Of course, some defendants skip out or even commit other crimes while released on bail, but we tolerate this to protect the rights of persons just like Manny. In fact, statistics show that a defendant who's been released on bail has a much better chance of being acquitted than one who's unable to make bail.

At Manny's arraignment, the judge sets his bail at $7,500. Most courts have a bail schedule, fixing a standard amount according to the severity of the crime. Somehow the money is raised, fortunately without Manny going back to Associated for another try at a loan. Probably Manny's family purchased a bail bond, in which a bail bondsman puts up the money in return for a nonrefundable fee of about 10 percent of the total bail. With a job, a family, a home, and no criminal record, Manny might have requested that he be released "on his own recognizance," meaning he wouldn't have to pay a bondsman anything. For a person charged with two armed robberies, however, release O.R. is unlikely.

When Manny and Rose visit O'Connor for the first time, they quite properly ask how they can afford him. O'Connor says, "We'll see about that later." Yeah, right. No criminal lawyer (even an inexperienced one like O'Connor) would dream of setting off on a difficult and time-consuming defense for a client who's already in debt without significant up-front money. That's why some defendants on bail commit other crimes—to raise the money to pay a lawyer because they don't want a public defender to represent them.

The police conduct a lineup in which two women from Associated unhesitatingly pick Manny out of a group of six similarly dressed white men. However, the lineup was not conducted fairly because the two women were standing together. The second woman heard the first identify Manny. The second witness should not have been present while the first one made her identification. As a result of this error, the second woman might be barred from identifying Manny at his trial.

The Wrong Man shows graphically how unreliable eyewitness identification can be. Though jurors tend to place great faith in eyewitness testimony, research into people's perceptions and memory suggests that eyewitnesses are often mistaken. Mistakes are more likely when a person is under stress, as is the case for many people who are the victims of or witness crimes. However, the Associated clerks saw the robber under almost ideal conditions—they got a good long look in a well-lit room. Many times, eyewitnesses catch only a fleeting glimpse of a poorly lit subject.

Nevertheless, they were wrong. Perhaps this isn't surprising. The actual robberies occurred many months' earlier and memories naturally fade. Besides, Manny looked scary as he came into the office with one hand in his coat pocket, and the women were terrified. Once they decided he was the robber, nothing was going to change their minds. At least, they weren't that far off—the real robber did closely resemble Manny.

In his opening statement, the prosecutor claims that he will present evidence that Manny needed money to pay his bookmaker. This was simply false; Manny never said any such thing. It suggests that the police were planning to lie about what he told them. This is troubling. Of course, police can and do lie just like other witnesses, but it isn't clear why they would want to when they have a case as strong as the one against Manny. In any event, the police and suspect are bound to disagree about what was said during an interrogation. This shows the importance of reducing a suspect's statements to writing and having him sign the statement.

The judge was correct in granting a mistrial. The juror's statement indicates that he had prejudged the case and didn't want to bother listening to the tedious cross-examination. If the judge had not aborted the trial, Manny would have had an excellent argument on appeal that he did not receive a fair trial. But the reality is that at the new trial, Manny would probably have been convicted. He has no provable alibi and the prosecution's case is quite solid.

The Wrong Man shows the criminal procedure machine grinding through its gears and the devastation that it can wreak in the life of an innocent man and his family. Hitchcock's great artistry makes this ultimate nightmare all too real. Despite every precaution to prevent it from happening, innocent people get accused and convicted of crime. When it happens, happy endings like the one in *The Wrong Man* are rare.

Trial Brief

Alone among Hitchcock's films, *The Wrong Man* is based quite literally on actual events that occurred in New York in 1953. Hitchcock was fascinated by the story because he had a lifelong terror of the police. Balestrero, the bassist at the Stork Club, was arrested for the robbery of the Prudential Insurance Co. and wrongly identified by three witnesses. His attorney, Frank O'Connor, later became district attorney of Queens. Balestrero faced thirty years in prison, but after a juror's outburst identical to the one in the film, a mistrial was granted. A week later, the real robber confessed. The locations in the film are the exact places where the real story occurred, including the very courtroom in Queens where Balestrero's trial took place.

Unusual Judges and Jurors

In actual trials, judges and jurors are the colorless sponges of the legal system. They soak up evidence and, when gently squeezed, are supposed to figure out what really happened. But play tricks with their role, and high drama may well unfold.

In *Twelve Angry Men,* for example, we barely see the defendant and the lawyers at all; the whole film takes place in the jury room where one courageous juror stands alone against all the rest. A juror in *Suspect* helps the public defender try her case. In *M,* the judges and the jury are the city's criminals. And in *The Ox-bow Incident* a posse conducts the trial, but not very well.

Anatomy of a Murder

Synopsis: An army officer is charged with killing a man who allegedly raped his wife. With a little prodding from his attorney, the officer claims that he was under the spell of an irresistible impulse.

Columbia Films/Carlyle (Otto Preminger). 1959. Black and white. Running time: 161 min.

Screenplay: Wendell Mayes. Original story: Robert Traver. Director: Otto Preminger. Jazz score: Duke Ellington.

Starring: James Stewart (Paul Biegler), Ben Gazzara (Lt. Frederick Manion), Lee Remick (Laura Manion), George C. Scott (Claude Dancer), Eve Arden (Maida), Arthur O'Connell (Parnell McCarthy), Kathryn Grant (Mary Pilant), Joseph N. Welch (Judge Weaver).

Anatomy of A Murder: Paul Biegler (James Stewart) displays the torn panties dramatically produced by surprise witness Mary Pilant (Kathryn Grant).

Academy Award nominations: Best Picture, Best Screenplay (Wendell Mayes), Best Cinematography (Sam Leavitt), Best Actor (James Stewart), Best Supporting Actor (Arthur O'Connell, George C. Scott), Best Editing (Louis R. Loeffler).

Rating: [4 gavels]

Surprise ending warning: Reading this summary may be hazardous to your enjoyment of the movie!

The Story

Army Lieutenant Frederick Manion and his wife Laura live in a trailer park near the wooded resort community of Thunder Bay. One night Manion walks from his trailer to the Thunder Bay Inn and shoots and kills its owner, Barney Quill. Manion then turns himself into the police. He is arrested for murder, and hires Paul Biegler to represent him.

Biegler would rather fish than practice law, and has a refrigerator full of trout and an unpaid secretary named Maida to prove it. Questioned by Biegler, Manion and Laura claim that Quill beat and raped her. When Manion found out what had happened, he blanked out, calmly walked to the tavern, and shot Quill. As the case goes to trial, the only issue is whether Manion was legally insane at the time he shot Quill.

Dancer is the big-city prosecutor brought in to help convict Manion. The contrast between Dancer's tough-guy attitude and Biegler's country-bumpkin charm enlivens the trial scenes. Dancer repeatedly insinuates that Laura was a lonely tramp who willingly made love with Quill. His questions imply that when the jealous Manion learned what Laura had done, he beat her up and killed Quill in anger. Together, they concocted the rape story to cover their tracks. Dancer finds support for his theory in the "missing panties," which Laura insists were torn off by Quill but have never been found.

Finally, Mary Pilant, a young woman who managed the Thunder Bay Inn for Quill, testifies as a surprise defense witness. Pilant dramatically produces Laura's torn panties. She says that she found them in Quill's dirty laundry, but didn't realize their significance until she heard about them at the trial. Immediately attacking, Dancer's cross-examination implies that she made up the panty story to get even with her lover, Quill, for fooling around with Laura. Reduced to tears, Pilant destroys Dancer's attack by revealing that Quill was not her lover, but her father. The shocked Dancer slinks away meekly and the jury finds Manion not guilty. Manion and Laura drive off without paying Biegler's fee, leaving behind an ambiguous note claiming that they were seized by an irresistible impulse and hinting that Manion did intentionally kill Quill.

Legal Analysis

Anatomy of a Murder is one of the grittiest and most dramatic trial movies ever made. Featuring eloquent attorneys who believe fervently in their causes and a calm judge whose rulings reflect both common sense and legal wisdom, the trial scenes have the power of a boxing match pared down to only the hardest exchanges of punches.

The trial focuses on the defense of "irresistible impulse." This defense allows a defendant to be found not guilty if a judge or jury believes that due to mental illness triggered by a powerful stimulus, the defendant was unable to stop himself from committing a crime even though he knew it was wrong to commit the crime. Thus, Manion might be found not guilty by reason of insanity even if he knew that killing Quill was wrong, if the shock of hearing that his wife had been raped made him powerless to control his desire to kill Quill.

The movie unrealistically shows Biegler and his boozy mentor Parnell knee-deep in musty law books, gleefully discovering that a Michigan court had authorized the irresistible impulse defense some seventy years earlier. The scene is charming, but as an experienced criminal lawyer, Biegler would know as much about the defense as about how to catch trout in northern Michigan. Even more unreal is Dancer's reaction. In a conference in Judge Weaver's chambers, Dancer pretends that Michigan does not allow the irresistible impulse defense. His position is grossly unethical; as a prosecutor, Dancer's job is not to win, but to see that justice is done. Dancer would have been severely reprimanded for trying to mislead the court, or at least booted from the office golf tournament.

The key to Manion's claim that he had an irresistible impulse to kill Quill is his belief that Quill raped Laura. Under the law, his reasonable belief that she was raped can constitute provocation for his actions, even if Laura lied to him when she told him that she had been raped. Since Manion's belief is what counts, everything he knew that lends credence to his belief that Laura had been raped is clearly relevant and admissible, such as what she told him and her bruised physical condition. Thus, the movie is highly misleading when at first, the prosecutor is able to prevent the jury from hearing any evidence about a rape. One of its dramatic high points takes place when Judge Weaver pauses, studies his pocket watch, then alters the course of the trial by ruling that the rape testimony is admissible. But the drama is entirely the moviemakers' creation; the rape evidence was admissible all along.

Dancer is a clever and powerful lawyer; he thoroughly dominates any witness he cross-examines. But his bombast covers up a dubious approach to the case. Dancer spends most of his time trying to disprove Laura's claim that she was raped, attacking her as a lonely seductress who enticed Quill into making love. Dancer's tactics would undoubtedly have led the jury to conclude that Manion is not guilty if they believe that Quill actually raped Laura.

What Dancer never makes clear to the jury is that even if Laura had been raped, and even if she told Manion that she had been raped, Manion can still be guilty of first-degree murder. Dancer should have squarely attacked Manion's irresistible impulse claim. He should have argued that regardless of whether Laura was raped, Manion shot Quill because he had a violent temper, not because he was powerless to control an irresistible impulse. Dancer has plenty of support for this theory: Manion was a war veteran with no record of mental illness; an hour elapsed between the time Laura told him what happened and the time he shot Quill; and Manion's claim to have been in a "daze" the entire time is suspicious at best. Dancer's theory allowed the jurors to find Manion not guilty if they believed Laura had been raped; he made a big mistake by never directly attacking Manion's irresistible impulse claim.

Biegler's tactics are also questionable. During his first interview with Manion, Biegler tells Manion that the "unwritten rule" is of no help to him. The "unwritten rule" to which Biegler refers exonerates a man (traditionally, it is men who claim the benefit of the rule) who catches someone in bed with his wife and kills him. There is no such rule. But if Manion acted in the heat of passion after learning that Quill had raped his wife, he might be guilty only of manslaughter, a much less serious crime than first-degree murder. The fact that an hour elapsed between the time Manion learned of the rape and the time he shot Quill makes the "heat of passion" argument much more difficult for Biegler, but doesn't destroy it. And jurors might be more willing to accept that Manion acted in the "heat of passion" than that he was suddenly rendered insane.

The origin of Manion's insanity defense illustrates the ethical pressures on criminal defense lawyers. When Biegler first interviews Manion, Biegler does not immediately ask what happened on the night Quill was killed. Instead, he delivers what Parnell calls "The Lecture." In The Lecture, Biegler helps Manion fashion a story by describing the possible defenses to a charge of murder and ticking off all of them as inapplicable except for "excuse." After Biegler repeatedly asks Manion for his excuse, and tells Manion that bad temper is no excuse, Manion finally says, "I must have been crazy."

For all his country-lawyer innocence, Biegler's lecture probably violates the attorneys' code of ethics. A lawyer can help a client tell a story in a credible way, but cannot create the story the client tells. But Biegler's lecture guides Manion towards the one story that might produce a not-guilty verdict. Of course, violations such as Biegler's rarely come to light. They take place behind closed doors, and are protected by attorney-client confidentiality. Ironically, for all the rules that regulate how evidence comes out publicly in court, stories typically take shape in lawyers' offices, out of the reach of those rules.

At the dramatic climax of the trial, Dancer meets his downfall when he violates one of the oldest tactical rules of trial. A cross-examiner is never supposed to ask a question to which he doesn't know the answer. In real life as in movies, the answer is almost always harmful. Here, Dancer does not know of the actual relationship between Quill and Mary Pilant. Yet after Mary tells of finding the panties in the hotel laundry, Dancer barges in and accuses her of being Quill's spurned lover. When Mary chokingly reveals that Quill was her father, a verdict favoring Manion is all but assured.

It is easy to fault Dancer: violate an ancient tactical rule of trial, get burned. But remember, Mary's testimony has severely undermined Dancer's theory. Her testimony strongly supports the defense claim that Quill raped Laura. So Dancer has to cast doubt on Mary's testimony, or he probably loses anyway. Since the scuttlebutt around town was that Quill and Mary were lovers, his attack on her motives for rushing forward at the last minute may have been a good gamble. After all, how likely was it that Mary was Quill's daughter?

Finally, Biegler's and Dancer's trial behavior furnishes a fine collection of what attorneys ought not to do if they want to avoid spending an evening in the county jail, courtesy of a trial judge's irresistible impulse. Dancer cross-examines Mary Pilant by yelling questions at her from a distance of three inches. When cross-examining Laura, he intentionally blocks Biegler's view of the witness. And of course, he tries to mislead Judge Weaver about the defense of irresistible impulse.

But Dancer does not wallow alone in the gutter. Biegler slams tables, accuses the prosecution of concealing evidence, threatens to strike Dancer, and deviously informs the jury that Laura passed a lie detector test. And when Biegler has a chance to cross-examine Dwayne Miller, a cellmate of Manion's who becomes a surprise prosecution witness, he commits a number of evidentiary sins. Miller testifies that while they were both in their cell, Manion boasted of how his lies would get him off scot-free. Enraged, Biegler asks for Miller's record of legal troubles, and attacks his credibility by reeling off his string of arrests and convictions. Unfortunately, most of this information is inadmissible in evidence. First, Biegler cannot attack Miller's credibility by showing that Miller has been arrested. No matter how often Miller has been arrested, arrests are flat-out irrelevant to credibility. Second, Biegler can attack Miller's credibility by showing that he has been convicted of serious crimes and misdemeanors, but not convictions for the petty misdemeanors which littered Miller's record. Despite Biegler's indignation about Miller's testimony, most of his cross-examination was grossly improper (see *Character Evidence,* p. 259).

Manion and Laura skip town without paying Biegler's fee, ensuring that the long-suffering Maida will have to endure at least one more month with a broken typewriter and a salary consisting of frozen trout. It's Biegler's fault for breaking the biggest Defense Lawyer's Rule of them all—get your money up-front. Actually, Biegler's entire fee arrangement with Manion was unethical. Manion agreed to pay Biegler—but only if Biegler got him off. This is a "contingency fee" arrangement. It is perfectly proper in cases involving broken legs and other civil matters, but improper in criminal cases.

Like many actual trials, the movie leaves us uncertain about what really happened. Did Quill rape Laura, or did she try to seduce him? Was it Quill or Manion who beat her black-and-blue? And was Manion temporarily insane when he killed Quill, or just plain angry? The jury's answer is not necessarily the correct one. But Judge Weaver saw to it that both sides had a fair shot, so bailiff, call the next case.

Trial Briefs

1. Robert Traver, the author of the book on which the movie is based, was a pseudonym for the late Justice Voelker, who wrote the book after his retirement from the Michigan Supreme Court.

2. Joseph N. Welch, unforgettable in the role of Judge Weaver, was not an actor by profession. He was an actual judge who gained national prominence when he represented the U.S. Army in the televised "Army-McCarthy hearings." The hearings were conducted by Sen. Joseph McCarthy to investigate supposed Communist infiltration of the army. Welch's handling of the defense, especially his repeated question to McCarthy, "Senator McCarthy, have you no decency? Have you no decency at all?" was widely credited with hastening the downfall of Senator McCarthy.

3. Because of its frank discussion of the physical act of rape and its focus on women's panties, many communities did not allow *Anatomy of a Murder* to be shown when it was first released.

4. Contrary to the movie, defendants found not guilty by reason of insanity are not normally set free. They typically have to serve at least a minimum amount of time in a medical facility, and are not released until they can show that they are no longer a danger to themselves or to others.

5. Irresistible impulse is not a permissible defense to a murder charge in all states. It developed as a more liberal alternative to the stricter "McNaghten rule," which began in England in the mid-1800s and is recognized in all states. Unlike the defense of irresistible impulse, the McNaghten rule allows a defendant to be found not guilty by reason of insanity only if a judge or jury believes that the defendant's mental illness prevented him from knowing that what he did was wrong.

6. The "McNaghten rule" and "irresistible impulse" are only two of numerous tests of insanity that have been in use at one time or another. Others include the "Durham rule" (announced in a 1954 Washington, D.C., case) and the "substantial capacity rule" (put forward by the American Law Institute in 1955). The varying tests reflect society's uncertainty about how to detect mental illness, and whether to incarcerate or even execute people who commit criminal acts as a result of mental illness. Many law school criminal law courses emphasize analysis of the different tests of insanity; any connection between this emphasis and the behavior of lawyers is presumed coincidental.

The Devil and Daniel Webster

Synopsis: The Devil's hand-picked judge and jurors have to decide whether a standard-form "sell your soul" contract is valid.

RKO/William Dieterle (Charles L. Glett). 1941. Black and white. Running time: 106 min.

Screenplay: Stephen Vincent Benet and Dan Totheroh. Original story: Stephen Vincent Benet. Director: William Dieterle.

Starring: Walter Huston (Mr. Scratch), Edward Arnold (Daniel Webster).

Academy Awards: Best Musical Score.

Academy Award nomination: Best Actor (Walter Huston).

Rating: —▮ —▮ —▮

The Story

Jamis is a poor New Hampshire farmer who in 1840 sells his soul to Mr. Scratch—better known as the Devil. Under their written contract, Jamis gets rich and the Devil is to get Jamis's soul after seven years. With gold coins obtained from this deal, Jamis pays off his debts and becomes greedy. Before long, the entire town is in debt to him. An adorable sweetie, sent by the Devil, bewitches him and he drives his loving wife and son away. As the seven years runs out, the Devil offers a contract modification. Jamis can save his soul if he gives up his son. Desperate, Jamis refuses the modification.

Fortunately, Daniel Webster is an old family friend. Webster takes on Jamis as a client in a last-ditch attempt to save his soul. When the Devil appears to claim it, Webster repudiates the contract and calls for a jury trial.

The Devil summons a judge and jury from hell—a series of brigands (including Benedict Arnold) who had previously sold their souls to him. There appear to be no lawyers in the bunch; apparently there are some souls that even the Devil won't take. The judge summarily rejects Webster's motion to disqualify the jurors and refuses to allow Webster to cross-examine. After an impassioned argument by Webster, the jury finds for Jamis and tears up the contract. The Devil is furious, telling Webster that he will never become president. Maybe it's also the Devil who guarantees that the Cubs will never win the World Series.

Legal Analysis

Webster's closing argument is masterful. Although one could not imagine a less sympathetic judge and jury, Webster turns matters around by a pure emotional appeal. He reminds the jurors of the simple things of life that they threw away by selling their own souls and pleads that they allow Jamis to get out of his unfortunate bargain. Surprisingly this works.

However, the reality is that Webster offered no arguments of legal substance on Jamis's behalf. Essentially he called for the jury to nullify the contract based on reasons of sentiment alone. The judge should have taken the case from the jury and held for plaintiff Devil, since he should have won as a matter of law. Jury nullification may be appropriate in a criminal case, but not in a breach of contract action. The Devil should consider an appeal. Normally, lawyers take cases "up" on appeal; the Devil probably would take this one down.

Webster's motion to disqualify the jury should have been granted. All of the jurors, as well as the judge, had previously sold their souls to plaintiff Devil. They were suffering the torments of the damned in hell. Since the Devil runs hell, the judge and the jurors might think that they would receive better treatment if they ruled for plaintiff Devil. This creates a clear conflict of interest and requires disqualification of the judge and jury. Impartiality of judge and jury is an essential element of due process of law.

Webster should have considered some other contract defenses such as unconscionability, fraud, or violation of public policy. Each of these defenses allows people to back out of agreements they've made. Unconscionability requires both unequal bargaining power and an offensively one-sided exchange. However, it can be argued that the parties were of equal bargaining power; this was not a take-it-or-leave-it situation like an insurance policy. The Devil appeared to be willing to bargain since he really wanted Jamis's soul. Nor is it clear that the second half of the equation is satisfied; an exchange of one's soul for seven years of wealth and good luck may not strike a judge as offensively one-sided. Lots of people would happily go for that deal.

Webster might have also argued that the contract was tainted by fraud. During the negotiation, the Devil told him that his soul was of no importance. This induced Jamis's reliance. However, it is likely that this defense would also fail, since Jamis knew or should have known that his soul was of great value. His reliance on the Devil's opinion on this point was not reasonable. The Devil's statement seems more in the nature of "puffing," like when a used-car salesman tells a male buyer that women will fall for him if they see him driving around in a bright red convertible. This sort of nonsense is not considered fraud even if a person is gullible enough to rely on it.

Webster's best argument might be that the contract violated public policy and thus was unenforceable. This defense works best if the public policy in question is stated in a statute passed by the legislature. For example, a contract to pay a bribe is unenforceable because bribery is a crime. We are not aware of any statutes that forbid selling one's soul, although you could probably find one somewhere.

A court might be willing to articulate such a policy as a matter of common law. For example, if your uncle pays you $100,000 in return for your promise not to get married for ten years, this promise is generally considered unenforceable. You can get married and keep the money. This is an example of judicial lawmaking to vindicate a widely held social policy in favor of marriage. A judge might also refuse to enforce a contract for the sale of one's soul out of a desire to discourage such transactions. While this argument would have little chance before the Devil's handpicked judge and jury, it might succeed on appeal.

The film has enormous fun with its amusing premise, but the legal principles of contract law go to the devil.

M

Synopsis: Everything's upside-down in this haunting German film. The crooks catch and try the killer and debate the insanity defense.

Nero Film (Seymour Nebenzal). 1931. Germany (in German with English subtitles). Black and white. Running time: 99 min. Remade in 1951.

Screenplay: Thea von Harbou, Paul Falkenberg, Adolf Jansen, and Karl Vash. Director: Fritz Lang.

Starring: Peter Lorre (Franz Becker), Otto Wernicke (Insp. Karl Lohman), Gustav Grundgens (Shranker).

Rating: —▮ —▮ —▮

The Story

A murderer of little girls is on the loose in a German town. The public is terrified and the police have no clue. However, they make life difficult for the underworld, busting dance halls and brothels every night. This business interruption is intolerable for the criminals. The leaders of the various underworld unions meet and vow to catch the killer themselves. The crooks are far better dressed and organized than the police. Of course, they earn a lot more.

The crooks enlist the beggars' union to watch the streets. Sure enough, a blind balloon salesman recognizes someone whistling Grieg's "Hall of the Mountain King" as the person to whom he sold a balloon on the day one little girl was killed. It is Becker, a solid though rather nerdy citizen. When spotted, Becker again has a child in tow. The beggars are off and running. One of them catches up with Becker, marking his coat with the letter "M" in chalk. Possibly the beggars suspect Becker of being half of the notorious crime duo of M & M.

Becker tries to hide in an office building, but the underworld finds him holed up in the attic. They haul him off to a huge abandoned brewery for his trial.

Becker's surrealistic trial takes place before a huge crowd of criminals. It is not, however, the U.S. Congress. The leaders of the underworld serve both as the judges and as prosecutors. All are experts on criminal law and procedure. Indeed, Shranker, the chief judge, is currently being sought for three murders himself. One of the crooks is appointed as Becker's counsel and he does an excellent job.

Becker is again identified by the balloon man; the lawyer is unable to puncture his story. Becker cracks and admits the crimes. He grovels on the floor, his eyes almost popping out with terror. Becker says that he can't help himself when he kills, and doesn't even remember the crimes. You are criminals because you want to be, he argues, but what choice do I have?

Becker's lawyer pleads insanity, arguing that it's improper to convict him for acts he could not prevent. As a result, Becker should be turned over to the state to be institutionalized and perhaps cured. The audience, no softer on crime than the rest of the citizenry, hoots insults at Becker. They want him snuffed out like a candle. A woman pleads for vengeance, arguing that nobody can know the suffering of a mother who loses her child. Before the judges can decide, the police arrive.

Legal Analysis

In the inverted world of *M,* the mob does much better police work than the police. They also stage a competent trial, conducted according to the so-called "inquisitorial" system of criminal procedure used in European civil law countries like France and Germany. In an "accusatorial" system, like that used in the United States or Britain, the evidence is presented through direct examination and cross-examination of the witnesses. The judge and the jury are neutral. They decide the case presented by the adversaries—namely, the prosecutor and the defense attorney.

Inquisitorial procedure is quite fair, nothing like that used in the Spanish Inquisition. The key difference is that civil law judges have a much greater responsibility for investigating a case than judges in an accusatorial system. In a pure inquisitorial system, a judge supervises the investigation and prepares a dossier that contains the evidence. All witnesses, including the defendant, are examined during this stage; the defendant has the right to refuse to answer questions or to give testimony (but not under oath). In some systems, the defendant's refusal to answer questions raises an adverse inference against him. The examining judge can decide to dismiss the case or let it go to trial. The assumption is that if things have gone that far, the defendant is probably guilty. However, there is no such thing as a guilty plea; the procedure is the same whether the defendant confesses or not.

Trials under the inquisitorial system are often shorter than our own. At the trial, a judge (or a panel of judges) reviews the evidence in the dossier and questions witnesses. The prosecutor and the defense lawyer have much less to do than under our system. They may ask witnesses a few questions (or ask the judge to pose the questions). There is no cross-examination. The accused will be questioned in detail (but not under oath). The main task of the lawyers is to make arguments about whether the defendant is guilty and what the correct sentence should be. Some systems use lay judges who sit together with the professional judge or judges at the trial. The lay judges are the continental version of our jury system. The judges (lay and professional) render a detailed written verdict.

The most important difference between Becker's trial and one that would have been conducted by the state is that the audience was permitted to heckle the defendant and to make statements. In this respect, the trial resembled more of a show or political trial than a normal criminal case.

Becker's counsel raises the insanity defense. In our system, as in civil law countries, a defendant cannot be convicted of crime unless he is mentally responsible for his actions. The theory is that it is wrong to punish people who are too mentally ill to control themselves or to know what they are doing.

The test most often used in America is the so-called McNaghten rule, based on an English case decided in 1843. Under McNaghten, a defendant cannot be found guilty if by reason of a mental illness he does not know the nature and quality of his act or, if he does know it, he does not know the difference between right and wrong. Some states recognize an additional "irresistible impulse" defense (see *Anatomy of a Murder*) which applies when a defendant cannot control his conduct. There are numerous other insanity formulas.

Becker may fall under the first part of McNaghten—he may not know the nature and quality of his act since he claims not to know what he is doing when he picks up and kills the girls. He may also fall under the irresistible impulse or similar tests, since he is unable to control what he is doing.

If acquitted on the grounds of insanity, a defendant is institutionalized until found to be no longer a danger to himself or to others. In a horrible case like Becker's, of course, he would probably be institutionalized for life or at least until old age.

The judges and the audience at Becker's trial conduct a vigorous debate about the insanity defense. Doesn't Becker deserve to die regardless of his mental state, as a matter of vengeance for his horrible crimes? What if Becker is faking—was he really unable to control himself? How do we really know if somebody is crazy anyhow? And if Becker is found insane and institutionalized, what if he escapes? Then he'll be on the loose again. We don't know how the criminals resolve these thorny issues, because the debate is cut short by the arrival of the police. Unfortunately for Becker, the rule against double jeopardy doesn't apply—he can and will be tried again in the regular courts.

M is a brilliant work of surrealistic art by the great director Fritz Lang. It is full of unforgettable scenes and great acting. In its topsy-turvy world, the police look like bumblers and the crooks look like respectable businessmen and seekers of justice. As experts in the criminal law, the mob does a respectable job of running a fair trial.

Trial Brief

Peter Lorre made his debut in *M* and was so unforgettable in the role that he became typecast for life. Lorre was Jewish and left Germany soon after the Nazis came to power. He once remarked: "The country was too small for two such monsters as Hitler and myself."

Becker is based upon Peter Kurten, a real child murderer known as the "Monster of Dusseldorf." Two months before Lang announced the film, Kurten's wife turned him in to the police at his request. Lang used real criminals as actors in the movie to make it more authentic; twenty-four of them were arrested for various offenses while the film was being shot. This is one way of keeping down a movie's production costs.

On Trial

Synopsis: When a man is charged with murdering his wife's former lover, the key direct examination is conducted by the jurors.

Warner Bros. 1939. Black and white. Running time: 60 min.

Screenplay: Don Ryan. Original Play: Elmer Rice. Director: Terry Morse.

Starring: John Litel (Robert Strickland), Margaret Lindsay (Mae Strickland), Janet Chapman (Doris Strickland), Edward Norris (Arbuckle), James Stephenson (Gerald Trask).

Rating: ⚖ ⚖

On Trial: The jurors wait to take matters into their own hands.

The Story

Robert Strickland is charged with killing wealthy Gerald Trask. The day of the murder, Strickland had paid Trask the $20,000 he had previously borrowed from Trask, in cash. District Attorney Gray's theory is that Strickland killed Trask to steal back the money from the wall safe in Trask's library. Strickland wants to plead guilty, but his attorney, Arbuckle, insists on a trial.

Gray's evidence suggests that Strickland has good reason for wanting to plead guilty. Mrs. Trask came to the library when she heard a noise, and saw Strickland shoot her husband. Glover, Trask's secretary, came running into the library when he heard shots and screams. Glover saw Strickland standing over the fallen Trask, gun in hand. Glover felled Strickland with a cane, and found a card with the combination to the wall safe in Strickland's pocket. Strickland tried to tear the card into pieces, but Glover pulled it away before he could do so and gave it to the police.

Again disregarding Strickland's wishes, Arbuckle calls Strickland's tearful five-year-old daughter Doris as a defense witness. The judge determines that Doris is competent to testify. Actually, the judge underestimates her. As Doris's testimony unfolds in a detailed flashback, she seems competent enough to recite *War and Peace.* According to

Doris, Trask came to the Strickland home and her daddy paid him $20,000 in cash. After Trask left, Strickland became angry with his wife Mae when he found out that Mae had spent the day with Trask, yet had tried to pretend that she had never met him. Strickland gets a gun and rushes out of the house. Later, Mae calls Trask's house, and Doris hears firecracker sounds through the phone. A panicked Mae runs out of the house, and neither Doris nor Strickland have seen her since.

A bailiff hands Arbuckle a letter, and the judge grants his request to recess the trial for a couple of hours. The local paper must produce a new edition every few minutes, because "Recess in Strickland Trial!" is headline news. The next edition would probably carry the headline, "Strickland Recess in 13th Minute!" After the recess, Mae dramatically enters the courtroom. She testifies that before she met Strickland, she was romanced by Trask. Mae ran out on Trask when she found out he was already married, and had not seen him again until Trask realized that she was married to Strickland. On the day Trask was killed, he had forced Mae to spend the day with him by threatening to reveal their old affair. If Strickland killed Trask, Mae says, he did it to protect her, not to steal back the money.

If anything, Arbuckle's defense has solidified Gray's claim that Strickland shot Trask. But in their deliberations, most of the jurors are sympathetic to Strickland and want to find him not guilty. One juror holds out for guilty, insisting that Strickland's attempt to tear up the card with the combination to the wall safe on it shows that his motive was robbery. To clear up their doubts, the jurors return to the courtroom and ask to question Strickland. He agrees to testify. In response to the jury foreman's questions, Strickland says that he didn't try to tear up the card, and couldn't have because he was in agony from being struck by the cane.

Sensing the road to victory, Arbuckle then questions Dr. Morgan, who examined Strickland just after the shooting. Dr. Morgan backs up Strickland, saying that the blow with the cane had paralyzed Strickland's entire right arm, and no way could he have used the arm to tear up a card. Arbuckle then recalls Glover to the stand and asks him to reenact what happened after he hit Strickland with the cane. The unsuspecting Glover, who did not hear the doctor's testimony, testifies that Strickland used his right arm throughout the struggle for the card and gun. Glover panics when the doctor's testimony is read back to him. He admits to stealing the $20,000 from the wall safe, but insists that he did not kill Trask. He's led away, and the jury immediately finds Strickland not guilty. Everyone is happy, including Gray and Mrs. Trask. Doris is so thrilled that she begins to recite the entire testimony.

Legal Analysis

Strickland gets away with murder, and the jurors seem to know it. Once they're convinced that Strickland did not kill for the money, but rather to avenge the abuse of Mae, they are sympathetic to him for taking out the Trask. Their not-guilty verdict illustrates the ultimate protection of the jury system in criminal cases. No matter what the "letter of the law," jurors are the conscience of the community and they have the power to disregard it. Jurors are never explicitly told that they have this power, and Arbuckle cannot ask them to exercise it, lest we end up with too much conscience and too little law.

Prosecutor Gray is not upset with the verdict. But even if he had thought that the jury thwarted justice, he would have been powerless to change the verdict. Once a jury declares a criminal defendant not guilty, its decision is binding forever. By contrast, in every other situation a judge has the power to overturn a jury's verdict. Thus, if a judge disagrees with a guilty verdict in a criminal case or with the verdict for either side in a civil case, she can order a new trial or even enter a different verdict.

The trial itself is a charming blend of reality and fantasy. On the reality side of the ledger is the judge's inquiry into Doris's competency as a witness. It doesn't take much for most people to qualify as a witness. As long as people understand the oath and are capable of communicating, they're in and it's up to the judge or jury to figure out if they're believable. But with young children like Doris, judges want to make sure that they know the difference between the truth and a lie and that it's wrong to lie. Thus, they may ask young children questions like, "If I were to tell you that I'm holding a pen right now, would that be the truth or a lie?" and "If I were to tell you that Santa Claus is a merchandising creation of a materialistic society, would that be the truth? Please, stop crying." Doris of course passes with flying colors by quoting one of the Ten Commandments. Thus, the judge correctly rules that she's competent to testify, though perhaps he goes too far by admitting her directly to Harvard.

Not so real is the jurors breaking off their deliberations to question Strickland. Undoubtedly, many jurors would love to hop out of the jury box to pursue evidence they think the attorneys are overlooking. But that would violate the ancient maxim, "Better to let ninety-nine guilty people go free than allow a juror to ask a question." In most courtrooms, jurors can't even submit written questions for a judge to ask. One reason for this caution is the fear that jurors will give more weight to the answers to their questions than to the rest of the testimony. Another is that jurors, unaware of evidence rules, will ask for improper information. That might give a litigant an unappetizing choice between revealing what the law says is inadmissible, or incurring the jurors' wrath by refusing to answer. A third reason is that, like the jurors in *On Trial,* the jurors will show up the legal profession by doing a better job of questioning than the lawyers.

As in many trial movies, the testimony in *On Trial* unfolds partly through flashbacks. The flashbacks are a useful reminder that we engage in a fiction when we swear witnesses to tell the "whole truth." Even little Doris would be unable to remember the detailed conversations, tones of voices, facial expressions, and the like that are part of the "whole truth" as presented in a flashback. Judges and jurors necessarily have to decide cases based on incomplete recreations of past events, and that is one reason that we don't force litigants, even a prosecutor in a criminal case, to prove their cases to an absolute certainty.

The Constitution assures a defendant of a "speedy trial." Coming in at an hour, this film assures viewers of a "speedy trial movie." Courts trying to reduce their backlogs should consider contacting the director's heirs.

Trial Brief

Elmer Rice, a lawyer, wrote the play on which the film is based in 1914. It was one of the first theatrical works to use the flashback technique. Before this film, the play was a silent picture in 1917 and an early talkie in 1928.

The Ox-Bow Incident

Synopsis: A posse turned lynch mob gives three men a summary trial, convicts them of murder, and hangs them. A haunting tribute to the value of due process.

Twentieth Century Fox (Lamar Trotti). 1943. Black and white. Running time: 75 min.

Starring: Henry Fonda (Gil Carter), Dana Andrews (Martin), Anthony Quinn (Martinez), Henry Morgan (Art Croft), Harry Davenport (Davies), Frank Conroy (Major Tetley), Leigh Whipper (Sparks).

Screenplay: Lamar Trotti. Novel: Walter Van Tilburg Clark. Director: William Wellman.

Academy Award nomination: Best Picture.

Rating:

The Story

It's Nevada, 1885. Nary a slot machine in sight. We're in Bridger's Wells, a wretched cowtown where there's nothing to do but drink, fight, play poker, fight some more, or visit the town's only prostitute. Carter and his sidekick Croft blow into town and settle down for serious drinking and brawling in the local saloon. News arrives that respected local rancher Larry Kincaid has been found murdered. There's been rustling in the area, and the killers were seen with Kincaid's cattle heading east. A posse forms to hunt down the bandits. Most members seem to join just to break the monotony. Sentiment is to catch the gunmen and hang them on the spot. The local brand of criminal justice is too slow and careless to bother with.

Only a few townspeople hold out against the mob. A storekeeper, Davies, tries to persuade the rabble to bring the killers back for a fair trial. Judge Tyler tries to calm the crowd but without his gavel and robes, he has no power. The sheriff, unfortunately, is away and Rich, the deputy sheriff, wants to prove himself as a lawman. He deputizes the whole mob.

Major Tetley, a former confederate officer, shows up in uniform to lead the posse. He wants to regain his lost military authority and also to toughen up his cowardly son. Ma Grier wants to show she is as tough as any man, though few would argue the point. Carter and Croft are uncomfortable with summary justice. But they ride with the posse anyway, believing that as strangers they are safer with the posse than being hunted by it. Sparks, a black man who seems to be the town preacher, is mostly ignored by everybody but rides along to pray for the killers. Luckily, the horses go along with the plan at no increase in pay.

The posse catches three men sleeping by a fire. Fifty head of cattle are nearby. Tetley conducts a rough-and-ready trial. Martin, the leader of the three men, protests that he bought the cattle from Kincaid. But he has trouble explaining the lack of a bill of sale; he claims Kincaid promised to mail one. Kincaid told someone else that he planned to sell no cattle this year. And Martin's statement that he paid $4,000 for a broken-down ranch is considered preposterous.

The second man is a senile old fellow who tries to blame Kincaid's murder on the third man, Juan Martinez, who at first seems unable to speak English. But someone identifies Martinez as a wanted criminal, and Martinez turns out to have Kincaid's gun, which he claims to have found on the trail. When Martinez tries to flee, he's shot in the leg. He then proves to speak excellent English.

It's majority rule. Davies cannot dissuade the mob. Carter is mostly passive (Henry Fonda was more successful in dissuading a mob in the jury room in *Twelve Angry Men* fourteen years later). Twenty-one of the twenty-eight vote to hang the three on the spot. Tetley grants a reprieve till dawn. Martin writes a letter to his wife, but won't let Davies read it to the crowd even if it might cause them to spare his life.

At dawn, the three are hanged. Shortly after, the sheriff arrives. Kincaid is not dead after all, and the sheriff has already caught the men who shot him. The three hanged men were entirely innocent. Who did this, the sheriff asks? All but seven, Davies replies.

In an epilogue, Martin's letter is read in the barroom. It is an eloquent testimonial to the values of due process of law. "Law is a lot more than the words you put in a book or judges or lawyers or sheriffs you hire to carry it out," Martin wrote. "It's everything people have ever found out about justice and what's right and wrong. It's the very conscience of humanity." Unfortunately, Martin's letter doesn't tell his wife where he hid the key to the outhouse.

Carter and Croft take up a collection from the barflies and ride off to deliver the letter and the money to Martin's wife.

Legal Analysis

Justice means a fair trial, in court, with lawyers, flags, and an impartial judge and jury. A fair trial can happen only after all the evidence has been carefully gathered and calmly presented. Nothing else will do. These simple themes have never been sounded more convincingly and movingly than in *The Ox-Bow Incident.*

The mob wants justice now, and cannot wait to gather evidence. Martin and his men are strangers, and strangers are suspect. Nobody can be bothered to check Martin's story about purchasing the ranch, or to search out witnesses among Kincaid's cowboys, or to wait for the sheriff who was known to have been at Kincaid's ranch that day. Doing justice right is indeed slow and uncertain. Impatient people don't want to take the time. They want to finish the business quickly.

The Ox-Bow Incident and *They Won't Forget* are the classic films about lynch mob justice. Audiences in 1943 must have thought back to the lynch mobs so recently prevalent in the South. Perhaps too they thought about Europe and about mobs of brutish thugs destroying the lives and property of innocent people. Others were wondering what an ox-bow might be.

The Ox-Bow Incident involves a "trial" in which circumstantial evidence makes up the whole case against Martin and his crew. There is no direct (meaning "eyewitness") testimony about Kincaid's death (see *Circumstantial Evidence,* p. 193). Here the items of circumstantial evidence raised powerful inferences of guilt: Martin had Kincaid's cattle, but no bill of sale. There had been a lot of rustling in the area. Kincaid had said that he would sell no cattle this year. Martinez had

Kincaid's gun and was identified as a wanted criminal. Martinez tried to flee and falsely pretended to speak no English. Martin's story about purchasing the broken-down ranch for $4,000 seemed absurd to men who knew the value of property in the area. All of this evidence raises inferences that in combination point solidly toward guilt. Yet every inference was wrong. Every bit of evidence had an innocent explanation. That is why we instruct jurors that if two inferences are equally possible, one pointing toward guilt and one toward innocence, they must adopt the latter inference. At a real trial, Martin would have had time to gather evidence of his own. Even assuming that Kincaid were really dead and that his real killers were at large, Martin might have been able to raise a reasonable doubt in the minds of the jurors. But he had no chance at all in a trial conducted by a vengeful and impatient mob at 3:00 on a cold morning at Ox-Bow.

The Star Chamber

Synopsis: Fed up with judges putting vicious crooks back on the street on some idiotic technicality? This film has a solution for you!

Twentieth Century Fox (Frank Yablans). 1983. Color. Running time: 109 min.

Screenplay: Roderick Taylor and Peter Hyams. Director: Peter Hyams.

Starring: Michael Douglas (Judge Steven Hardin), Hal Holbrook (Judge Benjamin Caulfield), Yaphet Kotto (Det. Harry Lowes), James B. Sikking (Dr. Harold Lewin), Sharon Gless (Emily Hardin).

Rating: —▮ —▮

The Story

Judge Hardin has to dismiss solid cases against vicious criminals because the Fourth Amendment requires him to exclude evidence obtained as a result of unlawful searches and seizures. Hector Andujar, for example, killed five old ladies to get their social security. The police chase Andujar and see him stick something into the trash can in front of his house. The cops wait until the garbage truck picks up Andujar's trash and places it in the scooper. Then they search the garbage and find the murder weapon. Judge Hardin excludes the evidence and dismisses the case—unlawful search and seizure. The police are lucky that the judge allows them to shower afterwards.

Later the case against Lawrence Monk and Arthur Cooms suffers the same fate. The police radio in and are told there are outstanding traffic warrants against a van. They stop the van and find the occupants extremely suspicious. They claim to smell marijuana. When they search the van, they find a bloody shoe. This shoe belonged to a young boy, Danny Lewin, who had been brutally murdered. Trouble is, the parking tickets had been paid at the time the police stopped the van, but the payments hadn't yet been entered into the police computer system. Therefore, the cops had no probable cause to stop the van, and all evidence discovered as a result of the search was suppressed.

These rulings leave the frustrated Hardin, D.A., and cops gnashing their teeth. For the first time, they realize that the Constitution was drafted by dentists. Dr. Lewin, Danny's father, is so devastated that he draws his gun and tries to kill Monk and Cooms but only succeeds in wounding a police officer. Judge Hardin is overcome with guilt but can see no way to avoid turning the vermin loose.

Hardin's former professor and fellow Judge, Benjamin Caulfield, inducts him into the Star Chamber. This group of nine angry judges meets secretly to consider the fate of criminals who got off on technicalities. Rule 1: If the Star Chamber votes guilty, hired killers dispose of the crooks. Rule 2: Everyone is guilty.

Will the conscientious Judge Hardin bring himself to join in the fun with this friendly bunch of judicial vigilantes? No way. He discovers that Monk and Coombs actually were not guilty of killing Danny Lewin, but the chamber says that it's too late to call off the hit people. After a series of silly chase scenes and narrow escapes, Hardin breaks up the Star Chamber.

Legal Analysis

The Star Chamber was an English court formed in 1347 to deal with complex cases. It was named aftr the gilded stars in the ceiling of its courtroom. Later, in the reign of Henry VIII, the court began to try criminal cases without juries, especially unpopular political cases. It specialized in such punishments as slitting of noses and severing of ears. It was widely detested and ultimately abolished. The words "star chamber" are still used to describe unfair and arbitrary judicial procedures, and the "court" in this movie stacks up well with the Spanish Inquisition.

The Fourth Amendment provides "The right of the people to be secure in their persons, houses, papers, and effects, against unreasonable searches and seizures, shall not be violated." Therefore, unless a search is "reasonable" or unless the police have obtained a search warrant, they cannot conduct a search for evidence.

What happens if the police violate this rule? Under the "exclusionary rule" of *Mapp v. Ohio* (1961), courts must exclude evidence obtained as the result of an unlawful search and seizure. Many people—cluding the makers of *The Star Chamber*—think that the exclusionary rule is wrong. Why, they ask, should the criminal go free because the constable blundered? But so far the courts have stuck with the rule, believing it is the only effective way to deter police officers from violating the Fourth Amendment whenever they want to.

Of course, there's a lot of law on what constitutes a "reasonable" search. Judge Hardin's reluctant rulings illustrate how technical the Fourth Amendment can be—and how difficult it is for police to keep up with it. Let's look at his rulings:

In the Andujar case, Judge Hardin suppressed the gun that the cops found in the defendant's trash can. That ruling was probably correct under California law at the time the movie was made. California courts had held that people have a reasonable expectation of privacy in their trash, so the cops can't search it without first getting a warrant. As precedent, this stunk. Later the U.S. Supreme Court changed that rule and held that once people put their trash outside to be picked up, it can be searched by the police even before it is mixed with other garbage (*California v. Greenwood,* 1988).

In the Monk and Cooms case, the police stopped the van because the computer erroneously informed them of outstanding warrants. Once they stopped the van, they smelled marijuana, searched the van, and found the bloody tennis shoe. The legality of the search depends on whether they had probable cause to stop the van in the first place.

Judge Hardin's ruling was correct at the time it was issued. Under former California law, the police had no probable cause for an arrest if the computerized information on which they relied is incorrect (*People v. Ramirez,* 1983). However, the U.S. Supreme Court has since ruled that if the police make an arrest in good faith reliance on information in a computer database, the arrest is valid even though the computerized information was wrong (*Arizona v. Evans,* 1995). Thus if the Monk and Cooms case came up today, the bloody tennis shoe could be admitted into evidence.

The suppression motions in this movie are realistic and they make a valid point. Reasonable people can criticize search and seizure law as impossibly complicated and too protective of criminals. Perhaps the police should be entitled to introduce evidence when they make a good faith error in arresting or searching someone. Maybe the exclusionary rule should be weakened or junked.

But a judge is required to follow the law, even if he or she finds it unjust or absurd. We can imagine that a judge who is really fed up with the Fourth Amendment might twist the facts a bit, refuse to exclude the evidence, and pass the buck to an appellate court. That court might quietly affirm without writing an opinion.

Sometimes the police lie to get around search and seizure law. For example, in the Monk and Cooms case, the police could have pretended to stop the van for an illegal left turn. In fact, the "smell of marijuana" excuse used by the police to search Monk's van is pretty suspicious. None of this is acceptable judicial or police behavior, but it goes on all the time.

It is inconceivable that American judges would condone vigilante justice, no matter how frustrated they felt about legal technicalities. Their training and professional moral code would prevent it. Besides, they'd have too much to lose if they get caught and it's likely they eventually would get caught.

And yet—there is quite a tradition of vigilante justice around the world. In many countries, the police or the army simply caused undesirable people to disappear. The "dirty wars" in Argentina, Chile, or El Salvador are just a few of many such examples. Judges often turned a blind eye to police terrorism. And you don't have to go too far back in American history to find lynch mobs and vigilante justice. They're well illustrated in *Fury, The Oxbow Incident,* and *They Won't Forget.* By the same token, *Judgment at Nuremberg* tells the story of judges who turned their courtrooms into official lynching machines.

So *The Star Chamber* may seem ridiculous, but a germ of truth lurks behind the nonsense. The rule of law sometimes leads to putting creeps back on the street. It is all too tempting for people—even judges—to take the law into their own hands.

Suspect

Synopsis: A public defender and a juror join forces to prove that a deaf-mute derelict did not commit a murder.

Columbia/Tri-Star Pictures (John Veitch). 1987. Color. Running time: 121 min.

Screenplay: Eric Roth. Director: Peter Yates.

Starring: Cher (Kathleen Riley), Dennis Quaid (Eddie Sanger), Liam Neeson (Carl Wayne Anderson), John Mahoney (Judge Matthew Helms), Joe Mantegna (Charlie Stella), Philip Bosco (Paul Grey).

Rating: —▮ —▮

Surprise ending warning: Reading this analysis could be hazardous to your enjoyment of the movie!

The Story

Justice Lowell hands an envelope to a government clerk named Elizabeth Quinn, then commits suicide. Not long afterwards, Quinn her-

Suspect: Kathleen Riley (Cher) cross-examines while Charlie Stella (Joe Mantegna) waits his turn.

self is floating in the Potomac River, stabbed to death. Carl Wayne Anderson, a disheveled, derelict deaf-mute holed up in a nearby tent, is quickly arrested for murdering Quinn when the police find him in possession of a knife and her purse.

When we meet her, Kathleen Riley is a Washington, D.C., public defender having a very bad day. She's attacked while driving in to work, given the thankless task of defending Anderson, and then struck by Anderson when she tries to interview him, not realizing that a Vietnam War–related illness has left him unable to hear or speak. They soon learn to communicate in writing, but all he can tell her is that Quinn was already dead when he found her and that a tattooed man named "Michael" had been poking around her body first.

Prosecutor Charlie Stella's opening statement tells the jurors that Anderson was about to enter Quinn's parked car to escape the December cold when she returned. He killed her, took her wallet and its $9, and dumped her into the nearby river. Riley's response is that while Anderson may be a lowlife who took Quinn's money, he didn't kill Quinn.

After Stella's expert doctor describes the fatal wound, the defense becomes a team effort of Riley and one of the jurors, Eddie Sanger. Sanger is a hotshot Washington lobbyist for milk producers who proves as adept at gathering evidence as votes. After studying the photos of

Quinn's fatal wound, Sanger anonymously phones Riley during a recess in the trial. Riley, who knew that the caller was Sanger, uses his tip to cross-examine the doctor. Riley gets the doctor to testify that the killer was right-handed. Then, proving that she prepared for trial by watching Atticus Finch defend Tom Robinson in *To Kill a Mockingbird,* she suddenly tosses a soft object to Anderson, who instinctively catches it with his left hand.

Sanger quickly becomes a sleuth that even Arthur Conan Doyle would have had trouble creating. Sanger examines Quinn's car, which the police have improbably allowed to remain in the same parking lot for two months (perhaps they validate). He also obtains a list of the license plate numbers of all the cars that were in the parking lot on the night Quinn was killed, chases Michael away when he attacks Riley with a knife, finds a key to Quinn's filing cabinet on Michael's dead body, and helps Riley with her legal research. He and Riley also break into Quinn's filing cabinet, and learn that before her death Quinn had been looking into old trial transcripts from 1968.

Riley and Sanger try to conceal their relationship, at least when they're not together in a public law library, the Department of Justice elevators, and an open courtroom. Nevertheless, Judge Helms becomes suspicious. Judge Helms is presiding over the trial after trading cases with another judge, expecting the Anderson trial to be over by the time Helms's expected presidential appointment to the Court of Appeal comes through. Helms orders the jury sequestered (kept together until the trial is over), in order to prevent Sanger from doing any more work on the case.

However, on the bus to the jurors' hotel, Sanger sees a car leaving the courthouse bearing the license plate of a car that was in the same parking lot as Quinn's the night she was killed. He thinks Riley is in danger, and escapes from the jurors' hotel. Meanwhile, Riley breaks into Quinn's car, which is still on the lot, and finds an audiocassette in the cassette deck. The tape contains Justice Lowell's last words, and describes a 1968 case in which Lowell and unnamed others had accepted a bribe to dismiss charges against a gangster named Cook. To find out who these others were, Riley rushes to the dark, empty courthouse and finds the lawbook containing the Cook case. She is chased off by a shadowy intruder, but saved by Sanger's sudden appearance.

In court the next morning, Riley identifies Judge Helms as Quinn's killer. Helms killed Quinn to keep her from blocking his promotion by revealing that he also had taken a bribe in the Cook case. Helms is arrested by Paul Grey, the red herring attorney general who until the end seemed to be the killer. Sanger and Riley then privately celebrate the eternal values of Truth, Justice, and Sexual Lust between Lawyers and Jurors.

Legal Analysis

Riley is a realistic public defender. She is dedicated to her job, but burned out by a daily treadmill of too many cases, little investigatory help, and clients who have a disturbing tendency to be guilty. She and her colleague Morty agree that what keeps them going is the chance to defend the rare innocent defendant. However, most public defenders do not measure success by the rate of "not guilty" verdicts. Giving a drug user a chance to avoid prosecution by entering a diversion program or securing mental health counseling for a client who must serve time are the sorts of outcomes that public defenders can look to as triumphs.

Even if she were unable to prove who really killed Quinn, Riley has a strong argument that Stella has failed to prove Anderson's guilt beyond a reasonable doubt. Stella has no eyewitnesses, Anderson is left-handed while the killer was probably right-handed, and nothing shows that Anderson's knife was the one used to kill Quinn. But like Riley, most defense attorneys try to do more than argue that the prosecution has failed to meet its burden of proof. They know that whatever the law says, many jurors are likely to believe that innocent people should be able to prove their innocence. Thus, even if they don't have Riley's success in fingering the real culprit, defense attorneys at least try to offer evidence of their clients' innocence.

In its basic plot, however, about the only thing real about *Suspect* is that the Potomac River does flow through Washington, D.C. As a devoted public defender who likes her job, Riley would not risk tossing away her career by even talking to Sanger during a trial, let alone meeting him repeatedly in public. The moment that Riley realized that Sanger was her anonymous tipster, she would have reported the improper contact to Judge Helms. Judge Helms would have immediately removed Sanger from the jury and appointed an alternate, or declared a mistrial and started all over again with new jurors. Sanger would probably have been permanently removed from the juror rolls, perhaps the result he was trying to achieve in the first place. Combining his experience as a milk lobbyist with his newly-developed detective skills, Sanger could then start a new company called "Moos and Clues."

Second, Riley ties Judge Helms to the Cook case bribery scheme by reading about the case in a volume of the *Federal Supplement*. But that's farcical. Most rulings by trial judges are never published; either they are oral, or if written they go into the court's and lawyers' case files and nowhere else. That's one reason that Judge Helms longs for a Court of Appeal position; he wants to write published opinions. Besides, there's no way that Judge Lowell, having taken a bribe, would have issued a written opinion. He simply would have entered an order dismissing the charges against Cook. Thus, there would have been no ruling for Riley to find in the *Federal Supplement* or anywhere else.

The tactics of both counsel are as suspect as the movie's title. Riley inexplicably waits two months to examine Quinn's car, and then does so by breaking in unlawfully. Of course, Riley had no need to break in. It's obvious that Quinn's car might contain relevant evidence; that's where Stella says she was killed. Thus, Riley should have inspected the car as soon as she took the case, and could have done so at any time simply by contacting Stella or the police. Riley's finding the tape is also silly; even the Keystone Kops would have found it immediately.

Riley's in-court techniques are no better. Cross-examining one of the police officers who arrested Anderson, Riley has the officer agree that the police don't determine guilt or innocence. The question is pointless, but perhaps the answer was a relief to the jurors, who would otherwise have wondered what their role was. Riley then asks the officer if he knows that at least 343 innocent people have been wrongly convicted, twenty-five of them executed. Where these figures come from is unclear, though given her trial technique it's possible that Riley is just referring to people that she's represented. Nevertheless, this information too is irrelevant to the issue of Anderson's guilt. Finally, there's Riley's direct examination of her client. She's supposed to ask questions. Instead she improperly becomes an unsworn witness, telling most of Anderson's story herself. At least Anderson personally denies killing Quinn, a dramatic moment when he utters his only sound.

Not to be outdone by Riley's mistakes, Charlie Stella commits reversible error before the trial is a minute old. During his opening statement, Stella tells the jurors that of the forty-three murder cases he's prosecuted, this one is the most horrible. At best, this is an improper thing to say during opening statement. Opening statement is only supposed to be a preview of Stella's evidence, not an argument. But Stella's remark would have been highly improper and prejudicial no matter when he made it. Stella not only injects his personal experience and credibility as a prosecutor directly into the case, but also he invites the jurors to compare Anderson to forty-three other murderers.

If a Court of Appeal had any doubts about Stella's prosecutorial misconduct, he removes them while cross-examining Anderson. Stella begins by telling Anderson that he deserves a medal for his direct examination "performance." This comment too is improper; Stella is supposed to ask questions and save his comments for final summation. Anyway, if Stella had been paying attention to Anderson's direct examination he would have awarded the medal to Riley, not Anderson, since Riley personally provided most of Anderson's defense.

Continuing his cross-examination, Stella shows the jury that Anderson is prone to violence. In response to Stella's questions, Anderson admits that while in Vietnam he beat a superior officer with a shovel, that another time he was arrested for assaulting a congressional aide, and that on still another occasion he spent six months in jail for beating a man who took his shoes. Unfortunately for Stella, not a single one of these events is admissible in evidence. It is improper for Stella to show that Anderson has been violent in the past, hoping that the jury will infer that he is just the sort of person who would have killed Quinn. The evidence rules barring character evidence protect defendants against being convicted for their past misdeeds, and Stella's questions are grossly improper (see *Character Evidence,* below).

Though the movie is entertaining, the plot of *Suspect* is one that even Aesop would have rejected as defying belief. The title is more relevant to the movie's depiction of trial rules than to the plot.

Sidebar: Character Evidence

Lawyers in trial films frequently try to improve their chances of winning by showing that a witness has an unsavory past, and is therefore just the sort of skunk who would commit murder, lie, or listen to country music. For example:

- In *Anatomy of a Murder,* the D.A. offers evidence that a defendant charged with murder previously attacked a soldier in a jealous rage. And the defense attorney offers evidence that a prosecution witness has been arrested for or convicted of a string of petty offenses.
- In *Suspect,* the D.A. offers evidence that a deaf mute charged with murder had previously beaten a man with a shovel and attacked a congressional aide.

In the colorful parlance of evidence rules, nasty past misdeeds constitute "character evidence." Character evidence confronts courts with difficult issues. In daily life we rely on character evidence regularly, whether choosing a baby-sitter or deciding which driver was at fault in an accident.

But character evidence can be highly prejudicial. Jurors may be too quick to assess blame according to past behavior, and not look carefully enough at how the specific events giving rise to the trial took place. And simple trials would turn into lengthy morality plays if lawyers were freely allowed to dredge up witnesses' pasts.

With some exceptions, the anti–character evidence forces have generally won the battle. For example, a party can offer evidence of a witness's past misdeeds to prove that the witness is a liar, but only if those misdeeds resulted in convictions for felonies or, if a nonfelony, crimes of dishonesty (e.g., theft). Thus, the defense attorney's cross-examination of the prosecution witness in *Anatomy of a Murder* is almost entirely improper. The lawyer refers to a string of arrests, which aren't even convictions. And what few convictions he mentions are misdemeanors not involving dishonesty.

A second possible use of past misdeeds is to prove that a person did whatever it's claimed he or she did (e.g., drove carelessly, committed a murder, etc.). To be admissible, the past misdeed has to be either identical to the act a party is charged with doing, or closely enough related to it to prove the party's intent or motive. Just showing that a party has been a rotter in the past won't do it.

In *Suspect,* for example, the D.A.'s character evidence is highly improper. Evidence that the defendant once hit a man with a shovel and attacked a congressional page are in no way identical to the murder he's charged with committing. Nor do they indicate that he intended to or had a motive to commit murder.

When you watch a film in which one of the attorneys triumphantly harpoons a witness or a party on his sordid past, you can be almost certain that the evidence would not have been allowed in an actual trial. Just another reason why it's more fun watching a movie than a real trial.

Trial by Jury

Synopsis: A jury tampering story told from the point of view of a juror whose choice is to play along or die.

Morgan Creek (James G. Robinson, Chris Meledandri, Mark Gordon). 1994. Running time: 107 min.

Screenplay: Heywood Gould and Jordan Katz. Director: Heywood Gould.

Starring: Joanne Whalley-Kilmer (Valerie Alston), Armand Assante (Rusty Pirone), William Hurt (Tommy Vesey), Gabriel Byrne (Daniel Graham).

Rating: —▮ —▮ —▮

Surprise ending warning: Reading this summary may be hazardous to your enjoyment of the movie!

The Story

Valerie Alston is a single mother and owner of a small business. When called for jury service she agrees to serve as a matter of civic duty. Everyone thinks she's nuts and, as things turn out, they're right. Prosecutor Daniel Graham is trying to convict a smooth but vicious gangland chieftain named Rusty Pirone. But Pirone's goons have rubbed out Limpy, a key witness who is being guarded in a hotel room by four police officers. These guys don't kid around.

Still uncertain of victory, the thugs find Alston at her son's soccer practice and force her into a van. Her job, explains Tommy Vesey, a crooked ex-cop, is to find Pirone innocent and hang the jury. Otherwise, she, her son, and her father will be killed. It's that simple. If she cooperates, Vesey explains, he will protect her. If not, forget it. And when she tries to hide the kid at her dad's place in the country, Vesey immediately presents her with photos of the farmhouse. However, at least Vesey doesn't charge Alston for the prints.

Even though the police are guarding the apartments of the jurors, Pirone himself sneaks into Alston's apartment. It is unclear how Pirone, who is being tried for murder, has gotten out on bail; normally murder is a nonbailable offense. Nor is it clear how he gets past the chain on Alston's door, unless Pirone is a part-time ghost as well as a mobster. But Pirone leaves no doubt that Alston is totally vulnerable. He explains that the game is not a matter of who dies, but who dies first. It's going to be her and the kid unless she plays along. And while he's at it, he rapes her.

Graham puts on a strong case against Pirone. By offering leniency to a series of convicts, Graham gets them to testify. He persuades Pirone's uncle to testify by threatening to disclose pictures of the uncle engaged in a homosexual act in prison. All in all, Graham's case—even without the unlucky Limpy—looks quite solid. Defense Attorney Greco can do little to discredit the prosecution's case except to call the various witnesses liars, killers, and thieves—which, of course, they are.

But Alston does her job. To the intense frustration of her fellow jurors, she holds out for a not guilty verdict. In the jury room, she argues that it was all a set-up and that Pirone's constitutional rights were violated. She steadily gains confidence, flirting with one of the men and getting one of the women to come to her defense. In fact, she turns out to be a much better advocate than Greco. Ultimately, four jurors vote for acquittal and a mistrial is declared.

Intensely frustrated by this defeat, Graham decides to find out what went wrong. From interviewing the jurors, Graham figures out that Alston was the main holdout and befriends her. Meanwhile, he has her apartment searched and finds an incriminating photo. When the mob's watchers see Graham come to Alston's home at night, they assume she's cooperating with Graham and decide to kill her immediately. Yet the murder attempt goes awry—Vesey has fallen in love with Alston and he shows up to save her. In the process he guns down the killers but is killed himself. His last words to her are that she must kill Pirone. Nothing like going out on a high note.

Looking nothing like the goody-two-shoes she was at the beginning of the movie, Alston contacts Pirone and goes to meet him at his country home. As they embrace, he tries to smother her, because it is too risky to let her live. She reaches for the knife in her purse and kills him. As the movie ends, she finally explains to Graham that she did what she had to do. Next time, she'll throw away the jury summons.

Legal Analysis

Trial by Jury shows how very difficult it is to convict organized crime leaders. It's army against army. Graham has a team of about five lawyers helping him, because the defendants have unlimited resources. They will call upon skillful and tenacious defense lawyers. The only living witnesses to the crimes of gang leaders are their few close associates, who are sworn to secrecy. Anybody who breaches their oath is killed.

Yet in recent years, numerous gangland bigshots have been convicted by the techniques used in this movie. By offering leniency or immunity to lower-level thugs, it is possible to get them to testify against the top guys. Then the witnesses are placed in a witness protection program and disappear. Loyalty just isn't what it used to be, and some gang soldiers aren't willing to spend life in prison just to keep their bosses on the street.

Graham clearly goes over the line in using the uncle's testimony against Pirone. It is unclear in the movie whether the sexual incident in the toilet was arranged by the prosecution to set up the uncle or a plumber. Even if the incident was discovered by accident, inducing a witness to testify by threatening to disclose embarrassing private information may be outrageous government misconduct that could require reversing a conviction. At a minimum, Graham was obliged to disclose to the defense how he got the witness to testify. Prosecutors must disclose evidence to the defense that can be used to impeach a witness to minimize the risk of false testimony. Of course, if it had been disclosed, the uncle would have refused to testify—so Graham confronted a catch-22 situation.

Whenever criminals are the witnesses against a defendant, the defense argues that such witnesses should not be believed. The witnesses are especially untrustworthy because they have usually made a deal with prosecutors that requires them to deliver incriminating testimony in order to hold up their side of the deal. These are indeed terrible witnesses, but without them, as Graham explains, it would be impossible to ever convict the wiseguys at the top of the organized crime heap. But as the incident with the uncle shows, prosecutors must observe at least a few basic rules of fair play when they turn criminal against criminal.

Jurors are notoriously unpredictable, and lawyers are always looking for some way to pick out which ones are likely to be sympathetic or antagonistic. As the jury is selected we see both sides being advised by their jury consultants. Greco's consultant has the easier job—find jurors who want to live. The use of consultants is now routine in important civil and criminal cases. It is not really clear whether jury consultants can produce a better jury than an experienced trial lawyer using his or her intuition. Still, nobody who can afford consultants dares to give them up. In this case, the consultants for both sides thought that Alston was a perfect juror.

Hung juries are a major problem in the criminal justice system. Although a case can be tried over again after a hung jury, retrials are costly to all concerned. Sometimes witnesses disappear, die, or change their stories between the two trials. In some cities, an increasing number of juries are hung, for reasons that can only be guessed at—possibly increasing distrust of the police or racial polarization.

The problem of jury intimidation is very real. Jury tampering carries a five-year maximum prison sentence under federal law, but it occurs just the same. Organized crime and gang defendants have the ability to seek out and kill anyone they choose, and jurors fear retribution if they vote someone guilty. What should someone like Alston do when she and her family are so plausibly threatened with death? Go to the police or the prosecutors? Of course—but as the picture shows, they might be unable to protect her. And at a minimum, if she reports the threat, she will have to go into some kind of witness protection program after the trial is over and her family and business life will be ruined.

Especially in gang and organized crime cases, the anonymity of jurors is protected so that it will be harder to find them. In fact, the jurors are anonymous in *Trial by Jury* but the mob finds Alston's name by following her to lunch and looking at her credit card receipt. She charges the lunch for everybody on the theory that she'd get a good tax deduction—showing that she knows as little about tax law as about the risks of serving on a jury in an organized crime case.

Sequestration of jurors is another technique that is often used to protect jurors both from attempts to influence them and from media publicity. Sequestered jurors have to stay together in hotel rooms throughout the trial. This is a huge hardship on jurors if the trial is lengthy. Sequestration makes it much harder to find jurors who are willing to serve and removes a lot of good potential jurors from the panel. Probably the judge in *Trial by Jury* should have sequestered the jurors as soon as there was any suspicion that tampering might have occurred.

Normally, the bait in jury tampering cases is money; the juror's vote is simply purchased for what seems like a fortune to an ordinary person but is pocket change to the defendant. There have been several successful prosecutions of jurors who were paid off, including one at the John Gotti trial in 1986. And Teamster boss Jimmy Hoffa was convicted of jury tampering in an earlier trial in which he had obtained a hung jury.

Trial by Jury effectively presents the dilemmas of fighting organized crime with our system of criminal due process. Even lowlives like Pirone get a fair trial and the right to an impartial jury. Yet they cannot be convicted unless we rely on possibly perjured testimony from vicious criminals who have been given immunity from prosecution. And we subject ordinary, vulnerable citizens like Alston to great inconvenience and sometimes to personal risk when they are called upon to serve as jurors. After seeing this movie, how many people will be willing to do it?

Twelve Angry Men

Synopsis: A jury deliberates the fate of a young minority defendant in a murder case. If you're ever on trial for your life, you'd better hope that someone like Henry Fonda is in the jury room.

UA, Orion-Nova (Henry Fonda and Reginald Rose), 1957. Black and white. Running time: 95 min.

Screenplay: Reginald Rose. Original play: Reginald Rose. Director: Sidney Lumet.

Starring: Henry Fonda (Juror), Lee J. Cobb (Juror), E.G. Marshall (Juror), Jack Warden (Juror), Ed Begley (Juror), Martin Balsam (Juror), Jack Klugman (Juror).

Academy Award nominations: Best Picture, Best Screenplay, Best Director.

Rating: —▮ —▮ —▮ —▮

The Story

The film opens as a bored judge instructs the jury. It's a Murder-1 case and the defendant goes to the chair if convicted. He's an eighteen-year-old Puerto Rican with a criminal record. He is accused of killing his father with a knife about midnight. The father often beat the boy and their relationship was bad.

As the jury deliberates, we learn what happened in the trial. The evidence against the defendant was strong. A woman who lived across the elevated train tracks testified that she was in bed at the critical moment. Through her bedroom window and through the windows of a passing train, she saw the defendant do the deadly deed. An old man who lived downstairs testified that he heard the defendant say "I'll kill you" and heard a body fall. The old man ran to his front door and saw the defendant running down the stairs. The knife used to do in the father was a switchblade like one the defendant had recently purchased.

The defendant's alibi was pitiful. He claimed he was at the movies from eleven until three in the morning, but couldn't even remember the names of the movies he had just seen. Apparently, they weren't memorable trial films.

The case seems open and shut and the all-male jury immediately votes eleven to one for conviction. The jury room is stifling. In a quaint echo of yesteryear, many of the jurors puff away on cigarettes (today, of course, smoking in the jury room would be punishable by five years on the chain gang). Everyone is sweating and cranky. There are no names; the jurors never introduce themselves. The deliberations are nasty and the remarks get personal. Only an architect

Twelve Angry Men: The jury debates the fate of a young murder defendant.

played by Henry Fonda holds out, indicating that he has some doubts.

Fonda gambles. He calls for another vote and says that he'll give in if nobody else will vote for acquittal. An older juror, respecting Fonda's independence, joins him in voting to acquit. Fonda begins probing the prosecution's case and various inconsistencies emerge. The shopkeeper who had sold the defendant the knife testified that he had never seen one like it; but Fonda produces an identical one and plunges it into the table (probably another severely punishable offense). He bought it at a pawnshop the night before. Fonda points out that the old man could not have heard the defendant yell over the noise of the passing train. He also shows that the lame old man could not have traveled the distance from his bed to the door in fifteen seconds as he had claimed. Other jurors begin to pick holes in the prosecution's case. For example, the woman who claimed she had seen the crime from across the tracks had small indentations on her nose that could only be made by glasses, but she obviously was not wearing her glasses in bed. The older juror points out that the old man really just wanted some attention. The cool E.G. Marshall cannot remember details of a movie he had just seen, tending to explain the defendant's failure to recollect and Hollywood's box office slump.

The juror played by Ed Begley is a racist, talking about how "these people" are violent and can't tell the truth. His racist arguments backfire, swaying undecided jurors toward a vote of innocence. One by one, the jurors switch from guilt to innocence. Finally, only the temperamental juror played by Lee J. Cobb holds out for guilt. He seems committed to executing the defendant. His estrangement from his own son has deepened his bitterness toward young people. In the end, even Cobb gives way as his various arguments crumble. The defendant is acquitted.

Legal Analysis

The defendant's lawyer did a terrible job. As Fonda points out, he was probably appointed to a case for which he was paid little and had nothing to gain. Apparently, he barely cross-examined the prosecution's witnesses. All of the inconsistencies were identified by the jurors, not by counsel at the trial. Moreover, the jurors know the defendant's criminal record—he attended reform school. But evidence of juvenile crimes would not be admissible, even if the defendant had testified, which apparently he didn't. It sounds like counsel fell asleep and failed to object to introduction of evidence about prior convictions (see *Character Evidence,* p. 259).

The defendant was on trial for his life (until 1963, first-degree murder carried a mandatory death sentence in New York). The sad reality is that it's difficult to find counsel to defend indigent defendants in capital cases, as well as to handle the lengthy and complex appeals that usually follow a death sentence. In order to do a good job in a capital case, an attorney must put in an enormous effort, yet the client is often a revolting personality, the chances of winning are slim, the public is disdainful, and the pay is inadequate. Public defenders are swamped with cases and often cannot put in the necessary effort to defend a capital case.

Twelve Angry Men is about the concept of reasonable doubt. It is the prosecution's burden to prove guilt beyond a reasonable doubt. None of the jurors who voted for acquittal, including Fonda, were convinced of the defendant's innocence. Indeed, the defendant probably was guilty. Let's not forget that he was identified by two eyewitnesses, his alibi was dubious, and the murder weapon was an unusual knife identical to one he had purchased. No suspect other than the defendant ever materialized.

Yet, the many questions and inconsistencies that cropped up during deliberations raised reasonable doubts in the minds of the jurors. Perhaps after all was said and done, the odds were ninety to ten in favor of guilt, yet that was not enough to convict the defendant of murder. Does this make sense? Considering the risk to society from turning a killer loose, is it worth acquitting ninety guilty people in order to avoid convicting ten innocent people? Or even ninety-nine killers to avoid convicting one innocent person?

Twelve Angry Men may be the best film about jury deliberations ever made. It contains many realistic insights about the jury system. Often, as in this case, jurors resent being stuck with the burdensome task of jury duty. They are paid little for their services. They sit around the jury room waiting to be picked for a jury. If they're lucky, they'll be able to entertain themselves with a thirty-year-old jigsaw puzzle missing several pieces. If they're picked as a potential juror, they must answer personal questions that even a daytime TV talk show host would hesitate to ask. Then they have to pay attention during a long and often tedious trial (without getting to hear some of the best bits which occur in the judge's chambers). Then they yawn through the judge's instructions which are phrased in legal mumbo jumbo. Finally, the really unpleasant part begins. The jurors are locked up with some pretty obnoxious personalities in sparse surroundings, especially before the introduction of air-conditioning. And they naturally want to wrap things up and get on with their lives.

In criminal cases, most states require unanimous jury verdicts (split decisions are acceptable only in civil cases and boxing matches). An eleven to one split in a criminal case is a hung jury and the case must be retried (or dismissed if the prosecution elects not to retry it). This means that twelve strangers must try to deliberate until everyone falls into line. Of course, it is very difficult to be a lone holdout, as Fonda was at first; a great amount of character is required to resist when one's cojurors are sure of their ground and impatient with any additional discussion. But jurors do take their work very seriously and perhaps it is not unheard-of for a single sturdy holdout to turn an entire jury around.

The jury in *Twelve Angry Men* was not well chosen. The defendant was a person from a minority group, probably Puerto Rican. Yet the jury consisted of eleven white Anglo males and one perhaps Hispanic male. There should have been a much larger minority representation on a jury drawn from a big-city panel. A skillful voir dire might have led to peremptory challenges of jurors like Begley and Cobb; on the other hand, they might have successfully covered up their attitudes and gotten onto the jury.

For all its gritty realism, the film misleadingly portrays important rules governing jury deliberations. Jurors are not supposed to perform experiments or develop evidence on their own. In one notorious evidence case, where the question was how long bite marks would last, one juror bit another one to find out. The appellate court sank its teeth into that one and threw out the conviction. Thus it was improper for Fonda to purchase the knife or to do an experiment about how long it would have taken the old man to run to the door.

Using juries to settle disputes is slow and clumsy and takes precious time from many people. Scratch any trial lawyer, and you'll hear some anecdotes about ridiculous jury verdicts. Of course, you can scratch any juror and hear equally good anecdotes about ridiculous trial lawyers. It would be much quicker and simpler if judges made the decisions—as they do in most legal systems around the world. Many people think the jury system (or at least the requirement of a unanimous verdict) is outmoded. *Twelve Angry Men* states the best case for keeping the jury system as it is. Juries can serve as the conscience of the community, as one final protection against the risk that the criminal law machine may grind up an innocent person.

Dollars and Sense

For obvious reasons, most trial movies are about criminal law. Somehow, the average viewer finds a murder trial more enthralling than an eight-week trial about whether Mary went through a red light before running into Terry. But that's a shame, because civil cases often pack every bit as much drama as criminal cases.

Civil cases aren't always contests over money. Fights over who gets custody of a kid will jerk your tears in *Kramer vs. Kramer* or *Losing Isaiah.* In *Whose Life Is It Anyway?* a quadriplegic fights for the right to die. These situations are every bit as dramatic as any criminal case.

But even fights over dollars can be very entertaining. *Class Action* is about an exploding gas tank; *Libel* is an enthralling mystery about whether a rich nobleman is really an imposter; and *The Verdict* is about medical care that nearly killed a woman in childbirth—and how the doctors and hospital try to cover it up. We guarantee that you'll find these trials just as much fun as your typical grisly murder case.

Class Action

Synopsis: A snarly consumer-crusading lawyer files a wrongful death lawsuit against a carmaker represented by his snarly, materialistic daughter. At the end, the makers of ethical rules have to do all the snarling.

Class Action: Michael Grazier (Colin Friels) and Jedediah Ward (Gene Hackman) flex their veins over the admissibility of evidence.

TCF/Interscope. 1990. Color. Running time: 109 min.
Screenplay: Carolyn Shelby, Christopher Ames, and Samantha Shad. Director: Michael Apted.
Starring: Gene Hackman (Jedediah Ward), Mary Elizabeth Mastrantonio (Maggie Ward), Lawrence Fishburne (Nick Holbrook), Colin Friels (Michael Grazier), Fred Dalton Thompson (Dr. Getchell), Jan Rubes (Dr. Pavel).
Rating: —▮ —▮

The Story

Jedediah Ward is an aggressive personal injury lawyer who specializes in "public interest cases." His clients are injured consumers who are victims of corporate greed. As a "bean counter" (an industrial accountant) explains, corporations can make more money by rushing goods into the marketplace and paying off the injured consumers who bother to sue than by investing the money necessary to design safe products. (Cigarette makers get to count the most beans under current laws. They get to kill people without having to compensate their victims.)

Jedediah files suit against Argo Motors on behalf of a client whose wife was killed when their Argo-made Meridian exploded into flames after a collision. Argo denies responsibility, insisting that the Meridian met or exceeded all federal safety standards. Argo's attorney is none other than Jedediah's daughter, Maggie Ward, who hopes to use the case as a stepping-stone to quick partnership in her corporate law firm. Maggie and Jedediah continuously hurl legal arguments, career choices, and family history at each other. The materialistic Maggie winds up ahead on points. Jedediah takes the case for a contingency fee, meaning that he collects a fee only if he wins, and then only a set percentage no matter how much time he spends on the case. Defense attorney Maggie bills by the hour, so she's undoubtedly passing the costs for all the hours she spends bickering with her father on to Argo.

Maggie's faith in Argo and its president, Dr. Getchell, begins to waver when she learns of a report prepared by Dr. Pavel before the Meridian went on the market. Dr. Pavel, an Argo engineer who has since retired, concluded that the Meridian would blow up if it was involved in an accident when its left turn signal was blinking. This means that the Meridian was not a danger on California freeways, where signaling drivers became extinct nearly two decades ago. At any rate, rather than spend money to replace the defective circuitry or train Meridian purchasers to use hand signals, Argo concealed the report. Maggie contacts Dr. Pavel, who confirms the defect and his report. But Dr. Pavel is well past it, and he has no idea of the report's whereabouts or much of anything else.

Thereafter, the report appears and disappears so often that it seems to have been written by Houdini rather than Dr. Pavel. Against the wishes of Dr. Getchell and Michael, her obnoxious supervising partner and lover, Maggie decides to turn the report as well as a mass of other documents over to Jedediah and his associate Nick, in compliance with their written demand for Argo's engineering reports. The report never gets to them, but it does show up in Maggie's desk drawer. When she next looks for it, it's gone again; Michael has destroyed it.

At trial, Jedediah calls Dr. Pavel to testify to the electrical fault that gives the Argo a disturbing tendency to explode. Maggie's cross-examination brutally destroys Dr. Pavel's credibility. She demonstrates that he not only has no idea where the report is, but also he is unable to remember his own phone number or social security number. Jedediah angrily accuses Maggie's law firm of destroying the report. To assure the court that it did no such thing, Maggie calls Michael as a witness to testify that he never saw a report questioning the Argo's safety. Jedediah then triumphantly calls the bean counter as a witness to testify that Dr. Pavel's report existed and that he discussed it with both Dr. Getchell and Michael. With this one witness, Jedediah scores a huge verdict for his client and subjects Michael to a likely conviction for perjury. Jedediah and Maggie, who together cooked up the whole charade in order to sock it to Argo and Michael, celebrate the new law partnership of Ward and Ward. In view of their past, their first piece of office equipment might be boxing gloves.

Legal Analysis

In order to defeat her father and further her climb up the law firm ladder, Maggie seems to accede to the destruction of a crucial report. Often trusted with important papers, lawyers are frequently in a position to alter a trial's outcome by making harmful papers disappear. Unfortunately, lawyers have sometimes given way to the temptation. In a major antitrust case a few years back, two senior members of one of Wall Street's best-known law firms were disbarred for concealing documents that would have harmed the position of their client, a well-known manufacturer of cameras and film. The ensuing publicity generated a lot of "negative" publicity for the law firm and the legal profession!

Much of the pretrial skirmishing between Jedediah and Maggie involves the process known as "discovery," in which each party to a civil case has an opportunity to force the opponent to reveal information. The theory of discovery is that if each party knows what the other is going to prove, settlements are more likely and trials will be less of a game. The theory breaks down because in practice, lawyers guard information the way piranhas guard their young. For instance, attorneys often refuse to answer an opponent's question by citing ambiguities in questions that a two-year-old would understand. And rarely do lawyers hand over information voluntarily. As in *Go Fish,* they turn over information only if the other side asks for the right stuff at the right time.

With the smoothness of Astaire and Rogers, Maggie and Michael abuse two of the most useful components of discovery, "depositions" and "motions to produce documents." A deposition is an oral proceeding in which an attorney can ask questions that have to be answered under oath. Judges are not present at depositions, which gives Maggie a chance to turn the deposition of Jedediah's client into the legal equivalent of the *Texas Chainsaw Massacre.* She verbally harasses him, and persists in showing him gruesome photos of the accident in which his wife died. She is so nasty that Jedediah and his client walk out of the deposition. Thus, Maggie abuses her power to ask questions. She also wastes her chance to find out what Jedediah's client will say at trial. Judged by any standard—moral, ethical, or tactical—Maggie's deposition technique is a flop.

Dr. Pavel's report begins its now-you-see-it, now-you-don't existence when Jedediah and Nick send Maggie a notice to produce documents. They ask her to turn over copies of the documents related to the Meridian's design. Maggie's firm invokes the classic Tsunami Response, which is designed to flood an opponent with so much information that the critical evidence is never found. Thus, the damning report is to be hidden amongst a truckload of other documents, perhaps including Maggie's high school algebra notes and the collected works of Pliny the Elder.

Unknown to Maggie, the Tsunami Response was unnecessary because Michael removed Dr. Pavel's report from the documents sent to Jedediah. When she learns this, Maggie becomes the heroine (or perhaps the "she-ro") for conspiring with Jedediah to take down Argo and Michael. But however noble her goals, Maggie behaves unethically at trial and puts her own career at risk. She and Michael could well wind up at a double disbar-ring ceremony.

First, Maggie improperly attacks the credibility of Dr. Pavel, who she knows is telling the truth about the report. In civil cases like this one (cases in which one private party seeks money damages from another private party), a lawyer cannot ethically attack the credibility of testimony that she knows to be true.

Maggie then violates another ethical principle by knowingly eliciting perjured testimony. Maggie calls Michael as a witness, knowing full well that he will lie about the report. By tricking him into committing perjury, she herself violates her position as an officer of the court.

Most importantly, Maggie violates her duty to Argo, her client, by secretly joining forces with Jedediah in the middle of trial. After "mama" and "dada," the third phrase learned by children who eventually go on to law school is "Thou shalt not represent conflicting interests." For better or worse she is Argo's attorney and she owes Argo a duty of loyalty. She cannot throw the case just because she finds out that it's a loser.

This does not mean that Maggie had to look the other way and pretend that nothing happened. The existence of the report and its destruction are devastating for Argo's position, and Maggie should have tried to control the fire rather than help Jedediah make it burn hotter. One way is by settling the case on the best terms she can get from Jedediah. This would benefit both Jedediah's client, who probably isn't anxious to go to trial, and Argo, which will be spared awful publicity. With this case behind her, she would advise Argo of its exposure for future accidents and urge Argo to take action to cure the electrical defect.

If the case continues to trial, Maggie would have to insist that Michael and Argo produce the report, or if it's been destroyed, a summary of it. If they refuse, how Maggie should proceed probably depends on whether Michael or Argo destroyed the report. If Michael destroyed it, she should report the misdeed to her state bar's Ethics Committee and to the judge. The former could disbar Michael; the judge could hold Michael in contempt of court and forward the matter to the district attorney for Michael to be charged with willfully destroying evidence. Maggie could continue to represent Argo by instructing Argo to prepare a new report summarizing the contents of the destroyed one, thus putting Jedediah in almost the same position he was in before the original report was destroyed.

Maggie probably has less of a chance to set things right if it was Argo that destroyed the report. She can't just turn in Argo like she could Michael, because she probably became aware of the destruction through a confidential meeting with Argo officials. Maggie would have to withdraw as attorney of record without telling the judge why she was doing so. She might try to hint at the cause of the problem: "Your Honor, a problem has arisen between my client and me about the evidence." Such a statement might lead the judge to question Argo, which might then come clean. But if Argo continues to stonewall, the judge might have to allow Argo to fight on with another lawyer. This is a great result for Argo and the lawyers. Lawyer No. 1, Maggie, is okay because she did the right thing by withdrawing. Lawyer No. 2 is okay because Argo will keep quiet about the destruction of the report, and therefore Lawyer No. 2 will know nothing about it. And Argo is okay because the plaintiff never gets the report. Who loses? Only the plaintiff, the public, and our system of justice.

Trial Briefs

1. A consumer class action is a lawsuit filed by a few people as representatives of a much larger group of individuals with nearly identical (and generally smallish) claims against the same defendant. For example, a few people who claim that an airline overcharged for coach tickets between January 1 and December 31 might file suit seeking return of the overcharges "for themselves and on behalf of all other coach passengers of the airline who purchased tickets between January 1 and December 31." Generally, the people who gain the most from a successful class action are the attorneys who file it. Don't be misled by the picture's title. It does not involve a class action. Jedediah has filed a garden-variety wrongful death claim on behalf of a single plaintiff.

2. The film is loosely based on the case of *Grimshaw v. Ford Motor Company,* involving a 1972 Ford Pinto that exploded when it was rear-ended. The jury awarded the plaintiff $2.5 million in actual damages and $125 million in punitive damages; the latter figure was reduced to $3.5 million on appeal. One of the documents offered into evidence in the *Grimshaw* case was an internal report prepared by Ford stating that the cost of adding safety equipment to every car would be much higher than the cost of paying victims who were killed or hurt because of the lack of the safety equipment.

It Could Happen to You

Synopsis: A police officer uses a lottery jackpot to enrich the lives of others, until a jury decides that all the money belongs to his grasping wife.

Tristar Pictures (Mike Lobell). 1994. Color. Running time: 101 min.

Screenplay: Jane Anderson. Director: Andrew Bergman.

Starring: Nicolas Cage (Officer Charlie Lang), Bridget Fonda (Yvonne Biasi), Rosie Perez (Muriel Lang), Wendell Pierce (Bo Williams), Isaac Hayes (Angel), Red Buttons (Walter Zakuto), Richard Jenkins (Harvey Hale).

Rating: ―■ ―■

The Story

Officer Charlie Lang is the World's Nicest Cop. He plays stickball with children in the streets of Queens and thwarts a robbery by tackling rather than shooting the gunman, so as to avoid injuring him. He is married to Muriel, a shrill and materialistic woman who makes Ebenezer Scrooge seem like Robin Hood.

At Muriel's urging, Charlie buys a lottery ticket. He chooses number 26, even though Muriel had told him to bet on 27, the day of their wedding anniversary. He then stops by a café for lunch, where he and his partner Bo are waited on by Yvonne. When an emergency suddenly calls them away, Charlie realizes that he has no money for a tip. Impetuously, he promises to return the next day and give Yvonne half his lottery winnings, should he get lucky.

Amazingly, that night Charlie and Muriel win $4 million in the lottery. Muriel is ecstatic; Charlie is uncertain about his moral obligations to Yvonne. He returns to the coffee shop the next day, and gives Yvonne a choice between a regular tip and half the value of his lottery ticket. Yvonne cynically selects the latter, and is amazed when Charlie tells her that he won and that he will make good on his promise by giving her $2 million.

It Could Happen To You: Charlie Lang (Nicholas Cage, right) finds out that courts can be meaner than the streets.

Muriel is furious with Charlie; she sees her furs, beach houses, and voice lessons disappearing before her eyes. But she agrees to go along with the bargain when Charlie points out the fame and commercial endorsements that her generosity is sure to produce. At a press conference, Muriel stands happily with Charlie and Yvonne as the lottery results are announced.

Muriel spends money on herself faster than she can count it; Charlie and Yvonne treat commuters to free subway rides, children to baseball games, and homeless people to free meals. Muriel is disgusted by Charlie's values, accuses him of having an affair with Yvonne, and starts divorce proceedings. Zakuto, Charlie's bumbling attorney, is no match for Hale, the sly conniving attorney hired by Muriel. Hale demands that all of the lottery winnings be given to Muriel, including the half that Charlie gave to Yvonne. Charlie willingly gives up any claim to Muriel's share of the prize, but refuses to let her have Yvonne's share. The case goes to court.

At the trial, Muriel testifies that the total prize was her property, and that Charlie had no right to give half of it away. Charlie and Yvonne admit to being in love, but testify that they had never met before he promised to split the winnings with her. The jury awards Muriel the entire amount, $4 million.

Charlie and Yvonne return to the café, which Yvonne had bought but is soon to lose. Yvonne is despondent. Charlie is just happy to be with Yvonne instead of Muriel; among other benefits, he's added ten years to his hearing ability. They offer food to a homeless person who wanders into the café. The person turns out to be Angel, a newspaper photographer in disguise. When the paper reports their kindhearted gesture, it's jackpot No. 2. Money pours in from everywhere. Muriel, meanwhile, is swindled out of her money, and winds up living with her mother and working in a beauty parlor.

Legal Analysis

Before the Soviet Union's breakup, much of the film would have made a perfect Soviet instructional film on the Evils of Capitalism. Muriel can spend an amount equal to the entire annual gross national product of Bulgaria before lunch. The legal system unjustly deprives the public-spirited Charlie and Yvonne of half the prize. And the lawyers offer a choice between an ineffectual boob (Zakuto) and an overbearing jerk (Hale). In this milieu, *It Could Happen to You* suddenly sounds more like a threat than a promise!

However, don't rush to give away half of your next big lottery prize on the theory that you can always get it back. Despite the jury's verdict awarding the entire prize to Muriel, Yvonne was legally entitled to keep her $2 million. In fact, if Charlie hadn't voluntarily given his share of the other $2 million to Muriel, he and Muriel would have ended up with a million dollars each. To understand why, you have to know a little bit about contract law and about how a couple's assets are divided when they divorce. Let's see how things should have worked out.

When he initially rushes out of the café, Charlie promises to split the lottery prize with Yvonne if he wins. Charlie feels a moral obligation to keep this promise, immediately rising above a few lesser saints. But had Charlie tried to renege, a court would not have enforced the promise. Charlie would be legally obligated to keep his promise only if Yvonne has given him "consideration." This means that Yvonne would have had to give up something of value in exchange for Charlie's promise. The Latins called it a "quid pro quo"; the Chinese did not. Yvonne did not give Charlie "consideration" for the promise; he was not even legally obligated to give her a tip. Thus, Yvonne did not have an enforceable contract; Charlie's splitting the prize with her was a gift. (One nice benefit for Yvonne: since it's a gift, not a tip, she wouldn't have to pay income tax on it!)

When Charlie and Muriel get divorced, they've got what's left of the other half of the prize, around $2 million. A New York divorce judge will divide this money "equitably" (fairly), no matter who earned it. This means that as a starting point, Charlie and Muriel each get half of the rest of the prize, one million each, just as if it was community property. But a judge doesn't have to split the money in half. A judge can award one spouse more than the other based on a number of factors, including the fact that Charlie gave away two million dollars.

Thus, a judge might well have decided to punish Charlie for his largesse by awarding Muriel the two million dollars they have left. So if you're keeping score at home, to this point, the score is Muriel $2 million; Yvonne, $2 million; Charlie, nothing.

But the game is not over yet. The final score would be changed by what happened at the press conference announcing the lottery results, an important event that Charlie's hack lawyer Zakuto neglects to bring up. Before the press conference, Charlie tells Muriel about the fame and endorsement contracts that will surely come her way if she shares the prize with Yvonne. Speaking of a dream that many of us have had but few of us have dared to utter, Muriel imagines the glory of selling dandruff shampoo on bus benches across the land. So it is that during the press conference, Muriel tells the whole world about her generous gift to Yvonne. By saying this and then standing by as Yvonne accepts half the prize, Muriel herself has joined in Charlie's gift to Yvonne and she cannot legally take it back. So in dividing Charlie's and Muriel's $2 million equitably, the judge would probably split it down the middle. The final divorce score would be Yvonne, $2 million; Muriel, $1 million; Charlie, $1 million.

This delightful movie pits heartstrings against pursestrings. It shows that generosity can bring its own financial rewards. Too bad it has to trample so many legal rules along the way.

Trial Brief

It not only could happen, it did happen to Bob Cunningham in 1984, though not exactly as depicted in the film. Bob, a middle-aged suburban New York detective, discovered that he had no money for a tip. Bob asked his waitress, Phyllis Penza, to choose the three numbers for the lottery ticket he had just bought, and promised to split the winnings in lieu of a tip. When the numbers Phyllis chose (7-9-29) turned up the winner, Bob won four million dollars. Bob fulfilled his promise to Phyllis and split his winnings with the full support of his wife, Gina. At the time of the film both Bob and Phyllis had retired and remained happily married to their longtime spouses.

Kramer vs. Kramer

Synopsis: Bring plenty of tissues as you watch mom and dad battle over custody of little Billy.

Columbia/Stanley Jaffe (Richard C. Fischoff). 1979. Color. Running time: 105 min.

Screenplay: Robert Benton. Novel: Avery Corman. Director: Robert Benton.

Kramer vs. Kramer: Joanna Kramer (Meryl Streep) fights for custody of her son.

Starring: Dustin Hoffman (Ted Kramer), Meryl Streep (Joanna Kramer), Jane Alexander (Margaret), Justin Henry (Billy).

Academy Awards: Best Picture, Best Actor (Hoffman), Best Supporting Actress (Streep), Best Director (Benton), Best Screenplay Adapted from Another Medium (Benton).

Academy Award nominations: Best Supporting Actor (Henry, the youngest person ever nominated), Best Supporting Actress (Alexander), Best Cinematography (Nestor Almendros), Best Editing.

Rating: ⚖ ⚖ ⚖

The Story

Ted Kramer, a busy advertising executive, pays little attention to the feelings and needs of his wife Joanna or to his six-year-old son, Billy. One fine day, Joanna walks out, leaving Billy behind. Once Ted realizes that she's gone for good, he painfully learns how to make french toast and eventually forms a close and loving bond with Billy. There are the inevitable accidents—as Ted talks with neighbor and soul mate Margaret, Billy tumbles from the playground bars while holding a toy and cuts his face.

A year and a half after her departure, Joanna returns and demands custody of Billy. Among other things, she accuses Ted of allowing Billy to become seven-and-a-half-years old in her absence. It's going to cost $15,000 to fight it, attorney Shaughnessy tells Ted, and Ted coughs up the money. Unfortunately, parental demands conflict with business deadlines and Ted gets fired. Knowing that he will surely lose the custody fight if he's unemployed, Ted uses all of his selling skills and lands a new job—at less salary than the old one.

Judge Atkins presides over the custody hearing. Joanna testifies that her marriage fell apart because Ted wouldn't let her go back to work. Now that she's recovered her self-esteem, she's working (earning more than Ted, for that matter), and ready to resume parenthood. She contends that Billy needs to be with his mother. On cross-examination, Joanna is asked about how many boyfriends she's had and whether she has a lover (she does).

Margaret testifies that Ted has been a wonderful father, but has to admit that she encouraged Joanna to leave Ted. Ted testifies that it would be best for Billy to stay where he is. A woman isn't necessarily a better mother than a man, he asserts. On cross-examination, Ted is grilled about losing his job and becoming downwardly mobile on the income ladder. He is also asked about Billy's fall from the bars. He is confronted with an unguarded admission he made to Joanna soon after the accident that he felt responsible for it. Joanna apologizes for having told her lawyer about this statement, claiming that she didn't want it brought out at the trial.

Judge Atkins goes for motherhood, by and for mothers, right down the line. Ted loses custody, must pay child support, and has to be content with seeing Billy every other weekend and one night during the week. Ted prepares Billy for the big change, as the audience uses up its supply of tissues.

In an unexpected Hollywood happy ending, Joanna tells Ted that she's changed her mind and doesn't feel ready to take custody of Billy after all. Ted is so grateful that he doesn't even ask Joanna for child support or a refund of his attorney's fees. Ted probably also doesn't want to think about the psychotherapy Billy will be going through when he figures out that his mom put him through an emotional roller coaster, only to reject him.

Legal Analysis

The standard in a child custody determination is "the best interests of the child." This means that the interest of the child prevails over that of the parents. A family court judge is expected to consider all the facts about the contending parents and their relationship to the child. This process leaves the trial judge with a great deal of discretion.

In *Kramer vs. Kramer,* both parents seem equally fit. Neither presents any danger to the child (if we dismiss the playground accident). Both have done a good job when they were primary caretakers. There are three relevant factors that the judge must balance: (1) Joanna abandoned Billy and Ted without any warning—this emotional instability might recur in ways that could be harmful to Billy; (2) Billy has been living with Ted for eighteen months and any change in the situation would be disruptive to Billy; (3) perhaps mothers are more suitable parents for young children than fathers.

Judge Atkins's decision relied entirely on factor three and found it outbalanced factors one and two. But there is no proof that mothers are better parents than fathers for seven-year-old boys; this was simply the judge's prejudice. Instead, factor two—the need for continuity— should have weighed heavily. Continuity is vital in the life of a small child and as between two equally fit parents, a child should probably stay put.

Atkins's decision reflects the traditional strong preference for mothers over fathers. This so-called "tender years" rule provided a strong presumption in favor of giving custody of a child under ten to the mother. By the late 1970s, when the movie was made, the tender years doctrine was definitely on the wane. It has been now been abolished in most states as illegal gender discrimination. An appellate court, at least today, would probably set the decision in *Kramer vs. Kramer* aside as an abuse of discretion.

Judge Atkins allows evidence about the number of Joanna's boyfriends and the fact that she now has a lover. This kind of evidence was traditionally allowed in divorce and custody cases, where issues of morality often played a major role. But by modern standards, the evidence is irrelevant and an invasion of Joanna's privacy. Single parents are going to have sex; the only issue is whether they will do so in ways that are harmful to the child. There is no reason to think Joanna will be indiscreet or careless in her personal relationships and therefore the testimony should not have been permitted.

When Shaughnessy tells Ted about the adverse result, they discuss an appeal. Shaughnessy tells Ted that he would have to put Billy on the stand. This is nonsense. An appeal is based on the written record of the hearing that has already occurred. There is no new evidence. Of course, if the appellate court tossed the case back to Judge Atkins for a new hearing, it would be possible to introduce new evidence. However, even in that case, Billy might not be called as a witness.

In cases involving children as young as Billy, the child's preference is not a major determinant, and there would be little need to put Billy on the stand and subject him to cross-examination. Having to choose between his mom and dad would be terribly damaging to such a small child. A better approach is for the judge to talk to Billy in chambers, out of the presence of the parents. Or a social worker might talk to him and submit a report to the judge. By contrast, if Billy were a teenager, his custodial preference would carry much more weight.

Repeatedly, the attorneys in this movie cross-examine by insisting that the witness answer yes or no. The witness isn't permitted to explain the answer, even though a yes or no answer is meaningless or misleading. For example, Ted is not allowed to explain the playground accident or the circumstances in which he missed deadlines at work to care for Billy. Especially in an informal setting like a nonjury custody hearing, the judge should allow a witness to explain an answer. At the worst, the lawyer who called that witness on direct exam is entitled to conduct redirect examination during which the witness can supply the necessary explanation.

Joanna claims that she told her lawyer not to ask Ted about his statement that he was responsible for Billy's accident. Clients are supposed to make the major decisions about what happens in their case—not attorneys. Even as to seemingly minor decisions, like what questions to ask on cross-examination, attorneys should respect their clients' wishes when the topic is important to the client. Joanna's attorney was wrong to override her decision.

How should we decide which parent should get custody when both parents want custody and both are fit? Certainly the best answer is a negotiated solution that both parents can live with. Courts should supply mediators to help the parents achieve an agreement. If that doesn't work, courts should consider joint physical and legal custody. Joint physical custody means the child lives with each parent part of the time. Legal custody means shared decision making. That way there's no clear winner or loser and both parents remain deeply involved in the child's upbringing.

The worst way to resolve the issue is to duke it out like Ted and Joanna in *Kramer vs. Kramer.* That requires a judge to decide that one parent is a clear winner and the other a clear loser. Such trials enrich the lawyers but impoverish the parents. Custody fights waste large amounts of court time and are emotionally wrenching for all concerned. Custody fights require the judge to exercise more wisdom than most human beings possess. And such decisions are devastating to the losing parent and often to the child. Not every loser will handle the defeat with the dignity and loving care that Ted somehow manages as he prepares to hand Billy over to Joanna.

Libel

Synopsis: Lord Loddon, an ex-POW, sues for libel after a tabloid publishes a letter from an old military buddy claiming that he is an imposter. A crackling mystery, both a "whodunit" and a "whoisit."

MGM/Comet. 1959. Black and white. Running time: 100 min.

Screenplay: Anatole de Grunwald and Karl Tunberg. Director: Anthony Asquith. Olivia de Havilland's costumes: Christian Dior.

Starring: Dirk Bogarde (Sir Mark Loddon, Frank Welney, Number 15), Olivia de Havilland (Lady Margaret Loddon), Paul Massie (Jeffery Buckenham), Robert Morley (Sir Wilfred), Wilfred Hyde White (Foxley), Richard Wattis (Judge).

Rating: —▮ —▮ —▮ —▮

Surprise ending warning: Reading this analysis might be hazardous to your enjoyment of the movie!

The Story

Sir Mark Loddon, Jeffery Buckenham, and Frank Welney were POWs in the same prison camp during World War II. Together they escaped, and became separated. Loddon eventually returns to his ancestral estate of Ingworth and marries Margaret, an American to whom he'd been engaged before the war. But he is constantly haunted by a nightmare in which he hears a tune and sees the image of a figure he can't identify.

Passing through London years later, Buckenham is shocked to see Loddon conducting a tour of Ingworth on the BBC. Buckenham fires off a letter that is printed in the sleazy *Daily Gazette.* The letter states that Loddon died during the escape attempt, and that the person claiming to be Loddon is really Welney. In the good old days, his lordship could probably have ordered Buckenham's head chopped off for such an impertinence. Now, at Margaret's urging, Loddon is reduced to suing the *Gazette* and Buckenham for libel.

To prove that the letter is false, Sir Wilfred has Loddon and his cousin testify that Loddon is who he says he is. But Loddon admits to a poor memory about his pre-escape life. Defense counsel Foxley's cross-examination of Loddon suggests how Welney could pass for Loddon. Loddon and Welney looked so alike that they probably were named "Most Likely to Pass for One Another" in the POW yearbook. Also, Welney was missing parts of two fingers on his right hand; Loddon's right hand is similarly afflicted. Loddon's explanation is that he lost the finger parts while escaping.

Foxley then has Buckenham testify that Welney was a nasty person

Libel: Sir Wilfred (Robert Morley) tries to persuade Lady Margaret Loddon (Olivia de Havilland) to testify for her husband.

who muttered about assuming Loddon's identity after the war. In flashback, Buckenham describes how Loddon died during the escape. Buckenham went to pilfer food, leaving Loddon and Welney together. He heard shots, saw Loddon's body on the ground, and heard German soldiers say he was dead. He also saw Welney running away. Though it was dark, he could distinguish Loddon from Welney because of their different jackets.

Foxley next produces a German doctor who operated on a severely brain-injured POW who was found where Buckenham last saw Loddon. He is a living corpse known only as No. 15, and has been locked away in bed since the operation. When No. 15 was found, he was wearing the jacket of a British major, Loddon's rank. Foxley offers the jacket into evidence, and then brings into court a ghastly, shuffling No. 15. He and Loddon appear to recognize each other, though neither says a word.

Fearing that the jury thinks that No. 15 is Loddon, Sir Wilfred convinces Margaret to testify. She shocks him by saying that her husband is an impostor. She had assumed that being a POW had changed Loddon and affected his memory. But when she saw her husband's reaction to No. 15, she knew he was a phony.

That night, a dejected and confused "Loddon" takes a walk along a river canal; the image and tune of his nightmare suddenly repeats. The next morning, he testifies that No. 15 is Welney. In another flashback, Loddon tells what really happened during the escape. When Buckenham went to get food, Welney tried to kill Loddon. They fought, and Loddon beat him severely about the head and knocked him out. Loddon exchanged his jacket for Welney's plain leather one, since a British major's jacket is a poor choice of dress before teatime or behind German lines. Loddon then ran off.

To prove his claim, Loddon picks up the British major's jacket that No. 15 was wearing when he was found. Loddon makes a slit in it, and dramatically pulls out a medallion given to him by Margaret before the war. Buckenham, realizing that only he and Loddon knew of the medallion, testifies that Loddon is indeed who he says. Foxley dismisses the jury, conceding defeat.

All ends happily. Loddon asks Sir Wilfred and Foxley to stick the *Daily Gazette* with a big enough settlement to provide for Welney's upkeep. Margaret and Loddon thank Buckenham for restoring their past. The German doctor finally knows who to send a bill to for his years of medical treatment.

Legal Analysis

Libel law protects people against false statements that damage their reputations. It is a form of protection that seems a bit incongruous in an era when people compete on national television to see whose lives are the most sordid. It is also a very complex and changing area of law, because in the United States a libel suit runs smack into the constitutional right of free speech.

A libelous statement is one that injures a person's reputation by exposing the person to ridicule or contempt, or lowering his esteem among the general populace. Buckenham's letter undoubtedly qualifies. Lord Loddon's reputation would go downhill quickly if people thought that he was dead. Restaurant reservations would be hard to come by, and he would never be a finalist in a magazine sweepstakes competition. On the other hand, he might get to attend an Elvis concert.

Buckenham's statement is libelous only if it is false. But in one of the many quirks of traditional libel law, Loddon doesn't have to prove that the statement is false; Buckenham and the *Gazette* have to prove that it is true. Therefore, Sir Wilfred need not have bothered to have Loddon and his cousin testify that Loddon is the real goods. He could introduce the newspaper clipping into evidence and leave it to Foxley to try to prove it true.

Another quirk of traditional libel law is that Buckenham and the *Gazette* can be "liable for libel" even if they acted from the purest of motives. Buckenham is not out to humiliate or blackmail his old friend; he honestly believes that Welney killed Loddon and took his place. And while the *Gazette* may have been guilty of trying to sell a few papers, all it did was publish Buckenham's letter. So the defendants weren't careless or evil. But they got their facts wrong, and under traditional libel law that's all that matters.

In most civil cases, a plaintiff has to prove actual injuries before he can be awarded any money. For example, even if Smith proves that Wesson carelessly struck him with his car, Smith can't be awarded any money unless Wesson actually injured him. But here comes another quirk of traditional libel law. Loddon wins his libel suit even though he doesn't prove that the libelous letter actually damaged his reputation. For example, Loddon doesn't have to bring people into court to testify, "I had planned to vote for Lord Loddon as Best Baron of the Year, but not now." Injury to reputation is presumed from the making of a libelous statement, and the jury could assess whatever damages it believed appropriate.

When No. 15 turns out to be Welney, Sir Wilfred might have another libel client on his hands, this time Welney. After all, Buckenham's letter falsely stated that Welney assumed Loddon's identity. Thus, Welney may be next in line to sue Buckenham and the *Gazette.* Of course, Welney's suit would raise an interesting question of whether someone who has been brain-dead for over a decade can be said to have a reputation. But the careers of many politicians suggest this is quite possible, so Welney might actually be entitled to damages. Loddon in effect accomplishes this goal by telling Sir Wilfred and Foxley to devote the money he gets from the *Gazette* to Welney's upkeep.

Lord Loddon would not be happy with the changes in libel law that have occurred in the United States, most of which favor the media. These changes date to the case of *New York Times v. Sullivan* (1964), in which the U.S. Supreme Court decided that libelous statements may be protected by the First Amendment guarantee of freedom of speech. Under U.S. constitutional guidelines, which don't exist in Britain, a "public figure" cannot sue for libel unless a person "maliciously" makes a false statement. This means that a person can make a false statement about a public figure and go scot-free unless he actually knows that it is false, or at least is totally indifferent to whether it is true or false. Loddon would find it almost impossible to prove that Buckenham or the *Gazette* acted out of malice. At most, they didn't investigate as thoroughly as they might have, but that's not malice. Thus, if he's a public figure, Lord Loddon comes away empty-handed as well as missing—fingered under modern U.S. libel law.

Loddon would not have much luck claiming that he's not a public figure. Ingworth, the family estate, is a mecca for tour buses. Tourists probably leave laden with apparel saying, "All whoever I am got from Ingworth was this lousy T-shirt." And when Buckenham sees him, Loddon is giving BBC viewers a guided tour of the estate, a show which probably drew a bigger audience than the finals of the sheep dog trials. This is enough to qualify him as a public figure.

But even if he's not a public figure, modern U.S. libel law makes things difficult for Loddon. Before suing, Loddon would probably have to ask the *Gazette* to print a retraction; if the paper did so, he couldn't get damages. And even if the *Gazette* refused to print a retraction, Loddon would be able to recover damages only if he could prove that the letter actually damaged his reputation. Unless the letter caused Loddon to be banished to the bleachers at Ascot, Loddon would still come away with nothing. Indeed, since Loddon ends up so grateful to Buckenham for restoring his memory of the past, perhaps the *Gazette* would countersue Loddon for the amount Loddon saved by not needing therapy from a counselor specializing in past life regression.

Though he loses the case, Foxley seems a much more resourceful barrister than Sir Wilfred. Wilfred is content to rely on the testimony of Loddon and his closest relatives, satisfied that their personal credibility will carry the day. He doesn't bother with objective proof such as fingerprints, blood tests, or military records. Had the tune and the sight of Patient No. 15 not miraculously restored his memory, Loddon would have been lucky to find work in the Ingworth gift shop. By contrast, good advocate that he is, Foxley doesn't accept Buckenham's story at face value. Realizing that Buckenham can't be certain that one of his companions died during the escape, or that the fallen companion was Loddon, Foxley investigates on the assumption that the companion survived. As a result, he turns up the evidence that almost pulls off a big upset.

Sir Wilfred is probably at his best when Margaret shocks him by testifying that her husband is an imposter. Most attorneys would be too stunned to say or do anything; those who could think at all would probably be wondering why they didn't take their parents' advice and go to dental school. But in the best barrister traditions, Sir Wilfred remains cool. He suggests that the sight of No. 15 has so unnerved Margaret that she is confused, and he gives her a second chance to confirm that her husband is Loddon. When she sticks to her story he insists on an explanation. If the explanation were weak, he'd at least have a basis for asking the jury to disregard Margaret's testimony.

After losing to Lord Loddon, the *Daily Gazette* decided there was no future in gossip and scandal, and sought respectability. It changed its name to the *National Enquirer.*

Losing Isaiah

Synopsis: Isaiah's Caucasian adoptive parents and his African-American birth mother wage an emotional battle for his custody. Bring whatever Kleenex is left over from *Kramer vs. Kramer.*

Paramount (Howard W. Koch Jr.). 1995. Color. Running time: 108 min.

Screenplay: Naomi Foner. Novel: Seth Margolis. Director: Stephen Gyllenhaal.

Starring: Jessica Lange (Margaret Lewin), Halle Berry (Khaila Richards), David Strathairn (Charles Lewin), Cuba Gooding, Jr. (Eddie Hughes), Samuel L. Jackson (Kadar Lewis), La Tanya Richardson (Caroline Jones), Marc John Jeffries (Isaiah).

Rating: —▮ —▮ —▮

The Story

Khaila Richards, an African-American crack addict, abandons her infant child Isaiah in a cardboard box next to a dumpster. Trash collectors spot him and rush him to a hospital. Margaret Lewin, a Caucasian medical social worker at the hospital, decides to adopt Isaiah. Her supportive husband Charles and her daughter Hannah reluctantly agree, the adoption takes place, and the Lewins grow to love Isaiah. His prenatal exposure to cocaine produces continuing behavior problems, including an inordinate fear of taking out the trash.

Khaila kicks her cocaine habit in prison and is released. She was never notified of the adoption and wants Isaiah back. She's represented by Kadar Lewis, a legal aid attorney, who believes that black children should not be adopted into white families. On Lewis's advice, Khaila moves to a nicer apartment and dumps her adulterous boyfriend Eddie Hughes, although not in a dumpster. The Lewins retain Caroline Jones, a black lawyer who is ambivalent about their legal position.

The custody hearing takes place in a shabby Chicago courtroom. Khaila testifies that she's free of drugs and is ready to be a good mother to Isaiah. On cross-examination, she admits she had been a prostitute and had left Isaiah to die, but insists that is all behind her. A social worker testifies that Isaiah would be better off in the long run

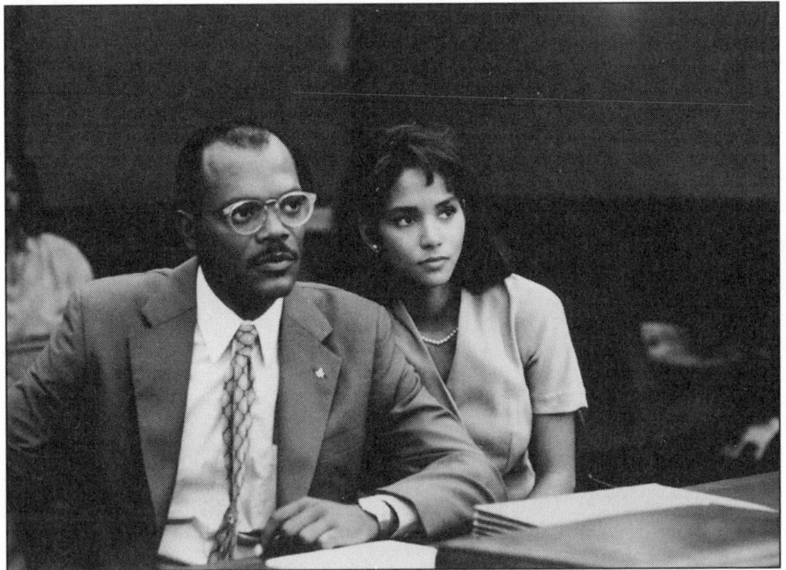

Losing Isaiah: Kadar Lewis (Samuel L. Jackson) and Khaila Richards (Halle Berry) fight for custody of Isaiah.

with a black parent, despite the short-term trauma of changing families.

Illustrating Sir Isaac Newton's theory, for every expert there is an equal and opposite counterexpert. The Lewins' expert testifies that it would be terribly damaging to Isaiah if he must leave the Lewins' home—especially in light of his cocaine-related behavior problems. The Lewins testify to their close bond with Isaiah. On cross-examination, Margaret admits that they have never read Isaiah any black children's literature. Also Charles admits to having spent a night with a female associate at his firm.

The judge rules that it would be in Isaiah's best interest to be returned to Khaila. But the transition is disastrous. Isaiah won't speak or eat. In despair, Khaila calls Margaret and asks her to take Isaiah back for the time being. *Kramer vs. Kramer 2* anyone?

Legal Analysis

The film takes it for granted that the Lewins had the right to adopt Isaiah when Khaila abandoned him. But Khaila has a fundamental right to raise her child. Before declaring Isaiah eligible for adoption, the state had to give Khaila time to get her act together. Before allowing the Lewins to adopt Isaiah, the state welfare agency would first make them foster parents, giving them only temporary custody.

Then, if Khaila made no contact with Isaiah for a substantial time period, the Lewins would be eligible to adopt Isaiah.

In order to strip a biological parent of the right to her child, the state must provide due process of law. And part of due process is to receive notice of the hearing which declared Isaiah free for adoption. Since Khaila was a crack addict without a permanent address, she was not served personally or by mail with notice of the termination proceeding.

The state attempted to give Khaila notice by "publication." In other words, somewhere in the back of a Chicago newspaper, perhaps after a classified ad for a "miracle drain de-clogger," was a legal notice telling Khaila and the world that a hearing concerning Isaiah's adoption was about to take place. Even if she were a devout hunter of used exercycles instead of a crack addict, she would probably have missed it.

The judge's ruling allowing Khaila to belatedly contest the adoption is probably right. The state should have made a greater effort to locate Khaila before publishing the newspaper notice. It could have checked with hospitals, prisons, welfare offices, and crack cocaine dealerships in an effort to locate Khaila. Since there's no evidence that Illinois took such steps, she did not get adequate notice of the hearing and was entitled to contest it. On the other hand, many states enforce a cutoff period in adoption cases so that after a year or two even an improperly noticed natural parent cannot overturn an adoption.

Procedural obstacles aside, the court had to decide whether Isaiah should stay with the Lewins or return to Khaila. The standard is "the best interests of the child." This doesn't provide much guidance, little better than the old adage to "buy low and sell high."

Losing Isaiah presents an important and unresolved social and legal issue: What is in the best interests of a black child? To stay in the only home he's ever known, with two Caucasian parents? Or to be raised by his same-race but less stable natural parent? This issue is emotionally wrenching for the persons involved and raises larger questions about the proper role of race in legal decision making.

As depicted in the film, many social work professionals believe that it is vital for a black child to be raised in a black household. They believe that a white family, no matter how loving, can only raise the child in a white environment. A child who never develops a black identity will be unprepared for the harsh realities of life as a black teenager and adult. In that case, the child is likely to suffer a personal crisis as he or she grows up. There have been numerous studies of the effect of transracial adoption on children, but the results remain unclear and disputed.

There is a strong custom in the social work field of discouraging adoption of black children by white parents. Indeed, the National Association of Black Social Workers is absolutely opposed to it. Several states (including California and Minnesota) have enacted racial preference statutes which provide that a child should be placed with a family of the same ethnic group if at all possible. As a result, in many communities it is extremely difficult for white parents to adopt black children out of foster homes, even when no black adoptive parents are available. The same would also be true for black parents seeking to adopt white children, but statistically that occurs much less frequently.

The judge's decision in Isaiah's case reflects the widely held philosophy against transracial adoption. However, the decision seems to disregard Isaiah's best interests. The decision might make sense if Isaiah had been with the Lewins only a short time or if they had only been foster parents. It is doubtful whether racial matching makes sense when a crack baby has been with his stable and loving family for three years in an apparently permanent placement. And, if the law is supposed to be "color-blind," making Isaiah's race the determinative factor may be unconstitutional. Not surprisingly, proposed federal legislation would forbid judges from taking race into account when making adoption decisions.

At the custody hearing, Lewis improperly questions Charles Lewin about the night he spent with a female associate. If it were shown that the Lewins' household was in danger of breaking up because of Charles's infidelity, the question would be relevant—not otherwise. Lewis's question only smears Charles's character, and it shouldn't have been allowed.

Losing Isaiah is a genuinely moving story that may well leave you in tears. The issues of interracial adoption are very real. The film does a good job of telling both sides. In the end, the film shows that it is often impossible to separate legal rulings from personal values.

Miracle on 34th Street

Synopsis: A Macy's department store Santa is cleverly proved to be the real thing.

Twentieth Century Fox. 1947. Black and white. Running time: 97 min.

Screenplay: George Seaton. Original Story: Valentine Davies. Director: George Seaton. Music: Alfred Newman.

Starring: Edmund Gwenn (Kris Kringle), Maureen O'Hara (Doris Walker), John Payne (Fred Gayley), Natalie Wood (Susan Walker), William Frawley (Charley).

Miracle on 34th Street: Kris Kringle (Edmund Gwenn) explains that his testimony would be more believable if the witness box had a chimney.

Academy Awards: Best Supporting Actor (Edmund Gwenn), Best Screenplay, Best Original Story.

Academy Award nomination: Best Picture.

Rating: ⚖ ⚖ ⚖

The Story

Doris Walker, a personnel manager for Macy's Department Store, hires a man with an uncanny resemblance to Santa Claus to ride on a float during Macy's annual Thanksgiving Day parade. The man, who gives his name as Kris Kringle, performs so well that she keeps him on as the department store Santa.

Kris soon shows that he may be as knowledgeable about marketing strategies as he is about getting an extraordinary amount of work out of little elves. To the consternation of Shellhammer, the manager of Macy's toy department, Kris tells customers about the best toys for their children, even if Macy's doesn't carry them. But even R.H. Macy himself applauds Kris when customers begin flocking to Macy's, confident that the store will point them toward the best deal, even if it's at a competitor's store.

Controversy arises when Kris becomes the first Santa to come out of the closet, openly telling anyone who asks that he really is Santa Claus. Doris, a hard-boiled realist who has the same disdain for imagination that Attila the Hun had for peasants, thinks Kris is bonkers and wants to fire him. His job is saved by the doctor from the Home for the Aged where Kris lives, who assures Doris that Kris's fantasy is harmless.

Proving that even saints can get testy, one day Kris bops a nasty Macy's employee named Sawyer on the head with his cane. Sawyer exaggerates his injuries, convincing Doris and Shellhammer that Kris might indeed be dangerous. They have Kris taken to the psychiatric ward at Bellevue Hospital. When Kris fails Bellevue's mental examination, the state prepares a petition to have him committed.

Coming to Kris's aid is Fred Gayley, Doris's next-door neighbor who has been wooing Doris with the help of her six-year-old child, Susan. Fred is one of filmdom's most unusual attorneys: He believes in Santa Claus, pleads with Doris and Susan to believe in the power of imagination, and represents Kris in the sanity hearing even though it costs him his cushy law firm job. If Santa could really have this effect on lawyers, undoubtedly more people would believe in him. At any rate, Fred asks Judge Henry Harper to hold a hearing before committing Kris to Bellevue. Judge Harper is unhappy about having to declare that there's no such thing as Santa Claus when he's up for reelection, but has to hold the hearing.

At the hearing, the state's attorney, Thomas Mara, triumphantly rests his case when Kris states under oath that he is the true Santa Claus. Mara asks for an immediate ruling committing Kris to Bellevue. Judge Harper consults with his good friend Charley, who reminds him of the dire consequences of an anti-Santa ruling. Doing the expedient thing, Judge Harper rules that since so many people believe in Santa, he'll give Fred a chance to prove that Kris is the real goods.

Unfortunately, Fred's only witnesses are R.H. Macy and little Thomas Mara Jr., who testify that they believe Kris is Santa. But their testimony means little, since Santa to them is simply a person who brings larger profits and toy trucks, respectively. But just as Fred is about to give up, help arrives from the post office. An eagle-eyed postal worker spies a letter written by Susan to Santa Claus, addressed to the courthouse. Though it is normally hard-pressed to deliver a letter across town in five days, the post office delivers thousands of letters addressed to Santa Claus to Kris within hours of finding Susan's letter. Fred argues that since the post office is a U.S. government agency, its conclusion that Kris is Santa should be binding on Judge Harper. Judge Harper is only too ready to agree, and orders Kris released.

Doris and Susan, who now believe in Santa and probably the Easter Bunny as well, celebrate Kris's release with Fred. With marriage in the offing, Doris, Fred, and Susan drive through idyllic, suburban Long Island, looking for a house to buy. Susan joyfully finds the house of her dreams for sale, a house that Kris said that Susan might someday have. Fred and Doris decide to buy it. As the film ends, we see Kris's cane leaning against the wall next to the fireplace.

Legal Analysis

One reason that trial movies are so enduring is that they typically concern the most serious, actual aspects of daily life. Neverthless, this fantasy film provides a useful insight into important aspects of our legal system.

We tend to think that trials represent one of the most rational parts of our culture, where all that counts is objective truth. For example, X may be charged with murder or rape, or sued for breach of contract, or negligently causing an automobile accident. Our first thought is that X's parents did a miserable job of raising X. Our second is that if X denies the claims, a trial would determine the objective truth—whether X really did commit the murder or breach the contract.

Nevertheless, the idea that a judge might someday be asked to decide whether a person really is Santa Claus is not sheer fantasy. Trials often involve subjective cultural beliefs. As long as our society collectively believes that a fact is true, a rational trial is possible regardless of whether that fact is objectively true.

For example, three hundred years ago, judges in Salem, Massachusetts, believed they were making rational, objective judgments when they decided whether some women were witches. Witches were real in their culture. Therefore, they could find evidence that a woman was a witch, such as the fact that some of a neighbor's cows took sick after the witch paid her neighbor a visit. Thus, they saw a rational connection between evidence (sick cows) and their social truth (witches).

Judge Harper engages in this same cultural process when he allows Fred to try to prove that Kris is really Santa. Judge Harper rules that since so many people in the country believe that Santa is real, he'll treat the existence of Santa as an objectively true fact. Once we accept this as a fact, the post office's delivery of mail to Kris can stand as rational support for the proposition that Kris is Santa.

It is tempting to blame the Salem witch trials on an ignorant culture that existed centuries ago, and to regard *Miracle on 34th Street* as an enjoyable fable that could never be real. But in fact our legal system converts cultural beliefs into objective truth all the time. Consider these everyday trial happenings:

• A psychiatrist testifies to an opinion that a killer was insane at the time he fired a fatal shot.

• A judge values the life of a person killed in an automobile accident at $1 million.

• A jury decides that two police officers acted properly in shooting an escaping suspect, because the officers reasonably believed that he was armed and about to fire on the officers.

None of these happenings constitute objective reality. The first reflects our culture's belief that there's a line between sanity and insanity, and that it's possible to measure a person's sanity at a given point in the past. The second reflects a cultural belief that money is the fairest way to compensate for a person's death, and that it's possible to fix the amount of money that a person was worth. Finally, the last reflects a cultural belief that officers act properly if they act reasonably, and that a group of citizens can stand in for the whole community when deciding what's reasonable. We'd talk about a fourth example, but our cultural belief seems to be that things occur in groups of three!

Our society may never get to the point where we believe it possible for someone to prove that he is Santa Claus. But that will be because our culture is unwilling to accept this as a fact, not because it is rationally impossible for Santa Claus to exist.

Setting aside the fantasy for a moment, *Miracle on 34th Street* does mislead us on the way to its happy outcome. During the hearing, the state attorney says that Kris has the burden of proving that he's Santa Claus. But the state is seeking to commit Kris to a mental institution, and the state has the burden of proving that Kris is dangerous either to himself or others. Even if Kris genuinely believes that he's Santa Claus, and even if the judge believes that Kris is mistaken, the state cannot commit Kris to a mental institution unless it proves that he is dangerous. Thus, when Mara impetuously rests his case (finishes presenting evidence) as soon as Kris testifies that he's Santa Claus, Judge Harper should have then and there set Kris free. Of course, that would have deprived the post office of a chance to show that neither rain, sleet, snow, hail, dark of night, nor the nonexistence of a real addressee can keep the mail from getting through; only the word "rush" stamped on an envelope can do that.

This is a wonderful feel-good movie. Santa is real; children can acquire their dream houses if they want them badly enough and are successful matchmakers; and Macy's is the best department store ever invented. With all this, who needs miracles?

Trial Brief

The film was remade in 1994, written by George Seaton and John Hughes and directed by Les Mayfield. It starred Richard Attenborough as Kris Kringle, Elizabeth Perkins as Doris, Mara Wilson as Susan, and Dylan McDermott as Fred. Macy's, which had much earlier ceased to represent the ultimate in chic shopping, was replaced by a generic department store.

Nuts

Synopsis: A hostile defendant in a manslaughter case insists on her right to be held responsible for her actions, not treated for mental illness.

Warner Bros. (Barbra Streisand). 1987. Color. Running time: 116 min.

Screenplay: Tom Topor, Darryl Ponicsan, and Alvin Sargent. Theatrical play: Tom Topor. Director: Martin Ritt.

Starring: Barbra Streisand (Claudia Draper), Richard Dreyfuss (Aaron Levinsky), Maureen Stapleton (Rose Kirk), Karl Malden (Arthur Kirk), Eli Wallach (Dr. Morrison), James Whitmore (Judge Murdoch), Robert Webber (Frances MacMillan).

Rating: —▮ —▮ —▮

The Story

Claudia Draper is a high-priced prostitute who has killed a client. She is charged with manslaughter, though flashbacks show she acted in self-defense. The immediate issue is not her guilt but her competence to stand trial. The film opens in a rushed and crowded courtroom. Middleton is Draper's lawyer, retained by her mother and stepfather. Middleton wants Draper committed to a mental institution for treatment. At the bench, Middleton, MacMillan (the prosecutor), and Judge Box discuss Draper's future as she sits fuming, unable to get anyone's attention. Drawing inspiration from the judge's name, Draper punches Middleton in the face and knocks him down. Understandably, he withdraws from the case. In desperation Judge Box orders legal aid lawyer Aaron Levinsky to represent Draper.

Draper is no happier with Levinsky, taunting him and refusing to cooperate. She takes it quite personally that the system is planning to institutionalize her indefinitely. Several psychiatrists have found

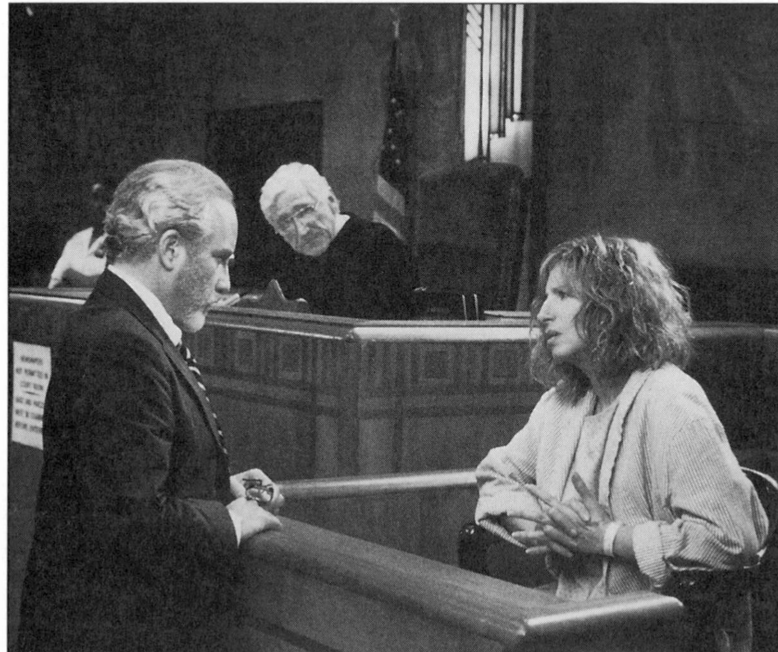

Nuts: Aaron Levinsky (Richard Dreyfuss) tries to prove that Claudia Draper (Barbra Streisand) is competent to stand trial.

Draper to be incompetent because she is so belligerent. In particular, Dr. Morrison sincerely believes that Draper needs treatment to modify her antisocial tendencies. She is, after all, a woman from an upper-class background who doesn't need to be a prostitute. Clearly, the shrinks believe, Draper cannot understand the proceedings against her and would be unable to cooperate in her own defense—the tests for competency to stand trial.

Eventually Levinsky breaks through Draper's wall of suspicion, and they prepare for the competency hearing in a courtroom at Bellevue Hospital before Judge Murdoch. Draper is her own worst enemy. She constantly interrupts the proceedings and seems unable to heed the judge's warnings to shut up. Her behavior reinforces the psychiatrists who think she is not competent to stand trial.

Draper's mother, Mrs. Kirk, is baffled by her daughter's condition. Perhaps psychiatric treatment is the answer. Draper taps on a water glass to prevent Levinsky from cross-examining. Mr. Kirk, Draper's stepfather, also thinks Draper should be treated rather than be humiliated in a public trial. On cross-examination, Levinsky goes after Kirk's offhand statement that he had bathed his stepdaughter. Until what age? Sixteen? Ultimately, Kirk is forced to admit that he is guilty of incest. Dr. Morrison comes across as a well-intentioned fool who cannot tolerate being challenged by a mere lawyer.

Testifying on her own behalf, Draper makes clear that she understands the proceedings and can cooperate in her own defense. On cross-examination, prosecutor MacMillan opens up the question of how Draper makes her living. Draper responds by telling MacMillan just what she could do for him, how it would feel, and how much each of the variations would cost. The prices seem high and MacMillan probably contemplates charging her with unfair business practices. Denying that she's crazy, Draper points out that many women marry men they despise in return for a Mercedes or summer in the Hamptons. Of course, most of them don't know about the variations.

Draper eloquently pleads with the judge to allow her to be held responsible for her own actions and stand trial. The judge wants to adjourn the proceedings and have Draper examined by a neutral psychiatrist. Rolling the dice, she refuses. Reluctantly, the long-suffering Judge Murdoch finds that Draper is competent and orders her released from custody pending her manslaughter trial. An epilogue tells us that Levinsky defends her and she is found not guilty. Dr. Morrison resigns as staff psychiatrist at Bellevue and takes a less stressful administrative job where no snotty lawyers can get near him. MacMillan probably buys a Mercedes and moves to the Hamptons.

Legal Analysis

Before Draper can stand trial for a crime, she must be mentally competent. This means that she must be sufficiently coherent to provide Levinsky with information necessary to construct a defense. In addition, she must be capable of comprehending the significance of the trial and her relation to it. As a practical matter, many defendants who might be able to establish an insanity defense at trial are diverted before trial into mental institutions because they are not competent to stand trial. Normally, as in *Nuts,* the determination of competence is made by a judge without a jury before the trial begins.

The rule requiring competence to stand trial serves important goals: it helps to assure a fair trial, since an incompetent defendant could not testify in her own defense or assist counsel in preparing a defense. It helps assure that the trial itself will proceed without disruption (a serious concern in *Nuts* since Draper could not keep her mouth shut). And finally, a defendant should know why she is being punished; this obviously depends on her understanding of what occurs at trial.

Nuts illustrates the difficulties a lawyer has with an uncommunicative client and how vital it is to persevere in order to win the client's confidence. Levinsky is only partially successful in achieving this. As a result, he stumbles through the hearing, apparently making up his cross-examination as he goes along. Not surprisingly, he unwittingly elicits damaging information, such as when Dr. Morrison reveals on cross-examination that Draper had punched a patient.

Similarly, Draper reveals nothing about incest or her relationship with her parents, since she believes that this is nobody's business but her own. It is implausible that Levinsky would have been able to uncover the incest while cross-examining Kirk. In fact, he probably would not have tried, since he would expect the stepfather to deny it. Thus the attempt to establish incest would probably have backfired.

Some of what happens at the competency hearing is dramatic but of marginal relevance to the narrow issue of whether Draper is competent to stand trial. For example, it is unclear just what her troubled childhood really tells us about her competence now. But the normal rules of evidence do not apply to a competency hearing, so perhaps the judge would let in all evidence that bears on Draper's mental competence.

The film dramatically presents the critical moral issue of whether a person whose behavior is antisocial and belligerent has a right *not* to be treated for mental illness. Many kind and protective people want to help Draper get her life back in order—her mother and stepfather, Middleton, MacMillan, the psychiatrists, and Judge Box. Perhaps some psychoactive medication could lessen her hostility; perhaps behavior modification and group therapy could persuade her to make a career change. Does it matter if a person wants to be *judged* and, if necessary, *punished,* rather than *treated?*

Draper argues that her lifestyle, profession, and personality are her own business. The state should not be allowed to treat people against their will who are not a danger to themselves or others, no matter what well-meaning professionals or parents might think. Yet, if she's mentally ill, how can she decide for herself whether she needs treatment? Our streets are full of homeless people who once would have been institutionalized against their will but who have been turned loose on the community to fend for themselves. Someone must be able to decide whether they are "nuts." But this film shows how careful we must be to avoid institutionalizing someone who may be nasty but who is nevertheless not "nuts" at all.

The Verdict

Synopsis: A burned-out personal injury lawyer finds moral redemption and pots of money when representing a young woman who went into a coma during childbirth.

Twentieth Century Fox (Zanuck-Brown). 1982. Technicolor. Running time: 128 min.

Screenplay: David Mamet. Original novel: Barry Reed. Director: Sidney Lumet.

Starring: Paul Newman (Frank Galvin), James Mason (Ed Concannon), Jack Warden (Mickey Morrissey), Charlotte Rampling (Laura Fischer), Milo O'Shea (Judge Hoyle), Lindsay Crouse (Kaitlin Price), Wesley Addy (Dr. Towler), Edward Binns (Bishop Brophy).

Academy Award nominations: Best Picture, Best Actor (Paul Newman), Best Supporting Actor (James Mason), Best Director, Best Screenplay.

Rating:

The Story

Frank Galvin is a boozy personal injury lawyer whose career has been a series of "bar" examinations. His practice consists of cases that he picks up by handing out business cards to bereaved family members during funeral services. But thanks to a referral from his semiretired mentor, Mickey Morrissey, Galvin has a "sure-fire winner." He represents a young woman who went to a hospital run by the Boston Archdiocese to give birth and ended up permanently comatose. Morrissey's judgment in referring the case to Galvin is as questionable as asking Henry VIII to write a book on dining table etiquette.

To succeed, Galvin has to prove that Dr. Towler gave the comatose woman the wrong kind of anesthesia. But with trial only two weeks away, Galvin's only preparation has been to figure out which bars are closest to the courthouse. Galvin is stirred to sudden sobriety by a visit to the comatose woman. He's determined to take the case to trial to atone for his past failings. He turns down a settlement of $210,000 offered first by Bishop Brophy and later by suave defense attorney Ed Concannon in the chambers of his crony, Judge Hoyle.

Galvin heads for the law library, one of the few places he's been to that doesn't stay open until two A.M. Concannon's preparation methods are not found in law libraries. He eliminates Galvin's key medical expert witness by treating him to a Caribbean vacation. He assigns one of his firm's lawyers, Laura Fischer, to charm her way into Galvin's head and bed. He makes sure that the Archdiocese's churches will have to pass the collection plates around a second time by putting enough of his firm's legal associates on the case to represent every

The Verdict: Judge Hoyle (Milo O'Shea) and Ed Concannon (James Mason) gang up on Frank Galvin (Paul Newman).

doctor in Boston. Finally, Concannon can depend on his pal Judge Hoyle not to run the trial according to his name.

Forced to find a last-minute substitute medical expert, Galvin unearths a kindly but ineffectual doctor who misreads the patient's chart and is bullied by Judge Hoyle into testifying that Dr. Towler wasn't negligent. A suddenly fearful Galvin goes after the settlement offer as if it were a full bottle of gin, but Concannon takes it off the table.

Back at trial, Dr. Towler, the author of a well-known anesthesia textbook, smugly defends his choice of anesthesia. He testifies that the anesthesia he used on the comatose woman was proper, since according to the admitting room form she hadn't eaten a full meal for nine hours. Her coma was an unfortunate and unforeseeable reaction to proper medication. Cross-examined by Galvin, Dr. Towler states that if the woman had eaten within an hour of the surgery, using the type of anesthesia he did would have been criminal negligence.

Galvin then produces a surprise witness, Kaitlin Price, the nurse who filled out the admitting room form. Nurse Price testifies that the form indicated that the woman ate a full meal within an hour of coming to the hospital, not nine hours. Dr. Towler had ordered Price to change the "1" on the form to a "9" when he realized that he had used the wrong anesthesia. On cross-examination, a sputtering Concannon charges Nurse Price with perjury. She dramatically pulls a piece of paper out of her purse, testifying that it's a photocopy of the original admitting form, showing the number "1." Concannon plays his last trump card: Judge Hoyle's friendship and ignorance. Upholding Concannon's objection, Judge Hoyle rules that the photocopy and all of Nurse Price's testimony is inadmissible, and orders the jury to disregard it. Nevertheless "the verdict" is for the comatose woman, with the jury foreman asking if the jury can legally award even more money than Galvin had asked for.

Legal Analysis

Frank Galvin is an all-too-typical figure in the modern-day legal profession. About half the lawyers who are disbarred or otherwise disciplined are addicted to drugs or alcohol. Soliciting clients by showing up at funerals would also probably get Galvin disbarred. That may be a bit surprising to TV viewers who have become used to seeing lawyers drum up business with commercials that make sales pitches for used cars and cubic zirconium diamonds seem sophisticated.

But *The Verdict* is only tuning up for the symphony of ethical and tactical snafus which follow. Never mind that Galvin neglects to take Dr. Towler's deposition, and violates a number of federal postal laws in his quest to locate Nurse Price. Galvin still seems a heroic figure when he twice spurns the Archdiocese's settlement offer of $210,000. Personal injury lawyers like Galvin often take cases on a contingency fee basis; their fees are strictly a percentage of what their clients collect, if anything. So at standard contingency fee rates, Galvin has turned down around $60,000 to $70,000, knowing that if he loses at trial he'll get nothing. But far from heroic, Galvin's refusals violate one of the cardinal ethical rules of law practice: Settlement decisions are to be made by clients, not by attorneys. Galvin has to convey the settlement offers to the comatose woman's legal guardian, even if he recommends against accepting them. Thus, the guardian is properly furious when she realizes that Galvin has given up sure money without consulting her. Had she reported Galvin to an attorney disciplinary committee, Galvin might have explained, "In order to feel good about myself again, I had to violate a cardinal ethical rule." Galvin would probably have been "disbarred," a term that would have terrified him into thinking that he couldn't drink any more.

Not to be outdone by Galvin, Concannon and Fischer would probably have been part of a double disbarring ceremony. On Concannon's orders, Fischer cozies up to Galvin and reports on his tactics. But Concannon is supposedly a brilliant lawyer. It's inconceivable that he would risk losing his career to win an ordinary medical malpractice case, especially one in which the boozy opponent has a longer losing streak than the Buffalo Bills in the Super Bowl. Concannon even personally writes out a check to Fischer as payment for her services, so the ethical committee can't possibly lose its disciplinary case (unless of course it was represented by Galvin). For her part, why would Fischer, an attorney trying to restart her career after a failed marriage, go along with Concannon's scheme? Isn't Fischer a wonderful role model for women seeking to advance in the legal profession? (See *Women Trial Lawyers in the Movies,* p. 90). "The Three Stooges Explain Thermonuclear Dynamics" would make more sense than this bumbling pair of lawyers.

The Archdiocese is itself a victim of Concannon's tactics. Unlike contingency fee plaintiff's lawyers, who collect a fee only if they win, defense lawyers like Concannon typically bill by the hour. Defense firms are experts at making paper mountains out of molehills, charging voraciously for every deposition, interrogatory, motion, and brief. The Archdiocese will pay dearly for Concannon's unnecessary marshaling of the resources of half of Harvard Law School's graduating class even if Concannon loses. With a trusting and naive client like Bishop Brophy, Concannon has every incentive to put enough padding in the bill to outfit the entire National Football League. After paying Concannon's law firm fees, the Archdiocese would be lucky to own an aspirin, let alone an entire hospital.

On the eve of trial, Concannon brings Dr. Towler to his law offices to prepare him to testify. Unlike English barristers, American lawyers regularly rehearse the testimony of clients and friendly witnesses. To the public, lawyers talk of helping witnesses present evidence credibly. To each other, they talk of "woodshedding" witnesses (figuratively beating them into saying the right things). The line between legitimately shaping a witness's testimony and improperly putting words in a witness's mouth is blurry. Not surprisingly, Concannon manages to cross it by creating testimony for Dr. Towler, not merely clarifying it. However, as in *The Verdict,* the "woodshed" is private and rarely does anyone, whether judge, adversary, or ethical committee, find out about what goes on inside it.

Though the film realistically portrays some of the seedier aspects of personal injury practice, it falls apart in the final dramatic trial scenes. Representing the plaintiff, it's up to Galvin to persuade the jury that Dr. Towler was negligent, meaning that Towler failed to meet the standard of care of physicians in the community. Galvin's only witness, the last-minute medical expert, is of no help; he concedes that Dr. Towler wasn't negligent. Since Galvin has no other evidence that

Dr. Towler was careless, Concannon should have immediately asked Judge Hoyle to stop the trial and enter a "directed verdict" for the Archdiocese and Dr. Towler. In civil cases, judges have the power to take a case from a jury if the jury could rationally arrive at only one result. Judge Hoyle would gladly have decided the case for the defendant and sent the jurors back to the jury room to watch TV and wonder what their role was supposed to be. But unfortunately for the Archdiocese, Concannon was played by "James" and not "Perry" Mason. Neither Concannon nor the members of his D-Day squadron thinks to ask for a directed verdict in favor of the doctors, so the trial continues. Nevertheless, the legally accurate name of the movie should have been *The Directed Verdict for the Defendant.* Well, maybe it was too long for the trailer.

The evidentiary bungling reaches a crescendo when Nurse Price provides evidence that Dr. Towler should have known that the patient had eaten within an hour of coming to the hospital, and thus used the wrong anesthetic. Price testifies that Dr. Towler confessed to her that he never looked at the information on the admitting room form, because he was tired after five surgeries. Judge Hoyle improperly rules that what Dr. Towler said to Nurse Price is inadmissible. Certainly, Dr. Towler's remark to Nurse Price is hearsay, and hearsay is normally not admissible in evidence (see *The Hearsay Rule,* p. 163). But one of the oldest exceptions to the hearsay rule is for "admissions." Under the admissions exception to the hearsay rule, anything said by a party to a lawsuit (like defendant Dr. Towler) is admissible in evidence when offered into evidence by the other party (like the plaintiff). Judge Hoyle may have gotten confused between evidentiary admissions and hospital admissions, though he'd never admit it. But since Dr. Towler's remark is so central to the issue of his carelessness, this single bad ruling would probably lead an appellate court to reverse a defense verdict.

But Judge Hoyle has more legal surprises up his long black sleeve. Nurse Price has in her lap the proof that Dr. Towler should have known that the patient had eaten within an hour of surgery. Price has a photocopy of the original admitting room form showing that she wrote a "1," not a "9." Concannon objects that the photocopy is inadmissible under the "best evidence rule." This is a remarkable objection, since the forgetful Galvin never offered Price's photocopy into evidence in the first place. Judge Hoyle, equally forgetful, upholds Concannon's objection to a photocopy that was never offered into evidence. Poor Nurse Price—the photocopy that she zealously guarded for four years never makes it out of her lap.

So it is that the best evidence rule, normally a rule of evidence about as exciting as an oil change, gets center stage of the drama. But despite Judge Hoyle's ruling, the best evidence rule would not have prevented Galvin from offering the photocopy into evidence. The rule provides that when a witness testifies to the contents of a document, the original document must be produced. But the best evidence rule was satisfied before Nurse Price even testified; the original admitting form is already in evidence. Galvin should have offered the photocopy to prove that the original was inaccurate. Of course, the best evidence rule would require Galvin to produce the photocopy, but it's right in his witness's lap. The jury would then simply have to decide which form was accurate, Concannon's original or Galvin's photocopy.

The Verdict pits a series of ethical and evidentiary nightmares against each other, and stirs in enough erroneous legal rulings to keep the Supreme Court going for two years. If justice is blind, justice got lucky in *The Verdict.*

Whose Life Is It Anyway?

Synopsis: An accident victim, paralyzed from the neck down, wants to die. The doctors insist that he be kept alive. It's up to a judge to decide.

MGM/Martin C. Schute, Ray Cooney (Lawrence P. Bachmann). 1981. Color. Running time: 118 min.

Screenplay: Brian Clark, Reginald Rose. Stageplay: Brian Clark. Director: John Badham.

Starring: Richard Dreyfuss (Ken Harrison), Christine Lahti (Clare Scott), John Cassavetes (Dr. Michael Emerson), Bob Balaban (Carter Hill), Kenneth McMillan (Judge Wyler), Thomas Carter (Orderly John).

Rating: —▮ —▮ —▮

The Story

Ken Harrison, a gifted sculptor, is horribly injured in a car crash. Six months later, it's clear that he will never move his legs or hands again. He dismisses his loyal girlfriend Patty, because seeing her each day makes him even more miserable. Though he preserves his sense of humor, Harrison decides that he wishes to die. Yet Harrison is so helpless that he cannot die if the hospital keeps him alive.

The chief of medicine, Dr. Michael Emerson, is unalterably opposed to letting Harrison die. Emerson is certain that Harrison will change his mind, accept his limitations, and want to live. Indeed, Emerson calms Harrison with Valium injections against Harrison's will.

Dr. Clare Scott, the physician in immediate charge of Harrison's case, struggles with the moral issue of whether to let him die. As a physician she is pledged to preserve life. But as a human being, she accepts Harrison's right to decide for himself. After a visit to Harrison's studio, where she observes what a great sculptor Harrison was, she brings herself to support him. Harrison also gets quiet support from Orderly John, a black reggae musician who sneaks him off for a concert in the hospital basement, and from a sympathetic novice nurse, Mary Jo Adler.

Harrison persuades Carter Hill, a cautious and somewhat bumbling personal injury lawyer, to represent him in asserting his right to die. This, Hill admits, is a case he could bear to lose. If you do, Harrison replies, it's a life sentence for me.

The hospital threatens to bring an involuntary commitment action against Harrison under the Mental Hygiene Law. To preempt this move, Hill brings an action for habeas corpus against the hospital. The theory is that it is holding Harrison without his consent and without any legal justification. If he wins, Harrison would be released from the hospital and could go off and die by himself. Judge Wyler conducts the hearing in an office at the hospital. Harrison hopes that Wyler is a hanging judge.

Emerson's defense is that Harrison is clinically depressed and therefore incompetent to decide whether he should die. In other words, Harrison must be crazy if he wants to die; therefore, he can't make the decision for himself. The hospital's psychiatrist, Dr. Jacobs, wisely supports Dr. Emerson, but Hill's psychiatrist, Dr. Barrows, predictably disagrees. Sure, Harrison is depressed, who wouldn't be? But he is not so depressed that he is irrational.

Harrison finally speaks, eloquently asserting his right to die. Without the ability to work, life is not worth living. In fact, he says, he is already dead. Imprisoned within his useless body, his mind will soon disintegrate. Let me die, he says, or come back in five years and see what a piece of work you've done today.

Judge Wyler, tortured by the decision, grants the writ. Emerson tells Harrison he doesn't have to leave; he can stay and the hospital will withdraw dialysis. Within a week or two, Harrison will be dead. Dr. Scott, John, and Adler bid Harrison farewell.

Legal Analysis

As a matter of constitutional law, a person has a basic liberty right to decide what to do with his or her body, if nobody else is harmed by the decision. Thus the state cannot prevent a person from buying or using contraceptives or from obtaining an abortion under certain conditions. Generally, this right covers a person's right to refuse treatment. As a result, Dr. Emerson's decision to inject Harrison with Valium against his will was wrong. Harrison would have been able to sue Emerson in a tort action for this unwanted treatment.

In the *Karen Ann Quinlan* case (1976) the New Jersey Supreme Court decided that a person has a right to die; it also said that a patient's parents have the right to pull the plug on a patient in a vegetative state whose wishes are not known. In *Cruzan v. Missouri Department of Health* (1990), the U.S. Supreme Court indicated that a competent individual has an absolute right to refuse life-saving food and water. But it left unclear whether family members can pull the plug on a vegetative patient when the state opposes that decision.

The constitutional right to decide what to do with one's body is not absolute. For example, state laws requiring motorcycle riders to wear helmets have been upheld, even though the state's primary interest is protecting the biker from his own stupidity. The helmet laws reflect society's ambivalence about how much control a person has over his body.

But how about a nonvegetative patient like Harrison? Does he have a right to die and must health care providers go along with his decision? Quite a few people, especially in the disability rights movement, would agree with Dr. Emerson that Harrison should not be allowed to commit suicide. This is an issue that is not settled, either legally or morally.

In this movie, Emerson does not claim that he can prevent Harrison from refusing treatment. Instead, he argues that Harrison is not mentally fit to make that decision. Surely, Emerson argues, society can prevent a disturbed or irrational person from killing him or herself. If, for example, a patient distraught over his marital problems comes to his doctor and demands barbiturates to kill himself, the doctor should not prescribe them. Instead, she should arrange for the patient to receive therapy and, if necessary, have him involuntarily committed.

Thus the issue comes down to Harrison's mental condition and that calls for a battle of the psychiatric experts. Needless to say, psychiatrists may have their own agendas. Dr. Jacobs is asked by Emerson to examine Harrison as a special favor. It's possible that Jacobs would incur serious professional problems at the hospital if he goes against Emerson's desires. Anyway, Judge Wyler correctly rules that Harrison's depression does not prevent him from making a rational decision about his own future.

Incidentally, Jacob's opinion is submitted at the hearing only in the form of an affidavit. Normally, this would be impermissible under the hearsay rule. Introducing testimony in affidavit form prevents Hill from cross-examining Jacobs (see *The Hearsay Rule,* p. 163). Nevertheless, the rules of evidence are not strictly enforced in this informal habeas hearing. Moreover, Hill does not object to the affidavit, so the point does not even arise.

Hill effectively uses the writ of habeas corpus to assert Harrison's right to get out of the hospital. This so called "great writ" comes down to us from hundreds of years of English practice. It's always available to force the government, or anyone else, who is holding someone against his will to establish the legal justification for the detention. It is, therefore, a great pillar of our civil liberties. The U.S. Constitution provides that habeas corpus cannot be suspended, "unless when in cases of rebellion or invasion the public safety may require it."

Whose Life Is It Anyway? forces us to imagine ourself in Harrison's place. Would we choose suicide instead of a life of utter helplessness, a burden to ourselves and everyone we know? Or would we try to overcome our disability and achieve a dignified and worthwhile life? If we choose life, society should make every possible effort to support that choice and provide us with the potential for meaningful existence. But the state or well-meaning doctors should not attempt to make the decision for us. Harrison should never have been required to put himself and others through the agony of the habeas hearing to be allowed to die with dignity.

The Young Philadelphians

Synopsis: A lawyer of uncertain breeding uses his abilities and social connections to rise to the top of the Philadelphia law firm aristocracy. He rekindles his independence from the social elite when he defends an old friend charged with murder.

Warner Bros. 1959. Black and white. Running time: 136 min.

Screenplay: James Gunn. Book: Richard Powell. Director: Vincent Sherman.

Starring: Paul Newman (Tony Judson Lawrence), Barbara Rush (Joan Dickinson), Brian Keith (Mike Flanagan), Alexis Smith (Carol Wharton), Diane Brewster (Kate Judson), John Williams (Gilbert Dickinson), Robert Vaughn (Chester Swynn), Paul Picerni (Louis Donetti), Billie Burke (Mrs. J. Arthur Allen), Otto Kruger (John Wharton), Frank Conroy (Dr. Shippen Stearnes), Robert Douglas (Morton Stearnes), Richard Deacon (George Archibald).

Academy Award nominations: Best Supporting Actor (Robert Vaughn), Best Cinematography.

Rating: —▮ —▮ —▮

The Young Philadelphians: Tony Lawrence (Paul Newman) hones in on the uncertain olfactory nerves of George Archibald (Richard Deacon).

The Story

Kate Judson marries William Lawrence, a member of one of Philadelphia's wealthiest and most powerful families. No sooner are they married than a miserable William confesses to Kate that he can't make her happy. (Modern Translation: "I'm gay.") He runs out on her, and within hours is killed in an automobile accident. Kate, meanwhile, seeks comfort with Mike Flanagan, the hard-working but socially unconnected man who had hoped to marry her. Mike gives Kate more than comfort; nine months later she gives birth to a son, Tony. Kate refuses the Lawrence money, but insists on giving her son the Lawrence name to help him achieve his rightful social position. In Philadelphia, only "Rocky" would have been a better choice.

Tony Lawrence grows up unaware of his real father's identity. Though a brilliant student, he never wonders why none of the Lawrence fortune finds its way into his hands or why Mike keeps coming to his graduations. During law school his playboy friend Chet introduces him to Joan Dickinson. Joan's father Gilbert is one of Philadelphia's top lawyers. Joan quickly falls in love with Tony, who is unlike the wealthy bores she usually dates. Tony, admirably setting aside any prejudice he might have against wealth and beauty, falls in love with Joan. They decide to elope. But the elder Dickinson intercedes by convincing Tony to postpone the marriage in exchange for a position in the Dickinson firm. Joan angrily dumps Tony and marries Carter, one of her aristocratic admirers.

Taking advantage of his mother's social connections, Tony outfoxes a law school chum, Louis Donetti, to secure a summer law job with John Wharton. Wharton is the head of a Philadelphia law firm that has even greater cachet than Dickinson's. Tony's skills at legal research and fending off Mrs. Wharton's amorous advances land him a permanent job with the Wharton firm.

After serving in the military during the Korean War, Tony becomes a Wharton tax specialist. He pulls off a coup by showing Mrs. Allen, a wealthy widow and Dickinson client, how Dickinson's ignorance of tax law has caused her to pay huge amounts in unnecessary taxes. Mrs. Allen becomes a Wharton client; Tony becomes a partner; the federal budget is slashed after the government loses Mrs. Allen's tax payments.

Everyone has big plans for Tony: Mike Flanagan and Louis Donetti want him to run for City Council; Dickinson wants him in his firm; and Joan, whose husband died in Korea, wants to marry him. All these plans are put on hold when Chet is arrested for the murder of his uncle, Morton Stearnes, who kept a tight rein on Chet's trust fund. Chet insists that Tony represent him. Tony is reluctant, as he has no criminal law experience. Moreover, Kate and Mike finally tell Tony who his father really is, and disclose that Dr. Stearnes, Morton's brother, has threatened to reveal that Tony is not a Lawrence unless Tony drops the case.

Tony does represent Chet, and faces his moment of truth when the D.A., Louis Donetti, calls George Archibald as his last witness. George is Morton's butler, and snootier than all the Lawrences and Stearnes put together. On the night of Morton's death, George heard Chet and Morton arguing in the study. On two occasions, Morton called George to the study to clear away empty drinking glasses. George could tell from the empty glasses that Chet was still there, because as a liquor expert he could distinguish the smell of the cheap rye that Chet drank from the fancy Scotch that Morton drank. Later that evening George heard a noise, and then a few minutes later a shot. He ran outside to find Morton dead, a gun beside him and Chet gone.

On cross-examination by Tony, George admits that he didn't actually see Chet in the study with Morton when he collected the empty glasses. Then, to show that George might be mistaken about the contents of the empty glasses, Tony asks George to smell three glasses and identify their contents. Seemingly bending over backward to be fair, Tony encourages George to take long sniffs so that he doesn't make a mistake. However, George does make a mistake with Glass No. 3: based on smell, he says it's water; after tasting it, he realizes it's gin. The shaken George concedes that he wasn't all that sure about Glass No. 2 either. Donetti objects to the whole experiment, claiming that having to smell one glass right after another probably upset George's sense of smell. The judge overrules the objections, rewarding Tony for his craftiness in getting George to take long sniffs.

Tony suggests to George that the noise he heard moments before the shot might have been Chet leaving through the garden gate; George isn't sure. Tony then calls Dr. Stearnes, who admits to having criticized Morton's financial competence and relieved him of many family duties just hours before Morton's death. Morton also had a brain tumor. Asked by Tony whether all of this might have caused Morton to commit suicide, Dr. Stearnes sadly nods "yes." The jury finds Chet not guilty.

The verdict produces smiles all around. Louis Donetti congratulates Tony on a fine job; Dr. Stearnes promises that the family will support Chet; Kate and Mike are proud of their son; and Joan and Tony make wedding plans. The only person with a reason to be unhappy is George, who has to return to Lemonade I and learn his drink smells all over again.

Legal Analysis

For anyone other than an oil mogul who learns about a new tax break, Tony's defense of Chet is the film's centerpiece. Tony proves as adept at finding holes in evidence as finding loopholes in the tax laws.

Nevertheless, Tony's strategy is extremely risky. Attorneys do not like to take chances on live courtroom experiments, especially with a hostile witness like George. Hanging around with Chet may have given Tony some insight into the effect of alcohol on the sense of smell, but he cannot be certain that George will make a mistake. In fact, the experiment nearly does backfire. To the relief of serious Scotch drinkers everywhere, George confidently and accurately identifies the contents of Glass No. 1 and No. 2. Not until he makes a mistake about Glass No. 3 does he volunteer the crucial information that he wasn't sure about Glass No. 2. Before George throws in this remark, Tony's experiment reinforces George's claim that he distinguished fancy Scotch from cheap rye on the night Morton died.

Though the experiment is dramatic, the film never makes clear Tony's purpose in conducting it. Most likely, Tony is trying to show that Chet left the house long before Morton committed suicide. That's why he makes a point of showing that George collected the glasses at the door to the study and didn't actually see Chet. George's unreliable nose would support Tony's argument that Morton was alone in the study, because all the glasses George carted off could have contained Morton's Scotch. (Conveniently, Morton is a fastidious drinker who doesn't like to refill glasses.) The only problem with Tony's argument is that it's illogical. On the one hand, Chet is gone long before Morton shoots himself; on the other, the noise George hears just moments before he heard the shot was Chet leaving through the garden gate. Unless the jurors' minds are clouded by the fumes created by Tony's turning the courtroom into the Honky Tonk Bar, they're bound to realize that Chet couldn't be two places at once. However, Tony may not be worried about this logical flaw. As the great Supreme Court justice Oliver Wendell Holmes pointed out, the life of the law has not been logic, but experience. For many jurors, any serious mistake by a prosecution witness will create reasonable doubt, even if the mistake doesn't fit in with the rest of the defense argument.

A better purpose for Tony's conducting the experiment is to suggest that even if Chet was still in the study, it was Morton who was doing all the drinking. This would support Tony's argument that Morton committed suicide, as it would show that he was distraught and acting strangely on the night he died. Moreover, it wouldn't require the jurors to play "Where's Waldo" with Chet; he's in the study until he leaves by the garden gate. To carry out this theme, Tony should have questioned George about Morton's morose demeanor and unusual behavior throughout the evening.

Whatever Tony's purpose, the judge's ruling allowing Tony to conduct the experiment seems correct. The results of the experiment are relevant if the courtroom conditions under which George has to identify liquor by its smell are similar to the conditions that existed on the night that Morton died. That night, George smelled two glasses at a time; in court, Tony asks him to smell three. If George had only been uncertain about Glass No. 3, which contained gin, the judge should have thrown out the whole experiment because neither Morton nor Chet were drinking gin. The critical testimony is George's admission that he was uncertain about Glass No. 2, containing Morton's brand of Scotch. If he's uncertain about the smell in court, he may have been equally uncertain at home. And Donetti can't complain that Tony rigged the experiment to spoil George's sense of smell, for in court as on the night Morton died, George smelled the glasses one right after the other.

Tony Lawrence and Louis Donetti reflect the experiences of many lawyers. In law school, they sweat for the grades that will allow them entry into the largest and most prestigious corporate law firms. Having achieved their goal, many quickly become disenchanted with the long hours and what they perceive as an unfulfilling lifestyle. Louis, for example, leaves his large law firm to go with a smaller, more active one that represents labor unions. When that doesn't provide enough action, he goes to work for the D.A. And Tony describes the Wharton firm as a "high-class graveyard." Apparently, even $200,000 tax loopholes lose their sex appeal after a while, hard as that may be to understand. Thus, taking on Chet's defense may reflect Tony's restlessness with tax law practice as much as it does his commitment to an old friend.

Still in the hospital after having given birth to Tony, Kate Lawrence assures William's mother that she will never ask the Lawrences to support Tony. Seemingly she couldn't do so anyway, for Tony was fathered by Mike. However, the law has traditionally tried to protect children against illegitimacy. At the time of Tony's birth, William would have been conclusively presumed to be the father if Tony was conceived while Kate and William were married and cohabiting. As a result of this rule, Tony might well have inherited a Lawrence corporation or two even though Mike was his biological father. Thus, the timing of events is crucial to determining who Tony's legal father is—if William's death took place after Tony's conception, then it's William; if William died beforehand, it's Mike. Since death and conception both took place on the same evening, Tony's financial claim to William's estate might well have hinged on whether Mike practiced lengthy foreplay.

In most states, the conclusive presumption that a husband is the father of a child conceived during wedlock has been greatly watered down. The change probably reflects both more reliable scientific means of determining a child's parentage, and less of a social stigma attached to being born out of wedlock. Today, even if Tony's conception preceded William's death, the Lawrences could probably prevent Tony from inheriting by showing that Mike was the biological father.

Tony's earning potential suddenly rises when the wealthy Mrs. Allen stumbles into his office in search of a lawyer who will prepare a will codicil leaving her dog Carlos to Joan. Tony agrees to draft the codicil; since he's still upset with Joan Dickinson, he probably wishes he could leave her a whole kennel. When Tony learns that Mrs. Allen is represented by Gilbert Dickinson, he expresses surprise that Dickinson never advised her to save taxes by using appreciated stock to make charitable gifts instead of cash. (Still sound advice!) Many lawyers would look at Mrs. Allen's balance sheet and not worry about charges of client-stealing. To his credit, Tony immediately offers to call Dickinson, and even tells Mrs. Allen that Dickinson can achieve the same tax savings for her that he can. Tony's actions are honorable; he goes beyond what the ethical rules require.

Tony also displays ethical sensitivity when Chet begs Tony to defend him. A lawyer is supposed to turn down a case if he lacks sufficient experience to do a competent job. Thus, Tony properly warns Chet that he is a tax attorney with no trial experience, and that Chet would be better off with the criminal law specialists that his family wants to hire. In light of their past friendship and Chet's strong wishes, Tony is justified in taking the case. But he would have been prudent to document Chet's consent in writing.

Tony winds up as the darling of the Philadelphia social elite. All he had to do was find gobs of tax breaks and pull off a miraculous criminal defense. But maybe even this wouldn't have been enough had word gotten out that he wasn't really a Lawrence.

Appendix of Additional Courtroom Movies

Have we whetted your appetite for courtroom movies? Here are some additional ones that may turn up on TV or in your local video shop.

Beyond Reasonable Doubt. New Zealand, 1980. David Hemmings. In this true story, the police frame and the prosecutor convict an innocent man who serves many years in prison before being pardoned. —■ —■

Body of Evidence. 1992. Madonna, Willem Dafoe. A sexaholic gold-digger is accused of loving a wealthy man to death as her lawyer tries to find the breast defense to murder. —■ —■

Brothers in Law. 1957. Richard Attenborough, Ian Carmichael. A light farce in which an inept new barrister finds himself in a chambers where the other lawyers are only slightly less daft than he is. —■ —■

The Case Against Mrs. Ames. 1936. Madeleine Carroll. A young widow acquitted of killing her husband has to battle for custody of her son. Opposing her is the husband's mother, her defense lawyer in the murder case, and the prosecutor still trying to prove her guilty. —■ —■

The Case of the Howling Dog. 1934. William Warren, Mary Astor. A dog that suddenly stops howling and then attacks its master allows Perry Mason to take a bite out of the District Attorney's murder case. The first Perry Mason film. —■ —■ —■

Criminal Court. 1946. Tom Conway. A lawyer defends his fiancée on a charge of murdering a mobster by offering evidence that the lawyer was the killer. —■ —■

Criminal Law. 1988. Gary Oldman, Kevin Bacon. A lawyer convinces a jury to acquit a murderer, then continues to represent him in order to prove his guilt. The film is more filler than thriller.

Defenseless. 1991. Barbara Hershey, Sam Shepard. An attorney conceals her own involvement in a crime by defending a friend charged with murdering her husband.

Disorder in the Court. 1936. The Three Stooges, called as witnesses in a murder trial, turn the proceedings into utter shambles.

A Dry White Season. 1989. Donald Sutherland, Marlon Brando. A rigged inquest reveals the brutal face of South African apartheid.

A Fish Called Wanda. 1988. John Cleese, Jamie Lee Curtis, Kevin Kline. Unexpected testimony from an alibi witness turns a trial into a shambles.

From the Hip. 1987. Judd Nelson, Elizabeth Perkins. A young lawyer finds success with ridiculous courtroom antics that suggest what might have been if a fourth Stooge had gone to law school.

How to Murder Your Wife. 1964. Jack Lemmon. A cartoonist plots the comic-strip murder of his action hero's wife, only to find himself charged with murder when his real wife disappears.

JFK. 1991. Kevin Costner. Jim Garrison tries Clay Shaw for conspiracy to murder the president. A disorganized jumble.

The Last Wave. Australia, 1977. Richard Chamberlain. A well-meaning lawyer represents five aborigines charged with homicide. After the trial, the world as we know it ends.

The Law of the Lawless. 1963. Dale Robertson, Yvonne DeCarlo. A judge dedicated to ridding the Old West of shootouts presides over the murder trial of an old friend.

Legal Eagles. 1986. Robert Redford, Debra Winger. D.A. and defense attorney join up in a silly piffle about art thefts and murder. The trial scenes run the gamut from unethical to unimaginable.

Madame X. 1966. Lana Turner. A woman who abandoned her family is defended by her unrecognizing son.

The Man Who Talked Too Much. 1940. George Brent, Virginia Bruce. A disillusioned D.A. sells his soul and courtroom tricks to the mob. When he tries to quit, the mob plants evidence putting his kid brother on Death Row. (Other Versions: *The Mouthpiece,* 1932; *Illegal,* 1955.)

Manhattan Melodrama. 1934. Clark Gable, William Powell, Myrna Loy. A D.A. prosecutes his childhood friend for murder, unaware that the victim was a blackmailer who intended to ruin the D.A.'s campaign for governor.

Marked Woman. 1937. Humphrey Bogart, Bette Davis. A group of Fallen Women screw up their courage to help a crusading New York District Attorney bring down a mobster.

Mountain Justice. 1937. George Brent, Josephine Hutchinson. Hillbillies seek revenge against an abused woman who kills her backwoods father in self-defense.

A Night of Adventure. 1944. Tom Conway. A lawyer defends a client on a murder charge; only trouble is, the lawyer did it. Not available on videotape or laser.

The Passion of Joan of Arc. Silent, 1928. Maria Falconetti. Joan of Arc is tried for heresy and burned at the stake. The judges are as grotesque as the procedure. Not available on videotape or laser.

The People Against O'Hara. 1951. Spencer Tracy. A burned-out lawyer goes to the limit and beyond in defending a client accused of murder. Not available on videotape or laser.

The People vs. Dr. Kildare. 1941. Dr. Kildare's roadside surgery saves an accident victim's life. Though it's more service than the AAA would provide he's sued for malpractice when the victim ends up paralyzed.

Physical Evidence. 1988. Burt Reynolds, Theresa Russell. A convoluted story about a public defender seeking to prove that a suspended police officer did not murder an informant. Both the officer's and the viewer's patience are put on trial.

A Question of Silence. Dutch, 1983. Three women who don't know each other kill a store clerk for no apparent reason. The trial is as baffling as the crime.

Roxie Hart. 1941. Ginger Rogers. A showgirl stands trial for murder to give her career a boost. Absolutely hilarious.

The Return of Martin Guerre. French, 1982. Gerard Depardieu.

Martin Guerre returns to his family, but is he really Martin or a clever imposter? Same story as *Sommersby*.

Serial Mom. 1994. Kathleen Turner. A farce in which a suburban mom massacres seven victims and the legal system.

Star Witness. 1931. Walter Huston, Chic Sale. The mob kidnaps and threatens to kill a young boy if his family testifies against a mobster boss.

State's Attorney. 1932. John Barrymore. A defense lawyer becomes the D.A. and prosecutes his former client. It's a primer on conflicts of interest. (Titled *Cardigan's Last Case* in Great Britain.)

The Story of Oiu Ju. China, 1992. Gong Li. A Chinese peasant woman seeks an apology from her husband's attacker and winds up with more justice than she really wants.

Stranger on the Third Floor, 1940. Peter Lorre. In Michael's scary nightmare, he's arrested and tried for a murder he didn't commit. Then it actually happens.

True Believer. 1989. James Woods. A lucky lawyer pulls a rabbit out of his hat to spring an innocent client. A contrived and unconvincing trial.

The Winslow Boy. 1950. Robert Donat, Margaret Leighton. A famous barrister convinces the British government to grant a hearing for a young naval cadet student expelled for stealing a five-shilling postal order.

Bibliography

We found these books helpful references on many of the movies reviewed in this book.

Cramton, Roger C., *Audiovisual Materials on Professional Responsibility* (American Bar Association, Section on Torts and Insurance Practice, 1987).

LaFave, Wayne R. and Austin W. Scott Jr., *Criminal Law* (West Pub. Co., 2d ed., 1986).

LaFave, Wayne R. and Jerrold Israel, *Criminal Procedure* (West Pub. Co., 2d ed., 1992).

Strong, John W., *McCormick on Evidence* (West Pub. Co., 4th ed. 1992).

Some invaluable reference books on movies:

Magill, Frank N., *Magill's Survey of Cinema* (Salem Press, 1980, 1981, and annual supplements).

Nash, Jay Robert and Stanley Ralph Ross, *Motion Picture Guide 1927–1983* (Cinebooks, 1985 and annual supplements).

Some journal articles on trial films:

Greenfield, Steve and Gary Osborn, "Lawyers in Film: Where Myth Meets Reality," 143 *New Law Journal* 1769 (December 17, 1993).

Mastrangelo, Paul J., "Lawyers and the Law: A Filmography," 3 *Legal Services Reference Quarterly* 31 (1983).

Rosenberg, Norman, "Hollywood on Trials: Courts and Films, 1930–1960," 12 *Law and History Revised* 341 (1994).

Verrone, Patric M., "The 12 Best Trial Movies," 75 *American Bar Association J.* 96 (November 1989).

Chapter 1

The Accused. Jonathan Friendly, "The New Bedford Rape Case: Confusion over Accounts of Cheering at Bar," *New York Times*

(April 11, 1984, Sec. 11, p. 19); Jesus Rangel, "Two are Convicted in New England Rape Case," *New York Times* (March 18, 1984, Sec. 1, p. 1).

A Cry in the Dark. Lindy Chamberlin, *Through My Eyes: An Autobiography* (Heinemann, 1991); Robert Cockburn, "Dingo Baby Couple Wins 540,000 Pounds," *The Times* (May 26, 1992).

I Want to Live! People v. Santo, 43 Cal. 2d 319, 273 P. 2d 249 (1954), cert. den. 348 U.S. 959 (1955) (Justice Douglas was of opinion that the writ should be granted); Application of Graham, 132 F.Supp. 69 (S.D. Cal. 1955); *Graham v. Teets,* 223 F. 2d 680 (9th Cir. 1955). Gale Cook, *A Penalty of Death, Montreal Gazette* (April 25, 1992, p. B6) (Cook was a journalist who witnessed Graham's execution).

Inherit the Wind. Note, 64 Chi. Kent L. Rev. 340 (1988); Lawrence M. Bernabo and Celeste Michelle Condit, *Two Stories of the Scopes Trial,* in Robert Hariman, ed., *Popular Trials: Rhetoric, Mass Media, and the Law* (University of Alabama Press, 1990). Special thanks for assistance to Professor Julian Eule.

Judgment at Nuremberg. "War Crimes: Finis," *Time* (April 25, 1949, p. 29); "War Crimes: The Last Judgments," *Newsweek* (April 25, 1949, p. 36); Telford Taylor, "Nuremberg Trials: War Crimes and International Law," *International Conciliation* 286–93 (April 1949); "Judgment at Nuremberg," 5 National Jewish Law Review (1990).

Let Him Have It. Iris Bentley, *Let Him Have Justice* (1995); "Bentley Given Part Pardon 40 Years After Being Hanged," *Daily Telegraph* (July 31, 1993, p. 7).

A Man for All Seasons. William Kinsella, "Thomas More: A Man for Our Time," 29 Catholic Lawyer 323 (1985); Hubertus Schulte Herbruggen, "The Process Against Sir Thomas More," 99 Law Quarterly Review 113 (1983); Thomas L. Shaffer, *On Being A Christian and a Lawyer* (Brigham Young University Press, 1981).

The Onion Field. People v. Powell, 67 Cal. 2d 32, 59 Cal. Rptr. 817 (1967); *People v. Powell,* 40 Cal. App. 3d 107, 115 Cal. Rptr. 109 (1974); *Smith v. Superior Court,* 68 Cal. 2d 547, 68 Cal. Rptr. 1 (1968); *In re Powell,* 45 Cal. 3d 894, 248 Cal. Rptr. 431 (1988); "Parole in 'Onion Field' case denied," *Los Angeles Times* (September 7, 1994, Metro Section, p. 3, col. 5).

Reversal of Fortune. Alan M. Dershowitz, *Reversal of Fortune* (Random House, 1986); *State v. von Bulow,* 475 A. 2d 995 (R.I. 1984).

10 Rillington Place. Ludovic Kennedy, *Ten Rillington Place* (Simon and Schuster, 1961).

The Thin Blue Line. Adams v. State, 577 S.W. 2d 717 (1979) (affirming

Adams's conviction); *Adam's v. Texas,* 448 U.S. 38 (1980) (reversing death sentence); *Adams v. State,* 624 S.W. 2d 568 (1981) (refusing new trial request); *Ex Parte Adams,* 768 S.W. 2d 281 (1989) (granting writ of habeas corpus and ordering new trial for Adams); *Harris v. State,* 784 S.W. 2d 5 (1989) (affirming Harris's conviction and death sentence). Daniel Cerone, "'Thin Blue Line' in a Different Court," *Los Angeles Times* (July 7, 1989, Calendar Section, p. 1); Donald P. Meyers, "The Next Life of Randall Dale Adams," *Newsday* (May 8, 1989). Orfield, *Criminal Procedure under the Federal Rules* (vol. 5, sec. 33; 2d ed., 1987).

Chapter 2

Billy Budd. Richard H. Weisberg, *The Failure of the Word,* ch. 8–9 (Yale University Press. 1984); 1 *Cardozo Studies in Law and Literature,* pp. 1–122 (1989) (numerous articles about *Billy Budd*); Christopher James Sterritt, "Ode to Billy Budd: Judicial Professionalism in Modern American Military Law," 38 *Federal Bar News* 208 (1991).

Breaker Morant. Sir Frank Fox, *Bushman and Buccaneer* (1902); Kit Denton, *The Breaker* (Washington Square Press, 1973); Lyman, "Echoes of Viet Nam and Breaker Morant Morality," *Washington Post* (August 9, 1981, Style Sec., p. G1); Thomas Pakenham, *The Boer War* (Random House, 1979).

The Court-Martial of Billy Mitchell. Isaac Don Levine, *Mitchell: Pioneer of Air Power* (Duell, Sloan and Pearce, 1943); Emile Gauvreau and Lester Cohen, *Billy Mitchell: Founder of Our Air Force and Prophet Without Honor* (E.P. Dutton and Co., 1942); Cathy Packer, *Freedom of Expression in the American Military* (Praeger, 1989). Special thanks for assistance to Professor Robinson Everett, David A. Brahms, and Christopher J. Sterritt.

A Few Good Men. Jacqueline Weaver, "Stage to Screen, Branford Lawyer's Story Told," *New York Times,* (November 8, 1992, Connecticut edition, sec. 13 CN, page 12, column 3); Bernard Weinraub, "Film: Reiner's March to a Few Good Men," *New York Times* (December 6, 1992, sec. 2, p. 1, col. 1). Dan Phelps, "A Few Good Men," *Needham Times* (February 1993); Bill Glauber, "Ex-Marine who felt 'A Few Good Men' maligned him is mysteriously murdered," *Baltimore Sun,* (April 10, 1994, p. 1). Special thanks for assistance to Professor Robinson Everett, David A. Brahms, Chief Judge Gene Sullivan (U.S. Court of Appeals for the Armed Forces), Major Nancy LaLuntas, Christopher J. Steritt.

Paths of Glory. Leonard V. Smith, "The Disciplinary Dilemma of French Military Justice, September 1914–April 1917," 55 *Journal of Military*

History 47 (1991). Special thanks for assistance to Professor Leonard V. Smith.

Prisoners of the Sun. C. Hosoya, N. Ando, Y. Onuma, and R. Minear, *The Tokyo War Crimes Trial* 37–42 (Kodansha Ltd. 1986); M. Bassiouni and V. Nanda, *A Treatise on International Criminal Law,* vol. 1, chapters 2 and 8 (Charles C. Thomas, 1973); Brian Williams, *Blood Oath* (Angus and Robertson, 1990).

Chapter 3

Women Trial Lawyers in the Movies. Cynthia Lucia, "Women on Trial: The Female Lawyer in the Hollywood Courtroom," 19 *Cineaste* 32 (1992); Carolyn Lisa Miller, "'What a Waste. Beautiful, Sexy Gal. Hell of a Lawyer.': Film and the Female Attorney," 4 *Colum Journal of Gender and Law* 203 (1994). Special thanks to Barbara Brudno for suggesting this sidebar.

The Advocate. The medieval practice of holding animals responsible for crimes is described in E.P. Evans, *The Criminal Prosecution and Capital Punishment of Animals* (1906), and in an essay by Paul Schiff Berman, "Rats, Pigs and Statues on Trial," *New York University Law Review,* pp. 288–326 (1995). The script in *The Advocate* is based on transcripts of medieval trials involving animals. Paul Sherman, "Advocate defends medieval madness," *Boston Herald* (September 4, 1994, p. O45).

Chapter 4

In the Name of the Father. Ronan Bennett, "The Big Screen Trial of the Guildford Four," *The Observer Review* (February 6, 1994, p. 2); Alan Travis, "The Report: Process Attacked from Beginning to End," *The Guardian* (July 1, 1994, p. 2).

The Life of Emile Zola. Louis Snyder, *The Dreyfus Case: A Documentary History* (1973).

Murder in the First. Stephen Farber, "A Drama That Puts Alcatraz on Trial," *New York Times* (January 15, 1995, Sec. 2, p. 12); "Corrections," *New York Times* (April 6, 1994, sec. A, p. 2); Gregory Lunes, "Truth Comes Last in Murder in the First," *Dallas Morning News* (March 10, 1995); Peter Stack, "Ex Con Disputes Film's Tale of the Rock," *San Francisco Chronicle* (January 21, 1995).

Sommersby. J. Clay Smith, Emancipation: *The Making of the Black Lawyer 1844–1944* (University of Pennsylvania Press, 1993).

To Kill A Mockingbird. Timothy Hoff, "Influence on Harper Lee," 45 *Alabama Law Review* 389 (1994); Thomas L. Shaffer, "The Moral Theology of Atticus Finch," 42 University of Pittsburgh Law Review

181 (1981). Special thanks to Edy Faal who provided assistance for this analysis.

Chapter 5

The Music Box. Paul Chutkow, "From the 'Music Box' Emerges the Nazi Demon," *New York Times* (December 24, 1989, sec 2, p. 11, col. 1).

Chapter 6

Fury. Jay Robert Nash and Stanley Ralph Ross, *The Motion Picture Guide 1927–1983* (Cinebooks, 1987).

They Won't Forget. Jay Robert Nash and Stanley Ralph Ross, *The Motion Picture Guide 1927–1983* (Cinebooks, 1987).

The Wrong Man. "All Around Town with 'The Wrong Man,'" *New York Times* (April 29, 1956); "Court is Turned into a Movie Set," *New York Times* (April 9, 1956).

Chapter 7

Anatomy of a Murder. Special thanks to Judge Robert Altman and to Professor Ken Graham for assistance with this analysis.

M. John H. Langbein, *Comparative Criminal Procedure: Germany* (West, 1977); John Henry Merryman, *The Civil Law Tradition,* 124–32 (1984); Abraham S. Goldstein, "Reflections on Two Models: Inquisitorial Themes in American Criminal Procedure," 26 *Stanfield Law Review* 1009 (1973); "Trial by Dossier," 142 *New Law Journal* 249 (1992).

On Trial. Magill's *Survey of Cinema* (1981).

The Star Chamber. Special thanks to Judge Robert Altman (whom Michael Douglas used as a model) who provided assistance for this analysis.

Twelve Angry Men. Bitemark case: *Miller v. Harvey,* 566 F 2d 879 (4th Cir. 1977).

Chapter 8

Class Action. Gary Schwartz, "The Myth of the Ford Pinto Case," 44 *Rutgers Law Review* 1013–1068 (1991).

Losing Isaiah. Elizabeth Bartholet, "Where Do Black Children Belong? The Politics of Race Matching in Adoption," 139 *University Pennsylvania Law Review* 1163 (1991); Asher D. Isaacs, "Interracial Adoption: Unlocking Racial Identity," *National Black Law Journal*—(1995); James G. O'Keefe, "The Need to Consider Children's Rights in Biological Parent v. Third Party Custody Disputes," 67 *Chicago-Kent Law Review* 1077 (1991). In the Interest of Ashley K., 571 N.E. 2d 905 (Ill. Ct. App. 1991). Special thanks for assistance to Joan Hollinger.

Whose Life Is It Anyway? Peter Steven Miller, "The Impact of Assisted Suicide on Persons with Disabilities—Is it a Right Without Freedom?" 9 Issues in *Law and Medicine* 47 (1993); Evan J. Kemp, "Paternalism, Disability, and the Right to Die," id. at 73; Note, "Liability for Improper Maintenance of Life Support: Balancing Patient and Physician Autonomy," 46 *Vanderbilt Law Review* 1255 (1993).

Index by Movie Title

Index by Number of Gavels

—▮ —▮ —▮ —▮

—▮ —▮ —▮

Index by Topics

Paul Bergman and Michael Asimow are Professors of Law at UCLA School of Law in Los Angeles. Bergman specializes in trial advocacy and evidence; Asimow in administrative law, taxation, and contracts. Both authors are avid tennis players and love old movies.